English Schools in the Middle Ages

NICHOLAS ORME

Methuen & Co Ltd

11 New Fetter Lane London EC4

First published 1973 by Methuen & Co Ltd
11 New Fetter Lane, London EC4
© 1973 Nicholas Orme
Printed in Great Britain by
T and A Constable Ltd
Hopetoun Street, Edinburgh

SBN 416 16080 0

Distributed in the USA by
HARPER & ROW PUBLISHERS INC
BARNES & NOBLE IMPORT DIVISION

For my family

Contents

List of maps   *page* viii
List of illustrations   ix
Acknowledgements   x
Preface   xi
List of Abbreviations   xiii

Introduction   1

1 **Education and society**   11
  The clergy, 12; kings and princes, 21; nobility and gentry, 29;
  administrators and lawyers, 36; merchants, craftsmen, artisans,
  43; villeins, 50; women, 52

Schools and their studies
2 The schools of medieval England   59
3 The study of grammar   87
4 Life in school   116
5 Patrons and schoolmasters   142

Historical developments
6 The schools from the twelfth century to 1400   167
7 The schools from 1400 to 1530   194
8 The religious orders and education   224
9 The schools under Henry VIII   252
10 The schools from Edward VI to Elizabeth   272

A list of medieval English schools, 1066-1530   293
Bibliography   326
Index   355

List of maps

1 Patrons of English schools, 1066-1400   *page* 147
2 English schools in the thirteenth century   171
3 Some fourteenth-century schools in Lincolnshire,
     Nottinghamshire and Yorkshire   191
4 Oxford in the fifteenth century   209
5 London schools in the fifteenth century   211
6 Endowed schools founded in England, 1330-1530   216
7 The dissolution of the chantries, 1547-8, in Gloucestershire,
     Herefordshire and Worcestershire   281

List of illustrations

Between pages 34 *and* 35

1 Reading (National Gallery, Hans Memling, 'The Donne Altarpiece')
2 Writing (British Museum, MS Cotton Vespasian F xiii, no 123)
3 A schoolmaster's notebook (Lincoln College, Oxford, MS lat 129, fo 197)
4 Early printed grammars I (*Equivoca*, ascribed to John of Garland)
5 Early printed grammars II (John Holt, *Lac Puerorum*, British Museum, C 33 b 4)

Between pages 130 *and* 131

6 Medieval schools I (aerial photograph of Ewelme, Oxon.)
7 and 8 Medieval schools II (outside: engraving of Wainfleet school from R. Chandler, *Life of Bishop Waynflete* (1811); inside: frontispiece from *The Shorte Accedence*, fragment in Exeter Cathedral library)
9 A medieval town and its schools (Bristol Museum, Georgius Hoefnagel, Map of Bristol (1581))
10 and 11 Schoolmasters (rubbing of the brass of Robert Londe, from a matrix formerly in the church of St Peter, Bristol; drawing of Cardinal Wolsey by Jacques le Boucq from the Bibliothèque d'Arras)

Between pages 226 *and* 227

12 and 13 Benefactors of schools: I – the clergy (drawing of Richard Fitz James from Merton College, Oxford, MS Merton 25 fo 1^R; drawing of John Colet from Cambridge University Library, MS Dd. VII. 3, fo 6)
14 Benefactors of schools: II – the nobility and gentry (effigies of Lady Katherine and Thomas Lord Berkeley from their tomb in Berkeley church, Gloucs.)

A*

Between pages 226 and 227

15 Benefactors of schools: III – the merchant class (rubbing of the brass of Joan and John Cook from the matrix in the church of St Mary Crypt, Gloucester)
16 The educational achievement (effigy of Bishop William Wainfleet from his tomb in Winchester Cathedral)

ACKNOWLEDGEMENTS

The author and publishers would like to thank the following for permission to reproduce the illustrations appearing in this book:

Aerofilms Ltd for no 6
Bibliothèque d'Arras for no 11
Bristol Museum for no 9
British Museum for nos 2, 4, 5, 7
Cambridge University Library for no 13
Exeter Cathedral Library for no 8
Lincoln College, Oxford for no 3
Merton College, Oxford for no 12
National Gallery for no 1
National Monuments Record for no 14
Victoria and Albert Museum for nos 10, 15
The Dean and Chapter, Winchester for no 16

Preface

It was on a summer afternoon twelve years ago, while exploring the village of Newland in Gloucestershire, that I came among the quiet houses which border its churchyard to a cottage called 'The Old Grammar School', and was moved to begin the inquiries which have led, much later, to the completion of this book. That I have found the history of medieval schools so congenial is very likely due to my own happy experiences in four crumbling Anglican seminaries, or to the tales I heard in youth of my parents' adventures in the private and elementary schools of England sixty years ago. Yet whenever we ponder our researches we soon become aware that greater forces move us than ourselves, and it is other scholars as much as I who have conceived the usefulness of this project and have helped to carry it out. My early progress was immeasurably assisted by my tutor, the late Mr K. B. McFarlane, who showed me the standards at which an historian ought to aim, and by Dr J. R. L. Highfield who patiently supervised my work after his ever-to-be-lamented death. More recently I have been fortunate in the advice and inspiration of Dr R. W. Hunt, which I am only sorry I have not turned to better use. Most of all I owe to the kindness of Dr A. B. Emden, who has not only offered unfailing encouragement and the benefit of his unrivalled knowledge of medieval education, but presented me with the notes he had himself assembled for a book on the same subject, and scholarship knows no greater generosity. Necessary visits to the Bodleian Library over a number of years have been made possible by the thoughtful co-operation of Professor Frank Barlow and of the University of Exeter, my employers, who have been ready and uncomplaining in meeting expenses. My stays in Oxford have been made pleasant by the hospitality of Magdalen College and more recently by the principal and students of Ripon Hall, in whose company I spent an agreeable term. I have also benefited from the advice and help of numerous other scholars who have answered my questions and communicated their discoveries, especially Brother Bonaventure, FSC, who kindly allowed me to read his thesis on 'The teaching of grammar in England in the later middle ages', Dr Antonia Gransden, Mr T. G. Hassall, Mr A. Jackson, Mr P. Lock, Mr W. Mitchell, Dr W. A. Pantin, the Reverend D. Powell, Mr I. Rowlands and Mr P. J. Wallis. To these must also be added my friends Dr J. S. Critchley and Dr M. C. E. Jones who have so kindly laboured to read and criticize my work. Faults remain, but without the advice and assistance here recorded there would have been many more.

Aylburton,
Gloucestershire
Easter 1973

List of abbreviations

Bodleian	Bodleian Library, Oxford
BM	British Museum, London
BRUC	A. B. Emden, *A Biographical Register of the University of Cambridge to 1500* (Cambridge, 1963)
BRUO	A. B. Emden, *A Biographical Register of the University of Oxford to 1500*, 3 vols (Oxford, 1957-9)
CCR	*Calendar of Close Rolls*
Complete Peerage	G. E. Cockayne, *The Complete Peerage*, ed. H. A. Doubleday and V. Gibbs, 14 vols in 15 (London, 1910-59)
Concilia	*Concilia Magnae Britanniae et Hiberniae, 446-1717*, ed. D. Wilkins, 4 vols (London, 1737)
Councils & Synods	*Councils and Synods, Part II: 1205-1313*, ed. F. M. Powicke and C. R. Cheney, 2 vols (Oxford, 1964)
CPR	*Calendar of Patent Rolls*
ECD	A. F. Leach, *Educational Charters and Documents, 598-1909* (Cambridge, 1911)
EETS	Early English Text Society
ESR	A. F. Leach, *English Schools at the Reformation, 1546-8* (Westminster, 1896)
EYS	A. F. Leach, *Early Yorkshire Schools*, 2 vols (Yorkshire Archaeological Society, record series, xxvii, xxxiii, 1899-1903)
LPFD	*Calendar of Letters and Papers, Foreign and Domestic, Henry VIII*, ed J. S. Brewer and others, 21 vols (London, 1864-1920)

PMLA	*Publications of the Modern Language Association of America*
PRO	Public Record Office, London
Reg.	*Register*[1]
SME	A. F. Leach, *The Schools of Medieval England*, 2nd ed. (London, 1916)
STC	A. W. Pollard and G. R. Redgrave, *Short Title Catalogue of Books Printed in England, 1475-1640* (London, 1926)
VCH	*The Victoria History of the Counties of England*

[1] For the sake of brevity, bishops' registers are noted with the name of the bishop first, then of the diocese. Thus *Reg. Chichele, Canterbury*, should be read, *The register of* [Henry] *Chichele, archbishop of Canterbury.*

Introduction

Perhaps no age has been more conscious than our own of the manifold
influences which natural surroundings and human society bring to the
making of man from childhood to maturity. If we set out to inquire how,
in the widest sense, men were *educated* in medieval times, a whole range of
possible influences will come to mind, including family life, social conditions, religious ideas and the tasks and preoccupations of adulthood.
Learning will thus be seen to include the acquisition of social habits, the
appreciation of nature and the mastery of trades, as well as the study of
letters in school; while schooling will appear as only one of the strands of
education, and one which in any case involved only a minority of people.
It is a necessary preliminary to the investigation of medieval schools to
remember the small scale of their impact compared with the other great
forces which wrought upon mankind. Yet although few went to school, and
although the schools were limited in their resources, their study has an importance and an application beyond the audience they reached. Other kinds
of education have left fewer traces either of their nature or their effects,
but the work of the schools is relatively well documented and, since it was
more formalized, far easier to reconstruct. It also provides an operational base
for the wider study of the life and education of medieval man. Schools have
always attempted to prepare their pupils for the world outside, and even in
medieval times their curriculum was not pursued merely for its own sake.
Not only did it seek to impart the literary techniques which the clergy, and
later many of the laity, needed for their adult work; it also tried to instil
religion and virtue, to teach an ethic of social behaviour and to stimulate the
imagination. The study of schools thus leads us insensibly to other aspects
of education and provides a good deal of material for understanding them.

Interest in schools among the wealthy and literate has never been lacking since the twelfth century, yet compared with the energy given to founding and managing them, their history has never attracted much attention, perhaps because of the tendency of educationalists always to undervalue the achievements of their predecessors. When the study of medieval history began in the seventeenth century, it fastened chiefly upon the excitements of political and constitutional history, the mysteries of the religious orders or the intricacies of genealogy and manorial history. Only a very few scholars thought to inquire into the history of medieval schools, among whom Christopher Wase and Anthony Wood are the most notable; indeed Wase deserves to be recognized as the first important historian of the subject, for he was the earliest to attempt a general inquiry into the origins and resources of the English schools and the succession of their masters.[1] His extensive collections however remained unpublished, and instead the easy fiction became current, and indeed remained so until the end of the nineteenth century, that medieval schooling had been mainly the work of the monks.[2] Little happened in the eighteenth century to dispel this assumption. A few local historians did bring to light instances of public, secular schools in the counties and boroughs of medieval England, but their discoveries failed to impinge upon the general notion of things.[3]

It was not until the beginning of the nineteenth century that the history of English schools was seriously reconsidered and as a subject worthy of investigation. By this period there was a growing feeling that the national facilities for education were inadequate, and this raised the question of whether the existing school endowments were being used to best advantage. Their origins and purposes began to be the subject of historical research. In 1818 Nicholas Carlisle published a private survey in which he attempted to list all the endowed grammar schools still extant and to describe their histories, in the course of which he incidentally drew attention to records of medieval schools anterior to the foundations with

---

[1] On Wase see P. J. Wallis, 'The Wase school collection: a neglected source in educational history', *Bodleian Library Record*, iv (1952), pp. 78-104, and Wase's own work, *Considerations Concerning Free Schools as Settled in England* (Oxford, 1678), pp. 28-41. Notes by Wood on schools appear in Bodleian, MS Wood D 11, folios 159-80v.

[2] e.g. John Aubrey, 'There were no free schools. The boys were educated at the monasteries.' (*Brief Lives and other Selected Writings*, ed. Anthony Powell (London, 1949), p. 6).

[3] See for example Richard Furney's MS 'History of Gloucester' (Bodleian, MS Top. Glouc. c. 4-5); Francis Blomefield's description of Norfolk; and Nicolson's and Burn's account of Westmorland and Cumberland.

which he was concerned.[1] In the same year Lord Brougham conducted a campaign for the reform of endowed schools, and this led soon afterwards to the establishment of a parliamentary commission to investigate schools and other endowed charities and to report upon their histories and activities. From this time onwards there was a steady growth of interest, both public and private, in the history of schools. Successive Charity Commissions published thirty-two reports between 1819 and 1840, and in 1853 the commission was put on a permanent footing. In 1864 the Endowed School Commission conducted even more searching inquiries, and its evidence, which ran to twenty-one volumes, contained a good deal of valuable historical material. At a local level the popular concern for education, and the reforms which this eventually produced, stimulated the production of a good many school histories, of varying quality, but testifying nevertheless to the strong sense of tradition that has been such a valuable influence on the modern English educational system.

The work of the Charity Commission was also responsible for inspiring the first research of an academic nature into medieval schools by A. F. Leach (1851-1915), the principal investigator of the subject. Leach's own education had been passed in medieval surroundings at Winchester and Oxford, where he distinguished himself by gaining a first class degree in *Literae Humaniores* and a prize fellowship at All Souls,[2] but it was not until 1884, when he was appointed an assistant charity commissioner and charged with investigating the history of the Prebendal School, Chichester, and the Grammar School, Southwell, that he suddenly became aware of the medieval origins of such schools and was fired to discover all that he could about them. The vague notions which he had hitherto entertained about medieval education being largely in the hands of the monks changed into a passionate desire to demonstrate, by contrast, the existence and importance of a large number of public, secular schools, run by secular priests and laymen, the ancestors of the schools of modern times. For the rest of his life he pursued this task with industry and enthusiasm.

Leach was not, in fairness to his contemporaries, the only historian who realized the potentialities of such research. As early as 1868 F. J. Furnivall had written a sketch of medieval English education as the foreword to an edition of poems on manners and meals for the Early English Text

[1] N. Carlisle, *A Concise Description of the Endowed Grammar Schools in England and Wales*, 2 vols (London, 1818).
[2] For Leach's career see Foster Watson's article in the *Dictionary of National Biography 1912-1921* (1927), pp. 327-8.

Society, and Leach acknowledged the generous help which Furnivall gave him in later years.[1] In 1894, the date of Leach's first important book on pre-Reformation schools, short accounts of the subject also appeared in two other works: J. H. Wylie's *History of England under Henry IV* and Mrs Green's *Town Life in the Fifteenth Century*.[2] But Leach alone applied the whole of his energies to the task and succeeded in publishing a large collection of materials for its study. His achievement in doing so remains impressive. During the twenty-one years between 1894 and 1915 he published nine volumes on the history of education alone, including general studies, collections of documents and local histories, as well as contributing more than fifteen lengthy articles on particular areas to the Victoria County History. In the course of this work he examined and brought to notice an enormous range of material, not only from printed sources but from charters and manuscripts in the British Museum, the Public Record Office and dozens of local archives and muniment rooms. He was therefore well qualified to write the histories of some 200 medieval schools which constitute his main achievement. He created the modern study of the subject and his writings remain indispensable for its pursuit.[3]

Leach's best work undoubtedly lies in his editions of local records, *Early Yorkshire Schools* and *Early Education in Worcester*, together with his detailed studies of Warwick School, Winchester College and St Paul's. Here were small, manageable subjects which he researched thoroughly and described on the whole judiciously, so that in general they are works which can still be used without fear. Much the same is true of his large collection of original records, *Educational Charters and Documents, 598-1909*, so long as allowance is made for the more accurate dates and texts which have been established since he wrote. The articles he composed for the Victoria County History are more variable. They seem frequently to have suffered from shortage of time, space and opportunities for research, which left them in some cases hasty and incomplete. This is particularly true of Yorkshire, where the short space allotted to Leach proved quite insufficient for the number of schools he had to describe. Worcestershire, where he had some good local assistance,[4] is far superior as a survey to Gloucestershire, the treatment of which is often sketchy and unreliable. The contributors to the VCH do not always seem to have pooled their

---

[1] *Manners and Meals in Olden Time*, ed. F. J. Furnivall (EETS, original series xxxii, part 2, 1868).
[2] These works are both listed below in the bibliography.
[3] There is no complete bibliography of Leach's writings, except for the list of those on medieval schools in *SME*, pp. vii-ix.
[4] *VCH Worcs.*, iv, 475 n 1.

discoveries, and Leach's own articles can sometimes be supplemented from elsewhere in the volumes, which are always worth checking with this in mind.[1] Much profit may still be gained from Leach's work in the VCH, but it can no longer be regarded as definitive, for the last sixty years have added much to what the author missed himself.

Leach however aspired to be more than a mere antiquary. He tried throughout his work to perceive it as a whole, and he wrote two books with the specific intention of summarizing the detailed research he had made. Both *English Schools at the Reformation* (1894) and *The Schools of Medieval England* (1915) were more ambitious than his other works, and both were the fruit of an unequalled knowledge of sources. They are not lacking in shrewd comments and valuable pieces of information including, in the latter volume, some of the local fieldwork which never came to be published elsewhere. At the same time, the two general works exhibit in larger measure than the others their author's defects as an historian. Not only are they limited by his failure to discuss topics in which he was not interested, but they suffer from the extravagance with which he extolled his theories and denounced his opponents, to say nothing of his careless regard for accuracy about dates and facts. His own contemporaries found these failings irksome. 'He gives the rashest judgment about the most disputable matters' complained F. W. Maitland of one of Leach's earlier works in 1900, and the reckless assertions which mar *The Schools of Medieval England* drew strong rebuke from R. L. Poole and A. G. Little. Far from crowning his reputation, his general studies clouded it; they brought the rest of his work under suspicion, and weakened the effectiveness of their author's whole achievement.[2]

Of the deficiencies in Leach's major works none is more serious than his treatment of the religious orders. Reacting too strongly against the opinion, once held by himself, that the monks were the schoolmasters of medieval England, he failed to give credit to the very real contributions to education which the religious orders had made. Although he often mentions the education of lay children in the monastic almonries and song schools, he gives little space in his articles and none in his general works to the schools which the monasteries kept for their own novices, schools small in numbers but ambitious and effective in their work. As to the

---

[1] e.g. Droitwich (ibid., iii, 76), and Tattershall (*VCH Lincs.*, ii, 237).
[2] For discussions of Leach's writings see C. H. S. Fifoot, *Frederic William Maitland, a Life* (Cambridge, Mass., 1971), pp. 240-3; A. G. Little's review of *SME* in *English Historical Review*, xxx (1915), pp. 525-9; and the articles by Joan Simon, W. N. Chaplin and P. J. Wallis in *British Journal of Educational Studies*, iv (1955-6), xi (1962-3) and xii (1963-4).

friars, the orders most committed to the pursuit of education, he is wholly silent. A great area of medieval education is thus absent from his work. It is easier to excuse his failure to discuss the curricula of the medieval schools, for this leads down unfrequented corridors that few have ventured to explore. Leach in fact chanced more than once upon relevant details, and many of the grammarians and authors used in the medieval schools were available when he wrote, but he never sought to penetrate what he called 'the darkness of our ignorance of the curriculum'. While we may pardon him this, who has taught us so much else, it remains a limitation which any successor must try to overcome.

Leach's excesses as an historian stand also in need of correction. One was an overestimation of the educational role of the collegiate churches in the middle ages, in particular of those great minsters and prebendal churches which in the eleventh and twelfth centuries were still staffed by secular canons. Having found schools at an early date in places such as Beverley and Hastings, Leach rashly concluded that all similar institutions had possessed such schools, and the theory became almost an article of faith to be recited on all occasions. No early collegiate church, however, ought to be credited with a school without specific information to that effect.[1] As for the collegiate churches of the later middle ages, communities of chantry priests or university scholars, Leach appears to have understood what is in fact the case, that some can be shown to have possessed schools and others not to have done. That he has been credited with making more claims about these collegiate schools than he intended arises from his own failure to observe clarity and precision in the statements he made.

The obsession with collegiate churches extended to Leach's treatment of the chantries, the educational importance of which he consistently overrated. Thus he supposed that many more chantries were founded to include schools during the fourteenth and fifteenth centuries than the evidence warrants, for chantry schools were a development of the *late* fourteenth century and became numerous only in the *second* half of the fifteenth. Many of the chantry priests mentioned as teaching school when the chantries were dissolved in 1548 had probably come to do so only recently.[2] Leach was right to point out that the dissolution of the chantries had an adverse effect upon the supply of education, in that such of their schools as were elementary were extinguished, while many of those which taught grammar suffered from having an income from land converted into

[1] As A. G. Little pointed out in his review. See also below, p. 176.
[2] For the present author's opinions see below, pp. 196-7.

a fixed stipend in an age of inflation. He made a necessary revaluation of the educational work of Edward VI, but once again his reaction was too strong and he gave this single episode too much importance in the history of Tudor education, a subject which he never indeed considered as a whole.

Leach's death in 1915 unmanned his favourite subject, since for all his efforts to popularize the medieval schools he never attracted many followers. Some of his ideas gained currency, but in general historians have continued to regard his work with reserve and few have been moved to enlarge or repair the edifice he built. Yet materials for the purpose have been steadily accumulating over the last sixty years. New editions of original records, both secular and ecclesiastical, have provided much incidental information; biographical data have become more plentiful as a result of Dr Emden's labours on university scholars; a number of good school histories have added their tithe as well. Much light has also been cast on the study of grammar in the middle ages, largely through the inspiration of Dr R. W. Hunt. Nevertheless, only two recent writers have reopened in general terms the history of the English schools before the Reformation, and both have concentrated on the sixteenth century. Mrs Simon has given us a most lucid and comprehensive survey of Tudor education, while Professor Jordan has done good service in describing the early history of the endowed schools in half a dozen counties, at least two of which were almost virgin territory.[1] It is hard, however, for a medieval historian to share his low opinion of the English schools at the end of the fifteenth century, particularly with regard to their numbers and continuity.[2] His concentration on the history of the 'free' or fully endowed schools leads him to overlook the larger number of other schools which always existed and to undervalue the institutions which they had developed to secure their continuity and to subsidize the expenses of their pupils.[3] What evidence has so far been collected points to a gradual increase in the number of known schools *throughout* the later middle ages, and the apparent absence of schools from many of the towns which Professor Jordan has investigated signifies no more than their absence from the records at present available to historians. The very accidents by which

[1] Joan Simon, *Education and Society in Tudor England* (Cambridge, 1966). Professor Jordan's major writings are listed below, in the bibliography.
[2] W. K. Jordan, *Philanthropy in England, 1480-1660* (1959), pp. 285-7; *The Charities of Rural England, 1480-1660* (1961), pp. 53, 151, 299-301. In Norfolk, for example, eight other grammar schools are known to have existed in the fifteenth century besides those mentioned by Professor Jordan, and in Yorkshire at least five (see below, pp. 324-5).
[3] This is the theme of chapter 6 in the present work.

most schools have left traces of their existence should make us beware of underestimating their number, especially when they occur in other towns of similar size and character to those with which we are dealing.

The present survey of English schools in the middle ages extends in time from the twelfth century to the accession of Queen Elizabeth, but is chiefly concerned with the years between 1200 and 1530. It begins with a sketch of the literary interests of the different classes of medieval society in order to suggest the conditions in which the schools grew up and the kinds of people whom they served. The next four chapters deal with the public, secular schools of this period – those which were staffed and attended by secular clerks and laymen, and which constituted the main source of literary education in medieval times. The different grades of these schools are described, as well as the studies they followed and the details of their management and internal life. Very little however is said about either the universities or the Inns of Court, which lie outside the scope of the work. This leads on to an account of the ways in which the schools developed historically during the middle ages. Two chapters follow the secular schools from their emergence in the twelfth century down to the eve of the Reformation, in what appear to be the main aspects of their history: their numbers, endowments and the interest they aroused among their contemporaries. This is followed by a summary of the educational work of the religious orders during the same period. Although the medieval era of English school history was already fading at the opening of the sixteenth century as the medieval curriculum changed into that of the Renaissance, constitutional changes were delayed until the Reformation. Two further chapters have therefore been added to show how, during the years 1534-60, the revolution in religion extinguished the schools of the religious orders and modified those of the cathedrals, the secular colleges and the chantries, while at the same time the mild educational jurisdiction of the medieval Church became a much tighter one, still exercised by the clergy but as an agency now of the crown. The work concludes with a list of the secular schools known by the author to have existed in England between the Conquest and the Reformation.

Education and society

Chapter One
Education and society

An inquiry into the English schools of the middle ages might well begin
with the question of why they existed at all. What were the literary needs
of the medieval community which led the schools to appear? How many
people, and of what ranks and occupations, had occasion to read or
write or to understand Latin grammar? The questions are easier to ask
than to answer, because of the perplexing nature of the evidence, at once
inadequate and overabundant. On the one hand there is a lack of contemporary comment before the sixteenth century on the extent of literacy
in England or its importance to the different classes of society. There is
little information from medieval school records, which include hardly any
surviving lists of pupils, to suggest who went to school at any particular
period, or why. On the other hand there exists from the twelfth century
onwards, and increasingly after the middle of the fourteenth, an enormous
mass of literary material, even considering only that which has survived:
charters, deeds, writs, registers, act books, court rolls, accounts, letters,
works of scholarship and imaginative literature. Obviously a good many
people were engaged in producing this material for a great many others to
read. So much literature, if it could be mastered, would tell us much about
the extent of literacy at the time, but the bulk is great and the details of
authorship and readership are hard to unravel. It needs a great deal of
patient research before enough of the individuals and institutions involved
in using literature can be identified to enable us to form conclusions about
society as a whole. In the meantime we can present only an outline of the
extent of literacy in medieval England, which is here based largely on
evidence of the fourteenth and fifteenth centuries. We shall examine the
society of this period, class by class, in the usual order followed by

medieval writers: first the clergy; next the military class, subdivided into the kings, the nobility and gentry, and the lawyers and administrators associated with them; and then the merchants, craftsmen and artisans. Our survey will conclude with two other groups whose educational opportunities present features of interest: villeins and women – for it is an obvious but fundamental fact that the medieval schools largely existed for and were dominated by the needs of men.

The clergy[1]

The clergy were, or should have been, the most literate of the three estates, and clerical life, if it were properly followed, involved both the use and understanding of written texts. All the clergy, whether in major or in minor orders, were expected to repeat the divine office: the eight daily services of praise and prayer to God. Those who were priests had also to celebrate a daily mass and, if necessary, to perform the other sacraments of the Church: baptisms, burials and so on. All these tasks involved the reading, or after reading the memorizing, of liturgical texts in Latin, and the ability to read letters alone was not sufficient for the purpose. A knowledge of plainsong was also necessary, so that psalms could be chanted and hymns sung, and Latin grammar had to be mastered so that the liturgy should not merely be rattled off parrot-fashion but be said with understanding and devotion. Nor was it intended that reading should be confined to the service books. In the thirteenth century widespread attempts were made, both in the religious orders and among the parish clergy, to encourage the reading and study of the Bible. 'Let all parish priests', wrote Bishop Grosseteste to the clergy of the diocese of Lincoln in about 1239, 'and those who have the cure of souls, when they have finished the divine office in church, attend diligently to the reading of holy scripture.' The ends he had in mind were that by assiduous reading they might nourish their power of prayer and be the better able to satisfy the questions of their parishioners concerning hope and faith.[2] The same ideal was still being sought at the end of our period, when in 1530 a decree of the reforming convocation of Canterbury ordered the clergy after completing the divine office to spend two or three hours, three times a week, in studying holy scripture or in reading one of the approved doctors of the Church.[3]

[1] Only the secular clergy are discussed at this point; for the religious orders see below, chapter 8.
[2] *Councils & Synods*, i, 269.
[3] *Concilia*, iii, 722.

Reading, song and Latin grammar, the last in particular, were all necessary accomplishments of the 'secular' clergy in the middle ages – those who ministered in the world as opposed to the members of the religious orders. Bishops, as we shall see, demanded that their clergy should be skilled in song and grammar; founders of colleges and chantries often stipulated that their occupants should be good grammarians;[1] Latin dictionaries were more than once bequeathed to parish churches for the use of the clergy who served them.[2] The depth of knowledge of Latin which a priest should have is suggested by William Melton, chancellor of York, in a sermon delivered to candidates for ordination in about 1510. No one should receive holy orders, he says, who has not gained at least a moderate knowledge of good letters, meaning Latin. He should be able to read a Latin book, especially the scriptures, readily and accurately. A priest ought to know enough grammar to be able to study from books and improve himself without the aid of other teachers.[3]

The reality was often quite different. Throughout the later middle ages their critics hastened to point out how far short the clergy fell of the standards of literacy expected of them. Their ignorance is a recurrent theme of writers from one century to another. Clerks and parish priests, declares Roger Bacon in the second half of the thirteenth century, recite the divine office 'like beasts', understanding little or nothing.[4] A hundred years later, the chronicler of Leicester Abbey tells how multitudes of men who had lost their wives in the plague flocked to take orders, 'of whom many were illiterate and like mere laymen, for in so far as they could read they could not understand'.[5] 'I have been priest and parson passing thirty winters', groans a repentant cleric in Langland's *Piers Plowman*, 'yet can I neither solfa nor sing, nor read saints' lives.'[6] 'They be so uncunning', cries a Lollard reformer of about 1400, 'that men scorn them for saying their service and reading their epistle and gospel.'[7] As late as the 1530s Thomas Starkey, the author and preacher, makes Reginald Pole, the future cardinal, attack the poor quality of those admitted to be parish

---

[1] See for example, A. Hamilton Thompson, *The English Clergy and their Organisation in the Later Middle Ages* (1947), p. 281; *CCR 1500-9*, pp. 146-7; *LPFD*, i, no 559.
[2] e.g. at All Saints, York, 1441 (*Testamenta Eboracensia*, ed. J. Raine, vol ii (Surtees Society, xxx, 1855), pp. 79-80); St Mary Crypt, Gloucester, 1454 (W. H. Stevenson, *Calendar of MSS of the Corporation of Gloucester* (1893), no 1138); King's Norton, Worcs., 1481 (*Testamenta Vetusta*, ed. N. H. Nicolas (1826), i, 367).
[3] *STC*, 17806; P. Hughes, *The Reformation in England*, vol i (1950), p. 85.
[4] Roger Bacon, *Opera Inedita*, ed. J. S. Brewer (Rolls Series, 1859), p. 413.
[5] Henry Knighton, *Chronicon*, ed. J. R. Lumby, vol ii (Rolls Series, 1895), p. 63.
[6] Langland, *Piers the Plowman*, ed. W. W. Skeat (1886), vol. i: B.v.422-3.
[7] *The English Works of Wycliffe*, ed. F. D. Matthew (EETS, 1880), p. 167.

clergy, 'for commonly you shall find that they can do nothing but patter up their mattins and mass, mumbling up a certain number of words, nothing understood'.[1] The charge indeed survived the Reformation and remained to be bandied about by Puritans in the seventeenth century.

Faced with these criticisms, it seems wise not to take clerical learning for granted. Yet if the charges cannot be altogether discounted, they can at least be put into perspective by a knowledge of how the medieval Church selected and supervised her recruits. For selection and supervision there certainly were, and their lack of complete success was not altogether due to the laxity of the ecclesiastical authorities. Deeply entrenched social attitudes towards the Church, such as are hardly encountered in modern times, also hindered their operation. Clerical life was seen not only as a vocation requiring knowledge and self-discipline, but as a career, offering freedom, status and wealth. Parishes were often regarded less as cures of souls than as benefices which could set up a poor man's son for life or keep a rich man's son in the style to which he was accustomed. Confronted by recruits whose motives for ordination were often more economic than religious, the most conscientious bishops found it hard to maintain standards of virtue and learning, while the more indolent were easily discouraged from doing so altogether.

It was by ordination that one entered the ranks of the clergy, and since early times the Church had tried to use the occasion to examine the candidates as to their suitability for clerical life.[2] Ordination was administered in several stages and therefore offered several opportunities for examination. The lowest degree was the first tonsure, which could be given to boys or youths and conveyed little more than clerical status at law. Next came the four minor orders culminating in that of acolyte, which seem usually to have been conferred together in medieval England. They too could be received at any stage and their recipients could, and often did, marry or take up lay employment without ever rising further in the clerical hierarchy. But the three major orders – subdeacon, deacon and priest – were taken much more seriously. They could only be administered one at a time, and a minimum age was stipulated: for a subdeacon eighteen, for a deacon twenty and for a priest twenty-five.

---

[1] Thomas Starkey, *A Dialogue between Reginald Pole and Thomas Lupset*, ed. Kathleen M. Burton (1948), p. 126.

[2] *Corpus Juris Canonici*, ed. E. Friedberg, vol i (1879), col 88: Decretum pars I dist. xxiv cap. v. The best modern discussions of ordination are by H. S. Bennett, 'Medieval ordination lists in the English episcopal registers', in *Studies Presented to Sir Hilary Jenkinson*, ed. J. Conway Davies (1957), pp. 20-34, and by P. Heath, *The English Parish Clergy on the Eve of the Reformation* (1969), pp. 12-18.

Moreover, each of the major orders involved an irrevocable vow of celibacy.

Ordination had to be administered by the bishop four times a year: on the third Saturday in Advent, on a Saturday during Lent, on the Saturday in Whitsuntide and on the third Saturday in September. The place appointed was usually the cathedral or the chapel of the manor where the bishop then happened to be staying. During the three days before the ordination, the candidates had each to be examined, a duty which originally pertained to the archdeacons of the diocese. When they were not available, or when the number of ordinands was too large, the bishop appointed other examining chaplains, generally senior clergy such as the chancellor of the cathedral or its prebendaries, his own diocesan officials or his chaplains. Ordinary parish clergy too were sometimes drafted for the purpose. The examiners had many things to ascertain, of which literacy was only one. Ordinands had to be freemen, sound in mind and body, without incurable disease or deformity. They must have received the necessary previous orders and have reached the stipulated age. They were required to be of good character and competent learning, and they had to produce a 'title' – evidence of a benefice or of private means with which to support themselves, lest after ordination they should compromise their clerical status by resorting to manual labour or to beggary.

The legatine council of London held in 1237 ordered that the names of those admitted to orders should be written down and kept, and from the middle of the thirteenth century onwards ordination lists do indeed survive among the contents of bishops' registers.[1] As a guide to the qualities of the candidates approved for ordination they are rather disappointing. They are chiefly lists of names, arranged under the orders each received, and sometimes subdivided into the unbeneficed, the beneficed clergy and the members of the religious orders. The only other information regularly recorded was the title, a care probably observed because the bishop was bound to maintain at his own expense any indigent clerks he was rash enough to ordain. Only a very little can be gathered from the lists about the learning of the ordinees. The names of candidates rejected on account of illiteracy were never preserved. It sometimes happened, however, that insufficiently learned clerks were ordained as

---

[1] *Councils & Synods*, i, 248. The earliest surviving lists include those of York, 1267 (*Reg. Giffard, York*, ed. W. Brown (Surtees Society, cix, 1904), pp. 187-98); Hereford, 1277 (*Reg. Cantilupe, Hereford*, ed. R. G. Griffiths (Canterbury & York Society, ii, 1906), pp. 299-312); and Canterbury, 1285 (*Reg. Pecham, Canterbury*, ed. F. N. Davis and Decima Douie (Canterbury & York Society, lxiv-v, 1968-9), i, 220-56; ii, 1-5).

subdeacons or deacons, and occasionally even as priests, on condition that they attended school for a year or two and did not take higher orders or hold a cure of souls in the meanwhile. Conditional ordinations of this kind were either granted infrequently or were not always recorded in the lists, for they occur only intermittently. The register of Walter Reynolds, bishop of Worcester from 1308 to 1313, is exceptional in listing ninety-two conditional ordinations of subdeacons, seven of deacons, and two of priests;[1] most other registers provide only a few examples of the practice. Thus Walter Stapledon of Exeter at an ordination in 1319 found three prospective subdeacons, two prospective deacons and one prospective priest unable to sing; he rejected the candidate for the priesthood and ordained the others conditionally.[2] Wulstan Bransford of Worcester ordered thirteen deacons to attend school in 1339 and two subdeacons on other occasions.[3] Thomas Brantingham of Exeter on two occasions in 1374 gave conditional ordination to two subdeacons, one deacon and five priests.[4] Again, Thomas Beckington of Bath and Wells let through between 1457 and 1463 two subdeacons, a deacon and two priests, but always with safeguards, the priests being threatened with annual examinations until they were found competent.[5] These instances, haphazardly and intermittently recorded though they are, do show that some attention was given on some occasions to clerical literacy, that exceptions could be made, but that candidates were expected to comply with the requirements in due course. As for the vast majority, ordained without comment, we have little means of knowing their literary powers. An exceptional list of remarks survives, however, about twenty-two priests ordained by Bishop Reynolds in 1310. Fourteen were noted as 'moderately literate', two as 'insufficiently literate'; eleven were, or looked, under age.[6] They were all admitted to the priesthood.

Once ordained, a priest might easily spend the rest of his life as an assistant curate, a domestic chaplain or even in a chantry, without ever again suffering an examination of his literary capabilities. If however he wished to hold a rectory or vicarage with cure of souls he would have to

[1] *Reg. Reynolds, Worcester*, ed. R. A. Wilson (Worcs. Historical Society, xxxvi, 1927; Dugdale Society, ix, 1928), pp. 102-47.

[2] *Reg. Stapeldon, Exeter*, ed. F. C. Hingeston-Randolph (1892), p. 523.

[3] *Reg. Bransford, Worcester*, ed. R. M. Haines (Worcs. Historical Society, new series, iv, 1966), pp. 186-8, 223, 240.

[4] *Reg. Brantyngham, Exeter*, ed. F. C. Hingeston-Randolph, vol ii (1906), pp. 787-9.

[5] *Reg. Bekynton, Wells*, ed. H. C. Maxwell-Lyte, vol ii (Somerset Record Society, l, 1935), pp. 512, 526, 540, 543.

[6] *Reg. Reynolds, Worcester*, pp. 122-3.

appear before the bishop or his official to be instituted to the benefice, thus providing a second opportunity for them to scrutinize his qualifications and to bar the unlearned at least from the cure of souls. Institution was no mere formality. The bishop required to be certified that the benefice in question was vacant, that the patron was entitled to present a candidate, that the latter was properly qualified as to age, character and learning, and was not otherwise beneficed. Sometimes the candidates appear to have brought written testimonials of their standing; at other times, at least with regard to their learning, they may have undergone an oral examination.[1]

Lists of institutions survive in episcopal registers from the beginning of the thirteenth century, but like the ordination lists they more often record the simple fact than the circumstances in which it took place. One of the earliest collections of episcopal *acta*, however, the rolls of Hugh of Wells, bishop of Lincoln from 1209 to 1235, is also one of the most informative about clerical learning.[2] As a source it has its deficiencies; the rolls are incomplete, and were kept in different ways at different times. They contain, however, some 1,958 institutions to benefices. The vast majority of these are recorded without comment, but in a minimum of 101 cases, at least 5 per cent of the whole, the candidates were found deficient in learning. Most of them were clerks in minor orders (fifty-seven), subdeacons (thirty-one) and deacons (seven), who had evidently secured benefices before their education was complete. Only four were priests. In all cases they were instituted conditionally upon their attending school, and were threatened with deprivation in future if they did not come up to standard. Unfortunately the lists of institutions are not sufficiently informative to reveal how many met this fate.

The rolls of Bishop Hugh give a not unfavourable picture of clerical learning. They show that the deficiency was among the young and those in minor orders who still had opportunities for improvement. The bishop was clearly interested in maintaining standards of literacy; that he did not make conditional institutions automatically is proved by the casual comment on four occasions that the previous candidates had been rejected altogether for insufficiency in letters. Hugh's concern was shared by his great successor, Robert Grosseteste, who ruled from 1235 to 1253. His rolls record the conditional institution of eleven subdeacons, one deacon

---

[1] *Councils & Synods*, ii, 775-6; *Reg. Drokensford, Wells*, ed. Bishop Hobhouse (Somerset Record Society, i, 1887), p. 218; *Reg. Stretton, Lichfield*, ed. R. A. Wilson (Wm. Salt Archaeological Society, new series x, part 2, 1907), pp. 58-9, 99-100, 184-6.
[2] *Rotuli Hugonis de Welles*, ed. W. P. W. Phillimore and F. N. Davis (Lincoln Record Society, iii, vi, ix, 1912-14), *passim*.

and four priests, together with other instances where ill-qualified applicants were merely granted pensions out of the livings they sought, to help them to study.[1] Grosseteste's correspondence shows the pressure a bishop faced from irresponsible patrons to institute unsuitable candidates, pressure he tried his hardest to resist. 'A certain monk', he writes, 'presented to me for a cure of many souls a deacon not tonsured, dressed against the statutes of the council in clothes of red and wearing rings, in the manner and style of a layman or rather of a knight and, as could be divined from his replies, almost illiterate.' The monk received a severe lecture for such temerity. To the treasurer of Exeter who reproached him for refusing a benefice to a certain clerk, he replied that he had done so because the presentee was under age and insufficiently learned, 'a boy, still only in his Ovid'. With equal firmness he turned away the relatives of the chancellor and the subdean of York for the same reasons. When Cardinal Otto, the papal legate, wrote to support the candidature of Thomas, son of the earl of Derby, for the church of Rand, the request was too powerful to refuse despite the boy's youth and lack of holy orders. But Grosseteste stipulated that an adequate vicar should be appointed, and put forward his favourite compromise that Thomas should receive a pension from the church and leave its care to a suitable rector.[2]

The experiences of Bishop Hugh and Bishop Grosseteste show how difficult it was to establish a high standard of learning among the clergy, given the prevailing social attitudes to a career in the Church. The authorities could not hope to eradicate these attitudes altogether, and merely sought to keep them within reasonable limits. The same policy was probably followed to a greater or lesser extent by later bishops, but their registers are not always as informative as the early rolls of Lincoln, making it difficult now to perceive which of them were lazier and which more active in enforcing clerical learning. Three examples from different dioceses in the early fourteenth century nevertheless show that in principle enforcement continued to be carried out. The register of Walter Stapledon, bishop of Exeter from 1308 to 1326, records five conditional institutions of insufficiently literate men, four of them clerks and one a priest. The bishop adopted different means of dealing with them: three he ordered to attend school, a fourth he entrusted to the rector of another parish and the fifth he commanded to hire a good chaplain to instruct him. Three of the candidates were made to report to the bishop for examination at a

---

[1] *Rotuli Roberti Grosseteste*, ed. F. N. Davis (Lincoln Record Society, xi, 1914), *passim*.
[2] Grosseteste, *Epistolae*, ed. H. R. Luard (Rolls Series, 1861), pp. 51, 63, 68, 151-4, 203-4.

later date, and at least one failed in the end to keep his benefice.[1] Staple-don's contemporary John Droxford, bishop of Bath and Wells from 1309 to 1329, made at least three conditional institutions, two of those concerned being sent to school and the third enjoined to hire a chaplain to teach him.[2] Lastly, in the register of Roger Martival, bishop of Salisbury from 1315 to 1330, we can detect a strong episcopal hand at work against the illiterate clergy. Four candidates were rejected altogether and are not heard of again. Ten others received conditional institution, Martival's usual practice being to order them to reappear for examination once or twice a year until they were found to be competent.[3]

In the fifteenth century there is a notable example of episcopal insistence upon clerical learning in the policy of Thomas Beckington, that enlightened and efficient ruler of the diocese of Bath and Wells from 1443 to 1465. His register, which is well kept and informative, lends confidence to the inquiries which it permits about the contemporary state of the clergy. It lists 671 institutions to benefices, excluding those attached to the cathedral itself. On the credit side we notice the appearance of a number of university graduates among the clergy, of whom at least 102 were instituted to 134 benefices during Beckington's reign.[4] Very roughly they formed about a fifth of the beneficed clergy in the diocese, although many of them, being occupied in study of administration elsewhere, were probably non-resident. Of the remaining 537 institutions to benefices, 30 involved men of insufficient learning. All were priests, suggesting that the problem, faced by the thirteenth-century bishops, of young candidates in minor orders whose education was still incomplete had been largely solved by a general rise in the age at which presentations to benefices were made. Two of these priests Beckington rejected altogether, the rest he instituted conditionally, generally ordering them to study for periods of between six months and two years and to appear later for re-examination. One was sent to the cathedral school, another to study under the rector of a nearby parish. At least one, and possibly two others, were deprived or resigned after being unable to meet the requirements, but the rest seem to have remained in possession.[5]

Apart from ordinations and institutions, a third way of checking on

---

[1] *Reg. Stapeldon, Exeter*, pp. 225-6, 229, 242, 268.
[2] *Reg. Drokensford, Wells*, pp. 119, 187, 200.
[3] *Reg. Martival, Salisbury*, ed. Kathleen Edwards, vol i (Canterbury & York Society, lv, 1959), p. 513, references sub 'Learning'.
[4] The figure may have been higher, since BAs are seldom identified as such at this time.
[5] *Reg. Bekynton, Wells, passim.*

B

clerical learning existed in the diocesan visitations which were periodically made by bishops, archdeacons and their deputies. In 1240 Walter Cantilupe, bishop of Worcester, charged his archdeacons and other officials to report to him the names of any rectors or vicars whom they found deficient in letters, and similar orders were made by other thirteenth-century bishops.[1] What such investigations might uncover was well illustrated when the dean of Salisbury, William de Wanda, made his celebrated visitation of the parish church of Sonning in Berkshire and its dependent chapels in 1222. Finding several chaplains serving in the parish who had never received his approval to do so, he summoned them each in turn to inquire into their ordination and their literacy. The sequel was astounding, as the dean immediately discovered when he examined the first to appear, Simon, chaplain to the vicar of Sonning:

> Being questioned about his orders, Simon said that he received the order of subdeacon at Oxford from an Irish bishop named Albinus who was deputising for the bishop of Lincoln. He also received from him the order of deacon. He received the order of priest four years ago from Hugh, who is now bishop of Lincoln. When tested on the gospel of the first Sunday in Advent, he was found ignorant, not understanding what he read. He was also tested on the canon of the mass, *Te igitur, clementissime Pater*, etc. He did not know the case of *Te*, nor by what part of speech it was governed. And when he was told to examine carefully what word might govern *Te* most suitably, he said *Pater*, for He governs everything. Asked what was *clementissime*, and what case, and how it should be declined, he did not know. Asked what was *clemens*, he did not know. Simon also knew none of the modes of the antiphons nor the music of the hymns, not even of *Nocte surgentes*; nor did he know any of the divine office or of the psalter by heart. He said that it seemed to him unfair that he should be tested before the dean, since he had already been ordained. Asked on what he was [examined] when he received the order of priest, he said he did not remember. He is sufficiently *il*-literate!

The next to appear, the chaplain of Hurst, 'a young man, and he knows nothing', refused the test with indignation, and when he rejoined the others who were waiting outside, they agreed to form a conspiracy of silence, which was only broken after great insistence from the dean. The results of the inquiry were only too clear. Of the seven chaplains in the parish, only one was judged of approved life and escaped being tested.

[1] *Councils & Synods*, i, 313, 609-10;, 721; ii, 1017-18.

The others were all found to be gravely deficient in song and grammar, and proved no better able to understand the liturgy than Simon had been.[1]

The Sonning case is an extreme one, for it is both early in date and involves the lowest stratum of the parish clergy, those unbeneficed chaplains who were hired for poor wages to deputize for rectors and vicars themselves. Nor can one altogether avoid the suspicion that their sense of outrage at the dean's officious behaviour clouded their willingness to demonstrate what they could do. And lest it be dangerous to leave this subject of clerical education with only the Sonning case in mind, let us at least redress the balance with a contrasting example, one from the end of our period, and involving a better class of clerical recruit, the beneficed clergy themselves. Between 1530 and 1533, Robert Joseph, monk of Evesham, who had been recalled to his abbey after enjoying several years of study at Oxford, found solace in his seclusion by keeping up a Latin correspondence with his friends and acquaintances, which he recorded in a letter book that still survives. Most of the correspondents were other monks, but some were secular priests, the occupants of the neighbouring parish churches in the vale of Evesham and the Cotswold hills: the vicars of Ombersley and Toddington, the rectors of Fladbury, Stow and Willarsey, the last a former schoolmaster. They appear as the recipients of Joseph's Latin letters, composed with all the elegance of the new learning, and some of them were evidently able to reply in kind.[2] It is between these extremes of learning and illiteracy that the clergy of the medieval English Church must be judged to lie.

Kings and princes

The history of the lives and educations of the English kings exhibits no simple transition from the unlettered warrior to the learned statesman, from a Saxon David to a Stuart Solomon. Nearly every monarch up to Henry VIII took the field at least once, and it was not until 1743 that a king of England accompanied his troops into battle for the last time. Literacy, on the other hand, was already a royal accomplishment by the twelfth century.[3] There is indeed no sign that the Conqueror himself could read or write, but he seems to have taken some trouble over the

[1] *The Register of St Osmund*, ed. W. H. R. Jones, vol i (Rolls Series, 1883), pp. 304-6.
[2] *The Letter Book of Robert Joseph*, ed. H. Aveling and W. A. Pantin (Oxford Historical Society, new series xix, 1967), pp. 269-85.
[3] On what follows see V. H. Galbraith, 'The literacy of the medieval English kings', *Proceedings of the British Academy*, xxi (1935), pp. 201-38, and on the twelfth century in particular, J. W. Thompson, *The Literacy of the Laity in the Middle Ages* (1939), pp. 166-95.

education of his sons. Robert, the eldest, certainly had tutors and may have received instruction in grammar,[1] while his youngest brother Henry I, though by no means the paragon of learning which later writers supposed him, was credited by two of his contemporaries, Orderic and William of Malmesbury, with having studied letters in his youth and being able to read.[2] His grandson Henry II passed part of his youth at Bristol under a schoolmaster by the name of Matthew, and both Peter of Blois and Walter Map testify to his knowledge of Latin and French.[3] That literacy in a king was not surprising but, on the contrary, held to be essential is suggested by the proverb, quoted by several twelfth-century writers, that an unlettered king is a crowned ass – *rex illiteratus, asinus coronatus*.[4]

After 1200 the literacy of the English kings ceases to be a matter for comment, either because it was taken for granted or because, if lacking, it would have been too impolite to mention, and for the next two centuries little can be gathered about royal education. Its main features during this period were probably, however, as follows. The heir to the throne was taken from his nurse at about the age of seven and committed to the care of an experienced and well-respected knight, who is usually described as his *magister* or *preceptor*.[5] Companions were provided for him from among the king's wards, noble youths being brought up at court under *magistri* of their own.[6] The prince's *magister* exercised a general supervision over his charge, forming his manners, administering encouragement and, when necessary, discipline, rather than acting as his schoolmaster – the function proper to a clerk. The education of princes was the theme of a number of treatises which circulated in Western Europe during the middle ages, including one said to have been compiled by Aristotle for his pupil Alexander the Great, and others by more modern writers such as Thomas

---

[1] C. W. David, *Robert Curthose* (1920), pp. 6-7.
[2] C. W. David, 'The claim of Henry I to be called learned', *Anniversary Essays by Students of C. H. Haskins* (1929), pp. 45-56.
[3] *The Historical Works of Gervase of Canterbury*, ed. W. Stubbs, vol i (Rolls Series, 1879), p. 125.
[4] For examples see Galbraith, 'The literacy of the medieval English kings', pp. 213-14.
[5] For royal tutors see as follows: Richard, King of the Romans (*Royal Letters of the Reign of Henry III*, ed. W. W. Shirley, vol i (Rolls Series, 1862), pp. 179-80); Edward I (Matthew Paris, *Chronica Majora*, ed. H. R. Luard, vol iv (Rolls Series, 1877), p. 553); Edward II (*CCR 1288-96*, p. 502; Hilda Johnstone, *Edward of Caernarvon* (1946), pp. 15-17); Edward the Black Prince (T. F. Tout, *Chapters in the Administrative History of Medieval England* (1920-33), v, 318-21); Richard II (ibid., iii, 330-1); Henry VI (*Proceedings and Ordinances of the Privy Council*, ed. N. H. Nicolas, vol iii (1834), pp. 294, 296-300); Edward, son of Henry VI (*CPR 1452-61*, p. 567); Edward V (*CPR 1467-77*, pp. 401, 417).
[6] Hilda Johnstone, op. cit., p. 43.

Aquinas and Giles of Rome.[1] The purpose of these works was chiefly moral and political. They sought to inculcate ideas of virtue, justice and statecraft and to give warning, from historical examples, of the fate of tyrants. The English princes were almost certainly brought up in this general European tradition, for Sir Simon Burley, the tutor of Richard II, possessed a French book 'of the government of kings and princes',[2] and the poet Hoccleve credited Henry V with having read both Giles and Aristotle. Hoccleve's own treatise in English verse, *The Regiment of Princes*, was composed in 1411-12 and was also intended for Henry's use as prince of Wales.[3] The medieval tradition was still alive a century later when another poet, John Skelton, compiled his *Speculum Principis*, or 'mirror of a prince', in 1501, the recipient of this brief Latin tract being Skelton's pupil, the future Henry VIII.[4]

Within this general education in morals and wisdom, the English princes must also have practised more specialized techniques such as riding and feats of arms, to say nothing of social accomplishments like harping and dancing. Reading, if it was not always part of their curriculum, was certainly so by the early fourteenth century. The literacy of Edward II is suggested by the purchase in 1300 of a primer, or elementary prayer book, for his use while he was still prince of Wales.[5] As to that of his successor Edward III there can be no doubt, for we know not only that he studied letters in his youth but also the name of his teacher, John Paynel, a royal clerk whom he later promoted to be chamberlain of Chester.[6] It is likely too that Edward retained a taste for reading when he grew up; in 1335 the royal exchequer bought an expensive book of romance for his use, and it was noted that the volume lay in the king's own chamber.[7]

Edward's literary interests are nevertheless outshone for us by those of his grandson Richard II. Richard too was undoubtedly literate, a point established by Froissart in his account of the occasion in 1395 when he presented the king with a richly bound and illuminated manuscript. 'The

[1] On this subject in general see L. K. Born, 'The perfect prince: a study in thirteenth- and fourteenth-century ideals', *Speculum*, iii (1928), pp. 470-504, and his translation of Erasmus, *The Education of a Christian Prince* (1936), pp. 99-130.
[2] PRO, E 154/1/19. It was probably the French translation of Giles of Rome, *De Regimine Principum*.
[3] Thomas Hoccleve, *Works*, ed. F. J. Furnivall, vol iii (EETS, 1897), pp. 1-197, especially p. 77, lines 2129-30.
[4] F. M. Salter, 'Skelton's *Speculum Principis*', *Speculum*, ix (1934), pp. 25-37.
[5] *Liber Quotidianus Contrarotularis Garderobae* (Society of Antiquaries, 1787), p. 55.
[6] *CCR 1327-30*, p. 573.
[7] F. Devon, *Issues of the Exchequer* (1837), p. 144.

king asked me what it was about, and I told him: "About love!" He was delighted by this answer and dipped into the book in several places and read, for he spoke and read French very well.'[1] Richard's liking for books has left several traces in the contemporary records, and his library must have been extensive. In 1380 when he was thirteen a Bible in French, *The Romance of the Rose* and romances of Percival and Gawain in one volume were purchased for him at a cost of £28.[2] Nineteen of his books are mentioned between 1385 and 1388, one of them like Edward's coming significantly from the king's private room, and four volumes of Richard's collection are still extant.[3] They include Roger Dymock's Latin treatise against the Lollards, two volumes of *Statutes* and, most interesting, a book containing three Latin tracts: one on the duties of kings, a second on dreams and their interpretation and a third on astrology and divination specially compiled in 1391 'for the solace of King Richard'.[4] The composition of a book to solace the king in Latin rather than in French or English makes it highly probable that Richard, besides his ability to read French, was familiar with Latin too.

Meanwhile from the reign of Edward III comes the earliest evidence that the king could write. This is the famous letter which the king sent to Pope John XXII in 1330, when he was still under the domination of Roger Mortimer, to say that the king's own personal requests for grants of benefices to his subjects would be addressed 'Pater Sancte' in the king's own hand. The letter itself was the work of a scribe, but Edward appended the two words in a painstaking hand to serve as a specimen.[5] In like manner Edward's eldest son, the Black Prince, was able to subscribe his writs of privy seal with his mottoes *Homout* (courage) and *Ich Dene* (I serve).[6] With Richard II the king began a regular practice of attesting documents with his signature or 'sign manual' instead of merely using a seal. The earliest surviving example is the king's letter of 1389 to William Wykeham, subscribed 'Le Roy R.S. saunz departyr'.[7] From this time

[1] Froissart, *Chroniques*, ed. Kervyn de Lettenhove (1867-77), xv, 167; translated by G. Brereton (1968), p. 408.
[2] F. Devon, op. cit., p. 213.
[3] Maude V. Clarke, *Fourteenth-Century Studies* (1937), p. 122; G. Mathew, *The Court of Richard II* (1968), pp. 40-1.
[4] Bodleian, MS Bodl. 581; *Summary Catalogue of Western MSS in the Bodleian Library, Oxford*, ed. F. Madan and H. H. E. Craster, ii, part 1 (1922), no 2191.
[5] Galbraith, 'The literacy of the medieval English kings', p. 223; C. Johnson and H. Jenkinson, *English Court Hand* (1915), i, 174-5; ii, plate xxiib.
[6] *The Museum of the Public Record Office: a Short Catalogue* (1956), p. 27.
[7] Galbraith, 'The literacy of the medieval English kings' p. 223; P. Chaplais, *English Royal Documents, 1199-1461* (1971), p. 71.

forward all the English kings accord with Alice's notion of a monarch, who is always busy 'signing things'.

The evidence for royal literacy and its place in the education of princes becomes much stronger with the rise to power of the house of Lancaster in 1399. There were already literary traditions in the family when Henry IV seized the throne, for his father, John of Gaunt, had been the patron and friend of Chaucer, and his grandfather, the first duke, was the author of a devotional treatise on an ambitious scale. Henry's own love of reading is attested by the study which was built for him at Eltham Palace soon after his accession, complete with two desks 'to keep the king's books in', and when he visited Bardney Abbey in 1406 we are told that he spent an afternoon in the monks' library, reading there from several books 'for as long as he wished'.[1] He was able to write both French and English, copies of which remain in his hand, and possibly even Latin, though the grim proverb which survives in his handwriting, *Nessescitas non habet legem*, suggests the school of life rather than a thorough grounding in orthography.[2] Henry V's accomplishments were as good if not better; he studied grammar in his youth, and in later life he also wrote both French and English. Twelve books on hunting were copied for his use in 1421, and he was a borrower (but not a returner) of other people's volumes. After his death in 1422 his executors restored *The Chronicle of Jerusalem* and *The Journey of Godfrey de Bouillon* to the countess of Westmorland, and the works of St Gregory to Archbishop Arundel.[3] His younger brothers shared his love of books. John duke of Bedford commissioned lavishly illustrated works of devotion and service books, and he took advantage of the English conquest of France to acquire the whole royal library of the Valois, some 843 volumes worth over 2,300 *livres*, apparently for a single payment only of 200 *livres*![4] The activities of Humphrey duke of Gloucester as a book collector and a patron of neo-classical scholars are too well known to require comment.[5]

The family tradition of learning ran true in the last two generations of the line. Henry VI began his formal education at the age of seven, when in 1428 he was put into the charge of the earl of Warwick to learn good

[1] *Johannis Lelandi Collectanea*, ed. T. Hearne (1715), vi, 300-1; H.M. Colvin, *The History of the King's Works* (1963), ii, 935-6.
[2] J. L. Kirby, *Henry IV of England* (1970), pp. 161, 203, 223, 254.
[3] C. L. Kingsford, *Henry V* (1923), pp. 14-15; Devon, op. cit., p. 368.
[4] Ethel Carleton Williams, *My Lord of Bedford* (1963), pp. 3, 198, 249-52; L. Delisle, *Recherches sur la librarie de Charles V* (Paris, 1907), i, 138-9, 399-402.
[5] On Gloucester see K. H. Vickers, *Humphrey Duke of Gloucester* (1907), pp. 340-425, and R. Weiss, *Humanism in England during the Fifteenth Century*, 3rd ed. (1967), pp. 39-70.

manners, letters and languages, which can be taken to mean by this date the ability to read, write and understand English, French and Latin.[1] The interest in education which grew out of these studies bore fruit in the foundation of Eton and King's, and in private life the king inherited the fondness of his ancestors for literature. His chaplain and biographer, John Blackman, records how he not only occupied himself continually with the reading of scripture and chronicles, but 'used also to address letters of exhortation to clerics, full of heavenly mysteries and most salutary advice, to the great wonder of many'.[2] Madness and civil war, however, dissipated these studious interests and Henry's own son Edward grew up in circumstances very different from his father's peaceful childhood. Born in 1453, he had scarcely left his nurse for a manly education in 1460 before the civil wars drove him to flee with his mother to Scotland, whence he only reached the safety of France in 1463. Yet his literary studies survived his distracted youth. Of his knowledge of grammar, Sir John Fortescue, his fellow exile in France, said that although he had not acquired perfection, he was nevertheless sufficiently learned to deserve the name of a grammarian.[3] It was in order to give him a thorough grounding in statecraft that Fortescue produced the two Latin treatises, *De Natura Legis Nature* on the power of rulers, and *De Laudibus Legum Anglie* in praise of the English legal system.[4] But the prince's promise was never to be fulfilled; he was not quite eighteen when he suffered a violent death at Tewkesbury in 1471.

The high standard of Lancastrian education was maintained by Edward IV in the arrangements he made for his own children, and no less care was given to the upbringing of the future Edward V than Henry's son had received. Born in 1470, Edward was only 3 years old when in 1473 he received the usual governor in the person of his uncle, Anthony Woodville, Earl Rivers, and as an additional mentor, John Alcock, bishop of Rochester, who was appointed his 'teacher' that he might be brought up in virtue and cunning.[5] At the same time, and despite his youth, a detailed timetable was drawn up for his daily lessons in the future.[6] He was to begin the day by hearing mattins and mass, with the whole of the divine

[1] *Proceedings and Ordinances of the Privy Council*, ed. N. H. Nicolas, vol iii (1834), p. 296.
[2] M. R. James, *Henry VI: a Reprint of John Blacman's Memoir* (1919), pp. 27, 28, 37.
[3] Fortescue, *De Laudibus Legum Anglie*, ed. S. B. Chrimes (1942), pp. 22-3.
[4] Ibid., pp. 3-21, 27.
[5] *CPR 1467-77*, pp. 401-17.
[6] *A Collection of Ordinances and Regulations . . . of the Royal Household* (Society of Antiquaries, 1790), pp. 27-9.

office on holy days, and a sermon at the principal feasts. After mass he breakfasted and spent the morning at his lessons until dinner. At table he was to hear readings from 'such noble stories as behoveth to a prince to understand', while the conversation in his presence was to be full of 'virtue, honour, cunning, wisdom, and deeds of worship, and of nothing that should move or stir him to vice'. After dinner he had further lessons, followed by sports and exercises. This led to evensong, supper and more 'honest sports' before he retired to bed at 8.00. His schoolmaster, when he came to learn grammar, was not however Bishop Alcock, but a professional by the name of Master John Giles, who had been in royal service ever since 1465 when he had begun teaching the young duke of Buckingham, then a ward in the queen's household.[1] He was giving instruction to Edward and to his younger brother Richard duke of York by 1476 when he received a generous grant for his services of £20 a year from the customs and subsidies of Dartmouth and Exeter.[2] If we can trust the account of Dominic Mancini, who visited England in 1483, Edward was a responsive pupil. 'In word and deed', says Mancini,

> he gave so many proofs of his liberal education, of polite, nay rather scholarly, attainments far beyond his age. . . . There is one thing I shall not omit, and that is his special knowledge of literature, which enabled him to discourse elegantly, to understand fully, and to declaim most excellently from any work whether in verse or prose that came into his hands, unless it were from among the more abstruse authors.[3]

Giles appears to have remained in attendance on the princes until Edward's succession to the throne in April 1483, which was followed by Richard's usurpation in June. The princes were last seen alive in the Tower during the late summer or autumn, and in November their old schoolmaster was paid off handsomely by Richard with a further annuity of £40 from the revenues of Coventry.[4] Was this not a sign that in more than one sense his pupils no longer required his services?

The emphasis of the Lancastrians and Yorkists on literary education continued under Henry VII, who followed his predecessors in this as in

[1] A. R. Myers, 'The household of Queen Elizabeth Woodville, 1466-7', *Bulletin of the John Rylands Library*, 1 (1967-8), pp. 471-2. For a probable identification see *BRUO*, ii, 842.
[2] *CPR 1467-77*, p. 592; *CCR 1476-85*, no 1. A reward in this form suggests that he was not in holy orders.
[3] C. A. J. Armstrong, *The Usurpation of Richard III*, 2nd ed. (1969), pp. 92-3.
[4] *CPR 1476-83*, p. 373, and cf. p. 481.

B*

so much else. Both his sons received the best education that the times could afford, Arthur, the elder, in particular. Born in 1486, he was one of the earliest English boys to be taught in the principles of the new learning, which itself suggests something of his father's wisdom and farsightedness. His first schoolmaster was John Rede, who after graduating as a master of arts from New College, Oxford, had been headmaster of Winchester before he was appointed chaplain and tutor to the prince.[1] Rede was responsible for teaching Arthur his grammar between about 1491 and 1496 when he was succeeded by Bernard André, the blind French poet and historiographer who was much esteemed at Henry's court.[2] André, who may have been the author of Arthur's up-to-date education on continental lines, remained his schoolmaster until about 1500 when he resigned, to be followed by an unnamed Scot who discharged the task until Arthur's death in 1502.[3] Besides his Latin lessons the prince also learned French from the Fleming, Giles D'Ewes, who was one of the principal teachers of the subject in England at that time.[4] André's description of Arthur's reading, if it is not false, is a remarkable one, for it comprises twenty-four Latin grammarians and authors. The grammarians were the new Italian masters now coming into fashion – Guarino, Perotto, Sulpizio and Valla – while the authors included a wide range of pagan orators, poets and historians: Caesar, Cicero, Livy, Lucan, Ovid, Pliny, Sallust and Virgil, to name only some. Homer and Thucydides also made their appearance in Latin translations. Of all these André reports 'he had either committed them partly to memory, or with his own hands and eyes had read them often and revolved them', and Arthur was only sixteen when he died.[5]

The education of Arthur's younger brother, the future Henry VIII, seems to have been no less careful, although in his case details of the curriculum are lacking. Like Arthur, Henry, who was born in 1491, had three schoolmasters in succession, none of whom had tutored his brother. The first of them was the poet John Skelton, who had already achieved fame as a rhetorician and translator when he was appointed Henry's tutor in about 1495.[6] Skelton taught him to spell, as well as composing the *Speculum Principis* for his use, on the virtues and vices of princes. In 1502, at about the time that Henry became heir to the throne, Skelton was replaced by John Holt, a distinguished grammarian, master of arts and

[1] *BRUO*, iii, 1555-6.
[2] Ibid., i, 33.
[3] *Privy Purse Expenses of Elizabeth of York*, ed. N. H. Nicolas (1830), p. 28.
[4] *Dictionary of National Biography*, sub nomine.
[5] *Memorials of Henry VII*, ed. J. Gairdner (Rolls Series, 1858), p. 43.
[6] *BRUO*, iii, 1705-6; W. Nelson, *John Skelton, Laureate* (1939), pp. 71-6.

friend of Thomas More. Holt had already taught Latin at Oxford, London and Chichester as well as composing an elementary Latin grammar on original lines called *Lac Puerorum*.[1] He died however in 1504, to be followed by William Hone, another Oxford MA who had been Holt's successor at Chichester. He probably tutored Henry for the next four or five years, thereafter continuing in royal service as schoolmaster to Henry's sister Mary.[2] From these schoolmasters Henry emerged, perhaps, more learned than any of his predecessors: a facile composer of Latin, a drafter of laws and statutes and a theological controversialist of determination, to say the least.

The education of the English princes is not easy to penetrate until the second half of the fifteenth century, and we should beware of too close criticism of a system of which so little can be known. Whatever the feats, the courtesy and the learning by which the members of the line of Plantagenet were trained, they produced in Edward I and his grandson kings of notable skill in war, in civil policy and in gaining public esteem. Yet the increasing amount of evidence about princely education during the fifteenth century is not wholly fortuitous; it suggests that this education was becoming much more formalized, and that literary studies were coming to occupy a larger place. An ex-chief justice wrote Latin treatises on law and government for the son of Henry VI; a careful timetable of studies and relaxations was drawn up for Edward V; the leading schoolmasters of the day were recruited to give the most modern literary education that the age afforded to the sons of Henry VII. It all bore fruit in the king's triumphant assertion of leadership over the clergy, the learned estate, in 1534.

Nobility and gentry[3]

Below the king came the 'second estate' or upper class of laymen, running from the royal family and the great magnates at the top down to knights and gentlemen of modest means at the bottom. There were many gradations of rank and wealth within the upper class, and during the fifteenth and sixteenth centuries a permanent division developed on parliamentary lines between the 'nobility' sitting personally in the House of Lords and the 'gentry' represented in the House of Commons; but throughout our

---

[1] *BRUO*, ii, 953, and see also below, p. 110.
[2] *BRUO*, ii, 956.
[3] Since this section was written, a valuable essay on the subject has been published in the late Mr K. B. McFarlane's posthumous book, *The Nobility of Later Medieval England* (Oxford, 1973), pp. 228-47.

period and for long afterwards the members of the upper class possessed more in common than divided them. As the terms 'noble' and 'gentle' suggest, they were considered, or liked to be considered, men of distinction and virtue; they were all men of leisure, unsullied by manual labour, living off the profits of their lands and offices; and together they formed a military class whose social role was to protect the kingdom against enemies from outside and to maintain law and order from within. They tried to place their children, when it was impossible to provide for them out of the family lands, in other careers which would give them a reasonable standard of life and the chance of self-advancement. Many were sent to school to be fitted for ecclesiastical careers or later, perhaps, to be trained as lawyers and administrators. Our present concern however is not with them, but with those who stayed at home to inherit the estates and the life that went therewith. What education was deemed suitable for them; what training was necessary to make a nobleman or a gentleman?

The members of the upper class clung to their military ethos, and it coloured their life deeply until the middle of the seventeenth century when the emergence of a professional army made it superfluous. Until that time it was the *sine qua non* for men of noble or gentle rank to possess horse, arms and armour, and to answer the call to arms in times of national emergency. The preoccupation with war extended even into their leisure, of which the active pursuits – jousting and hunting – were a training for combat, and even the passive ones – heraldry, chess and the reading of histories and knightly deeds – recalled the field. Skill in riding and arms was therefore an essential element of a noble or gentle education. Yet it would be wrong to dismiss the upper class as nothing but a pack of rude fighters or obsessive huntsmen at any period after the Conquest. Chivalry, originally a term of war, came also to mean a code of good manners at home. The perfect knight was expected to behave with courtesy to women, with deference to the great and with politeness even to the lower orders. Gentle youths, growing up in their own or in some other household, were expected to give their attention to personal hygiene, deportment, the rules of social precedence and etiquette at table. Helpful manuals were written to explain the conventions in these matters.[1] When the tables were cleared and the company withdrew to make merry in hall or chamber, other accomplishments were desirable: the ability to sing and dance, to play on the harp or pipe. These social arts formed the second important branch of noble or gentle education.

[1] For examples see Furnivall's collection, *Manners and Meals in Olden Time*, and also below, pp. 105-6.

The addition of a third branch, the study of letters, was made necessary by the gradual transition of English society from the heroic age into the age of settled government and constitutional development. Even in the twelfth century the knights were coming to be the governors of the kingdom in peace as well as its defenders in war. The great magnates became associated with royal government; they were summoned to attend the king's council and in due course the meetings of his parliament; they held office in his household, helped carry out his policies in the localities and went on diplomatic missions for him. The lesser knights and gentlemen of the shires did not escape being drawn into the royal administration either. They too were charged with bearing office in their counties as sheriffs, coroners, collectors of subsidies, commissioners for special inquiries, members of the House of Commons and justices of the peace. The strong desire for political and social reasons to take up these offices, many of which involved contact with written records, offered one obvious incentive for the members of the upper class to become literate. Their own affairs provided others. As the organization of households and estates became more complex, as records of income and expenditure came to be kept, contracts and leases to be filed and letters to be exchanged, the noble and gentle proprietors were almost obliged to become acquainted with the documentation of their affairs. How else could they have kept a check on the stewards, clerks and bailiffs who discharged the day-to-day tasks of administration? Not to do so would have been to risk losing power and to invite dishonesty.

Furthermore, literature came to have an important place in the leisure of the upper classes. More than one of the fourteenth-century magnates whom we know best for his stormy career in war or politics appears to have sought in books a quiet retreat from the strains of public life. Guy Beauchamp, earl of Warwick, had a collection of twenty-eight volumes, chiefly romances and lives of the saints, until in 1306, for some reason or other, he gave them to the Cistercians of Bordesley Abbey in Worcestershire.[1] His better-known contemporary, Thomas earl of Lancaster, also mollified a turbulent life with a taste for literature. Just before his execution at Pontefract in 1322 he asked his confessor to arrange for the return of a French Bible which he had borrowed from a clerk of York and was to be found in his treasury 'among his other books'.[2] In the political

---

[1] H. J. Todd, *Illustrations of the Lives and Writings of Gower and Chaucer* (1810), pp. 160-2.
[2] R. L. Atkinson, 'A French Bible in England about the year 1322', *English Historical Review*, xxxviii (1923), pp. 248-9.

struggles of Richard II's reign, the king's old tutor, Sir Simon Burley, and his uncle, Thomas duke of Gloucester, were on opposite sides and both met violent deaths, yet their bibliophile tastes could hardly have been more civilized. A list of Burley's goods in 1388 mentions twenty-one of his books including a Bible and seven volumes of romances, all in French,[1] while the inquisitions concerning Gloucester's property in 1397 reveal no less than eighty-four volumes in the duke's castle of Pleshey in Essex and a further eleven at his house in London. They included romances, histories, lives of saints, service books and Bibles, mostly in French save for a few on law and science in Latin.[2] These noble libraries were only the precursors of many more in the fifteenth century, even before the invention of printing had multiplied the number of available books.

Nor were their owners readers only. More than one medieval knight and nobleman embarked upon literary compositions of his own, and on a wide variety of subjects. The earliest of these gentle authors wrote in French. Walter of Bibbesworth, a knight of Hertfordshire who flourished in 1270, composed two treatises in verse, one on the crusades and the other on the education of children.[3] His namesake and contemporary, Walter of Henley, produced his *Husbandry*, a guide to estate management, between about 1276 and about 1290.[4] Of him we know little more than that he was probably a knight of Buckinghamshire who in later life entered the Dominican order. In the middle of the fourteenth century no less a person than Henry of Grosmont, first duke of Lancaster and father-in-law of John of Gaunt, exercised himself in writing the devotional treatise, *Le Livre de Seyntz Medicines*, which he finished in 1354.[5] A year or two later Sir Thomas Gray of Heton, an English knight of Northumberland, took advantage of a spell of captivity at Edinburgh to begin composing the *Scalachronicon*, an ambitious chronicle of British history in five books, perhaps the first historical work by an English layman since Saxon times.[6]

These are only isolated figures, but by the reign of Richard II it is

[1] PRO, E 154/1/19; BM, MS Add. 2549, p. 206.
[2] Viscount Dillon and W. H. St J. Hope, 'Inventory of the goods of Thomas duke of Gloucester', *Archaeological Journal*, liv (1897), pp. 275-308; *Calendar of Inquisitions Miscellaneous*, vi (1963), no 372.
[3] Kathleen Lambley, *The Teaching and Cultivation of the French Language in England* (1920), pp. 11-15, and see below, p. 72.
[4] Dorothy Oschinsky, *Walter of Henley and other Treatises* (1971), especially pp. 144-8.
[5] *Le Livre de Seyntz Medicines*, ed. E. J. Arnould (Anglo-Norman Text Society, ii, 1940), p. 224.
[6] *Dictionary of National Biography* (1908), viii, 464.

possible to discern a whole literary circle of noblemen and gentlemen centred on the court, owning books, keeping company with poets and writing prose or verse themselves. Besides the figures already mentioned – Richard II, Simon Burley and Thomas of Woodstock – it is worth while noting the group of friends and acquaintances whom contemporaries, rightly or wrongly, suspected of anticlericalism and even heresy: the 'Lollard knights'.[1] Sir John Clanvowe (d. 1391) was certainly the author of *The Two Ways*, a short devotional treatise of ten folios in English prose, and very probably of the English poem called *The Boke of Cupide*, a debate on love between the cuckoo and the nightingale.[2] Sir Lewis Clifford (d. 1404) was a close friend of Chaucer and apparently also of the French poet, Eustace Deschamps, who refers to him twice in his verses.[3] In 1393 the duchess of York bequeathed him a book 'of vices and virtues'.[4] Sir John Montague, later earl of Salisbury (d. 1400), was praised by a contemporary French writer as a maker of ballads, songs, roundels and lays,[5] while Sir Richard Stury (d. 1395), the friend of Froissart and an acquaintance of Chaucer, owned a manuscript of the *Roman de la Rose* which was bought after his death by Thomas duke of Gloucester.[6] Sir Philip la Vache (d. 1408), another of the circle, was also a friend of Chaucer who addressed to him the poem *Truth*, a 'balade de bon conseyl'.[7] Henceforward instances of nobles and knights as patrons, authors and book collectors become so numerous that to list them all would be to write a whole history of English literature.

The three main elements in the life and education of the English upper class in the later middle ages were therefore the exercise of arms, social accomplishments and the ability to read. Exactly when the study of letters became a normal part of this curriculum is difficult to define, and the attention given to it must have varied from family to family even within the same century. Messrs Richardson and Sayles have collected numerous

[1] On the knights in general see K. B. McFarlane, *Lancastrian Kings and Lollard Knights* (1972), pp. 139-226.

[2] V. J. Scattergood, 'The authorship of "The Boke of Cupide"', *Anglia*, lxxxii (1964), pp. 137-49; ' "The Boke of Cupide" – an edition', *English Philological Studies*, ix (1965), pp. 47-83; '*The Two Ways*: an unpublished religious treatise by Sir John Clanvowe', ibid., x (1967), pp. 33-56.

[3] G. L. Kittredge, 'Chaucer and some of his friends', *Modern Philology*, i (1903-4), pp. 6-13.

[4] K. B. McFarlane, op. cit., p. 185.

[5] J. Webb, 'Translation of a French metrical history of the deposition of King Richard II', *Archaeologia*, xx (1824), pp. 72, 320.

[6] BM, MS Royal 19 B xiii (Sir G. F. Warner and J. P. Gilson, *Catalogue of Royal and King's MSS in the British Museum* (1921), ii, 328).

[7] Edith Rickert, 'Thou Vache', *Modern Philology*, xi (1913-14), pp. 209-25.

examples of earls and knights of the twelfth century who were reputed learned and in some cases evidently knew Latin;[1] on the other hand prejudice against literary as compared with physical prowess had not altogether disappeared even in the sixteenth century. Richard Pace, the humanist writer, tells an amusing anecdote of an English dinner party in 1515 when the conversation turned to the education of children:

> There happened to be present one of those whom we call gentlemen, and who always carry some horn hanging at their backs, as though they would hunt during dinner. He, hearing letters praised, roused with sudden anger, burst out furiously with these words . . . 'A curse on those stupid letters! all learned men are beggars. . . . I swear by God's body I'd rather that my son should hang than study letters. For it becomes the sons of gentlemen to blow the horn nicely, to hunt skilfully, and elegantly carry and train a hawk. But the study of letters should be left to the sons of rustics.'[2]

Sixteen years later Sir Thomas Elyot conceived the existence of similar prejudices when he censured those who 'affirm without shame that to a great gentleman it is a notable reproach to be well learned and to be called a great clerk'.[3] It is however likely that the ability at least to read the vernacular was generally mastered by the upper class from Richard II's reign onwards, if not in youth then in later life. This is suggested by the literary interests already mentioned, by the increasing survival at this date of autograph letters, wills and other personal documents, and the numberless activities, in public and private, which personality and experience alone could scarcely have discharged without literacy. Chaucer's portraits of the upper class of his day depict not only a knight skilled in war, but a squire who can 'purtreye and write', and a franklin who has held one civil office after another: sheriff, accounter, knight of the shire and justice of the peace.[4]

The extent to which Latin was studied is more of a problem, but there are indications that it was becoming common among the upper class by the fifteenth century, although whether as a necessary skill or as a mental discipline or merely to acquire the 'glamour' that it conferred upon clerks

[1] H. G. Richardson and G. O. Sayles, *The Governance of Medieval England* (1963), pp. 263-84.
[2] R. Pace, *De Fructu* (Basel, 1517), p. 15, translated in *Manners and Meals in Olden Time*, ed. Furnivall, pp. xii-xiv; compare John Skelton, *Poetical Works*, ed. A. Dyce (1843), i, 334-5.
[3] Elyot, *The Boke Named the Gouernour*, ed. H. H. S. Croft (1883), i, 99, and cf. 104-5, 113ff.
[4] *The Works of Geoffrey Chaucer*, ed. F. N. Robinson, 2nd ed. (1957), pp. 17-18, 20.

1 *READING*

Elizabeth (d. 1508), wife of Sir John Donne of Kidwelly, using a service book. Religious devotion was an important stimulus towards literacy among the laity.

2 *WRITING*

The signature of the young Edward V during his short reign in 1483, followed by those of his uncle, Richard duke of Gloucester (motto: Loyalty binds me), and Henry duke of Buckingham (motto: Let me be often mindful). Shortly afterwards Richard seized the throne. Buckingham, although consistently mindful of his own interests, was executed later in the year.

3 *A SCHOOLMASTER'S NOTEBOOK*

Vulgaria—English sentences with Latin translations – studied in the grammar school of Master Robert Londe (plate 10) over the Newgate in fifteenth-century Bristol (plate 9). The heading 'Wotton' may indicate material borrowed from the nearby grammar school at Wotton-under-Edge.

(Right) The opening lines of the *Equivoca*—a grammatical poem on homonyms, attributed to John of Garland. The initial A is missing; the text trickles through an exhaustive commentary.

(Below) *Lac Puerorum*, 'milk for children', an elementary grammar by John Holt, *c.* 1496. Its use of visual aids to explain the declension of 'hic magister' is typical of late medieval efforts to make grammar easy and interesting.

Uguſtus/ti/to/ceſar vel menſis habeto.
Auguſtus/tus/tui/vult diuinatio dici.
Mobile cum fiat auguſtus/nobile ſignat.
Augeo dat primū/dant guſtus auilcʒ ſecundunt.

[In ſuperiori libro tractauit autor de ſynonymis: quibus ſufficienter ſm ordinem alphabeti tractatis. Ja iſto ſecundo libro ſuo τ vltimo de equiuocatōe nominum τ verborum aliarumcʒ partiū orationis eode ordine (qui ſuper i us eſt ſeruatus) intendit plenius edocere. In primo igitur agit de equiuocatione hanus dictois Auguſt: τ dicens qʒ plura ſignificat. Sed qʒ ſin diuerſam ſignificatione illius dicere vario variaſ: docet autor primo eius declinationem. quia cognita eius ſignificatio facilius cognoſcef. Ponit ergo differentiam inter auguſtus qd eſt ſecunde declinationis nominum: τ auguſtus quod eſt quarte declinationis n. minuē: imo tamen ſubſtantiua. Et Auguſtus tatum.tam primū. qʒ ſecunde declinationis: τ eſt adiectiuum. Dicens qʒ hic Auguſtus tis ſecunde declinationis: ſiut quidam imperator: homanorum ſic dictus: ab augeo eo. quia poſt victoriam obtentā ab hoſtibus quos deuicit. Antonium videlicet τ Cleopatram: multipliciter auxit rem rempublicam' Unde tanta prerogatiua meruit dignitatis: extolli: qʒ ipſe τ quilibet imperator pot eum ſuo nomine cenſeretur. Unde ſic ſcribitur imperator: ſemper Auguſto. quia quilibet imperator vocatur Auguſtus. quia auget rem publicam: vel haberet ſiue haberet voluntatem ſecundo.

[Item Auguſtus euidem declinationis ſecunde: vocatur q̄ quidam menſis. anglice the mounth of Auguſt. quia in eo menſe augentur fructus. Uel quia in illo menſe natus fuerat ille imperator. Uel quia in illo menſe de hoſtibus triumphauit qui menſis ante vocabatur Sextilis. quia eſt ſextus menſis ab imbre: id eſt a Martio. ſicut September dicitur ſeptimus ab imbre: τ ſic de ceteris. Hic Auguſtus tus tui. quarte declinationis eſt quedam ſpecies diuinationis. anglice a v vj teller a tre: facta per auguſtum auium: quando aliqʒ predicat futura per garritum auium. Soleba̅t enim antiquitus eſca ſparge re gallinis. τ in guſtu τ acceptione illius eſce ſolebant capere diuinationem/ q̄ Auguſtus dicitur. Et tunc componitur ab hoc nomine auis: τ hic guſt⁹ tus anglice a taſte. Unde auguſtus quaſi auis guſtus.

[Auguſtus ta.tum.id eſt hic τ hec nobilis τ hoc le. Omnibus. Uox precor auguſtas pro me tua mollitat auree. Et etiam tunc componitur ab aue τ guſtus quia ſolis nobilibus ſicut olim guſtare aues. Et tunc componit Auguſtus au guſto. auguſtiſſimus.

[Conſtrue. Auguſtus ceſar vel menſis.i.exiſtens ceſar vel menſis habeto.i. habeat ti.to.iſtas inflectiones t.in genitiuo: τ to in datiuo: Auguſtus in nomi natiuo Uel ut pot exponi. O tu ceſar vel o ti menſis: habeto.i.habe auguſtus id eſt hoc nomē auguſtus facies: et in gtō: τ to in dtō ſed mihi prior conſtructio magis placet. Secundū verſi ſic conſtrue. Auguſtus facie τ tus in gtō τ tui in dtō: vult dici diuinatio.i.quedā ſpēs diuinationis q̄ ſit p guſtu auiū. Tercium verſum ſic conſtrue. Et cū auguſtus fiat.i.ſit factū mobile.i.adiectiuū ſic decli naf. Auguſtus ta.tum. ſignat.i.ſignificat mobile.i.illud qd hic τ hec nobilis et hoc le. ſignificat. Augeo dat τc. Conſtrue. Au eo.i. hoc verbū augeo auges: atʒi augere eſt primū auguſtū.i. auguſtus qñ idē: qd impator ceſar vt men ſis.i.deriuaf de augeo. Suſtus: qʒ p et.τ ams dant ſcdm auguſtū i. augnitus qñ idem e qd diuinatio: vel qñ eſt nomē adiectiuū: ſic cōponif de hoc nomine auis. τ guſtus tus tui.]

Prima pars

[Here is to be noted/that in euery plurell nombre the vocatyf ſhall be lyke the nominatyf/and the abla tyf lyke the datyf. Alſo whan the nominatyf ſingu ler of this declenſon endeth in as or in es/thou ſhalt put awaye s.to make the vocatyf/as hic Thomas/ hic Anchiſes o thoma.o anchiſe. In all other of this declenſon the vocatyf ſhall be lyke the nominatyf as hic poeta:o poeta.

The ſynguler. Hec muſa:huius muſe :huic muſe. hāc ſam.o ſa.ab hac ſa. The plurell he muſe. harū ſarum his ſis.has ſas.o muſe:ab his muſis.

[Here is to be noted that theſe. vii. nownes in this verſe maketh the datyf and ablatyf plurell bothe in is and in abus

Filia nata deas liberta ſtulabus equabus.

Alſo the ſcrypture vſeth aiabus:famulab⁹:dſiabus/ the whiche of all ſuche other be not of vſe

[Theſe nownes of Hebrewe Paſcha:manna : zizai nia.and mammona.be the neutre gendre and of no declenſon. Though we fynde in holy ſcrypture the ge ntyf and datyf in e.more of vſe than of rule/and ly ke wyſe Adam and Abraham. As for alpha and iota and generally all names of letters they be both neu tre and vndeclyned And ſome lettred men ſaye hoc paſcha paſchatis. And polenta is the feminyne gen dre: vt Plautus. Ubi nequam homines polentam pranſitant/how be it Ouide vſeth hym in the neutre gendre/as Dulce dedit teſta quod coxerat ante poi lenta.]

Opuſcul.

[Examples of the ſeconde declenſon.

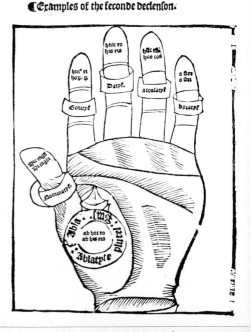

and learned men, is hard to say. Thomas of Woodstock was learning grammar in 1366 when he was eleven, and the future Henry V, then only the son of the earl of Derby, in 1396 at the age of nine.[1] In 1413 William Lord Ros of Belvoir Castle made provision in his will for a chaplain to be hired to teach grammar to his sons, of whom there were five, and in 1419 a London grammar master was paid a year's fees for teaching Walter House, a royal ward and heir to the manor of Ashfield in Suffolk.[2] There was a regular grammar master in the royal household by 1449 to teach the king's wards and the other boys whom he received to be trained,[3] and in 1467 the sons of the duke of Buckingham, Henry and Humphrey Stafford, then in the queen's wardship, were receiving a similar tuition in grammar.[4] In so educating their wards, those responsible were doing no more than their own fathers would have done had they been alive.

There are even instances of noble boys being sent to pursue their studies in the universities. This had long been so of those who were destined for the Church, and it is not surprising to find the practice extended to elder sons who aimed merely at becoming educated laymen. If later testimony may be trusted, the young Henry V, a year or two after we have seen him learning grammar, continued his studies at Oxford under the tutelage of his uncle, Henry Beaufort, the chancellor of the university, where he lived in a chamber over the front gate of the Queen's College. The story, if it is true, must belong to the year 1398 when Henry was twelve.[5] A generation later two noble youths and their tutors came in turn to reside in University College: Robert Hungerford, heir to the barony of Hungerford, from 1437 to 1438 and John Tiptoft, son and heir of the first Lord Tiptoft, from 1440 to 1443.[6] Neither boy was more than a paying guest in the college, and in neither case is the course of studies known, but the fact that each had a graduate tutor suggests that far from merely engaging in spelling and reading, they were learning grammar or even arts. It may well have been these studies that suggested Hungerford's appointment as English ambassador to the council of Basel in 1446, while his coetanean, Tiptoft, was stimulated in later life to study at Padua and to become a notable patron of learning. Towards the end of the century, when Thomas Grey, son and heir of the marquess of Dorset, and his two

[1] Devon, op. cit., p. 189; C. L. Kingsford, *Henry V*, pp. 14-15.
[2] *Reg. Chichele, Canterbury*, ed. E. F. Jacob, vol ii (1937), pp. 23-4; Devon, op. cit., p. 359.
[3] On this subject see below, pp. 217-19.
[4] *Bulletin of the John Rylands Library*, l (1967-8), pp. 471-2.
[5] *BRUO*, ii, 909-10.
[6] Ibid., ii, 985; iii, 1877-9.

younger brothers came to be educated in Oxford, the university authorities, proud of the honour, spent 2s. 6d. on wine and wafers to entertain them on their arrival in 1495. They were subsequently put under the tuition of the future cardinal, Thomas Wolsey.[1] In 1497 Sir Thomas Markenfield, a knight of Yorkshire, made similar arrangements for Ninian, his son and heir, to spend two years at Oxford before going on to the Inns of Court.[2] Instances of this kind are not numerous until the middle of the sixteenth century, and they should not be overrated, but they nevertheless provide yet another sign of the growing interest of the upper class in literary studies and, like a shadow of coming events, presage the great invasion of the universities by the aristocracy after the Reformation.[3]

Administrators and lawyers

The literary concerns of the king, the magnates and the gentry were not however limited to their own education or their private libraries. The administration of their property and their role in the life and affairs of the community caused them to employ other literate men to serve them as secretaries, clerks and agents. The household of servants with which every great man surrounded himself, whether bishop or abbot, earl or knight, contained a significant proportion of men engaged in literary tasks, to say nothing of the stewards, receivers and bailiffs in charge of the lord's estates, whose work also involved them with documents to a greater or lesser extent. Because of the literary demands which it made, royal and private administration both stimulated the spread of literacy and provided employment for the literate, thus foreshadowing on a smaller scale the role that is played by business and professional life today.

In all England it was the king whose affairs were most important, whose possessions most extensive and whose administration was in consequence the largest and best developed. It is difficult to give an exact census of the clerical posts in the royal administration at any one period, but most of the departments have left some details of their size from which a general impression may be gained concerning the later middle ages. The royal household, of which the fullest picture comes from Edward IV's reign, contained three main clerical divisions at that time.[4] The secretarial department – the signet office – consisted of a secretary, four clerks and

---

[1] *BRUO*, ii, 824-5.
[2] Ibid., p. 1222.
[3] On the later history of noble education see J. H. Hexter, *Reappraisals in History* (1961), pp. 45-70.
[4] A. R. Myers, *The Household of Edward IV* (1959), *passim*.

probably three apprentices.[1] The jewelhouse or treasury of the chamber maintained a single treasurer with a clerk to assist him. The counting house, the centre of household economy, was presided over by three great officers – steward, treasurer and controller – but since they were often absent on royal business, the day-to-day work devolved on the cofferer and his six assistants, while another thirteen clerks assigned to the household below stairs kept the accounts of the kitchen, the stable and so on. The total strength of the clerical staff in the royal household probably reached thirty or thirty-five during the fifteenth century.

Next came the administrative departments which had in previous centuries 'moved out of court', or split away from the royal household itself. The largest of these was the chancery, the senior staff of which comprised in the fourteenth century the chancellor himself, twelve clerks of the first form, twelve of the second and twenty-four cursitors. Since however the clerks of the first form were each allowed to employ three assistants and those of the second form two or one, the whole clerical strength of the office probably topped 100.[2] The privy seal office was much smaller, with a keeper and four clerks in the fourteenth century, rising to five in the fifteenth when there were also half a dozen assistants, say a dozen in all.[3] The staff of the early fourteenth-century exchequer included seven great officers (the treasurer, chancellor and four or five barons) and between twenty and thirty lesser ones, including the two remembrancers, the engrosser, auditors, chamberlains, tellers and sundry clerks.[4] The great wardrobe required a keeper and half a dozen clerical assistants, others being maintained in the various local warehouses where the wardrobe staff supervised the storage of the king's possessions.[5] The courts of common law had also their complements of clerks. The king's bench employed a minimum of twenty-three in 1317, and by the end of the century there were about fifteen seniors, whose underlings and assistants probably brought the strength of the department to thirty.[6] The clerks of the court of common pleas with their quaint denominations –

---

[1] Jocelyn Otway-Ruthven, *The King's Secretary and the Signet Office in the Fifteenth Century* (1939), pp. 110-13.
[2] Chaplais, *English Royal Documents*, pp. 20-3.
[3] A. L. Brown, 'The privy seal clerks in the early fifteenth century', in *Essays Presented to Kathleen Major*, ed. D. Bullough and R. L. Storey (1971), pp. 261-2.
[4] T. Madox, *History and Antiquities of the Exchequer* (1711), pp. 564-87, 713-42.
[5] Tout, *Chapters*, vol iv (1928), pp. 386-7.
[6] *Select Cases in the Court of King's Bench*, ed. G. O. Sayles, vol v (Selden Society, lxxiv, 1958), pp. ix-xvii; vol vii (ibid., lxxxviii, 1971), pp. xvi-xviii.

prothonotaries, filacers and exigenters – added up to a similar number.[1] In all, the various departments of the royal administration centred in London and Westminster probably employed between 200 and 250 clerical officers during the later middle ages, but this, although the largest concentration, was not quite the whole story. At a local level each of the sheriffs had the assistance of a clerk or two – a receiver of moneys and a keeper of writs;[2] there were also the stewards and receivers of crown lands, while the collection of customs and taxation, though usually performed by representatives of local communities who were not full-time employees of the crown, nevertheless involved more clerical work and acted as a further stimulus towards national literacy.

No private administration could equal the size and complexity of the king's, but everyone of consequence possessed one, from the queen and the other members of the royal family, through the bishops and lay magnates, to the gentle occupants of two or three manors and the aggregate of their affairs, the servants they employed and the records to which they gave rise was very much greater than that of the king. Private administration naturally varied in size and scope with the wealth and concerns of the lords concerned, which also fluctuated through marriages, the endowment of children and changing political fortunes, but certain features are common to the administrations of the great magnates, from the Black Prince and John of Gaunt in the fourteenth century to the earl of Northumberland and Cardinal Wolsey in the early sixteenth.[3] In the household itself a steward and a chamberlain usually exercised general supervision, while a number of knights and gentlemen attached to the lord's chamber bore him company and did his errands. A treasurer, a controller and a cofferer paid wages and expenses, supervised the purchase and consumption of supplies and kept the household accounts. A chapel of priests, clerks and choristers provided religious services and was probably also a source of literate servants, the chaplains being seconded

---

[1] Margaret Hastings, *The Court of Common Pleas in Fifteenth-Century England* (Ithaca and New York, 1947), pp. 107-8.
[2] W. A. Morris and J. R. Strayer, *The English Government at Work, 1327-1336*, ii (1947), pp. 100-1.
[3] See in general G. A. Holmes, *The Estates of the Higher Nobility in Fourteenth-Century England* (1957), pp. 58-84, and in particular, Margaret Sharp, 'The central administrative system of Edward the Black Prince', in Tout, *Chapters*, vol v (1930), pp. 289-400; S. Armitage-Smith, *John of Gaunt* (1904), pp. 221-7; R. Somerville, *History of the Duchy of Lancaster*, vol i (1953), pp. 90-110; Margaret Aston, *Thomas Arundel* (1967), pp. 236ff, 410-14; *The Regulations of the Household of the Fifth Earl of Northumberland*, ed. T. Percy (1770), pp. 43-6; George Cavendish, *The Life and Death of Cardinal Wolsey*, ed. R. S. Sylvester (EETS, 1959), pp. 18-21.

and the choristers promoted for this purpose when necessary. Lastly the menial servants carried out the multifarious tasks of housekeeping and were styled, according to rank, yeomen, grooms and pages or children.

The lord's own household, however, like that of the king, was only part of his administrative machine. His wealth and power came from his estates and these required their own system of management. At the lowest level there were reeves and bailiffs in charge of individual manors and estates. These were grouped by counties or some other convenient arrangement under receivers (originally clerics) responsible for finance, and stewards (usually gentlemen) who held the lord's courts and supervised the lesser officers in their jurisdictions. Higher still came a receiver-general who in most large administrations from the fourteenth century onwards exercised supreme control over the receipt and payment of moneys, a chief steward or steward of lands, and often special auditors to tour the estates and help compose and check the local accounts.

It is more difficult than might be expected to ascertain how many members of these organizations were literate, and in any case the whole list of staff has rarely survived. While reeves and bailiffs probably received clerical assistance in order to understand written instructions and to prepare accounts, household servants not apparently concerned with such things may have been literate nevertheless. Dr Margaret Aston has shown that the household of Thomas Arundel, when he was bishop of Ely, contained ten or eleven clerks between 1381 and 1384, but the twenty-three yeomen included one man described as 'clerk of the wardrobe' and two others who had previously been choristers in the bishop's chapel and were able at least to read.[1] The household roll of Henry Percy, earl of Northumberland, in 1512 numbered 166 of whom a minimum of 50 were probably literate, including 4 great officers, a chapel establishment of 22, a surveyor, a secretary and 14 clerks.[2] A decade or so later Cardinal Wolsey's household was reckoned at almost 500 strong before his fall in 1529, the literates again numbering at least 80, with 4 great officers, a chapel of 46, 2 secretaries, at least 9 assorted clerks, and 3 others seconded from the royal chancery.[3]

Medieval administrators were recruited in two ways. Some rose from the ranks, beginning their careers as choristers or children in the great private households, or in the royal administration as menial assistants to the senior clerks who drilled them in the methods of the department. The

[1] Margaret Aston, op. cit., pp. 252-6, 410-14.
[2] T. Percy, op. cit., pp. 43-6.
[3] George Cavendish, op. cit., pp. 18-21.

seniors of the medieval chancery trained the apprentices in this way, while in the privy seal office Dr A. L. Brown has noted that 'the normal method of entry was to begin work under an established clerk ... and progress to an established clerkship with a privileged position in the office'.[1] Others entered the world of administration at a higher level after a university career, frequently of a distinguished kind. Thus John Stratford, the future archbishop of Canterbury, was a DCL of Oxford when he first appears as deputy treasurer of the exchequer in 1326-7, while John Thoresby, after graduating in arts from the same university, was appointed an exchequer clerk in 1330 after which he became in turn keeper of the rolls in the chancery, keeper of the privy seal and finally archbishop of York – the seal of a successful career.[2]

The two meanings of the word 'clerk' remind us of the frequency with which ecclesiastics discharged administrative posts in medieval times, especially those which involved secretarial work and accounting. Until 1371 the great officers of state – chancellor, treasurer and keeper of the privy seal – were ecclesiastics to a man except for a short period after 1340 when Edward III tried the experiment of appointing laymen.[3] The clerks of the royal administration were generally unmarried men in major or minor orders during the fourteenth century, and in 1388 those of the chancery were specifically forbidden to take wives.[4] Ecclesiastics made themselves so indispensable in private administration that they often doubled as receivers and stewards, and might in the latter office discharge the duties normally done by gentlemen. The role of the clergy in this respect did not however escape criticism, especially during the last third of the fourteenth century, a period of unusually fervid anticlericalism. In 1371 the laity in parliament petitioned successfully for the removal of ecclesiastics from the three great offices of state, apparently through vague fears of inefficiency and malpractice in waging the war in France.[5] Not long afterwards a more generalized attack on the employment of clerics as administrators appeared in the second version of Langland's *Piers Plowman*, composed between 1376 and 1377, on the grounds that it led them to neglect their canonical duties. 'Their masses and their mattins and many of their hours are done undevoutly; it is to be dreaded lest

---

[1] T. F. Tout, 'The household of the chancery and its disintegration', in *Essays Presented to R. L. Poole*, ed. H. W. C. Davis (1927), pp. 72-5; Brown, op. cit., pp. 262-3.
[2] *BRUO*, iii, 1796-8, 1863-4.
[3] For lists of these officers see F. M. Powicke and E. B. Fryde, *Handbook of British Chronology*, 2nd ed. (1961), pp. 83-93.
[4] *Essays Presented to R. L. Poole*, pp. 82-3.
[5] *Rotuli Parliamentorum* (1767-77), ii, 304.

Christ at the Judgment accurse full many.'[1] The argument was repeated
with more venom and at greater length by the Lollards. 'Lords do great
wrong and guile', runs one of their tracts, 'for they make priests stewards
of their household, clerks of their kitchen, auditors, treasurers, almoners,
and stewards of their courts as though no man could discharge worldly
offices but they.' 'Might not lords', concludes the writer, 'find true laymen
in their lordships to rule their households and worldly offices?'[2]

These criticisms seem to have had little immediate effect. The laymen
who took office under Edward III in 1371 were no more successful than
their predecessors, and by 1377 the clergy were again in control of the
three great offices. Thereafter the great and the privy seals were hardly
ever out of their hands until the Reformation. Yet a gradual increase in
the number of married clerks, lay rather than ecclesiastical in their way of
life, is perceptible from the end of the fourteenth century onwards. The
office of treasurer of England itself was normally held by laymen after
1422. Married men gradually infiltrated the chancery, despite the prohibition of 1388, until at last in 1523 even the six senior clerks were permitted
to marry; in the privy seal office the poet Hoccleve was married by 1410.[3]
The magnates too were tending to charge laymen more frequently with
secretarial work and accounting,[4] and if they held back it was often
because it cost more to employ them than it did priests who could be
given benefices at the Church's expense. William Worcester (1415-*c.* 1480)
was an early forerunner of the senior administrators of Tudor and Stuart
times, with his spell at Oxford followed by marriage and employment as
secretary to Sir John Fastolf, but he did not reap great rewards from his
service. Hence the wry humour with which he remarked to John Paston
in 1454, 'I have five shillings yearly, all costs borne, to help pay for bonnets
that I lose. I told my master so this week, and he told me yesterday he
wished me to have been a priest, so I had been disposed, to have got me a
living by reason of a benefice.'[5]

The work of the medieval administrators demanded a working knowledge of Latin, and until the early fifteenth century of French.[6] The chief

[1] Langland, *Piers the Plowman*, ed. Skeat, vol i: B Prol. 95-9; cf. C Prol. 93ff.
[2] *The English Works of Wycliffe,* ed. Matthew, pp. 168, 247.
[3] *Essays Presented to R. L. Poole*, pp. 82-3: A. L. Brown, op. cit., p. 270.
[4] K. B. McFarlane, 'William Worcester: a preliminary survey', in *Studies Presented to Sir Hilary Jenkinson*, p. 199; B. P. Wolffe, *The Royal Demesne in English History* (1971), pp. 161-8.
[5] *The Paston Letters*, ed. J. Gairdner (1904), ii, 334.
[6] On this topic see Helen Suggett, 'The use of French in the later middle ages', *Transactions of the Royal Historical Society*, 4th series, xxviii (1946), pp. 61-83.

language employed in the chancery was Latin, in which most of the charters and letters were composed, though French documents were occasionally issued too. The rolls of parliament, drawn up by chancery clerks seconded for the purpose, were usually kept in Latin until the early fourteenth century and thereafter in French until it was in turn replaced by English at the beginning of the fifteenth. The exchequer and the royal household produced their accounts in Latin, but the privy seal made more use of the vernacular. Its writs were wholly in Latin only until about 1300, after which French was principally employed until the 1420s when, as elsewhere, English crept in. Administrators in private households must also have been familiar with both Latin and French until at least 1400, since the two languages were used interchangeably during the fourteenth century for such documents as conveyances, contracts, private letters and wills. Private accounting too was conducted in French on occasions. At the end of the century students of business techniques at Oxford were still mastering French and Latin, and French indeed retained some currency for the purposes already mentioned until as late as the 1430s. Meanwhile, however, English became steadily more popular; it was beginning to be used for deeds by the 1370s, wills by the 1380s and private letters soon after 1400, although not until the middle of the fifteenth century was it finally established as the second language of business.

Latin and French, together with English after the middle of the fifteenth century, were also the working languages of the common law and hence the literary requirements of those other men of affairs, the common lawyers.[1] Of the three, Latin had dominated the first two and a half centuries of legal history after the Conquest. It was the language of the older treatises such as Bracton and Fleta, of the statutes until about 1300, of most legal writs and of the enrolments of pleas and judgements in the records of the courts of common law. French had come to establish itself during the thirteenth century as the medium in which the pleas were actually conducted both in the king's courts and those of the private jurisdictions. Consequently the yearbooks of leading cases were also written in French, as were most of the statutes from 1300 until 1487, and the later treatises on law such as 'Britton' (*c.* 1291-2) and Sir Thomas Littleton's *Tenures* (*c.* 1475). English made a rather late appearance in the legal world. It was used for some parliamentary petitions after the end of the fourteenth century and for most of the petitions to the chancellor to

[1] Sir John Fortescue, *De Laudibus Legum Anglie*, ed. S. B. Chrimes (1942), pp. 114-17; F. Pollock and F. W. Maitland, *The History of English Law before Edward I*, 2nd ed. (1898), i, 79-87; W. S. Holdsworth, *History of English Law*, 3rd ed. (1923), ii, 477-82.

use his equitable jurisdiction by the middle of the fifteenth. Parliamentary statutes however did not appear in the language until 1484, and as is well known, French continued to be widely used by the English common lawyers until Hanoverian times.

Consequently any who wished to study the common law, whether for professional reasons or merely to gain a useful familiarity with its procedures, needed first to master Latin, and many instances may be found of boys being sent to grammar school as a prelude to legal studies. Thus in 1380 John Melburne of London promised as part of a marriage contract to maintain his son William at Oxford until he had learnt sufficient grammar, after which he was to study the law of the land in the king's courts.[1] Nine years later William Tonge, alderman of London, arranged in his will for his elder son to practise the common law when he was well seen in grammar.[2] The sequence of school and legal training in London is also illustrated in the history of the Paston family of Norfolk. William, the founder of their fortunes, was said by his enemies to have been the son of a 'good, plain husbandman' of Paston, who sent him to school in the 1390s, after which he went to 'court' in London to study law, and became successively serjeant and justice of the court of common pleas. Whatever William's origins, there is no reason to doubt the account of his career.[3] The justice did better than this for his own children, three of whom proceeded to Cambridge where they apparently studied both grammar and arts, and John, the eldest (1421-66), proceeded to the Inner Temple.[4] An acquaintance with the common law, as he later discovered, was only too desirable for the management and defence of one's lands, and like the fifteenth-century noblemen who went to Oxford, his journey from Cambridge to the Inns of Court anticipated what was to become a common procedure among the English upper class in Elizabethan and Stuart times.

Merchants, craftsmen, artisans

The literary concerns of the king and the aristocracy had their parallels lower down in society, where other groups of people developed, albeit to a less ambitious degree, need the or the taste for reading. The towns in particular were nurseries of literacy. Just as the magnates discharged public

[1] Edith Rickert, *Chaucer's World* (1948), p. 55.
[2] Ibid., pp. 111-12.
[3] *Paston Letters and Papers of the Fifteenth Century*, ed. N. Davis, vol i (1971), pp. xli-ii, lii-iii.
[4] Ibid., pp. 41, 234.

and private affairs which stimulated them towards the study of letters, so too the leading inhabitants of the towns were called upon to take their turns in the exercise of municipal government – administering the community as mayors, bailiffs and sheriffs; presiding over the borough courts; negotiating with the king; collecting taxation; representing the borough in parliament – all tasks with which literacy was closely involved. Like the aristocracy in the countryside, the town oligarchies also needed permanent officers to whom they could depute some of these duties, and hence there evolved an administration to help them, headed by the town clerk, or 'common clerk' as he was generally known in medieval times. The origins of this office go back at least to the early thirteenth century,[1] and during the next 300 years it developed into a post with multifarious and important duties – secretarial, legal and financial.[2] In his secretarial capacity the common clerk dealt with the correspondence received by the corporation; he issued writs and deeds on its behalf and had them copied into registers. He kept accounts of municipal expenditure, and was often responsible for recording the pleas and judgements of the borough court. In the fifteenth century he sometimes turned antiquary, collecting and codifying the charters, privileges and customs of the borough. The *Liber Albus* of the city of London compiled by John Carpenter in 1419 is a work of this kind, and so is *The Mayor of Bristol's Calendar* which Robert Ricart drew up sixty years later.[3] Town clerks were often lawyers by training and much of their work involved knowledge of the common law, but most towns came also to employ a second, more specialized legal officer, the recorder, who could both assist the mayor in judging the pleas in the borough court and represent the borough when necessary in the courts of the crown. A third officer, the common attorney, was often required as well to plead in the borough court on behalf of the corporation.

The greatest developments in town administration during the later middle ages naturally took place in London, where a sophisticated organization of permanent officials and clerks had evolved by the fourteenth century.[4] The common clerk himself kept the city muniments, enrolled deeds and issued writs, while the chamberlain supervised the

---

[1] e.g. J. W. F. Hill, *Medieval Lincoln* (1948), p. 196.
[2] On the office of town clerk see Alice Stopford Green, *Town Life in the Fifteenth Century* (1894), ii, 257-64.
[3] H. T. Riley, *Munimenta Gildhallae Londoniensis*, vol i (Rolls Series, 1859) and *Liber Albus: the White Book of the City of London* (1861); Robert Ricart, *The Maire of Bristowe is Kalendar*, ed. Lucy Toulmin Smith (Camden Society, new series, v, 1872).
[4] G. A. Williams, *Medieval London: from Commune to Capital* (1963), pp. 93-6.

property belonging to the city and admitted freemen to its privileges. The recorder, 'one of the most skilful and virtuous apprentices at law in the kingdom', sat at the mayor's right hand when pleas were judged, and the 'common countour', or common serjeant-at-law, was the secondary legal officer who appears to have acted as pleader on behalf of the city. The administration of London also required the services of large numbers of clerks – two for the mayor, as many as six or nine for the sheriffs, one each for the aldermen, the chamberlain and the recorder, and at least two for the common clerk – perhaps as many as thirty-five in all.[1] The clerical staff in London was exceptional, and must have diminished in size in cities and towns of smaller population, wealth and affairs. In Bristol, one of the largest of the provincial towns, with a population of some 9,000 during the later middle ages, we hear of the common clerk and three legal officers: the recorder, the steward of the court of Tolsey and the common attorney, and doubtless they had the assistance of some other menial clerks.[2] In smaller places probably only a common clerk and a recorder were absolutely indispensable, and it is by no means certain that even they were always full-time employees, but may have had other legal and administrative concerns. Yet in general the point remains that town government provided a further modest stimulus towards the general advancement of literacy.

The private as opposed to the public affairs of the merchants and prosperous craftsmen of the towns were equally favourable to the pursuit of letters. Wise merchants would keep records of their stocks, their orders and their sales, and if their trade was anything more than local it would involve correspondence with suppliers and the sending out of bills to customers. Probably the merchant himself discharged these tasks, although on rare occasions we do hear of clerks,[3] and doubtless servants and apprentices often helped out. Some of the activities of trade must have involved the use of Latin, but not all, and it seems rather unlikely that all merchants, let alone craftsmen, were competent grammarians. Merchants' letters are generally in French until the end of the fourteenth century and in English or French thereafter, depending on the country of the correspondent.[4] Accounts, like those of the London merchant Gilbert Maghfield

[1] Ibid., p. 96, n 3.
[2] On Bristol see Robert Ricart, op. cit., p. 75; *The Little Red Book of Bristol*, ed. F. B. Bickley (1900), i, 48-9; *The Great Red Book of Bristol*, ed. E. W. W. Veale, vol i (Bristol Record Society, iv, 1933), pp. 119-21.
[3] e.g. Sylvia Thrupp, *The Merchant Class of Medieval London* (1948), p. 163; *The Great Orphan Book and Book of Wills, Bristol*, ed. T. P. Wadley (1886), p. 10.
[4] e.g. *The Cely Papers*, ed. H. E. Malden (Camden 3rd series, i, 1900).

which survive from 1390 to 1395, might also be kept in the vernacular, in this case French.[1]

Like the magnates, the merchant class were not only impelled towards literacy by their business concerns but also in their hours of leisure. Here again their tastes were not usually such as demanded much knowledge of Latin. For scholarship they seem to have had less time, opportunity or ambition than had the aristocracy. The possession of learned books by the citizens of London does not seem to have been common. It was perhaps only one more side of an exceptional character that led Sir William Walworth, the stalwart fishmonger who slew Wat Tyler in 1381, to acquire the twenty-three Latin volumes, mostly works of theology or canon law, which he bequeathed in his will four years later.[2] Nor can we regard as typical the book collection of John Carpenter, the common clerk already mentioned, which included twenty-two works in Latin and two in French in 1442, again mostly of a moral and theological nature.[3] Bibliophile interests such as these must have been rare in any English town. The commonest books to be mentioned in townsmen's wills, and even they do not occur very frequently, are missals and breviaries, the texts respectively of the mass and the divine office.[4] The use of a service book in that religious age was of course one of the chief applications of literacy in every class of society, and the English habit of taking books to church was sufficient to arouse the interest of the Venetian observer of 1500 who wrote the account of England known as the *Italian Relation*. 'They all attend mass every day', he writes with a traveller's exaggeration, 'any who can read taking the office of Our Lady with them, and with some companion reading it in the church, verse by verse, in the manner of churchmen.'[5] Curiously, however, the evidence of townsmen's wills suggests that it was not so much the office of Our Lady or other elementary prayer books that were carried to church, but the same missals and breviaries used by the clergy themselves. Such a wish to accompany, even if not fully to understand, the Latin services is rather striking.

Apart from liturgical books, Bibles, lives of the saints and mystical or

---

[1] Edith Rickert, 'Extracts from a fourteenth-century account book', *Modern Philology*, xxiv (1926-7), pp. 111-19, 249-56.
[2] S. Bentley, *Excerpta Historica* (1831), pp. 134-41.
[3] T. Brewer, *Memoir of the Life and Times of John Carpenter, Town Clerk of London*, 2nd ed. (1856), pp. 131-44.
[4] See for example R. R. Sharpe, *Calendar of Wills Proved in the Court of Husting, London*, vol ii (1890), pp. 103, 114-15, 302-3, 312, 344, etc.; T. P. Wadley, op. cit., pp. 73, 117, 126-7, 132, 159, 177.
[5] Charlotte A. Sneyd, *Italian Relation of England* (Camden Society, xxxvii, 1847), p. 23.

devotional works account for most of the volumes mentioned in townsmen's wills, and even these seem to occur less frequently than in the wills of the wealthier, more leisured aristocracy.[1] No doubt it is wrong to estimate the extent of literacy in the towns or the guiding tastes of the literate from wills alone. In most towns the literary interests of the burgesses must have advanced well beyond things liturgical and devotional. Over most of England, but more particularly in the Midlands and the north, guilds of townspeople enacted miracle plays, sometimes in the form of elaborate cycles, which though religious in their subject yet bore the stamp of art and imagination. Amateur historiography was also popular, at least among the citizens of London, and several chronicles (rather rudimentary by continental standards) were composed there during the fifteenth and early sixteenth centuries by men such as the skinner William Gregory (d. 1467), the draper Robert Fabyan (d. 1513) and Richard Arnold (*fl.* 1473-1521), who was apparently a haberdasher.[2] Finally in the commonplace book of Richard Hill we have perhaps the fullest guide to the literary tastes of a prosperous city merchant. Born in 1490, Hill was trading as a grocer in London during the years 1518-26, during which time he transcribed into a narrow paper volume, much like an account book, a whole anthology of useful and entertaining material, chiefly in English but with about a dozen of the items in Latin.[3] The contents include personal memoranda, commercial notes, practical treatises on farriery and medicine, religious poems and tracts and large numbers of secular pieces: tales from Gower's *Confessio Amantis*, lyrics, satirical and humorous poems, and verses on courtesy and etiquette. Unique though the book may be in the range of its contents, the evident transcription of many of the pieces from collections already existing, together with the survival of similar commonplace books of the same date, suggest that the compiler was by no means alone in the possession of such literary tastes.

The evidence already discussed seems to suggest that the literacy of the merchants and craftsmen of the later medieval towns meant primarily the ability to read and write in the vernacular, meaning French and English. Knowledge of grammar, meaning Latin, although suggested by the survival of the language in law and accounting, by the evidence about

[1] Thrupp, *Merchant Class of Medieval London*, pp. 161-3.
[2] C. L. Kingsford, *English Historical Literature in the Fifteenth Century* (1913), pp. 70-112.
[3] Oxford, Balliol College, MS 354; R. A. B. Mynors, *Catalogue of the MSS of Balliol College, Oxford* (1963), pp. 352-4. The contents of the book are more fully discussed and partly edited in *Songs, Carols and other Miscellaneous Pieces from Balliol MS 354*, ed. R. Dyboski (EETS, 1908).

service books and by a few of the items in Richard Hill's book, was probably more sketchy and less common. This estimate of urban literacy is confirmed on the whole by evidence about particular trades and crafts in London during the fifteenth century, and London is not likely to have been excelled in this respect by any other English town. Thus in 1402 a Yorkshire knight, Sir John Depeden, left £20 for the education of a boy named John FitzRichard, with instructions that when he could read or write he should be sent to London to learn the craft of the fishmongers, grocers or mercers.[1] In 1422 the guild of brewers resolved henceforth to keep their records in English, observing that many of their craft knew how to read and write it but were ignorant of French and Latin.[2] In 1450 an apprentice haberdasher, Thomas Bodyn, claimed that eight years before, when he had signed his indentures, his master had promised to send him to school for a year and a half to learn grammar and half a year to learn writing; Bodyn went so far as to petition the chancellor because of the alleged failure to perform the obligation.[3] By the 1490s it had evidently become normal among the goldsmiths for apprentices to learn reading and writing, and this became compulsory by an ordinance of the company in 1498.[4] Perhaps only the scriveners, with reason, insisted on their apprentices possessing the 'perfect congruity of grammar' needful for writing deeds and copying books. In their ordinance, also of 1498, they commanded their apprentices to be 'completely erudite and learned in the books of *Parvula*, genders, declensions, preterites and supines, *Equivoca* and synonyms, with the other petty books'.[5]

Something of the extent of literacy among the non-noble classes in England during the later middle ages can be gathered from the history of benefit of clergy, the privilege which permitted clerks accused of secular crimes in a secular court to be transferred for trial and judgement to an ecclesiastical tribunal. This could be claimed by clerks of any degree, whether they were in major or in minor orders, and even if they had received no more than the first tonsure. The historian of the institution in England, Dr Leona Gabel, has shown how the original tests of who was and who was not a clerk lay in the possession of a tonsure, clerical garb or a certificate of ordination, but that these, after the beginning of

[1] *Testamenta Eboracensia*, ed. J. Raine, vol i (Surtees Society, iv, 1836), p. 296.
[2] R. W. Chambers and M. Daunt, *A Book of London English* (1931), p. 39.
[3] PRO, Early Chancery Proceedings, C 1/19/491.
[4] W. S. Prideaux, *Memorials of the Goldsmiths' Company* (no date), i, 28, 31-2, 34, 36.
[5] *Scriveners' Company Common Paper, 1357-1628*, ed. F. W. Steer (London Record Society, iv, 1968), p. 51. For the grammars mentioned see below, pp. 90-1, 108.

the fourteenth century, gave way to a simple test of literacy.[1] A prisoner in the secular court who claimed benefit of clergy was handed a Latin service book and asked to read two verses aloud after which, if he succeeded, he was handed over to the ecclesiastical authorities. Since the latter were generally more lenient than their secular counterparts, there was a strong incentive for a lapsed clerk and even for a mere layman to prove his clerical status if he could. Yet literacy was for long so restricted to the clergy that Dr Gabel notes very few men in secular occupations successfully claiming the privilege by means of the reading test during the reigns of the first three Edwards. Only towards the end of the fourteenth century does a change become noticeable. From this time onwards the records of the secular courts provide numerous examples of merchants, craftsmen and even agriculturalists claiming to be clerks and establishing their status by means of the literacy test.

> Selected at random from rolls dating from 6 Richard II to 1 Edward IV, there appear literate clerks described as 'former servant', 'mercer', 'servant', 'tailor'. 'spicer', 'fishmonger', 'hosier', 'smith', 'fisher', 'shipman', 'chapman', 'yeoman', 'butcher', 'husbandman', 'mason', 'walker', 'webster', 'cooper', 'vestmentmaker', and relatively numerous instances of literate labourers.[2]

It is evident that either clerks have taken up secular employment after receiving the first tonsure and learning to read, or else literate laymen are exploiting a privilege originally intended merely for the clergy. In either case it argues a significant extension of lay literacy. During the fifteenth century benefit of clergy became clearly established as a privilege for the literate as well as the clergy, and in 1489 this was formally recognized by a statute which introduced a different degree of immunity for persons merely literate from that available to the clergy proper.[3]

The incidence of lay literacy is equally apparent from the numbers of witnesses in the ecclesiastical courts whom the records describe as 'literates'. Bearing in mind what has been said about the learning of London merchants, their 'literacy' was probably the simple ability to read rather than a grammatical understanding of Latin. In 1373 fourteen lay witnesses appeared in a suit between the hospital of St Cross, Winchester,

[1] Leona C. Gabel, *Benefit of Clergy in England in the Later Middle Ages* (Smith College Studies in History, xiv, 1928-9), pp. 62-91. See also Holdsworth, *History of English Law,* iii, 293-302.
[2] Leona C. Gabel, op. cit., 81.
[3] *Statutes of the Realm* (1816), iii, 538.

and the diocesan bishop, William Wykeham; eleven of the fourteen were described as literate.[1] In an inquiry of 1466 in Norfolk touching Sir John Fastolf's will, nineteen lay witnesses appeared, of whom eight were literate. They included two merchants, a mariner, a husbandman, an agricultural labourer and a former schoolmaster. The illiterate were of similar status, and comprised a gentleman, two husbandmen, three labourers and five other artisans and servants.[2] Furthermore, of 116 male witnesses who appeared in the consistory court of London between 1467 and 1476, 62 were described as 'literate' and 6 as 'somewhat literate'. All were artisans and tradesmen, and they exhibited the same mixture of literacy and illiteracy among men of similar occupations. Thus six of the tailors were literate and nine were not, while the figures for the shearmen were five and two, for the drapers four and one and for the grocers four and none.[3] Why some of these could read and some could not demands knowledge of age and ability, rank and property, ambition and complacency which we no longer possess.

Villeins

Despite the steady growth of literacy among the higher estates and conditions of men, there were others whose opportunities for education remained limited. They included the class, still numerous until the fifteenth century, of bondmen or villeins, the unfree tenants of the countryside. It was a mark of their servile status that besides the obligations of service which they owed to their lords, villeins also suffered restrictions on their personal freedom: they were forbidden to leave their manors, marry their daughters or send their sons to school without their lord's permission. This restriction on the education of villeins was not primarily intended to keep them illiterate, since their literacy in itself could have harmed no one. It existed rather because schooling presupposed a career in the church or in some trade or profession, and hence departure from the manor and the acquisition of free status. The lord would lose the services of an educated villein, and should he ever come to inherit the family holding, he might be unable to supply the services which that holding had been accustomed to render. For this reason, lords of manors insisted on their right to control the education of their villeins, while at the same time they did not seek to forbid it altogether.

When a villein wished to send his son to school he was obliged to

1 *VCH Hants.*, ii, 255.
2 *The Paston Letters*, ed. Gairdner, pp. 236-45.
3 Thrupp, *Merchant Class of Medieval London*, p. 157; Leona Gabel, op. cit., pp. 82-4.

procure a licence from his lord, and those who were discovered evading the obligation were liable to be fined or to suffer distraint of their goods.[1] Sometimes the licence was a limited one, permitting the licensee to be educated for so many years and to be tonsured after the manner of scholars, but not to receive any higher orders of clergy. This enabled the lord to reassume control if the villein failed to make enough progress in learning to qualify for holy orders, and to make a final, perpetual grant of freedom if he did. Thus in 1314 the prior of St Germans in Cornwall manumitted or freed two boys so that they could be tonsured and study for three years.[2] The usual practice on the manors of St Albans Abbey during the fourteenth century seems to have been to permit villeins to go to school provided they were not the eldest sons and that they did not receive ordination beyond that of the tonsure itself.[3] In other cases, however, complete freedom was granted from the first. In 1333 the cellarer of Gloucester Abbey, as lord of the manor of Coln Rogers, gave full manumission to Walter son of Henry atte Yate, enabling him to learn letters and to proceed to holy orders. But even this involved a saving clause, that should he ever return to a life of manual labour, he would again become of servile status.[4]

Fees were generally exacted for the licence. In this respect the monks of St Albans were among the most lenient, usually charging their tenants only 6d. or 1s. in the fourteenth century. 'The sums', as Dr Levett observed, 'are in no way prohibitive; they serve as a registration informing the lord what has become of his villeins' boys.' In consequence requests for schooling were not uncommon among the abbey tenants: nine boys were licensed at Norton near Baldock between 1331 and 1333, and six at Hexton in 1348.[5] Other lords charged more, either because they disapproved of the education of villeins or sought to exploit it. Sums of 3s. 4d., 5s. 0d. and 13s. 4d. were paid for licences between 1361 and 1371 on the Warwickshire manor of Wolston which belonged to the Turvill family.[6] Still higher was the 20s. exacted from a villein at Sevenhampton in Wiltshire in 1283, which lay in the possession of the notorious usurer Adam of Stratton.[7] It may be, however, that these larger sums purchased

---

[1] e.g. *VCH Middx.*, iv, 224.

[2] *Reg. Stapeldon, Exeter*, p. 494.

[3] A. Elizabeth Levett, *Studies in Manorial History* (1938), p. 246.

[4] *Reg. Bransford, Worcester*, p. 179.

[5] Elizabeth Levett, op. cit., p. 246.

[6] J. Thorold Rogers, *History of Agriculture and Prices in England*, vol ii (1866), pp. 615-616.

[7] *Court Rolls of Wiltshire Manors of Adam de Stratton*, ed. R. B. Pugh (Wilts. Record Society, xxiv, 1970), p. 77.

complete freedom, not only to attend school but to take priests' orders as well.

It has often been assumed that the restrictions on the education of villeins came to an end as a result of the Statute of Apprentices of 1406, but this appears to be doubtful.[1] The chief concern of the statute was to re-enact earlier legislation which forbade men to apprentice their children in towns unless they owned land to the value of at least 20s. a year. It does indeed contain the clause 'that any man or woman, of whatever estate or condition, be free to put his son or daughter to learn letters at any school in the kingdom', but this would seem to apply only to the matter in hand: the restrictions on apprenticeship are not to prevent those who lawfully may from sending their children to school.[2] It is highly unlikely that the governing class would so casually have surrendered control over the education of their villeins and in fact permission to go to school continued to be required of them after 1406. In 1410 two boys were reported to have left the manor of Barton in Bedfordshire to attend school without permission, and as late as 1465 the jurors of the manor of Methley near Leeds were fined for omitting to report that one of the villeins had been placed at learning without the lord's consent.[3] The obligation to obtain permission probably fell into disuse only along with the other incidents of villeinage as the fifteenth century wore on.

Women

The other great section of society limited in its opportunities for education was the second sex. Everywhere the schools were orientated towards the needs of men, more even in England than in France and Italy. Women had little place in the educational system; their contribution to life, though indispensable, was social and economic rather than literary or scholastic. Thus among the clergy, the learned estate *par excellence*, women were represented only by the orders of nuns and a few anchoresses. The English nunneries remained fairly steady in number from 1200 until the Reformation with between 140 and 150 houses, but their inmates, who are reckoned at about 3,300 in the peak period before the Black Death and

---

[1] The assumption made by Leach in *ECD*, p. xxxviii, and *SME*, p. 236, has generally been followed by subsequent writers.

[2] *Rotuli Parliamentorum*, ii, 601-2; *Statutes of the Realm*, ii, 157-8.

[3] T. W. Page, 'The decline of English feudalism'. *Publications of the American Economic Association*, 3rd series, i, no 2, (1900), p. 77, quoting PRO, Court Rolls, SC 2/179/50; H. S. Darbyshire and G. D. Lumb, *The History of Methley* (Thoresby Society, xxxv, 1934), p. 182. See also *Modus Tenendi Cur. Baron* (1510, reprinted for the Manorial Society, ix, 1915), p. 4.

at just over 2,000 afterwards, were never more than a fifth of the total population even of that half of the clergy who belonged to the religious orders. Only two nunneries, Shaftesbury and Syon, can be counted among the twenty-eight religious houses which in 1535 enjoyed an income of over £1,000 a year. Many of the other establishments were very small and poor.[1] The inferiority of the nuns with respect to wealth and numbers is also apparent when it comes to learning. Whereas the norm among monks and friars by the fourteenth century seems to have been the knowledge of reading, song and grammar, extending in many cases to an acquaintance with theology, most nuns were able merely to read and sing the Latin necessary for the divine office.[2] It was not even expected that they should possess a grammatical understanding of the language. Most bishops who had to deal with nuns wrote to them in the vernacular language of the day, French or English, and if they wrote in Latin assumed that the letters would be translated for the nuns to understand. Bishop Stapledon of Exeter probably gauged their capabilities accurately in his injunctions of 1319 for the nuns of Canonsleigh and Polsoe, where he ordered that any sister who wanted to speak during the periods of obligatory silence should use Latin words, but not grammatically, such as '*candela, liber, missale . . . est, non, sic,* and other similar words'.[3]

Among the laity the literary attainments of women were equally limited.[4] Most were fully occupied in ministering to their families or employers and in bearing the burdens of work and marriage, bed and board. The wives and daughters of the wealthy and well-born alone enjoyed the leisure and carried the kind of responsibilities that would have benefited from a knowledge of letters. Reading offered such women several advantages. It freed the religiously inclined from the limitations of the rosary and made available the hours of the Virgin, the psalter and other pious works. It permitted the more frivolous to read aloud from poetry and romances when no one else was available to do so, an invaluable accomplishment on wet and wintry days. For women of property, charged with running affairs for an absent husband or left by his death in sole control, it gave the power at least to read letters of instructions and the reports of servants, without which wealth could scarcely be managed

---

[1] On these statistics see M. C. Knowles and R. N. Hadcock, *Medieval Religious Houses*, 2nd ed. (1971), pp. 251-89, 493-4.
[2] On the learning and education of nuns I have followed the excellent account of Eileen Power, *Medieval English Nunneries* (1922), pp. 237-84, 568-81.
[3] *Reg. Stapeldon, Exeter*, pp. 95, 316.
[4] On this subject in general see Dorothy Gardiner, *English Girlhood at School* (1929), pp. 1-140.

successfully. But when all is said, no woman had any strong incentive to do more than learn to read and understand her mother tongue and possibly to read Latin. A knowledge of Latin grammar or the study of higher subjects was quite outside her sphere. Blue stockings were as yet unworn.

How did women attain a knowledge of letters? In this respect the nunneries had a role to play, but it should not be exaggerated. Their limitations as places of literary education have been judiciously summarized by Professor Eileen Power.[1] There were not many houses of nuns, and only a minority of these took in children at all. They did not restrict themselves to girls but frequently admitted infant boys as well. Moreover, the presence of children in nunneries was disliked by the bishops, who thought it subversive of the religious life and usually forbade them to stay after a certain age, varying from five to eleven for boys and from ten to fourteen for girls. The numbers involved were also small, the largest examples including the eighteen children mentioned at Stixwould Priory in 1400, the twenty-six girls boarding at St Mary's Abbey, Winchester in 1536 and the thirty to forty children said in 1537 (probably with exaggeration) to have been normally maintained at Polesworth.[2] Most other nunneries supported much smaller numbers, nine or six or even less. Wealth and breeding were the criteria for entrance: the list of girls at Winchester was headed by Lady Bridget Plantagenet (whose father was Viscount Lisle), the daughters of three knights and girls of old-established Hampshire families such as Dingley and Tichborne. The education such children received probably concentrated on manners and morals; the study of letters seems to have been elementary and restricted to reading. 'In fine,' Professor Power remarks, 'though nunneries did act as girls' schools, they certainly did not educate more than a small proportion even of the children of the upper classes, and the education which they gave them was limited by their own limitations.'[3]

Those girls who did not learn their letters in a nunnery must either have picked them up informally from the chaplains and other literates with whom they kept company, or have learnt them in public elementary schools. We hear of such a school in London between 1504 and 1515 under the conduct of an elderly priest, William Barbour, who was teaching the *paternoster, ave* and *credo* 'with further learning' to thirty young children when he was accused, somewhat improbably, of raping the 8-year-old Elizabeth Garrard.[4] There were also at least a few schoolmistresses, whose duties must have been meant for young children of both sexes. One of

[1] Eileen Power, op. cit., 261-2.   [2] Ibid., pp. 263-6.   [3] Ibid., p. 262.
[4] PRO, Early Chancery Proceedings, C 1/290/78.

these, Matilda Maresflete of Boston, is described as *magistra scolarum* in 1404, and there are two instances in London: a certain 'E. Scolemaysteresse' to whom a wealthy grocer bequeathed 20s. in 1408, and an 'Elizabeth Scolemaystres' who appears living in Cripplegate in 1441 when she contributed to a subsidy levied upon aliens.[1] The presence of school-mistresses in fifteenth-century England is in fact less notable than their fewness in numbers, for there were many more in the great continental towns where the education of women was taken more seriously. At Paris, for example, twenty-one schoolmistresses were licensed to teach in 1380 by the cantor of Notre Dame.[2]

As within the nunneries, the literary education of girls outside was probably restricted to the reading of their mother tongue, and perhaps the study of French after that language ceased to be a vernacular in England. It was reported in 1463 of Margaret Rocliffe, the grand-daughter of Sir William Plumpton, 'that she speaketh prettily, and French, and hath near hand learned her psalter'.[3] Writing was a different and much rarer accomplishment, as Professor Davis has ably demonstrated with regard to the women of the Paston family in the fifteenth century.[4] Whereas the men were all able to write 'with differing degrees of competence and elegance', the letters apparently emanating from the women were in fact the work of other hands. The Paston women could probably have read the letters they received from their absent husbands, but when they needed to reply they called on whichever literate member of the household was available to write for them. In only one of them, Margery (d. 1495), the wife of John Paston III (d. 1504), can be discerned a halting ability to write. Three of the six surviving letters written for her are subscribed 'Be yowre servant (and bedewoman) Margery Paston', in what Professor Davis calls 'the same distinctively halting and uncontrolled hand, as of someone beginning to learn to write'. Margery was evidently unable to compose a legible letter in a reasonable space of time, and she is the only one of the Paston women who has left evidence of her ability even to write her own name.

*　　　*　　　*

The brief survey of medieval society which we have made should serve

[1] *VCH Lincs.*, ii, 451; Thrupp, *Merchant Class of Medieval London*, p. 171, and 'Aliens in and around London in the fifteenth century', *Studies in London History presented to P. E. Jones*, ed. A. E. Hollaender and W. Kellaway (1969), p. 269.
[2] Michael Felibien, *Histoire de la Ville de Paris* (Paris, 1715), iii, 449, where they are styled *rectrices*.
[3] *The Plumpton Correspondence*, ed. T. Stapleton (Camden Society, iv, 1839), p. 8.
[4] *Paston Letters and Papers of the Fifteenth Century*, ed. Davis, vol i, pp. xxxvi-viii.

to remind us of a few important points. The Church was the original centre of literacy, and the need for a literate clergy was the principal cause of the appearance and existence of schools in England until the sixteenth century. Clerical life involved not only reading but the understanding and use of Latin, hence the development of different grades of schools to teach reading, Latin grammar and higher studies such as arts and theology. It was the ancient connection of the Church with the schools that led educational matters to come under ecclesiastical jurisdiction throughout the middle ages and even for long after the Reformation. In time there also grew up alongside the clergy another large and important body of Latinists: the administrators and lawyers who staffed the institutions of royal government, the towns and the great private households. Outside these groups, Latin formed part of the education of at least some of the nobility, gentry and the more ambitious burgesses by the fifteenth century, while the ability to read in the vernacular was still more widespread and reached further down the social scale to some artisans and across it to the wives and daughters of the well-to-do. By the time Bosworth Field came to be fought, literacy had gained a hold among some people of almost every district, rank and occupation, although another 400 years were to pass before its triumph was complete.

Schools and their studies

Chapter Two

The schools of medieval England

Now that we have gained some idea of the importance of literary education in medieval society, we can proceed to examine the institutions by which such education was provided. In medieval times any such institution was usually described as a 'school'.[1] Not only was the word used indiscriminately of what we would now call primary and secondary schools, but it was also applied to those institutions of higher study which we know as universities. One went to 'school' at Oxford, where in the 'schools' or lecture rooms one heard one's seniors expound the precepts of the 'schoolmen', Peter Lombard, Duns Scotus and Aquinas. When they wanted to distinguish a particular kind of school, medieval writers usually qualified the word by an adjective referring to the grade of study there, thus evolving the terms 'song school', 'grammar school' and 'school of logic' or 'of theology'. As an alternative they defined a school according to its constitution not its curriculum. The terms 'high school', 'general school' and 'public school' are all found in medieval times to denote a school open to all comers as opposed to a private school, just as 'free school' also occurs, meaning an endowed school where education was given gratis as opposed to the usual kind of school where fees were paid. Modern writers, seeking to classify the medieval schools by their constitutions, have evolved other expressions such as 'endowed school', 'chantry school', 'cloister school' and 'almonry school'. Either method of classification, by curriculum or constitution, is quite permissible so long as the two methods are not confused, and no attempt is made to draw false

[1] In medieval Latin the form *scola* is most commonly found, generally in the plural *scole* and *scolas*, even when only one school is meant. Hence the usual term for a schoolmaster, *magister scolarum*, which also means a master of one, not many, schools.

distinctions between, say, a chantry school and a grammar school which were sometimes the same thing and sometimes not.

The most widespread, prominent and best-attended of the medieval English schools, and hence the chief subject of our attention in this book, were those which may be called public and secular. By 'public' we mean that they were not confined to any particular class of persons but were open to all who could afford to attend them, and by 'secular' that their masters and pupils were secular priests or clerks, and later on laymen too, rather than members of the religious orders. From the twelfth century onwards these were the schools *par excellence* of medieval England, embracing a far greater proportion of the population than did the private schools in the households of the nobility or the schools of the religious orders, both of which we shall examine in due course.[1] As a class the public secular schools may be conveniently subdivided into four smaller groups according to their curricula and courses of study: song schools, grammar schools, business schools and schools teaching higher studies such as arts and theology. These subdivisions are somewhat artificial and they cannot be applied with complete accuracy, but they do at least suggest the various grades of medieval schools and make clearer the different stages of the medieval educational system.

The first and lowest grade of medieval schools consisted of those which we would call 'primary', and which contemporaries usually termed 'reading' or 'song' schools. The children who attended them were probably in the region of seven to ten years of age; Chaucer, who described such a school in *The Prioress's Tale*, made the schoolboy hero who had not long begun his studies there 7 years old.[2] In the same period William Wykeham in his statutes for Winchester College of 1400 ordered that the scholars should be admitted between the ages of eight and twelve, and that they should be already competent in reading, song and elementary grammar.[3] He thus presupposed the existence of elementary schools at which these subjects had been mastered. If this was the normal time for beginning one's education, we must also remember that many people, whose need, desire or opportunity for education came only in later life, must have learnt their first letters at a much later age.

Learning in an elementary school began with the alphabet, the form of

---

[1] For private secular schools see below, pp. 217-21, and for the schools of the religious orders, below, chapter 8.

[2] *The Works of Geoffrey Chaucer*, ed. Robinson, p. 161, line 1693.

[3] T. F. Kirby, *Annals of Winchester College from its foundation in the year 1382* (1892), p. 457.

which was already well established by the fourteenth century, and was usually set down in manuscripts as follows:

+A.a.b.c.d.e.f.g.h.i.k.

l.m.n.o.p.q.r.ꝛ.ſ.s.t.

v.u.x.y.z.&.9.∴.est amen.

In other words it began with a cross, followed with a capital A, and then gave the rest of the Latin alphabet in minuscule, black-letter script, with alternative forms for 'r', 's' and 'u'. Next came the abbreviations for *et* and *con*, then three dots or tittles and lastly the words *est amen*.[1] The reasons why this form evolved are obscure, and they were not even clear to those writers who in the sixteenth and seventeenth centuries first tried to explain them. But the alphabet continued to be generally presented in this way until the sixteenth century, and with only a few variations until the eighteenth. The contemporary English word for it was 'abc' or 'abece', or alternatively the 'cross row' in allusion to the prefatory symbol.

More than one method was probably employed for presenting the alphabet to children for their attention. It may have been written up in black upon the whitewashed classroom wall, like the three English alphabets of the sixteenth century which can still be seen on the vestry wall of the church of North Cadbury in south Somerset. It seems often to have been inscribed upon a small board for the child to handle, like the hornbooks of later times. 'You know', observes the Dominican friar Robert Holcot who died in 1349, 'that boys when they are first instructed are not able to learn anything subtle, but only simple things. So they are first taught with a "book" of large letters affixed to a piece of wood, and progress afterwards to learning letters from a more advanced book.'[2] From the description given in a fourteenth-century English poem on the Passion, such a 'book' or tablet appears to have consisted of a parchment leaf bearing the alphabet, decorated with red paragraph marks, and fixed to a board.[3] The use

[1] This version of the alphabet is from Bodleian, MS Rawl. C 209 fo 1, of the fifteenth century. An earlier version, written in the late fourteenth, is in Glasgow University, Hunterian Museum Library, MS 472 fo 1. Both are followed by the *paternoster* and other prayers in English.

[2] Beryl Smalley, *English Friars and Antiquity in the Early Fourteenth Century* (Oxford, 1960), p. 332.

[3] The poem appears in the commonplace-book of John Grimestone, OFM, written by 1372 (Edinburgh, National Library of Scotland, MS Advocates 18.7.21 fo 122b; C. Brown, *A Register of Middle English Verse*, part 2 (1920), nos 899, 925). Another version is printed from BM, MS Harley 3954 fo 87a in *Reliquiae Antiquae*, ed. T. Wright, vol i (1841), pp. 63-4. For an exhaustive but eccentric treatment of early alphabets and hornbooks see also A. W. Tuer, *History of the Horn Book*, 2 vols (1896).

of a piece of transparent horn to cover the tablet is not mentioned by the earliest writers, but it is apparent that in most other respects these early manuals were very similar to the well-known hornbooks of the sixteenth, seventeenth and eighteenth centuries.

A third method of learning the alphabet was from a small book of several pages called a primer, of which numerous copies were produced both in Latin and in English from at least the thirteenth century onwards. The primer was a religious miscellany containing the basic prayers and elements of the faith, and the more simple liturgical devotions for the laity to follow, such as the hours of the Virgin Mary. These primers often began with the alphabet, thus serving in effect as a textbook of elementary education, for there are several indications that the learning of the basic prayers followed the mastery of the alphabet. Bishop Grandisson of Exeter in 1357 spoke of scholars learning to read and write the Lord's Prayer, the Ave Mary, the Creed and the mattins and hours of the Virgin, and wished that they be taught to translate and understand such things before being taken on to higher studies.[1] Likewise Bishop Alcock of Ely observed in the 1490s that children, when they were set to school, were taught to serve God, to say grace, to help the priest to sing and to repeat 'Our Lady mattins'.[2] The arrangements for the chantry school at Childrey in Berkshire, made by William Fettiplace in his will of 1526, provided that children should first be taught the alphabet, the three basic prayers and all things necessary for serving the priest at mass, as well as the collects, psalms and prayers for the dead, and graces at meals. They were then to learn in English the articles of the faith, the ten commandments, the seven deadly sins, the seven sacraments and other useful precepts.[3] In this way elementary education reflected the religious preoccupations of the day, and came to possess a religious as well as a literary motive.

Besides learning to say the basic prayers, children who knew the alphabet gained practice in reading from church service books such as the psalter and the mattins book. In the absence of any real textbooks or readers specially designed for elementary instruction, these service books provided a useful substitute. They were readily available, since every church and chapel was supposed to possess them, as also did many of the clergy themselves and some even of the wealthier and more pious laity.

---

[1] *Reg. Grandisson, Exeter*, ed. F. C. Hingeston-Randolph, vol ii (1897), pp. 1192-3; *ECD*, pp. 314-17.

[2] E. F. Rimbault, 'Two sermons preached by the Boy Bishop', *Camden Miscellany VII* (Camden Society, new series, xiv, 1875), p. 10.

[3] PRO Prob. 11/23 (PCC 6 Jankyn); *VCH Berks.*, ii, 275-6.

They tended to be written in a large, clear hand, with the letters separate not cursive, so that the words were easy for young eyes to distinguish and understand. Lastly they prepared the child for higher studies. If he intended to go on to learn Latin grammar, an early ability to read Latin words at sight was highly desirable. Even if he aimed only at being able to read English, the practice at recognizing words would be useful, and the ability to read a Latin service book a valuable accomplishment in performing religious devotions later in life.

Closely connected with reading (which in medieval times was probably always performed aloud) was the study of song; indeed it so dominated the elementary schools that they were generally known to contemporaries as 'song schools'. 'Song' meant plainsong such as the clergy used for reciting the psalms and hymns of the divine office, rather than any more elaborate polyphonic music. The importance of song in medieval schools is easily understood. It helped to teach a clear, correct pronunciation of words, instead of the mumble into which ordinary reading aloud is liable to deteriorate. 'Without knowledge of music', said William Horman, the early Tudor grammarian and schoolmaster, in 1519, 'grammar cannot be perfect.'[1] Moreover, since a high proportion of all schoolchildren at any time before the Reformation were being educated for a career in the Church, the study of plainsong helped to prepare them for the daily repetition of the divine office, which was the basic duty of all the clergy, whether monks, friars, secular priests, or merely clerks in minor orders. Children who learnt to sing the psalter and other Latin hymns did not of course yet understand the meaning of the words they repeated; their knowledge extended only to the sound. This is made clear in Chaucer's description of the song school. The little 'clergeon' who sits in school at his primer, apparently learning the alphabet or the basic prayers, hears the older children singing the *Alma Redemptoris Mater* in praise of the Virgin. But when questioned as to the meaning of the hymn, an older boy can only give the gist for, as he says, 'I lerne songe, I kan but smal grammeere.'[2] The remaining subject taught in the elementary schools was probably writing, although as references to it are very uncommon before the early sixteenth century, it may often have been postponed until later on. However, the requirement in the 1518 statutes of St Paul's school, London, that candidates for entry should be able to read and write suggests that the art of calligraphy could be acquired at an elementary stage.[3]

[1] William Horman, *Vulgaria*, ed. M. R. James (Roxburghe Club, clxix, 1926), p. 146.
[2] *The Works of Geoffrey Chaucer*, ed. Robinson, p. 162, line 1726.
[3] J. H. Lupton, *A Life of John Colet* (1887), p. 285.

Where was the elementary education of the song schools available in medieval times? In the twelfth and thirteenth centuries there is evidence for the teaching of song in connection with the nine English secular cathedrals, those which were staffed by a chapter of secular canons.[1] At five of these – Exeter, Lincoln, London, Wells and York – the song schools came under the care of the precentor, the dignitary who had general charge of the musical life of the cathedral. At three others – Hereford, Lichfield and Salisbury – the schools were supervised by the precentor's deputy, or succentor. At most of these cathedrals a special master ruled the song school, but at two of the smaller establishments, Exeter and Hereford, the succentor himself acted as teacher in addition to his other duties. Special buildings for the song school are mentioned at Exeter, London and York, and probably existed elsewhere too, the school at London being held in the church of St Gregory which abutted on to the south-west side of St Paul's. These cathedral song schools were not confined to the choristers and others who ministered in the church, but were evidently intended to be open to the locality as well. At Hereford the choristers were indeed chosen from among the boys who resorted to the song school, and the precentors of Lincoln and York who claimed the sole right of appointing song schoolmasters in these cities took care to prevent the chaplains and parish clerks of the neighbourhood from teaching song and thereby infringing the monopoly of the cathedral song school.[2] Yet apart from Lincoln and York there is a strange silence about the cathedral song schools after 1300, suggesting that most precentors and succentors found them not worth bothering with, and either left the teaching of song to the cathedral grammar schoolmaster or permitted boys other than their own choristers to be educated by the local clergy, in contradistinction to Lincoln and York.

There were song schools too in other towns and cities. Sometimes the local house of regular or secular canons came to provide or to supervise such education. Thus at Canterbury Archbishop Lanfranc between 1077 and 1087 gave the schools of grammar and music in the city to the canons of St Gregory, who at that time were seculars but later adopted the Augustinian rule.[3] There was a song school at Huntingdon by the reign of Henry I when the historian Henry of Huntingdon, who was also arch-

---

[1] On the cathedral song schools see also Kathleen Edwards, *The English Secular Cathedrals in the Middle Ages*, pp. 166-8.

[2] *VCH Lincs.*, ii, 423-4; *EYS*, i, 22-3.

[3] *The Cartulary of St Gregory, Canterbury*, ed. Audrey M. Woodcock (Camden 3rd series, lxxxviii, 1956), pp. 1-2.

deacon of the place, presented the control of the school which had come into his possession to the canons of Huntingdon, acknowledging that it belonged by right to them.[1] At Warwick in the fourteenth century the master of the music school was appointed by the dean of the collegiate church and had to attend mass every day with two of his scholars in the Lady chapel of the college.[2] In other places there were other recognized patrons who insisted on their rights to appoint the authorized school-masters of song. At Bury St Edmunds between at least 1268 and 1426 the right was exercised by a local religious guild, the Congregation of Twelve, while in the Yorkshire towns of Howden and Northallerton, which were peculiars belonging to the prior of Durham, the prior is recorded appointing schoolmasters both of song and of grammar during the fourteenth and fifteenth centuries.[3]

The facilities offered by these schools were supplemented and perhaps even supplanted by the numerous foundations of chantries and collegiate churches which characterized the period from 1300 to 1500. The colleges frequently supported choirs of clerks and boy choristers, and even small chantries of a single priest often needed the assistance of boys in the celebration of the mass. Some founders were therefore careful to make arrangements for a supply of boys and for their training in song. Arch-bishop Chicheley's college of Higham Ferrers, founded in 1422, supported six choristers and provided tuition for them in song by one of the chaplains or clerks of the college.[4] Similarly the foundation statutes of Edmund Mortimer's college of Stoke by Clare, issued in the following year, mentioned five choristers and a master to teach them reading, plainsong and descant.[5] Sometimes tuition in reading and song was offered to outsiders as well. The statutes of Sibthorpe College in Nottingham-shire, issued in 1335 and revised in 1343, provided that the clerk of the church, who was to be qualified in reading and song, should teach the boys of the parish when he had time, and others who wished to learn their letters, taking reasonable payment for his pains.[6] Likewise at Tattershall College in Lincolnshire the statutes, drawn up in about 1460, permitted four poor boys teachable in song and reading to be admitted to help the

[1] Mary Bateson, 'The Huntingdon song school and the school of St Gregory's Canterbury', *English Historical Review*, xviii (1903), pp. 712-13.
[2] A. F. Leach, *History of Warwick School* (1906), p. 66; *ECD*, pp. 274-7.
[3] *VCH Suffolk*, ii, 309-11; *EYS*, ii, 60-2, 84-7.
[4] *CPR 1416-22*, p. 441; *VCH Northants.*, ii, 219.
[5] Sir William Dugdale, *Monasticum Anglicanum*, ed. J. Caley, H. Ellis and B. Bandinel (1817-30), iv, 1419.
[6] Thompson, *The English Clergy and their Organization*, pp. 256, 267.

six choristers of the collegiate establishment.[1] Several small chantries also provided teaching at an elementary level. Thomas Langley, bishop of Durham, founded two chantries in his cathedral church in 1414, one of the priests of which taught song to all comers and the other grammar, taking nothing from the poor and charging moderate fees from those who could afford to pay.[2] In 1443 John Abbot, citizen and mercer of London, willed lands to found a chantry in his native village of Farthinghoe, Northamptonshire, for a priest to instruct the children of the parish in what other evidence suggests to have been the elementary subjects.[3] A generation later in 1489 another Northamptonshire man, William Chamber, endowed a chantry in the church of All Saints, Aldwinkle, whose chaplain was to teach spelling and reading to six poor boys of the parish without charge.[4] A number of similar chantry foundations came into existence between this date and the dissolution of the chantries in 1548.

Apart from the long-established song schools of the cathedral cities and other towns, and besides the newer facilities associated with chantries and colleges, a good deal of elementary education was provided privately and informally all over the country by ordinary chaplains and parish clerks. In 1367 Archbishop Thoresby, acting at the request of the precentor of York, censured certain chaplains and clerks who were keeping song schools in parish churches and private houses in the city to the prejudice of the cathedral song school.[5] Similarly in 1395 the chapter of Lincoln Cathedral summoned a local chaplain named John Austin to explain why he had kept a number of boys in the exchequer of Lincoln to teach them singing, without licence from the cathedral song school-master. Austin, who confessed to having taught nine boys, was made to swear not to do so in future without permission. A few years later in 1408 one of the vicars choral of Lincoln was also accused of teaching three boys in the close and was made to pay a small fine for the offence.[6] We hear less of such teaching outside the places where it was restricted and hence attracted attention, but it certainly existed. In about 1500 a Somerset chantry priest giving evidence in a tithe dispute recalled that in about the 1460s he had lodged in the vicarage of Bridgwater where the parish chaplain had taught him to 'learn, read, and sing' at the command of the

---

[1] *Historical MSS Commission, De Lisle and Dudley MSS*, vol i (1925), p. 182.
[2] *VCH Durham*, i, 371-4.
[3] *ECD*, pp. 414-17; *VCH Northants.*, ii, 280-1.
[4] *ECD*, pp. 434-5; *VCH Northants.*, ii, 281-2.
[5] *EYS*, i, 22-3.
[6] *VCH Lincs.*, ii, 423-4.

vicar.[1] In 1489 a gentleman of Ticehurst in Sussex left a house to the church for the use of any priest or clerk who was willing to teach children.[2] Later, in 1529, the convocation of clergy in the province of Canterbury actually recommended the parish clergy to engage in teaching in their spare time, and the chantry certificates of 1548 suggest that some at least of the chantry priests had begun to do so.[3]

Besides parish priests, there is also evidence that elementary education was widely available from parish clerks, those clergy in minor orders who assisted the parish priests to sing the divine office, celebrate mass and administer the occasional offices such as baptisms and burials. That such clerks should teach was indeed encouraged by the canon law. The *Decretals* of Gregory IX issued in 1234, repeating the decree of a much earlier council of Mâcon, ordered that every priest with cure of souls should have a clerk to sing with him, read the epistle and hold schools.[4] Teaching of this kind is found in England by the middle of the thirteenth century, but it was not always regarded favourably when it clashed with the rights of an established school. In 1268 the abbot of Bury St Edmunds prohibited any clerk in Bury from teaching the psalter or singing without the licence of the Congregation of Twelve who presided over the authorized song school.[5] The determination of the precentors of Lincoln and York, already mentioned, to defend their song schools in the fourteenth century was in part provoked by the competition of local parish clerks. Elsewhere however it was generally recognized that a clerk had at least the right to teach boys from his own parish, a privilege indispensable for the organization of choirs and the training of boys to serve at mass. This right was expressly conceded to the parish clergy and clerks of Lincolnshire by Bishop Alnwick when in 1442 he drew up a revised set of statutes for the cathedral, although he admitted the precentor's right to license every other kind of song school in the county.[6] So we find casual allusions to teaching by parish clerks in several places. At Westminster, for example, the clerk who kept the image of the Virgin in the chapel of St Mary de Pew was teaching children in 1451 when one of his pupils caused a fire

[1] Bridgwater, Corporation MSS, vol x, no 1, document no 115; *Historical MSS Commission, Third Report*, p. 312.

[2] *Transcripts of Sussex Wills*, ed. R. G. Rice, vol iv (Sussex Record Society, xlv, 1940-1), p. 244.

[3] See below, pp. 272, 280.

[4] *Corpus Juris Canonici*, ed. E. Friedberg, vol ii (1881), col 449: Decretal III tit. 1 cap. iii.

[5] *VCH Suffolk*, ii, 311.

[6] *VCH Lincs.*, ii, 422-4; *Lincoln Cathedral Statutes*, ed. H. Bradshaw and C. Wordsworth (1897), ii, 157; iii, 299.

through negligence in snuffing out a candle.[1] Teaching in the church of St Nicholas, Bristol, is suggested by an entry of 1481 in the church book forbidding the clerk to take books out of the choir for children to learn from without the churchwardens' permission.[2] Similarly the instructions for the parish clerks of Faversham, which date from 1506, direct that one of them shall teach children to read and sing in the choir and to do service in the church, taking fees for the purpose.[3]

In such ways, formally from well-established song schools and less formally from the clerks and chaplains of parish churches, was elementary education obtained in pre-Reformation England. It would only be fair to conclude that compared with the education provided at a higher level in grammar schools and universities, the elementary stage was rudimentary in its organization and of little repute as a branch of learning. It possessed no special manuals or textbooks for instruction except for the primer and the humble hornbook. It attracted comparatively little attention from educational benefactors, the number of endowments made to provide elementary education being but a fraction of those applied for the support of grammar and of university studies. Even at the Reformation, when at least some care was taken at the dissolution of religious houses and chantries to save the grammar schools associated with them, whatever elementary teaching these foundations had provided was allowed to perish unrescued.[4]

The same cannot of course be said of the grammar schools which formed the second tier of the medieval educational system. The study of grammar could be traced back through a long tradition of scholarship to classical times. It possessed a large body of works dealing with both its theoretical and its practical side, which even in the later middle ages scholars were still seeking to improve and to popularize. Grammar schools, compared with their elementary inferiors, were more sophisticated in their organization and attracted much more attention from patrons and benefactors. So much more plentiful are the sources for the curricula and organization of the medieval grammar schools that they demand and will receive separate treatment in the following chapters of this book.[5] Here it will be enough to observe that the grammar schools taught the Latin language and literature, in which they endeavoured to impart the ability to read, write, speak and understand.

[1] C. L. Kingsford, *English Historical Literature in the Fifteenth Century* (1913), p. 372.
[2] J. R. Bramble, 'Records of St Nicholas Church, Bristol', *Clifton Antiquarian Club Proceedings*, i (1884-8), p. 148.
[3] F. F. Giraud, 'On the parish clerks and sextons of Faversham, 1506-1593', *Archaeologia Cantiana*, xx (1893), p. 205.
[4] See below, p. 282.
[5] See in particular below, chapters 3 and 4.

Although song and grammar were different stages of the educational curriculum, this did not necessarily mean that they were taught and studied in different institutions. Sometimes indeed this was the case. At Warwick in the early fourteenth century the song schoolmaster was restricted to the teaching of reading and song while the study of Donatus, author of the standard elementary Latin schoolbook, only began in the grammar school.[1] Parents bringing their children for admission to St Paul's school after 1518 were told by Colet 'If your chylde can rede and wryte latin and englysshe sufficiently, soo that he be able to rede and wryte his owne lessons, then he shal be admytted into the schole for a scholer.'[2] This clearly suggests mastering the rudiments in an elementary school before going on to the cathedral grammar school. Similarly at Bruton grammar school, founded by Colet's enemy Bishop FitzJames in 1519, the statutes declare that the schoolmaster 'shall not teche his scolers song nor other petite lernynge, as the crosse rewe, redyng of the mateyns or of the psalter or such other small thyngs, nother redyng of Englissh, but such as shall concern lernynge of gramer'.[3]

On the other hand there are far more references to suggest that the stratification of education had not proceeded very far even by the beginning of the sixteenth century. Grammar was certainly taught in some schools whose range was otherwise elementary. At Canterbury the rector of St Martin's church was permitted to keep a school for any number of boys learning the alphabet, the psalter and song, and for up to thirteen boys studying grammar; in 1321 he was sued for exceeding this number by the master of the city grammar school.[4] The teaching of Donatus was frequently begun in the elementary, not the grammar school. In 1377 the vicar of Kingston-on-Thames was licensed to keep a school for boys learning reading, song and Latin up to Donatus.[5] The 1400 statutes of Winchester College, followed in 1447 by those of Eton, both of which were grammar schools, nevertheless expected their scholars to arrive already knowing Donatus.[6] At the same time several of the new grammar schools founded during the fifteenth and early sixteenth centuries per-

[1] Leach, *History of Warwick School*, pp. 65-6; *ECD*, pp. 274-5.
[2] Lupton, *Life of Colet*, p. 285.
[3] F. W. Weaver, 'Foundation deed of Bruton School', *Somerset and Dorset Notes and Queries*, iii (1892-3), p. 245.
[4] *ECD*, pp. 260-7.
[5] *Reg. Wykeham, Winchester*, ed. T. F. Kirby, vol ii (Hants., Record Society, xiii, 1899), p. 287.
[6] Kirby, *Annals of Winchester*, p. 457; *The Ancient Laws . . . for King's College Cambridge and . . . Eton College*, ed. J. Heywood and T. Wright (1890), p. 479.

mitted the entry of 'petty' scholars still at the elementary stage. The grammar school of Newland in Gloucestershire founded in 1446 was open to boys learning the alphabet, mattins book and psalter, besides those who came to study grammar.[1] A year or so later the grammar master of Ewelme school was envisaged as teaching a reading class as well.[2] When Robert Sherborne, bishop of Chichester, founded Rolleston grammar school in 1524, he ordered the master to take special care over teaching his better pupils so that they might deputize for him in instructing such as came to school ignorant of the alphabet and the first elements of learning.[3] In the same way the 1525 statutes of Manchester grammar school required the master to appoint one of his scholars for a month at a time to teach the abc and the primer to the infants who sat at one end of the same schoolroom as the grammarians.[4] Such examples as these suggest that a strict organization of song and grammar into different schools, though practised in a few places, was not fundamental or universal over the country as a whole.

The chief aim of most grammar schools was to give a good general grounding in the Latin tongue, with special concentration upon the structure of language and upon literature, especially poetry. Many people who studied grammar, however, were less interested in its linguistic and literary aspects than in its practical uses in the administrative and commercial spheres of life, for which their studies were intended to qualify them. To satisfy the needs of such people there evolved during the later middle ages a class of schoolmasters who specialized in the more practical aspects of Latin, of which the principal one was the study of dictamen, the art of composing letters. This art, which was studied to some extent in all grammar schools, was highly developed by the specialists, who taught how to compose every kind of letter both formal and informal that men of affairs or their deputies might wish to send on any occasion. Most of these teachers dealt also with the related techniques for drafting deeds and charters, and many of them extended their range to cover other subjects which were not strictly grammatical but belonged to the same world of commerce and administration for which they were preparing their pupils: conveyancing, the composition of court rolls and other legal records and the keeping of accounts. During the fourteenth century these

[1] *Reg. Spofford, Hereford*, ed. A. T. Bannister (Canterbury and York Society, xxiii, 1919), p. 282.
[2] *Historical MSS Commission, Ninth Report*, p. 218, section 21.
[3] Chichester Diocesan Record Office, Cap 1/14/5 fo 28.
[4] *VCH Lancs.*, ii, 584.

studies and the institutions where they were pursued came to form a definite subdivision of English education, which we may call that of business studies. Their place in the educational hierarchy was somewhat equivocal. In some respects they could be ranked above the grammar schools, because the advanced study of dictamen could only properly come after learning the rudiments of grammar, and some of the pupils who attended business schools were, as today, youths and men older than schoolboys who came to be crammed for some special kind of job. Yet the business schools were also tainted by their concern with humble subjects like accountancy, and contemporaries generally rated their practical motives far lower than the humane and scholarly intentions of the study of grammar.

One other subject came during the fourteenth century to be closely associated with the arts of business, and that was the study of French.[1] Generally speaking, the period between the twelfth and fifteenth centuries saw the French language in England change from a vernacular widely spoken and naturally acquired into a foreign tongue, unknown by most of the population and studied artificially by lawyers and merchants for professional reasons. The Norman Conquest had made French the language of the English court and of the lay aristocracy. During the twelfth and thirteenth centuries its currency had spread widely among the native English gentry, the clergy and even among merchants and tradesmen. It was also the accepted vernacular language of the law courts, and of the schools and universities when one was not speaking Latin. Yet French never succeeded in displacing English entirely, and by at least the middle of the thirteenth century the anomalous situation was developing whereby French was still widely used by the upper classes for conversation and literary purposes and by lesser men at least for legal and commercial reasons, while many of the population who were ambitious to enter and take part in these spheres had been brought up to speak only English. Unlike the French themselves and the children of upper-class families in England, who still learnt French from birth in the thirteenth century, other Englishmen were faced with the prospect of mastering it artificially when they went to school, or when occasion demanded it in later life.

It was therefore at this time that the first manuals were produced for teaching French, aimed at those who had been brought up to speak English. Compared with the complicated and systematic grammars of Latin, these early French manuals were only short and simple, presupposing that the language was still a flourishing vernacular. The

---

[1] The following section is largely based on Kathleen Lambley, *The Teaching and Cultivation of the French Language in England* (1920), especially pp. 3-57.

earliest survivor, which apparently dates from before 1250, is a short treatise in Latin of only two pages on the tenses of the verb *aimer*, showing how they are formed and how they correspond to their Latin equivalents. From the second half of the century come two Latin tracts on French orthography. The first, which is generally known as the *Orthographia Gallica*, was intended to help people to write French correctly from dictation, and to pronounce it properly at sight. The second, usually called the *Tractatio Orthographiae*, which covers very similar ground was the work of a certain 'T. H.' student of Paris. It remained in use until at least the second half of the fourteenth century when it was revised by a doctor of law in the university of Orleans, Canon T. Coyfurelly, and continued to circulate in England in this new version.

The later thirteenth century also saw the composition of a useful manual for teaching vocabulary by Walter of Bibbesworth, the Hertfordshire knight who flourished in the 1270s and who produced it at the request of a noble lady named Denise de Mounchensy. The work was a poem in rhyming couplets which aimed to introduce children to a wide variety of words by describing common scenes and objects to which they referred. It begins with an account of how children are born and reared, goes on to distinguish the parts of the body, describes the tools and implements found in and around the house, and proceeds to treat of such subjects as hunting, beasts and birds, flowers and trees. English equivalents of the French words were written in between the lines of the poem. Not content with a mere vocabulary, the author often digressed to deal with similar or equivocal words to show how they differed in gender, spelling, or meaning:

> *a lippe and an hare*
> Vus avet la levere, et le levere,
>   *a pound*   *a book*
> Et la livere, et le livere;
> La levere si enclost les dens;
> Le levere en boys se tent dedens;
> La livere sert en marchaundye;
> Le livere sert en seynt eglise,
> Et le livere nous aprent clergye.

In short, the treatise tried to convey information in a useful and amusing way, and a large number of manuscripts testify to its popularity and success. It also served as the model for many imitations.[1]

At the beginning of the fourteenth century French was still holding its

---

[1] The treatise is printed in T. Wright, *A Volume of Vocabularies* (1857), pp. 142-74.

own in England. When Ranulf Higden, monk of Chester, composed the great history of the world which he began in the 1320s, he observed that French was still widely current in England. It was the only vernacular language permitted in schools, the children of gentlemen still learnt it from the cradle and social climbers who wished to be reputed gentlemen spoke it with great assiduity.[1] Sixty years later such a statement was quite out of date. In the interim, during the reigns of Edward III and Richard II, English developed at an enormous rate to rival French as a religious, literary, commercial and conversational medium. When John Trevisa came to translate Higden's *Polychronicon* into English, a task he finished in 1387, he pointed out that since the year 1349 English had come to displace French as the vernacular language in schools, and that in his time it was very little known by schoolchildren.[2] In 1362 a parliamentary petition alleged that many difficulties were caused in the law courts because French was now 'too little known' in the realm, and attempted, but without success, to replace French by English for pleading and by Latin for the keeping of records.[3] In the following year the chancellor for the first time opened parliament in English.[4] Throughout the second half of the fourteenth century a spate of literature in English testifies to the great revival of the language in every field: devotional and religious treatises, poetry, letters, translations of the Bible and of works of scholarship. French on the other hand was fast deteriorating into the French of Stratford-atte-Bowe and the French of the farthest end of Norfolk, so humorously treated by those very English writers, Chaucer and Langland.

Far from approving the decline of French which accompanied the English revival, contemporaries viewed it with concern and made what attempts they could to halt the process. The foundation statutes of the three Oxford colleges founded in the first half of the fourteenth century – Exeter (revised 1325), Oriel (1326) and Queen's (1341) – were all careful to prescribe the use only of Latin or French in the community.[5] The university itself, in statutes compiled before 1380 for the guidance of its grammar masters, ordered that they should use both French and English when they translated Latin words or explained their meanings, 'lest the

---

[1] Ranulph Higden, *Polychronicon*, ed. C. Babington, vol ii (Rolls Series, 1869), pp. 158-161.
[2] Ibid.
[3] *Rotuli Parliamentorum*, ii, 273; *Statutes of the Realm*, i, 375-6.
[4] *Rotuli Parliamentorum*, ii, 275.
[5] *Reg. Stapeldon, Exeter*, pp. 309-10; *Statutes of the Colleges of Oxford* (1853), vol i: Oriel p. 8, Queen's p. 14.

French language be altogether lost'.[1] Froissart believed that in 1337 Edward III had commanded noblemen, gentlemen and burgesses of the good towns to teach their children French so that they would be more familiar with it in time of war.[2] And even Trevisa when noting in the 1380s the decline of French in schools felt that the advantages were balanced by the disadvantages which would come to those who travelled abroad without knowing the language.[3]

In any case there continued, even after 1400, to be a need and hence a demand in England for a knowledge of French. Quite apart from its lingering use in letters and deeds up to the 1450s, it remained indispensable for the study and practice of the English common law, for those who engaged in commercial dealings with foreign countries and for those who travelled abroad for the purpose of pilgrimage, diplomacy or war.[4] Although the thirteenth-century tracts of orthography and vocabulary still continued to circulate in their original or in revised versions, the general background of spoken French in England which they had presupposed had now all but disappeared, and new textbooks became necessary which would give much more help than before to students of the language. In place of the manuals on orthography more ambitious works appeared which taught the accidence or morphology of nouns and verbs and took as their model the corresponding elementary textbook of Latin, the *Ars Minor* of Donatus, following its simple and attractive method of explaining the rules by means of questions and answers. At least two such works circulated in England during the early fifteenth century, and it is significant that they both claimed to teach the 'douce françois de Paris', in other words French as a foreign language. One, *Le Donait*, was the work of a certain R. Dove, while the other, the *Donait François*, was compiled so its preface explains by certain clerks at the command and expense of John Barton, who was born and bred in Cheshire, who studied at Paris, apparently in the early fifteenth century, and who intended it principally for the use of children.

Likewise the older vocabularies in verse were replaced by dialogues and conversations in prose, some in French alone, some in both French and English, which were intended to make the reader fluent in everyday French without any tears at all. With an eye to their audience they featured

[1] *Statuta Antiqua Universitatis Oxon.*, ed. Gibson, p. 171.
[2] Froissart, *Chroniques*, ed. de Lettenhove, ii, 419.
[3] Higden, *Polychronicon*, ii, 161.
[4] On the persistence of French in fifteenth-century England see Helen Suggett, 'The use of French in England in the later middle ages', *Transactions of the Royal Historical Society*, 4th series, xxviii (1946), pp. 61-83.

children or merchants in scenes which they were likely to experience when using the language. A typical example of such dialogues, and an attractive one, is a set compiled in the 1410s by William Kingsmill, scrivener and teacher of business studies first at London and then, after 1420, at Oxford. Two travellers meet and, after trying out different kinds of greetings and salutations, fall into conversation about the battle of Agincourt. They ride from Tetsworth to Oxford, where they put up at 'The Mill on the Hoop' in Northgate Street. Inquiries are made there about board and accommodation, after which the innkeeper's wife presents her son, aged twelve, whom a traveller proceeds to question about his knowledge and education. This gave Kingsmill the opportunity for a little self-advertisement:

> 'My child, have you been to school?'
> 'Yes, sir, by your leave.'
> 'At what place?'
> 'Sir, at the house of William Kingsmill, scrivener.'
> 'Fair child, how long have you been dwelling with him?'
> 'Sir, for less than a quarter of a year.'
> 'That is only a short while, but what have you learnt there during that time?'
> 'Sir, my master has taught me how to write, to endite, to count and to speak French.'
> 'And what can you say in French?'
> 'Sir, I know my name and how to describe my body.'

This the prodigy proceeds to do with relentless detail, and the conversations conclude with a rapid rehearsal of various other words on miscellaneous subjects.[1] Dialogues and narratives of this kind continued to be popular throughout the fifteenth century, and the first works in French to be printed in England belonged to this class. These were the *Dialogues in French and English*, which are actually narratives, published by Caxton in about 1480, and *A good boke to lerne to speke French*, issued two or three times after 1497 by the rival printers Richard Pynson and Wynkyn de Worde. They held the field in England until the appearance of a new and improved series of textbooks in the 1520s.[2]

The chief centre during the later middle ages for the teaching of business studies was Oxford, where a succession of masters gave instruction in dictamen, accountancy, French and even the principles and

[1] P. Meyer, 'Les manuscrits français de Cambridge', *Romania*, xxxii (1903), pp. 47-58.
[2] *STC*, nos 24865-8.

procedures of the common law.[1] These subjects did not form part of any course of study for a university degree, and their establishment in Oxford rather reflected the popularity of the city as a resort of scholars of all kinds, just as nowadays the university attracts the presence of secretarial and commercial colleges upon its fringes. The origin of business studies in Oxford goes back to at least the time of King John, from whose reign there survives an early legal formulary for teaching the drafting of letters and documents, although in this case orientated towards the clergy rather than the laity. It is probable that such practical studies were continuously followed in Oxford from then until the middle of the fifteenth century. In about 1280 a certain John of Oxford, whose works show a familiarity with the town, was the author of several tracts on the keeping of courts, conveyancing, accounting and the writing of model deeds and letters. Similar treatises with an Oxford connection also survive from the reign of Edward II (1307-27).

In the second half of the fourteenth century the leading exponent of commercial subjects in Oxford, and indeed in the whole country, was Thomas Sampson, a married man whose career in the city stretched from about 1350 until about 1409. That we know more than usual about his teaching and the kind of clientele for which he catered is due to the survival of a number of his formularies of model letters and deeds, in which for the sake of greater interest he frequently alluded to his work, his pupils and the city where he taught. In this way we learn that he was principally a teacher of dictamen, the composition of letters and deeds in both Latin and French; doubtless he was also able to teach either language when asked to do so. Writing, accountancy and conveyancing were others of his specialities. His pupils were of varying ages. One model letter relates that Sampson 'has newly come to Oxford to teach *boys* dictamen and writing', and these boys may have followed something similar to a course in grammar, albeit with a more practical bias. Other pupils were older and came rather to be crammed for some special purpose. One letter mentions a youth who has transferred from the university arts course to learn to write and endite under Sampson, after which he is to go into the service of an earl.[2] Another, purporting to come from a man who has been

---

[1] The following section is based largely on the work of H. G. Richardson, *An Oxford Teacher of the Fifteenth Century* (1939), reprinted with corrections from *Bulletin of John Ryland's Library*, xxiii (1939), pp. 436-57; 'Business training in medieval Oxford', *American Historical Review*, xlvi (1941), pp. 259-80; 'Letters of the Oxford *Dictatores*', in *Formularies which Bear on the History of Oxford*, ed. H. E. Salter *et al.*, vol ii (Oxford Historical Society new series, v, 1942), pp. 329-450.

[2] *Oxford Formularies*, ii, 407.

appointed steward of a household, asks his brother to learn to write and count, and then to come and help him with the office.[1] The cramming course for older pupils was much shorter than a grammar course at an ordinary school, and six months is once mentioned as a period needed to become competent.[2] It was also expensive, and sums of £2 and £5 are mentioned as being sent to pay Sampson's fees.[3] Still, he seems to have been a popular and successful master; his formularies for teaching letter writing circulated widely and were frequently copied or adapted by later masters in the same line.

Other practitioners continued his work in early fifteenth-century Oxford. From the reign of Henry V there survive the formularies of a teacher who identifies himself only as Simon O., who taught conveyancing and letter writing as Sampson had done. In about 1420 William Kingsmill, the London scrivener whose French dialogues have already been mentioned, moved to Oxford where he proceeded to engage in teaching the usual range of business studies. There were still a number of such teachers in 1432 when the university passed a statute designed to bring them and their students into closer touch with the more literary studies of the arts course. The statute provided that scholars who were learning the art of writing and speaking French, composing deeds, writing, the holding of lay courts and the English method of pleading, should all frequent the university lectures on Latin grammar and rhetoric. It also ordered that the teachers of these subjects should come under the supervision of those university masters who were delegated to supervise the grammar schools of the city.[4] But by the second half of the fifteenth century the study of dictamen and its associated subjects had withered away in Oxford, due in part perhaps to the declining interest in the particular forms these subjects had taken, and in part to the development of new institutions for teaching them, such as the Inns of Court at London.

It is probable that at least the rudiments of legal drafting and accountancy were taught by orthodox grammar masters in some other towns. A grammatical miscellany of the 1420s which belonged to a Bristol schoolmaster contains two short tracts, one explaining the Latin words used in deeds and charters, and the other describing the Arabic numerals and relating them to their Latin equivalents.[5] Moreover, in the century before the Reformation, when a large number of new endowed grammar schools were being founded in England, one or two founders made provision

---

[1] Ibid., pp. 371-2. [2] Ibid., p. 372. [3] Ibid., pp. 397, 407.
[4] *Statuta Antiqua Universitatis Oxon.*, ed. Gibson, p. 240.
[5] Oxford, Lincoln College, MS lat. 129 pp. 46, 61-5.

for the teaching of commercial subjects as well as for grammar itself. The earliest attempt to endow a commercial school seems to have been made by Simon Eyre, citizen and draper of London, who died in 1459 and left his vast fortune to establish a college and school at the Leadenhall for masters teaching song, grammar and writing, which latter probably meant drafting and scriveners' work rather than the simple ability to write which was learnt in the grammar course.[1] Eyre's foundation was unfortunately abortive, but similar schemes were conceived by two benefactors of education in Yorkshire in the 1480s: Robert Stillington, bishop of Bath and Wells, and Thomas Rotherham, archbishop of York. Both founded large endowed schools in their native places, the former at Acaster shortly before 1483 and the latter at Rotherham in that year.[2] Both schools maintained three masters to give free instruction to all comers in song, grammar and writing which in Stillington's foundation was coupled with 'all such things as belonged to scrivener craft' and in Rotherham's with the teaching of reckoning or accountancy. Rotherham said that he included tuition in writing so that the many able youths of the area who did not wish to enter the priesthood could be better fitted for the mechanical arts and other concerns of the world. The history of Acaster school is obscure, and when we next hear of it in 1546 the writing school had disappeared, but at Rotherham writing continued to be taught until the college was dissolved in 1548. The lowliness of the subject however, even in Rotherham's eyes, is shown by the small salary of £5 6s. 8d. he gave to its master, as against £6 13s. 4d. for the teacher of song and £10 for the grammar master. Much the same view was taken by Bishop Sherborne in the statutes for his grammar school at Rolleston in 1524. Although Sherborne was chiefly concerned with promoting a liberal education through the study of grammar, he nevertheless recognized that boys who were dull or lazy might come to school and these he ordered the master to improve as best he could by teaching them to read, write and cast accounts.[3]

It is also likely that writing and the composing of letters and deeds could have been learnt in pre-Reformation England from scriveners, those professional exponents of the art. William Kingsmill had described himself as one when he was offering lessons in French, dictamen and accountancy. A Nottingham pupil in about 1532 was sent for five weeks to learn writing from a scrivener dwelling in the Long Row.[4] Nor should we

[1] J. Stow, *A Survey of London*, ed. C. L. Kingsford (1908), i, 154.
[2] *EYS*, ii, 89-96, 104-85.
[3] Chichester Diocesan Record Office, Cap 1/14/5 fo 28.
[4] *VCH Notts.*, ii, 222.

forget how many people must have picked up a knowledge of business techniques not formally in a school, but informally from their seniors in some merchant's house or great household. Although the kind of personal records which are alone likely to reveal such training hardly survive from medieval times, Dr E. W. Ives has recently drawn attention to an illuminating example from the early sixteenth century.[1] This is a testimonial written by John Fairchild on his own behalf to his uncle, Cardinal Wolsey, in 1515 when he sought appointment as clerk of the works at Tournai. Among his attainments Fairchild claimed that he could file writs, enter pleas and engross legal records; he could act as an attorney or solicitor and he could conduct the business of a court. He had learnt the theory of such things at Gray's Inn and had practised them while working for his father. He could audit accounts and act as a household officer, secretary, comptroller, clerk of the kitchen or clerk of the works, and this he had also learnt with his father in the service of the duchess of Norfolk. By such ways, as well as in school, a young man might qualify himself in law and administration.

The fourth and highest grade of medieval schools were those which dealt with the 'higher studies' to which grammar itself was only a preliminary: the seven liberal arts, canon and civil law and theology, 'the queen of the sciences'. The appearance of masters teaching these subjects in public and gathering students about them is a characteristic of the twelfth century. Some of the earliest groups are found around the nine secular cathedrals: Lincoln, Salisbury, York and so on, where the cathedral and the bishop's household offered patronage and facilities as well as a potential audience of clerks. Other scholars, to whom ecclesiastical supervision was perhaps more irksome, settled in towns which were centrally placed and easy of access, well provided with food and lodgings and not too close to bishops or cathedrals – conditions which were all forthcoming at Northampton, Oxford and to a lesser extent Cambridge. The twelfth century in which these gatherings of masters and students originated was followed by the thirteenth in which they acquired organization and institutions. The gatherings in the towns, eventually restricted to Cambridge and Oxford, became universities which, being national rather than local institutions and providing indeed the material for many large tomes in themselves, will not come under consideration here. Those in the cathedral cities developed into more humble institutions, the chancellor's schools of theology and canon law, which nevertheless

[1] E. W. Ives, 'The common lawyers in pre-Reformation England', *Transactions of the Royal Historical Society*, 5th series, xviii (1968), p. 152; *LPFD*, ii, part 1, no 1368.

because of their long history and their importance in the provision of education locally, deserve some treatment.[1]

The scholars who taught at the English cathedrals in the twelfth century were generally canons of the church or other *protégés* of the bishop, and dealt with any one of a large variety of subjects: philosophy, law, medicine or theology. The number of students they attracted around them fluctuated with their reputations and probably sank with their deaths or departures. The tendency in the thirteenth century was for the range of studies to become contracted to two, theology and canon law, and for a definite officer of the cathedral to be made responsible for teaching them. This imposed limitations but it also brought stability. Students of arts or medicine would find better facilities for study at the universities, but the local clergy provided an obvious audience for lectures on theology and canon law, including as they did some men desirous of higher education who were unable to attend university, and many whose education was greatly in need of improvement. The development of special institutions of higher education at the English secular cathedrals may also have been influenced by the decrees of the two general councils of the western Church which met at the Lateran in Rome in 1179 and 1215. The first of these ordered that each cathedral should provide a grammar master, the second added that each metropolitan cathedral, the seat of an archbishop, should also provide a master to teach theology and that both masters, the grammarian and the theologian, should be given prebends for their support in the cathedral concerned.[2] The decrees of 1215 would only have involved the provision of theological lecturers at Canterbury, which was a monastic cathedral, and York, but in the event many more schools of theology were organized than the council had demanded. During the thirteenth century most of the nine English secular cathedrals, influenced more perhaps by their own traditions of education than by the council, evolved and organized permanent schools of theology under specially deputed teachers.

The official who became responsible at most of these cathedrals for teaching theology was the chancellor, whose office dated back to the beginning of the twelfth century, who acted as librarian and secretary to the chapter and who supervised the teaching of the cathedral grammar school by a deputy schoolmaster. During the thirteenth century he also

---

[1] On the higher studies in the cathedrals see in general Edwards, *English Secular Cathedrals*, pp. 185-205, to which the following section is greatly indebted.

[2] J. D. Mansi, *Sacrorum Conciliorum Nova et Amplissima Collectio* (1778, reprinted 1961), xxii, cols 227-8, 999-1000. See also below, pp. 174-5.

became responsible for teaching theology, a development which had taken place at Lincoln by 1200, Salisbury by 1240, York by 1250 and London by the end of the century. At only two cathedrals were different arrangements made: Chichester, where a special office of theologian was created and endowed with the prebend of Wittering during the reign of Bishop Ralph Nevill (1224-44), and Hereford where the duty of lecturing is found in 1356 annexed to the office of penitentiary.[1] The chancellor or his equivalent was expected to deliver lectures personally in either theology or canon law, but he was usually permitted to appoint a deputy if necessary. Sometimes too the chancellor allowed his place to be taken temporarily by a visiting scholar, or by a local cleric who wished to expound his views on subjects of current interest.

The duty of lecturing, however, was subject like so many other institutions of the medieval church to a good deal of interruption and neglect. The difficulties experienced in getting the chancellors of Salisbury to lecture during the fourteenth century have been clearly demonstrated by Dr Kathleen Edwards.[2] At Wells too the bishop found the chancellor negligent in 1335 and ordered him to resume lecturing; in the following years, care was taken to impress the importance of the duty upon succeeding dignitaries.[3] In 1365 the bishop of Chichester was moved to complain to Pope Urban V that although the prebend of Wittering was reserved for a lecturer in theology, former popes had provided to it candidates who were not theologians, so that the intention of the foundation was defrauded. This elicited a papal promise that in future only theologians should hold the benefices.[4] In the early sixteenth century Richard FitzJames, bishop of London, found that his chancellor had omitted his duties, apparently on the ludicrous grounds that he was bound to lecture 'continuously', which was impossible! FitzJames was quite equal to this and provided his chancellor with a careful gloss on the word, declaring that it meant regular lectures three times a week during certain seasons of the year, which he was also careful to specify.[5] Still, as these examples make clear, the authorities did not permit the institution of lecturing to languish unopposed; negligence, when it came to light, encountered resolute action, and however tenuous the records of

[1] Edwards, *English Secular Cathedrals*, pp. 197-8.
[2] Ibid., pp. 201-2.
[3] *Reg. de Salopia, Wells*, ed. T. S. Holmes, vol i (Somerset Record Society, ix, 1895), pp. 255, 341.
[4] *Calendar of Papal Letters 1362-1404*, pp. 189-90.
[5] *Registrum Statutorum et Consuetudinum . . . Sancti Pauli Londinensis*, ed. W. S. Simpson (1873), pp. 413-15.

lecturing in any one cathedral, there can be no doubt that the institution in general continued to function during the fourteenth and fifteenth centuries.

Something can be gathered from scattered references of the circumstances in which the chancellors delivered their lectures. A special building for the purpose is mentioned more than once; at Salisbury the chapter built a new range over the west side of the cloister in 1454 for a lecture room and library,[1] while at London in 1465 the school was held in a room under the chapter house.[2] Lecturing varied in frequency from time to time and from place to place; once a fortnight is mentioned at Salisbury in 1454, and three times a week at London in the early sixteenth century.[3] There were also terms and vacations. The chancellor of Wells was bound to lecture from 15 October until 3 July, while FitzJames's ordinance at London bound him to hold forth from the autumn until Advent, from Epiphany to Quinquagesima and from Whitsun to the beginning of August.[4] Exactly who turned up to hear the lectures is not always clear, but they seem usually to have included the clergy of the cathedral and city, and those of their brethren from elsewhere who stood in need of education. We find Bishop Hugh of Lincoln (1209-35) commanding the vicar of Barton-on-Humber to study theology at Lincoln for two years, while in 1293 Archbishop John Romeyn of York permitted the rectors of his diocese to reside away from their cures in order to attend the lectures in theology at York.[5] These lectures were still attracting a local audience in 1365 when Simon Langham, bishop of Ely, after visiting the hospital of St Leonard, York, arranged that those of the brethren who were apt and wished to study should attend the theological school of the city and be provided with parchment for writing down 'what might seem devout and notable'.[6]

The subjects prescribed for study in the chancellors' schools were simply defined as theology or canon law, but sometimes we have more precise knowledge of the topics covered. Robert Winchelsey, canon of St Paul's and later archbishop of Canterbury, disputed at London between 1283 and 1293 on the nature of the Trinity and the relations between its

[1] Edwards, *English Secular Cathedrals*, p. 202; *VCH Wilts.*, iii, 178-9.
[2] *Historical Collections of a Citizen of London*, ed. J. Gairdner (Camden Society, new series, xvii, 1876), pp. 230-1.
[3] *VCH Wilts.*, iii, 178-9; W. S. Simpson, op. cit.
[4] *Reg. de Salopia, Wells*, i, 341; W. S. Simpson, op. cit.
[5] *Rotuli Hugonis de Wells*, ed. F. N. Davis, vol iii (Lincoln Record Society, ix, 1914), pp. 101-2; *EYS*, i, 17.
[6] PRO, Chancery Miscellanea, C 47/21/4 mm 2, 6. I owe this reference to Br. Bonaventure.

persons; these were questions which he had already discussed in the schools of Oxford.[1] In 1355 two friars, a Franciscan and a Dominican, disputed in the chancellor's school at York about the conception of the Virgin, which the Franciscan held to be immaculate.[2] From Wells there survives a set of lectures on the Apocalypse which John Orum, doctor of divinity and canon of the cathedral, gave there in the early fifteenth century.[3] At London the chancellor's school also served as a forum in 1465 for the great controversy which broke out in the city between the friars and the secular clergy on the poverty of Christ. It was on this occasion that William Ive, master of Whittington College, lectured in the school in cap and gown, attended by a verger bearing a silver wand, and read, says a contemporary witness, 'many full noble lessons to prove that Christ was lord of all and no beggar, and he did it after the form of schools'.[4]

The secular cathedrals were not the only institutions to maintain lectures in the higher studies. During the thirteenth century the friars developed an elaborate and effective system of schools and lectures in arts and theology for their own members, and they were imitated in this, albeit with less zeal, by the greater houses of monks and regular canons. These facilities will be noticed in a later chapter;[5] they were primarily intended for the members of the houses and orders concerned, but sometimes outsiders may have been admitted. When the abbot of Westminster complained at the beginning of the fourteenth century to the monks of Worcester Cathedral for allowing the cessation of lectures there, he observed that it was to the loss of both regulars and seculars, and there is some evidence too that the friars may have admitted seculars to the lecture rooms of their orders.[6]

A new kind of institution for the study of theology appeared in the early fifteenth century with the opening of the Guildhall Library in London. The foundation was carried out by the executors of Sir Richard Whittington and William Bury, both citizens and mercers of London who died in 1423, the leading spirit among the executors being John Carpenter, the clerk to the corporation of the city. Whether Whittington originated

[1] A. G. Little, 'Theological schools in medieval England', *English Historical Review*, lv (1940), pp. 624-30.
[2] A. G. Little, *The Grey Friars in Oxford* (Oxford Historical Society, xx, 1892), p. 242.
[3] BRUO, ii, 1405-6.
[4] *Historical Collections of a Citizen of London*, ed. Gairdner, pp. 230-1. Notes of Ive's lectures survive in Bodleian, MS Lat. th. e 25, folios 24-7, a reference I owe to the kindness of Dr R. W. Hunt.
[5] See below, pp. 226-43.
[6] A. F. Leach, *Documents illustrating Early Education in Worcester, 685-1700* (Worcs. Historical Society, xxxi, 1913), pp. 29-34; see also below, p. 233.

D

the scheme or whether the disposition of his money towards it was Carpenter's idea is not now easy to say; both were men of experience and vision. Nor do the foundation statutes survive, but it is possible from stray references to form an idea of the way in which the institution worked. Opened in or shortly before 1425, it was a chained library, chiefly devoted to works of theology and open to the public. Two priests were retained to act as its keepers, and we are told that it was a resort of students who wished to be educated in holy scripture. The foundation must have been popular for it received several benefactions of money and books during the fifteenth century, and the library continued to function until the beginning of Edward VI's reign when the college of priests at the Guildhall, whose members had staffed it, came to an end with the dissolution of chantries and colleges in 1548. At the same time, according to the historian of London, John Stow, the books were sent for by the Lord Protector, Edward duke of Somerset, and loaded onto three carts 'with promise to be restored shortly', but they were never returned.[1] This assertion is to some extent borne out by a minute of the corporation of London in 1549 permitting Somerset's secretary, William Cecil, to borrow certain volumes, including the works of St Augustine, with a request that they should be returned when he had finished reading them.[2]

The Guildhall Library was the model for two similar foundations at Bristol and Worcester executed by another John Carpenter, who was bishop of Worcester from 1443 to 1476 and a devoted patron of learning throughout his life.[3] Carpenter's early career as a secular priest in London and his close friendship with his namesake, the town clerk, must have made him well acquainted with the Guildhall scheme, while his reign as bishop of Worcester, in which he distinguished himself by his conscientious administration, gave him the opportunity for reproducing it in his diocese. Both Worcester and Bristol were in need of educational facilities, for Worcester with its monastic cathedral lacked a chancellor to lecture on theology, while Bristol presented problems of another kind. It was the largest town in England without a cathedral or a resident bishop and lay on the edge of the diocese, making supervision difficult. It supported nearly 100 secular clergy for whom some sort of instruction was desirable,

---

[1] Stow, *Survey of London*, ed. Kingsford, i, 275.
[2] On the history of the Guildhall Library see T. Brewer, *Memoir of the Life and Times of John Carpenter*; *Calendar of Plea and Memoranda Rolls of the City of London 1458-1482*, ed. P. E. Jones (1961), pp. ix-xiii; R. Smith, 'The library at Guildhall in the 15th and 16th centuries', *Guildhall Miscellany*, i (1952), pp. 3-9, vi (1956), pp. 2-6; and E. M. Borrajo, 'The Guildhall Library', *Library Association Record*, x (1908), pp. 380-4.
[3] For Carpenter's career see also below, p. 200.

and being infected by Lollardy it was strongly in need of orthodox teaching. Carpenter used two existing foundations as the basis for his schemes: the carnary chapel on the north side of Worcester cathedral, and the House of Kalendars, a chantry of four priests attached to the church of All Saints at Bristol. In 1464, with the consent of the patrons concerned, he established in both places a library of chained volumes, apparently of theological works, each library being open to the public on weekdays from 10.00 until 2.00. Responsibility for the libraries was to lie in the hands of the carnary chaplain and the prior or master of the House of Kalendars, both secular priests. Each was in future to be a university graduate and if possible a bachelor of theology, and their duties besides supervising the library included expounding obscure and difficult points of theology to the readers and delivering a theological lecture in the library once a week.[1] The carnary library remained in being until the Reformation. It was served by a succession of graduate chaplains, and weekly lectures were still being delivered there in 1539 when the foundation came to an end as a consequence of the dissolution of the monastic cathedral.[2] The success of the library at Bristol on the other hand is more difficult to gauge; it seems still to have been in existence in 1480, and the priors were nearly all graduates until the house was dissolved as a chantry in 1548. The survey of the chantries carried out in that year however says nothing of either library or lectures.[3] Yet whatever the fate of his foundations, one cannot but pay tribute to the originality of Carpenter's vision and the utility of his schemes.

It was still possible, therefore, in the fifteenth century for a secular clerk to study theology at an elementary level without going to a university, in one of the dozen or so local centres which we have mentioned, and the same applied to monks and friars for whom the local schools of their orders were available. The historian John Rous writing in about 1486 declares that 'today, fruitful lectures and disputations are held in cathedral churches and some noble colleges, and in the friaries of the four mendicant orders'.[4] A quarter of a century later, in 1509-10, Edmund Dudley painted a less favourable picture and asked what had become of the famous men

---

[1] For the ordinances of the House of Kalendars see Worcs. Record Office, Reg. Carpenter vol i folios 197-8, and for those of the carnary chapel, ibid., Reg. Silvestro de Gigli folios 132v-3v.

[2] PRO, Exch. Augm. Misc. Books, E 315/101 fo 147.

[3] *Itineraria Simonis Simeonis et Willelmi de Worcestre*, ed. J. Nasmith (1778), p. 229; Sir John Maclean, 'Chantry certificates, Gloucestershire', *Transactions of the Bristol and Gloucs. Archaeological Society*, viii (1883-4), p. 246.

[4] John Rous, *Historia Regum Angliae*, ed. T. Hearne (1716), p. 73.

who had once read divinity in the cathedral churches and in great monasteries.[1] Yet despite one or two failures of which Dudley may have known, the teaching of theology on a local basis continued to find approbation even during Tudor times. When Henry VIII decided in 1539 to found a large number of new secular cathedrals out of the old cathedral priories and other religious houses, the draft schemes for the new foundations included provision for at least one reader of divinity in each.[2] In the event, the Henrician cathedrals set up in 1541-2 were on a more modest scale and lacked the projected lecturers, but interest in religious education continued strong during the succeeding years, and under the regimes of Edward VI, Mary and Elizabeth care continued to be taken by the authorities that lectures should at least continue in the old secular cathedrals, while some attempt was made to introduce them to the new foundations. In this, as in many other respects, a medieval institution continued to be influential in the new age.[3]

[1] Edmund Dudley, *The Tree of the Commonwealth*, ed. D. M. Brodie (1948), p. 62.
[2] On this subject see below, p. 263.
[3] *Visitation Articles and Injunctions*, ed. W. H. Frere (Alcuin Club, xiv-xvi, 1910), ii. 133, 250, 311, 377; iii, 31, 42, 49, etc. See also, on Lichfield, *VCH Staffs.*, iii, 167.

Chapter Three

The study of grammar

Now that we have noted the main features of the medieval system of education, let us return to the area which will be our chief concern – the study of grammar. This study has already been defined as that of the Latin language and its literature, but the definition embraces a wide variety of activities. At an elementary level grammar involved correct spelling and pronunciation, the mastery of the basic inflexions and constructions and the assimilation of vocabulary. At a more advanced stage it included the art of composition, both of prose and verse, and the pursuit of a clear and elegant style. Literary criticism was another branch, the study and interpretation of Latin texts, with reference when necessary to related topics such as mythology and history. At the highest level of all, grammarians interested themselves in the structure of the language and tried to elucidate the rules by which it operated. They studied the origins and meanings of words and engaged in what we would call philology, lexicography and linguistic philosophy. The study of grammar began in school, where boys learnt the elements of the language, composition and literary criticism. It continued at university where grammar at a more advanced level formed part of the arts course. Higher still, as material for philosophical speculation and original research, it occupied some very able minds of the twelfth and thirteenth centuries, not only the specialists whose grammatical works we shall consider shortly, but men of universal learning, of whom Roger Bacon, Robert Grosseteste and Robert Kilwardby are good examples.

If it be asked why Latin was the chief study of the medieval schools rather than French or English, the answer is simple. Latin was the language of the Christian religion, in which its sacred texts, its liturgy, theology and law were all inscribed. It was equally the language of scholarship and of the principal textbooks of all the liberal arts, philosophy, the natural sciences and the civil law. Since even the teaching of these subjects was generally conducted in Latin, the mastery of the language was an essential preliminary to all higher studies. Latin was also the language of a great deal of humane literature both classical and medieval including history, poetry and letters, which were considered as repositories of wisdom and virtue. Moreover, despite the challenge of French and later of English, it long remained a medium of administration and commerce, in which charters were drafted, accounts kept, letters written and negotiations conducted, especially when foreign countries were involved. No wonder then that grammar was considered to be the most fundamental of all studies. 'Experience plainly teaches', wrote William Wykeham in the foundation deed of Winchester College in 1382, 'that grammar is the foundation, gate, and source of all the other liberal arts, without which such arts cannot be known, nor can anyone arrive at practising them. Moreover, by the knowledge of letters justice is cultivated and the prosperity of the human condition is increased.'[1]

Let us begin with the textbooks from which Latin was studied during the later middle ages. The standard elementary grammar used in the medieval schools was the *Ars Minor* of Aelius Donatus, the teacher of St Jerome, who flourished at Rome in the middle of the fourth century.[2] This was a brief account, only a dozen pages long, of the eight parts of speech, explaining their characteristics and describing their inflexions without too much concern over irregularities. Its method of exposition was by means of simple questions and answers, which could easily be repeated by masters and their pupils:

> How many are the parts of speech? Eight. What are they? Noun, pronoun, verb, adverb, participle, conjunction, preposition, interjection. What is a noun? A part of speech with a case, properly or commonly signifying a body or a thing. How many characteristics have nouns? Six. What are they? Quality, comparison, gender, number, form, and case,

and so on, until each of the characteristics of nouns had been discussed and the commonest inflexions had been given. In this way the *Ars Minor* both taught the basic accidence and imparted a good many definitions at the same time. It was highly esteemed as an elementary schoolbook throughout the middle ages, and was translated into English in the

[1] Kirby, *Annals of Winchester College*, p. 441; *ECD*, pp. 320-1.
[2] Printed in *Grammatici Latini*, ed. H. Keil, vol iv (1844), pp. 355-66.

fifteenth century. During 1,000 years of use, however, the text inevitably suffered a great many modifications, both of rules and definitions, as the study of grammar changed and developed. Thus whereas the *Ars Minor* treated only of the first three conjugations and declensions, the late medieval *Donet*, as it was called, described four and five respectively, and departed in other details from the text that St Jerome would have studied.

The *Ars Minor* offered no more than an introduction. Longer and more detailed works were required to build upon its foundations and to explain all the irregularities of accidence, the properties of words and their relations with one another. As an advanced school textbook the most popular work of the later middle ages was the *Doctrinale* of Alexander de Villa Dei, of Ville Dieu in Normandy, who was writing in about 1200.[1] The *Doctrinale* was a verse treatise of some 2,650 hexameters, divided into four sections which dealt in turn with the parts of speech, syntax, quantity and metre, and figures of speech. It was widely used all over Western Europe during the later middle ages, both in schools and universities, and its popularity, surviving well into the age of printing, led to the appearance of over 260 editions between 1470 and the 1520s. By this time however it was falling out of fashion; the scholars of the New Learning treated it with scorn, and subsequent historians of education have generally concurred with their judgement.

In order to understand why medieval students found Alexander so useful, let us take as a brief example the author's treatment of the nouns of the first declension, with which his work begins:

> Rectis as es a dat declinatio prima,
> atque per am propria quaedam ponuntur Hebraea,
> dans ae diphthongon genetivis atque dativis.
> am servat quartus; tamen en aut an reperimus,
> cum rectus fit in es vel in as, vel cum dat a Graecus.
> rectus in a Graeci facit an quarto breviari.
> quintus in a dabitur, post es tamen e reperitur.
> a sextus, tamen es quandoque per e dare debes.
> am recti repetes quinto, sextum sociando.[2]

> > The nominative ends in as, es, a,
> > But certain Hebrew proper nouns in am.
> > The genitive and dative end in ae,
> > The accusative in am, but en or an

---

[1] *Das Doctrinale des Alexander de Villa Dei*, ed. D. Reichling (Berlin, 1893).
[2] Ibid., p. 8.

> For nominative es or as, and an
> For Greek nouns with a nominative a.
> The vocative is a, but es makes e;
> The ablatives are also a and e;
> But nominative am remains the same
> In both the vocative and ablative.

If this information were arranged in tables in the manner of Kennedy's *Latin Primer*, it would be at once apparent that in nine lines Alexander has taught us the singular number of every possible Latin noun of the first declension, as well as those of Greek and Hebrew origin. Having read it we can decline not only *mensa* and its companions but personal names such as Aeneas, Atrides, Cybela and, what is more to the point in Christian Europe, Adam and Thomas. This introduces us to one of Alexander's basic preoccupations – completeness – the achievement of which helped to make his work so valuable. It might be argued that the information would be better understood in tabular form, but medieval teaching methods, at a time when classes were large and books were few, tended to be oral rather than visual, and another great merit of the *Doctrinale* was that it could easily be chanted aloud and committed to memory.

The popularity of the *Doctrinale* was shared by a similar work, the *Grecismus* of Évrard of Béthune.[1] Of the author little more is known than that he was probably a Fleming by origin, and was also active at the beginning of the thirteenth century. Like the *Doctrinale* the *Grecismus* is a treatise in verse, some 4,500 lines long, which deals somewhat haphazardly with all four branches of grammar (orthography, prosody, accidence and syntax) and with figures of speech. While it has something to say on most matters, its special concern is less with basic accidence than with the derivations, meanings and characteristics of words. Thus when treating of nouns, Évrard arranges them in lists under their genders, and he also gathers together the names proper to classical mythology with explanations. The most distinctive feature of the *Grecismus* is the eighth chapter, 'concerning nouns of Greek origin', which gives lists in alphabetical order with meanings, hence the title of the book and the author's proud appellation of 'the Grecist'.

Third in this popular genre of grammars in verse come two poems of the early thirteenth century called *Synonyma* and *Equivoca*, which are in fact the two halves of a single work. The poems, which also had a European circulation, were ascribed in most of the English editions to John of

---

[1] *Eberhardi Bethuniensis Graecismus*, ed. J. Wrobel (Breslau, 1887). The early printed editions are listed in *Gesamtkatalog der Wiegendrucke*, vol vii (Leipzig, 1938), nos 9211-9228.

Garland, the greatest English grammarian of the thirteenth century, who made himself an international reputation as a teacher at Paris and Toulouse. The authorship has not however been established beyond doubt, and the poems may even be older than Garland's career.[1] In the prologue the author declares his intention of giving milk to children and of teaching the elements of Latin to those who know only their mother tongue. After explaining the difference between synonyms and *equivoca*, or homonyms as we would now call them, he promises to give lists of both in alphabetical order. This order he nevertheless observes only as far as the first letter of each word. In the *Synonyma* key words are taken, such as *anima*, *avis* and *aqua*, and their synonyms are listed, often with indications of the specialized senses in which they are used. In the *Equivoca* lists of homonyms are given, beginning with the word *augustus* which if second declension may mean an emperor, a month or a coin, but if fourth declension relates to a species of divination. The two poems were very popular in England and occur in many of the manuscripts used by school-masters, where they are sometimes accompanied by a prose commentary ascribed to a certain *Magister Galfridus Anglicus*.

At a higher level than the verse treatises, there were grammars of an advanced nature in prose, which were detailed guides to the whole study of Latin rather than textbooks for the use of schoolboys. Such a work was the grammar of Priscian, who had taught at Constantinople in the years around 500.[2] His long and detailed study was arranged in the order which the classical grammarians had developed and which their medieval successors usually followed. This divided grammar into four parts: the study of the letter, the syllable, the word and the clause, or to use the technical terms, orthography, prosody, accidence and syntax. The first three of these divisions were covered by Books I-XVI of Priscian's grammar, which in medieval times were together known as *Prescianus in Majore*. Book I treats of the letters of the alphabet, their sounds and values, while the beginning of Book II deals with the quantities of syllables. The remainder of the first sixteen books is devoted to the eight parts of speech, their characteristics and the regular and irregular forms of their accidence.

---

[1] The early English editions of these works are listed in *STC*, nos 11601-17. They are each about 700 lines long. The *Synonyma* is also printed in Migne, *Patrologia Latina*, vol cl (1854), cols 1577-90. On these works and their authorship see B. Hauréau, 'Notices sur les œuvres authentiques ou supposées de Jean de Garlande', *Notices et extraits des mss de la bibliothèque nationale*, xxvii, part 1 (Paris, 1879), pp. 55-64; and L. J. Paetow, *Morale Scolarium of John of Garland* (Memoirs of the University of California, vol iv, part 2 (1927), pp. 133-4).

[2] Printed in *Grammatici Latini*, ed. H. Keil, vols ii-iii (1855-8).

D*

Here, as everywhere, Priscian gives numerous examples of the usages of words from a wide variety of classical authors. Books XVII and XVIII, which deal with syntax, were usually called *Prescianus in Minore* or *Prescianus de Constructionibus*, and were frequently published and consulted independently of the rest of the work.

Priscian's grammar was too advanced for ordinary school work. It was indeed the prescribed text for the grammatical section of the arts course at university, and in school its role was probably limited to that of a reference work, or something that was known only by the master. The same may be said of two other important grammars in prose which circulated during the later middle ages. These were the *Summa super Prescianum* by Peter Helias, who was teaching at Paris in about 1140-50, and the grammar of the Italian Dominican, John Balbi of Genoa, which forms the first part of his *Catholicon* or dictionary, completed by 1286.[1]

As well as grammars in the limited sense of works on accidence and syntax, the study of Latin needed dictionaries in which the forms and meanings of large numbers of words would be easily available for consultation. It was in this field that medieval scholars made one of their most useful contributions to knowledge by inventing and developing the notion of the dictionary as it is understood today.[2] The story begins with Isidore of Seville (*c.* 560-636) whose *Liber Etymologiarum*, frequently consulted during the middle ages, was an encyclopedia in which the different branches of knowledge were described and the terminology of each one traced and explained.[3] Isidore opens by discussing grammar and the other liberal arts, afterwards proceeding through such topics as law and chronology, God, the Church, geography, Man and the animal kingdom, providing not only information on the words proper to each subject but also discussing their etymologies. Isidore's work nevertheless remained an encyclopedia rather than a dictionary, and it was not until the eleventh century that a recognizable specimen of the latter was first produced. This was the *Elementarium* of Papias, a Lombard of Pavia, who tells us in his preface that many others had previously been engaged upon the task and that he had given ten years to completing it, which he probably achieved in about 1053.[4] The *Elementarium* consisted basically of a word list in alphabetical order. 'Anyone', says the author, 'who wishes to

---

[1] The work of Peter Helias has not been printed. For the *Catholicon* see below, p. 93.
[2] The following paragraphs are much indebted to Ll. W. and B. A. Daly, 'Some techniques in medieval Latin lexicography', *Speculum*, xxxix, (1964), pp. 229-39.
[3] *Isidori Hispalensis Episcopi Etymologiarum sive Originum*, ed. W. M. Lindsay (1911).
[4] Some early printed editions of the *Elementarium* are listed in L. Hain, *Repertorium Bibliographicum* (1831), vol ii, part 2, nos 12378-81.

find anything quickly must also notice that this whole book is composed according to the alphabet, not only in the first letters of the words but also in the second, third and sometimes even the fourth determinative arrangement of the letters.' In other words, Papias claimed to carry his alphabetical arrangement to at least the third letter of every word. He also promised to explain the genders and declensions of nouns, the conjugations of verbs and the quantities of doubtful syllables and to cite the books and authors he had consulted. In fact the execution of the work, at least in the surviving copies, does not always measure up to the promises, but the *Elementarium* none the less remains as a pioneer work, struggling to evolve the techniques of arrangement which are taken for granted by us. It was widely used in medieval times and survived to be printed on several occasions in the late fifteenth century.

The two other standard dictionaries of the later middle ages were also the work of Italian scholars. The *Derivationes* of Hugutio of Pisa, bishop of Ferrara, who died in 1210, gave particular attention to the origin of words. Taking key words in turn, it discussed their etymologies and meanings, and then provided lists of their compounds and derivatives, together with similar or related words and roots.[1] As a work of reference however the *Derivationes* was far less easy to consult than the *Elementarium*, because the alphabetical arrangement took account only of the first letter of the word (it begins with *augeo*), and the compounds were not arranged according to their own spelling but followed that of the parent word. For this reason manuscripts of the work were frequently provided with finding-lists of words in a fuller alphabetical order along with references to their places in the text. The third of the great lexicographers was the Dominican John of Genoa, or *Januensis* as he was usually called, whose *Catholicon*, finished by about 1286, contained besides the grammar already mentioned a comprehensive Latin dictionary. The *Catholicon* marked a great improvement on its predecessors. The order was alphabetical down to the last letter of every word, and the entries indicated stems, principal parts, etymologies and meanings, the execution of the work being of a high standard. The *Catholicon*, which seems to have reached England by the end of the thirteenth century, soon established itself in Western Europe as *the* dictionary, and it was printed far more frequently in the fifteenth century than any of its rivals.[2]

[1] There are no printed editions of the *Derivationes*. MSS are listed in A. Marigo, *I Codici Manoscritti delle 'Derivationes' di Uguccione Pisano* (Rome, 1936).
[2] The MSS of the *Catholicon* are listed in ibid., pp. 31-40, and the early printed editions in *Gesamtkatalog der Wiegendrucke*, vol iii (Leipzig, 1928), nos 3182-205.

One other thirteenth-century dictionary deserves to be mentioned before we leave the subject of lexicography. The *Summa Difficiliorum Vocabulorum Biblie* was the work of the Franciscan William Brito of Lyons who completed it between 1249 and 1272.[1] It was a glossary, also rigorously alphabetical, of some 2,500 difficult words in the Bible, with detailed commentaries on their origins and meanings, and citations from a large number of other authors both classical and medieval. This was a more advanced work than schoolboys would have used, but it was often consulted and cited by schoolmasters and grammarians in their researches, so that it came to be influential in the study of grammar as well as of theology.

The various works discussed above were the chief textbooks and authorities for the study of grammar in the later middle ages, their circulation extending over most of Western Europe. Excepting the three works of the late and post-classical eras, they were all produced during a period of just over 200 years, from about 1053 to about 1286, which therefore constitutes a golden age of grammatical studies. Four of the authors were French and three were Italians; the English contribution, though by no means negligible, was a more modest one.[2] It was therefore largely a continental movement of the twelfth and thirteenth centuries that shaped the way in which grammar was studied and taught in England from 1200 until the beginning of the sixteenth century. All the works which have been mentioned circulated widely in England during this period. They dominate the grammatical sections of medieval library catalogues, including those of the few schools for which details have survived. They are constantly quoted as authorities by the English scholars who wrote on grammar, and the shorter works appear frequently in the grammatical miscellanies which masters compiled for their own use in school.[3]

Yet useful and comprehensive though the standard grammars were, they did not preclude the carrying out of further work on the subject in England during the later middle ages. Schoolmasters often found it necessary to abridge or to simplify the authorities for class consumption,

---

[1] Brito's work was printed under the title *Vocabulorum Biblie* and attributed to Henricus de Hassia (Ulm, J. Zainer, *c.* 1473). A new edition by Dr Ll. W. Daly is in preparation. On Brito see B. Hauréau in *Histoire littéraire de la France*, vol xxix (1885), pp. 583-602.

[2] Besides John of Garland, the twelfth-century grammarians Alexander Neckham and Osbern of Gloucester had a European circulation. See R. W. Hunt, 'The "lost" preface to the *Liber Derivationum* of Osbern of Gloucester', *Medieval and Renaissance Studies*, iv (1958), pp. 267-82.

[3] On their pre-eminence see R. W. Hunt, op cit. below; Br. Bonaventure, 'The teaching of Latin in late medieval England', *Medieval studies*, xxiii (1961), pp. 11-12; and on medieval libraries, below, pp. 124-6 and 250.

and they were also moved to write discussions and commentaries of their own on the problems with which the great grammarians had dealt. Hence a considerable number of grammatical treatises were produced in England during this period, usually shorter and more limited in scope than the authoritative works. Their circulation was also much smaller, and until the invention of printing no native English grammar achieved the currency of the great continental masters, even in England.

The leading grammar schools of medieval England were those of Oxford, and of the masters who taught there four have left identifiable treatises, from Richard of Hambury who flourished at the end of the thirteenth century to John Leland who died in the early fifteenth.[1] The grammar schools of Oxford were frequented, independently of the university, by pupils from many parts of the country, and at least two of the Oxford masters seem to have enjoyed more than a local reputation for their work. We have already noticed how the currency of the French language in England was reflected by its use for vernacular purposes instead of English in the schools.[2] According to the Oxford scholar and translator John Trevisa writing in 1385, John Cornwall (who flourished at Oxford between 1344 and 1349) was the first master to replace French by English as the language of instruction in school. This observation is borne out by the fact that Cornwall's *Speculum Grammaticale*, which was written in 1346, is the earliest extant treatise on grammar to include explanations in English. Trevisa goes on to explain how Cornwall's innovation was copied by Richard Penkridge, another Oxford master of the 1360s, and then by other men, 'so that now [in 1385] . . . in alle the gramere scoles of Engelonde, children leveth Frensche and construeth and lerneth an Englische'.[3] A generation later another Oxford master, John Leland, who was teaching there by 1400 and died in 1428, enjoyed a reputation far wider than his own city, and was called by his contemporaries 'flos grammaticorum', 'the flower of grammarians'. Manuscripts of his work reached such places as Beccles, Bristol, Worksop and possibly also Bridport and Norfolk during the fifteenth century.[4] The esteem in which Leland was held apparently rested on his simplification, 'not to say

---

[1] The standard treatment of this subject is by R. W. Hunt, 'Oxford grammar masters of the later middle ages', *Oxford Studies Presented to Daniel Callus* (Oxford Historical Society, new series, xvi, 1964), pp. 163-93.
[2] Above, pp. 71-3.
[3] *Polychronicon Ranulphi Higden*, ed. C. Babington, vol ii (Rolls Series, 1896), pp. 158-161.
[4] For Leland's works see Hunt in *Oxford Studies Presented to Daniel Callus*, pp. 169-70, 181-4; and *BRUO*, ii, 1129.

debasement', of older and more complicated grammars, and his surviving works are neither many nor of a high standard. Yet few other English schoolmasters possess even the slight indications of fame and influence which can be claimed by Leland and Cornwall.

Although Oxford kept its primacy in the study and teaching of grammar until the early sixteenth century, the masters of some other towns produced treatises which had more than a local circulation. One such scholar was the Cambridge grammarian Nicholas of Brackendale, who after a spell in the bishop of Ely's prison on a charge of homicide in 1255, engaged in the gentler task of writing a metrical treatise on deponent verbs, several copies of which circulated in later times.[1] Another work which found favour with grammarians was the *Memoriale Juniorum* of Thomas Hanney, who began it, according to the preface, at Toulouse on 20 April 1313, and completed it at Lewes on 28 November of the same year, 'at the instance of Master John Chertsey, rector of the schools in that place'. The treatise, which discusses all four parts of grammar in 160 pages, was widely used during the fifteenth century, when it was known to John Leland and is found in the hands of both the regular and the secular clergy.[2] There are other lesser instances of the transmission of methods and treatises from one town to another. A grammatical miscellany used at Bristol in the 1420s, for example, contains besides one of Leland's tracts a work on heteroclite nouns, 'according to the use of London'.[3]

Much of the work of the English grammarians of the later middle ages was related to the growing importance of English as a linguistic and literary medium. By the fifteenth century it was evidently becoming thought too difficult for boys to begin learning grammar from works like those of Donatus and Alexander which were written wholly in Latin. Elementary grammars began therefore to be produced in English. We have seen that the *Speculum Grammaticale* of John Cornwall is the first surviving treatise to include explanations in the vernacular, though these are limited to little more than the English translations for the inflexions of the verbs. But by the 1430s treatises wholly in English begin to survive in grammatical manuscripts. They include versions of Donatus on the

[1] *BRUC*, p. 90.
[2] For Thomas Hanney see Hunt in *Oxford Studies Presented to Daniel Callus*, p. 175, who lists the surviving MSS of his work. There were also copies in the following medieval library catalogues: Mary Bateson, *Catalogue of the Library of Syon Monastery* (1898), p. 6; M. R. James, 'Catalogue of the library of Leicester Abbey', *Transactions of Leics. Archaeological Society*, xxi (1940-1), p. 13; and Bridport parish church (J. Hutchins, *History of Dorset*, 3rd ed. (1863), ii, 29).
[3] Oxford, Lincoln College, MS lat. 129 pp. 66-71.

eight parts of speech, as well as a tract on comparison and another on the translation of English sentences into Latin. They thus anticipate the similar works in English which, under the name of John Stanbridge, were widely used in the schools of early Tudor England and have often been considered the first of their kind.[1]

The English grammarians of the fifteenth century must also be credited with producing the first Latin and English dictionaries.[2] The *Medulla Grammatice*, an alphabetical list of Latin words with English meanings, was probably compiled in the first third of the fifteenth century and exists in a large number of manuscripts.[3] Its successor, *Ortus Vocabulorum*, drawn from the *Medulla*, the *Catholicon* and other collections, was first published in 1500 and appeared frequently until the early 1530s.[4] Whereas the Latin to English dictionaries had at least a great precedent in the *Catholicon*, the production of an English to Latin volume was a much more difficult and original task. It seems first to have been accomplished by a Dominican recluse of King's Lynn, known as Geoffrey to the bibliographers of the sixteenth century, who completed it in 1440.[5] His *Promptorium Parvulorum* was drawn from the authorities on etymology already mentioned – Hugutio, Brito and John of Genoa – and was arranged alphabetically, except that it listed the verbs separately from the other parts of speech. A Latin equivalent, and sometimes more than one, was given for each English word, together with its principal parts. The *Promptorium* exists in several manuscripts and was printed at least six times between 1499 and 1528.[6] Yet is was not the only effort made in this direction, for another work, the *Catholicon Anglicum*, survives in two

---

[1] English tracts from four MSS have been printed by S. B. Meech: 'John Drury and his English writings', *Speculum*, ix (1934), pp. 70-83; 'Early application of Latin grammar to English', *PMLA*, l (1935), pp. 1018-32; 'An early treatise in English concerning Latin grammar', *University of Michigan Publications: Language and Literature*, xiii (1935), pp. 81-125. To these may be added Aberystwyth, National Library of Wales, MS Peniarth 356, by information of Dr R. W. Hunt. It includes tracts on the parts of speech, syntax and comparison (the latter similar to that printed in *Speculum*, vol ix).

Early dates for tracts in English include 1432 (*Speculum*, ix, 70-83). There was another at Winchester College, 2nd fo 'Ablatyf cas', in *c.* 1433 (W. H. Gunner, 'Catalogue of books belonging to the college of St Mary, Winchester', *Archaeological Journal*, xv (1858), p. 74).

[2] On Latin-English and English-Latin dictionaries see *Promptorium Parvulorum*, ed. A. Way (Camden Society, vols xxv, liv, lxxix, 1843-65), vol iii, pp. xiii-lxxi.

[3] A copy was bequeathed by Master James Bagule, rector of All Saints, York, in 1438 (*Testamenta Eboracensia*, ed. J. Raine, vol ii (Surtees Society, xxx, 1855), pp. 79-80).

[4] *STC*, nos 13829-37.

[5] *Promptorium Parvulorum, passim.* The authorship is revealed in vol i, p. 1.

[6] *STC*, nos 20434-9.

manuscripts of which one is dated 1483.[1] It was never printed. Though it contains fewer words than the *Promptorium*, it is often more ambitious in providing Latin synonyms, sometimes with illustrative quotations.

Something can now be said of the range and methods of teaching in the English schools before 1500. The grammars, both those of the great authorities and the adaptations made by the English masters, used two obvious means of making their material easy to digest. Some were written like the *Doctrinale* in hexameters, and others followed Donatus in explaining rules and definitions by means of questions and answers. Much information was probably got by heart in this way. Attention was also given to the recognition and parsing of words by the pupils. In 1357 Bishop Grandisson of Exeter talks of boys 'replying as to the parts of speech' as a necessary part of their education.[2] The fourteenth-century statutes for the Oxford grammar schools advise the masters to ask what parts of speech are the words in a certain expression, so that the pupils may identify each one and then decline it in its parts.[3] At a more advanced level there were also disputations on grammatical rules and questions. These are reflected in the textbooks of writers like John Cornwall, who debates whether the noun *leopardus* is to be declined as one or two words and marshals the theories and authorities on either side.[4] This could easily have been reproduced in class. At Eton College a solemn disputation was held between two of the scholars every 7 July in the chapel nave, with the whole school looking on.[5]

Latin composition was practised by means of sentences in English, called 'vulgars' or *vulgaria*, which the pupils rendered into 'latins' or *latinitates*, several collections of these *vulgaria* surviving from the fifteenth and sixteenth centuries with the model translations in Latin written beneath the English for the master's use.[6] The term 'latin' (*latinitas*) was

[1] *Catholicon Anglicum*, ed. S. J. H. Herrtage (EETS, 1881).
[2] *Reg. Grandisson, Exeter*, ii, 1192-3; *ECD*, pp. 314-17.
[3] *Statuta Antiqua Universitatis Oxon.*, ed. Gibson, p. 171.
[4] Hunt in *Oxford Studies Presented to Daniel Callus*, p. 176.
[5] *Ancient Laws*, ed. Heywood and Wright, p. 527.
[6] Early examples of *vulgaria* come from Bristol, *c.* 1427-35 (Oxford, Lincoln College, MS lat. 129 pp. 187-201); Beccles, 1432 (*Speculum*, ix (1934), pp. 70-84); and apparently Lincolnshire, temp. Edward IV (BM, MS Harl. 1587 folios 64v-83, 104-5v – a reference I owe to Br. Bonaventure). There are two early sixteenth-century examples from Oxford in the British Museum: MS Arundel 249, folios 9-61 (*A Fifteenth-Century School Book*, ed. W. Nelson (1948)), and MS Royal 2 B xx, folios 35-49.

Early printed collections include those of John Anwykyll, 1483 (E. Gordon Duff, *Fifteenth-Century English Books* (Bibliographical Society Monographs, xviii, 1917), p. 109); John Stanbridge, 1508, and Robert Whittinton, 1520 (*The Vulgaria of John Stanbridge and Robert Whittinton*, ed. Beatrice White (EETS, 1932)); and William Horman, 1519 (*Vulgaria*, ed. M. R. James (Roxburghe Club, 1926)).

also used for Latin sentences which masters devised to illustrate points of grammar and syntax, and which their pupils also probably studied or learnt by heart. It has often been observed that the earliest printed *vulgaria*, those of the early Tudor schoolmasters, show a consistent attempt to interest their readers by taking themes from everyday life, contemporary events and even schoolboy humour, but this method of enlivening lessons was not an invention of the Tudor period and was indeed far older. It was used by English schoolmasters from at least the middle of the fourteenth century, and even they were only repeating what Ælfric of Eynsham had done about the year 1000. Thus an example of the use of comparison in John Cornwall's *Speculum Grammaticale* runs, appropriately for the year of Crecy, 'Would than no man in France were stronger than I, and if it be so, I know well that our king (whom God preserve) should have the upper hand (or, should acquit himself well) over Philip, who holds himself to be rightful king of France.'[1] By taking subjects of topical interest, the medieval schoolmasters both stimulated their pupils and trained them in a Latin which was still a living language, able to be turned to everyday use as well as to understanding the works of long-dead authors.

For this reason the fifteenth- and sixteenth-century *vulgaria* collections are a treasury of allusions to the life and interests of the time, which deserve a wider audience than historians of education alone. They include, for example, a store of popular proverbs. 'Better is a bird in hand than four out', 'it is evil to teach an old dog courtesy', 'need maketh the old wife to trot', 'the blind eateth many a fly'. There are schoolboy sallies and flashes of classroom wit. 'His nose is like a shoeing horn', 'thou art a false knave', 'I had as lief be served with a kale-stalk as a herring on a flesh day'. There are glances at public events ('the king of England shall wed the emperor's daughter of Almayne'); at economic history ('he made a hospital for lazars with the plunder that he won in war'); and at religious controversy ('our parson shall shrive me in Lent, holiest of times, and not a friar nor none other religious man'). Other exercises preserve delightful glimpses of ordinary life and landscapes. A fair manor house stands with its drawbridge and encircling moat; a garden grows full of nettles; children walk out into the meadows on a holiday. A large water pot is purchased from the potter of Boston; an illuminator buys an ounce of azure to decorate a missal; an appealer and a defendant fight a judicial combat upon Tower Hill. Men ride into the town on market days; pilgrims go off to Canterbury to worship at St Thomas's shrine; a well-apparelled company of knights sets out for the lands of the heathen. In

[1] Hunt in *Oxford Studies Presented to Daniel Callus*, p. 175.

church a cantor teaches young choristers; a clerk rings the bell sweetly; a fervent preacher rages in the pulpit, pleasing the laity but giving offence to wise and learned men. They gleam, these fragments of the past, among the pages of the old grammars, like pressed flowers from summers long ago: not the lilies and roses of an Augustan garden, but the homelier blooms of English lanes and fields.[1]

Pupils also learnt to write longer and more ambitious pieces of prose and verse. The late fourteenth-century statutes for the Oxford grammar schools recommend the masters to set verses and model letters every fortnight, containing words apt and not prolix or overlong, but full of succinct and beautiful clauses and plain metaphors. The pupils must then write out these verses and letters on the next holiday, if not before, and on returning show their transcriptions and render the pieces by heart.[2] The study of dictamen, or the composition of letters, has already been noticed in the last chapter.[3] It probably received some attention in all grammar schools, and there existed both treatises on composition and books of model letters to serve as examples. Handwriting was doubtless practised too. A grammatical miscellany of Edward IV's reign, which may have originated in Lincolnshire and later came into the hands of a monk of Christ Church, Canterbury, includes several folios on which somebody has been copying exemplars. The texts selected for the purpose deal, like the *vulgaria*, with subjects both moral, practical and amusing: one of the distichs, or moral couplets, of Cato; English and Latin charters and petitions; and an epitaph in four lines of rhyming Latin verse on Scogan, the famous jester of the period.[4]

Higher and more difficult still was the writing of verse, the mastery of which seems to have been regarded as setting the seal upon the school career. In 1312 Nicholas Picot, alderman of London, directed that his sons should be put to school until they could compose letters and versify properly.[5] Similarly in the 1393 statutes of the little college of Bredgar in Kent, the ability to 'read, sing, construe, and compose twenty-four verses on one subject in a single day' qualified the scholars of the foundation to take part in the chapel liturgy.[6] William Paston, who was still at school at Eton in 1479 when he was nineteen, apparently stayed on to master versifying 'whyche', he wrote to his brother John, 'I troste to have wyth

---

[1] The examples are a random selection from the *vulgaria* listed above.
[2] *Statuta Antiqua Universitatis Oxon.*, ed. Gibson, p. 171.
[3] See above, p. 70.
[4] BM, MS Harl. 1587 folios 189-215.
[5] R. R. Sharpe, *Calendar of Wills in the Court of Husting, London* (1889), i, 233-4.
[6] *Literae Cantuarienses*, ed. J. B. Sheppard, vol iii (Rolls Series, 1889), p. 19.

a lytyll contynuance'. He could not resist including one of his exercises in the letter, on the theme

Quomodo non valet hora, valet mora?

in order to show off the epigram he had written, complete with what classical taste would regard as a terrible false quantity:

Arbore jam videas exemplum. Non die *possunt,*
Omnia supleri; set tamen illa mora.

'And thes too verse a-fore seyde be of myn own makyng'![1]

Nor did the schools merely teach proficiency in the writing of Latin. Although English became a medium of instruction in school after the 1340s, its use was almost certainly restricted to the elementary stages. After mastering the rudiments with the help of an English accidence, the pupils would still have gone on to deal with grammatical material entirely in Latin, and at least in the best schools they would also have been expected to speak it without lapsing into English. 'If I had not used my English tongue so greatly', admits a schoolboy in the Magdalen College school *Vulgaria* of about 1500, 'for which the master hath rebuked me oft times, I should have been far more cunning in grammar. Wise men say that nothing may be more profitable to them that learn grammar than to speak Latin.'[2] At the visitation of Southwell Minster in 1484 one of the complaints against the grammar master was that his boys spoke English, not Latin, in school.[3] In boarding establishments the use of Latin may well have extended further, as at Wells where the choristers were warned in 1460 that when at dinner or supper they should 'ask for anything they want in Latin, not in English'.[4]

In the fourteenth century the successful completion of the grammar course was marked by special ceremonies in some places. At St Albans the school statutes of 1309 provide for the elevation of such youths to the dignity of bachelors. Anyone who wished to rise to this dignity had to take a proverb from the master and compose verses, model letters and a *rithmus* on the subject, as well as carrying on a disputation in the school. The candidate, if he was successful, offered sixpence to St Nicholas, and drinking and other customs marked the occasion.[5] At Beverley, where

[1] *Paston Letters and Papers of the Fifteenth Century*, ed. Davis, i, 650-1.
[2] *A Fifteenth-Century School Book*, ed. Nelson, p. 22.
[3] *VCH Notts.*, ii, 185.
[4] *Dean Cosyn and Wells Cathedral Miscellany*, ed. Dom. A. Watkin (Somerset Record Society, lvi, 1941), p. 106.
[5] *Reg. John Whethamstede*, ed. H. T. Riley, vol ii (Rolls Series, 1873), p. 312; *ECD*, pp. 244-5.

bachelors were also made, we hear in 1338 that they presented gloves to the officers of the church.[1] The St Albans statutes speak of the privileges of the bachelors, but no information is forthcoming about them, nor about the status of this baccalaureate in ecclesiastical and scholarly circles in general.

As well as the mastery of the language itself, the medieval school curriculum involved the reading and appreciation of good literature. This began, as has been noticed, at an early age in the song school with the basic texts of the Christian faith, the hours of the Virgin and other prayers and hymns.[2] In the grammar schools the literature read consisted largely of Latin poetry, as indeed it had done since late antiquity. No curricula exist before 1528 to show exactly what texts were studied and for how long, but some idea can be gathered from the regular appearance of certain works in the anthologies which represent the teaching collections of medieval schoolmasters. In England as elsewhere in the thirteenth century, a set of six Latin authors appears frequently in manuscripts and was probably widely read in schools: the *Sex Auctores*. They included Cato, Theodulus, Avianus, Maximian, Claudian and Statius in the order usually followed.[3] The most popular of these texts was the *Distichs of Cato*, an anonymous third-century compilation of moral precepts fathered onto the great Roman stoic philosopher.[4] The work begins with a preface and fifty-eight short precepts in prose, such as 'Pray to God', 'Love thy parents', 'Respect the magistrates', and 'Say little at banquets'. These were called the 'small Cato'. They are followed by four books of hexameter couplets, making up some 306 lines of verse, and known as the 'great Cato'. The couplets offer pieces of moral advice and comfort, of which the following are examples:

> Be given more to wakefulness than sleep,
> For long rest supplies food for vices.

> Give way to a greater, for the time being.
> We have often seen the victor overcome by the vanquished.

> Since Nature created you a naked infant,
> Remember to bear poverty with patience.

---

[1] *ECD*, pp. 294-7. Compare also J. R. Magrath, *The Queen's College, Oxford* (1921), i, 323: 'pro sirothecis datis eis tempore versificandi'.
[2] See above, pp. 62-3.
[3] On these authors see M. Boas, 'De librorum Catonianorum historia atque compositione', *Mnemosyne*, new series, xlii (1914), pp. 17-46.
[4] *Catonis Disticha*, ed. M. Boas and H. J. Botschuyer (Amsterdam, 1952).

Though pagan in origin, these sentiments had been modified in the course of transmission and their morality was now of an acceptable Christian kind. Their great popularity is clearly seen from the manifold quotations and reproductions found in medieval literature, and they survived in the school curriculum even after the coming of the Renaissance.

The ninth-century *Eclogue of Theodulus*, also anonymous, is the debate of Pseustis, an Athenian shepherd, with Alithea, a beautiful virgin of the line of David, who contrast scenes from classical mythology with episodes from the history of the Jews.[1] The antagonists take a quatrain apiece alternately, and some very happy comparisons are made: Hercules and Deïaneira with Sampson and Dalilah; the Tower of Babel with the attack of the giants on Olympus. Of course the true history of the chosen people wins the debate against 'vain fables of the Gentile sect', and this outcome doubtless did much to maintain the reputation of the poem against any hostility towards classical culture. The *Eclogue* continued to be widely read in England until the sixteenth century, and it was also well known outside school.

The remaining four authors offered other species of Latin poetry. Avianus, who had flourished about the year 400, contributed the *Fabulae*, a set of forty-two short fables on human and animal subjects. Maximian's work was the six *Elegies*, dating from the sixth century, a curious set of love poems from a frustrated old man, hardly appropriate for classroom reading and censured as such by Alexander in the *Doctrinale*. Claudian, a contemporary of Avianus, was represented by his poem *De Raptu Proserpinae* in three books, and Statius who lived from *c.* 45 to *c.* 96 contributed epic poetry. His unfinished poem *Achilleis* in two books treats of the hero's youth, his seclusion in the household of Lycomedes, his discovery by Ulysses and ends with the embarkation for the Trojan War.

These authors preserved a not inconsiderable fragment of classical culture, with something of its morality, its erotic and epic poetry, and some of the famous scenes from its mythology. But although they still maintained their popularity in the thirteenth century, it is rare to find them together in manuscripts of later date. By 1300 changing tastes in Western Europe were leading to the disuse of the pagan poets and the formation of a new group of texts for use in school. These were the famous *Auctores Octo*, widely used on the continent until 1500, among whom only Cato

[1] *Theoduli Eclogam*, ed. J. Osternacher (Linz, 1902). The work is discussed by G. L. Hamilton, 'Theodulus, a medieval textbook', *Modern Philology*, vii, no 2 (1909), pp. 1-17.

and Theodulus remained from the earlier set, their former companions being replaced by new poems, mostly dating from the twelfth and thirteenth centuries, which displayed moral and religious tones of a more obviously Christian character.[1] In England similar changes can be seen. In the teaching collections of the fourteenth and fifteenth centuries Cato and Theodulus alone survive to represent the classical tradition, and they are now accompanied by examples of modern poetry similar to those which were popular on the continent.

The most directly religious of the new poems was the one entitled *Liber Penitencialis*, or from its opening words *Peniteas cito*:

> Sinner, repent swiftly, since one who pities you
> > Will judge you; and let these five things be noted:
> The hope of pardon, a contrite heart, confession of your fault,
> > A satisfactory penance, and a flight from evil.[2]

The poem is an admonition to penance and explains the need for confession, how best to achieve it and how then to make satisfaction. It is almost certainly the work of William de Montibus, an English scholar of the early thirteenth century, who after studying at Paris became chancellor of Lincoln and lecturer in theology there until his death in 1213.[3] The poem reminds us that schoolmasters worked with a religious as well as a scholastic purpose, a later example of this being the English treatise on penance which John Drury of Beccles composed in 1432 for the edification of his pupils during Lent.[4]

Moral poetry is represented by the *Liber Parabolarum*, also known as the *Parvum Doctrinale*, usually ascribed to Alain de Lille, the French poet who died in 1203.[5] This work is a set of more than 300 proverbs in verse couplets, somewhat in the manner of the *Distichs of Cato*:

[1] The *Auctores Octo* included Cato; Theodulus; the *Facetus* (*Cum nihil utilius*); *Cartula* (*De contemptu mundi*); the *Liber Parabolarum* (the three latter being mentioned below); the story of *Tobias* by Matthew of Vendôme; the *Fables* of Aesop; and the *Floretus*, a religious poem on faith, virtue, sin, the sacraments and so on. Early editions are listed in the *Gesamtkatalog der Wiegendrucke*, vol iii (Leipzig, 1928), pp. 27-42.

[2] *Incipit: Peniteas cito, peccator, cum sit miserator*. Printed in Migne, *Patrologia Latina*, vol ccvii (1855), cols 1153-6.

[3] H. Mackinnon, 'William de Montibus, a medieval teacher', *Essays in Medieval History Presented to Bertie Wilkinson*, ed. T. A. Sandquist and M. R. Powicke (Toronto, 1969), pp. 32-45.

[4] *Speculum*, ix (1934), pp. 76-9.

[5] *Incipit: A phebo phebe lumen capit*. Printed in Migne, *Patrologia Latina*, vol ccx (1855), cols 581-94. Texts are listed in Hans Walther, *Carmina Medii Aevi Posterioris Latina*, vol i, part 1 (Göttingen, 1969), no 71. On the ascription to Alain de Lille see Marie-Thérèse d'Alverny, *Alain de Lille: textes inédits* (Paris, 1965), pp. 51-2.

As Phoebe takes her light from Phoebus, so a fool
His sense from a wise man, sparkling as if with light.

Do not take everything for gold that gleams like gold,
Nor suppose every beautiful apple to be good.

Caesar was everything, but Caesar's glory
Has ceased to be, and his tomb was scarce eight feet.

Moralizing is also the theme of the *Cartula*, so named from its opening word, a poem which dates from the twelfth or thirteenth century and is of uncertain authorship.[1] Despite its ornamental style, with both internal and end rhymes, the *Cartula*, otherwise known as *De Contemptu Mundi*, is a sombre series of reflections on the vanity of human life and the things of the world, in the best medieval manner:

Each precious thing, each beauty of the world,
Is like a flower, adorned by Nature's hand
Only to wither and to be destroyed,
No longer flower to blow or smell to breathe.
So royal state and all terrestrial power,
Prosperity of things and length of days,
All pass without delay; the hour of death
We do not know, but death itself is sure.

The poem concludes by exhorting the reader to have faith in Christ for the better rewards that this will bring.

Another group of poems popular with schoolmasters were those which dealt with good manners and social behaviour, and which were known indiscriminately by the name of *Facetus*. The version most often read in England was the one beginning *Est nihil utilius*.[2] 'I believe', says the unknown author, 'that there is nothing more useful to the welfare of man than to know the rules of life and to practise good manners.' He begins with the duty of man to God, his obligation to honour God's Church and clergy and the importance of good behaviour in church. He deals subsequently with such topics as respect for parents, marriage, self-discipline, good manners towards others and etiquette at meals. Other poems on

---

[1] *Incipit: Cartula nostra tibi mandat, dilecte, salutes*. Printed in Migne, *Patrologia Latina*, vol clxxxiv (1859), cols 1307-14; see also Walther, no 2521.
[2] Continental texts of the poem begin *Cum nihil utilius* (Walther, no 3692), *Est nihil utilius* (Walther, no 5777) being apparently confined to England. The name *Facetus* was also given to two other poems: *Doctrine vivum propere diffundere rivum* (Walther, no 4683) and *Moribus et vita quisquis vult esse facetus* (Walther, no 11220).

etiquette are sometimes found in teaching collections, one of the most popular being *Stans puer ad mensam*, a short work of forty-odd lines, usually ascribed to Robert Grosseteste, bishop of Lincoln from 1235 to 1253.[1] It contains a list of things for boys to remember when waiting at table or eating there themselves: do not cram your mouth full or wipe your knife on the table cloth; beware of stroking dogs at mealtimes, and so on.

The anthologies characteristic of the fourteenth- and fifteenth-century schoolbooks thus preserve far less of the classical culture than had been true before 1300, and even the remnants which survived in Cato and Theodulus had been heavily Christianized. Nevertheless the literary value of the poetry commonly studied in the later middle ages should not be altogether underrated. Not all the pieces are of equal merit, but from the best the pupils would get at least some idea of the elegant expression of ideas and observations in verse, particularly of a didactic nature. With its emphasis on piety, wisdom and good manners, the reading programme of the later medieval schools reveals an awareness of the need to educate the whole man that is hardly different from that of the Renaissance.

The next period of change and development in the English school curriculum may be said to begin during the last quarter of the fifteenth century, when new educational ideas began to reach England from Renaissance Italy. The revival of interest there in the great classical authors was of profound importance for education, since they began to oust the medieval reading texts from their place in the schools and soon became established as the models for grammar and literary style against the laws and opinions of the great thirteenth-century grammarians. Two of the leading exponents in Italy of the new grammar related to the classical authors were Lorenzo Valla (1407-57) and Niccolo Perotto (1429-80), both of whom came ultimately to exercise much influence in England. Valla's work on grammar, the *Elegantiae Linguae Latinae*, had reached Oxford by 1474 when a copy occurs in the library list of Lincoln College through the gift of Robert Fleming, the English diplomatist and traveller in Italy.[2] Perotto's *Rudimenta Grammaticae* with explanations in English was printed at Louvain in 1486, evidently for the English market.[3] Very few editions of the Italian grammarians were ever published in England itself, although in 1487 Caxton printed the *Donatus Melior*, a

---

[1] A version of *Stans puer ad mensam* is printed in *Manners and Meals in Olden Time*, ed. Furnivall, part 2, pp. 30-2; see also Walther, no 18581.
[2] R. Weiss, *Humanism in England during the Fifteenth Century*, 3rd ed. (1967), pp. 168-170; 'The earliest catalogues of the library of Lincoln College', *Bodleian Library Quarterly Record*, viii, no 94 (1937), pp. 349 no 69, 356).
[3] Duff, *Fifteenth-Century English Books*, no 346.

revised edition of the old master by Antonio Mancinelli of Velletri, and the *Opus Grammaticum* of Giovanni Sulpizio of Verona came out at least four times between 1494 and 1505.[1] Continental editions of the new grammarians could however be imported without much difficulty.[2]

The first English grammarian to show an interest in these Italian masters seems to have been John Anwykyll, who after studying grammar at Cambridge in the mid-1470s was appointed headmaster of the new grammar school at Magdalen College, Oxford, in about 1481.[3] Some two years later a treatise by him entitled *Compendium totius Grammaticae* was published in Oxford, where it ran into two editions. This work, a discussion of the four parts of grammar, was notable in that it drew not only on the established work of Alexander and Evrard but on the new Italian masters Perotto and Valla, and gave citations from Cicero, Horace, Quintilian and other classical authors. Anwykyll also compiled a novel set of *vulgaria*, more model sentences in Latin and English, but which, instead of being as usual the author's own invention, were taken from the plays of Terence. That his work was valued by the fellows of Magdalen is clear from an indenture of 1487 in which the college retained his services for the next fifteen years and praised his labours 'concerning a new and most useful form of grammar, conceived and prescribed by him for the school'.[4] He died however in the following year, but his grammar survived to be published at Deventer in 1489 and at Cologne in 1492, suggesting not merely an English market but also a certain amount of interest in continental circles.[5]

Anwykyll was the earliest member and perhaps the founder of an important group of grammarians who taught or studied at Magdalen College school in the years around 1500, and who dominated the educational scene in England up to the Reformation.[6] The second in seniority to Anwykyll himself was John Stanbridge, who was born in north Oxfordshire in about 1463 and educated at Winchester and New College, graduating in due course as an MA and taking priest's orders. In 1487 he became Anwykyll's deputy in the college school, and succeeded him as

---

[1] Mancinelli's *Donatus Melior* is listed in Duff, nos 129-30; *STC*, nos 7013-14. Sulpizio's *Opus Grammaticum* is in Duff, nos 388-90, and *STC*, nos 23425-7a.

[2] The Oxford bookseller, John Dorne, stocked Perotto, Sulpizio and Valla in 1520 (F. Madan, 'The daily ledger of John Dorne', *Collectanea I*, ed. C. R. L. Fletcher (Oxford Historical Society, v, 1885), pp. 172, 175).

[3] For Anwykyll's life see *BRUO*, i, 39.

[4] J. R. Bloxam, *Register of Magdalen College Oxford*, vol iii (1863), pp. 7-9.

[5] For editions of Anwykyll's works see Duff, op. cit., nos 28-31.

[6] On the school and its masters see R. S. Stanier, *A History of Magdalen College School Oxford*, 2nd ed. (1958).

headmaster there from 1488 to 1494. His movements during the next seven years are not known, but in 1501 Bishop Smith of Lincoln decided to turn the decayed hospital of St John at Banbury into a grammar school and appointed Stanbridge as master of the hospital with responsibility for teaching the school. He held the post for nine years, during which time the bishop rewarded him with two other benefices, until his early death in 1510 at the age of forty-seven.[1]

Stanbridge was credited by his contemporaries with six works, all fairly short and of an elementary nature. The first of these, the *Accidence*, was attributed to him in two printed editions during his lifetime and reissued after his death in a modified version as 'ex stambrigiana editione'.[2] This is an English tract of some thirty pages on the eight parts of speech, similar to and ultimately deriving from Donatus. Although neat in construction and easy to understand, it has little claim to originality, for it is only one variant among the large number of English versions of the *Ars Minor* which were circulating at the time, some of which were older than Stanbridge himself. Two other short English tracts supplemented the *Accidence*: *Gradus Comparationum* on the comparison of adjectives and *Sum es fui* on the forms of a few irregular verbs: *sum*, *fero* and their compounds. They are credited to Stanbridge in two editions of about 1515.[3]

The fourth work generally attributed to him was the *Parvula*, a short English tract on elementary syntax, written like the *Accidence* in question and answer form and intended to help pupils translate English into Latin. The textual history of the tract is complicated, for it exists in three versions the earliest of which, the *Long Parvula* of fifteen pages, was first printed at Oxford during the early 1480s when Stanbridge would seem to have been too young to claim the authorship, which is not revealed. A second shorter version of ten pages, also anonymous and entitled simply *Parvula*, was printed several times after about 1495. The third version seems first to have appeared in 1510-11 after Stanbridge's death. It is entitled *Parvulorum Institutio* 'ex stanbrigiana collectione' and is a revised version of the *Long Parvula* of twenty-two pages, with marginal references to the classical authors showing the rules of syntax in operation. The authors cited include Cicero, Ovid, Pliny, Sallust, Terence and Virgil, as well as

---

[1] For Stanbridge's life see *BRUO*, iii, 1754-5.

[2] The editions of the *Accidence* attributed to Stanbridge during his lifetime are *STC*, 23140 and 23143. Editions of the *Accidence* 'ex stambrigiana editione' include *STC*, 23145 and 23147.

[3] Editions of the *Gradus Comparationum* and *Sum es fui* are listed by Edith Pafort, 'A group of early Tudor school books' *The Library*, 4th series, xxvi (1946), pp. 227-61.

Valla. As with the *Accidence* it would seem that Stanbridge did not originate the form of the *Parvula* but revised its usages to accord with the classical authors coming into fashion, assuming that the classical citations are from his own and not another hand.[1]

Lastly there are the *Vocabula* and the *Vulgaria*. The earliest known edition of the former comes from 1510 and of the latter from about 1508, and both bear Stanbridge's name upon their title pages. The first is a vocabulary of Latin words arranged in hexameters, with the English meanings interlined, and covers such topics as the human body, the family, trades, agriculture, animals, plants, war and musical instruments. Several other similar lists had already circulated in medieval times.[2] The *Vulgaria* is yet another collection of short English sentences relating to ordinary life with model translations into Latin.[3]

Stanbridge enjoyed a considerable success with his teaching. He was the first English grammarian whose works, by means of the new printing presses, achieved a really wide circulation. During the first thirty years of the sixteenth century, edition after edition came forth, revised perhaps in some cases by other hands. His works were in use at one time or another at all the leading English schools: Eton, Magdalen, St Paul's and Winchester, and in many other of the new foundations. As a grammarian he owed much to his English forerunners. The use of the vernacular in school textbooks had become well established during the fifteenth century, and versions of the *Accidence* and the *Parvula* which he modified were already circulating before he began to teach. His *Vocabula* and *Vulgaria* also accord in form with other long-established types. Much of the originality with which modern historians have credited him belongs more justly to his predecessors. Indeed the elementary nature of his published work makes it difficult to decide his place in the English Renaissance, and it may be that some of his popularity arose from his use of traditional and well-known methods. Nevertheless the wide circulation of his works after his death, the use made of them by grammarians as late as the seventeenth century and the knowledge that he possessed copies of the works of Cicero and Plutarch all suggest that he deserves his reputation as a master of the New rather than the Old Learning.

[1] Editions of the *Parvula*, the *Long Parvula* and the *Parvulorum Institutio* are listed by Edith Pafort, op. cit.
[2] See the examples in T. Wright, *A Volume of Vocabularies* (1857).
[3] Editions of the *Vocabula* and the *Vulgaria* are also listed by Edith Pafort, op. cit. A modern edition of the *Vulgaria* is *The Vulgaria of John Stanbridge and . . . of Robert Whittinton*, ed. Beatrice White (EETS, 1932).

Two other early productions of the Magdalen school of grammarians are also worth attention. The first is the elementary grammar *Lac Puerorum* or *Mylke for Chyldren* written in about 1496 by John Holt, who after serving as usher under Stanbridge in the college school, became successively grammar master to Archbishop Morton's boys at Lambeth, headmaster of Chichester school and finally tutor to the young Henry VIII, then prince of Wales. The grammar, which dates from its author's days at Lambeth, is an English tract on accidence and elementary syntax, with some ingenious features to make the subject interesting and easy. Thus Holt deliberately added simple meanings to the technical terms – 'the shewynge mode or indicatyf', 'the byddynge mode or imperatyf', 'the wysshynge mode or optatyf' – and he introduced graphic diagrams showing the five declensions and their endings arranged on the fingers of the hand, and, in one case, on the sheaves of a fan or pulley. Holt was evidently a man of parts, and would doubtless have done much had not he also suffered an early death in 1504.[1]

Impressive in another way is a set of *vulgaria* apparently compiled after 1498 for use in Magdalen College school but never published at the time.[2] It can properly claim nevertheless to be the best example of its kind ever written, in which the *vulgaria* tradition reached its apogee, never to be surpassed, so that what began as school exercises became here a minor classic of literature. Like most of their kind the model sentences of the Magdalen *Vulgaria* deal with everyday life in and out of school, but hardly any of the others can match their variety, wit or imagination, and seldom has the world of childhood and its emotions been so well realized.[3] The passages are both longer and more ambitious than was usual for such exercises, and must have been intended for senior boys of some competence. The author has been conjectured as one of the Magdalen schoolmasters of the period, perhaps Stanbridge or possibly Holt, but this is still unresolved.[4] What is clear is the place of the work at the watershed when the habitual deference to the medieval grammarians was being challenged and disturbed by the moderns. 'Ther is so great diversite of autors of gramer and of eloquence', runs one of the passages, 'that I cannot tell to whom I may inclyne, for theis new auctors doth rebuke the noble dedes of them that ben before them, therfore oure myndes be plukkyde by ther and

---

[1] For Holt's life see *BRUO*, ii, 953-4, and for his work, *STC*, nos 13604-6.
[2] *A Fifteenth-Century School Book*, ed. Nelson.
[3] See below, pp. 138-9 for an illustration and discussion of this.
[4] There seems no reason, however, why he should not have been one of the fellows of the college itself.

thither, but we be so variable and wandrynge of mynde that we covett the newer thynges and tho thei be worse.'[1] The habit of allegiance to the medieval past was evidently still strong.

It would not be so much longer. By 1500 the classical revival was beginning to spread through the English schools. The Magdalen College *Vulgaria* itself quotes Cicero, Ovid, Terence and Virgil, as if the pupils were already studying them. The education of Henry VII's elder son, Prince Arthur, who died in 1502, was a thoroughly modern one, based on Perotto, Sulpizio and Valla, and on a wide range of pagan classical authors.[2] It was not however until the second decade of the sixteenth century that the medieval school curriculum finally gave way to the on-slaught of the New Learning. By this time Holt and Stanbridge were dead and a new generation of grammarians was coming to the fore. Like their predecessors they were Oxford men – indeed John Colet and Thomas Linacre were contemporaries of Stanbridge and William Lily had been his pupil – but all three had left Oxford to travel abroad in France and Italy where they probably gained a closer acquaintance with the latest developments in education than was possible at home.[3] In about 1508 Colet began to establish his ambitious new school at St Paul's, and it is significant that he desired for its use an entirely new grammar, different from those already available. This led to the publication of a fresh series of textbooks. Colet himself prepared the *Aeditio*, a treatise on accidence, in 1510, and he commissioned Linacre to produce an elementary grammar, though he rejected it when finished as being too difficult for children.[4] William Lily, whom Colet chose to be the first headmaster of St Paul's, also set to work on two books of syntax: an elementary *Rudimenta*, and a more advanced *De Constructione* which, after being given to Erasmus for revision, was published in 1513.[5] The two other leading English gram-marians of the day were also advocates of the new theories. The elderly William Horman, who had been headmaster of both Winchester and Eton and who published his large new *Vulgaria* in 1520, was a close associate of William Lily.[6] The Stanbridgian tradition was represented by Robert Whittinton, a pupil of the old master whose works he engaged in revis-ing during the 1510s and 20s as well as writing others on his own

[1] *A Fifteenth-Century School Book*, ed. Nelson, pp. 19-20.
[2] See above, p. 28.
[3] For Colet see *BRUO*, i, 462-4, and for Linacre and Lily, ibid., ii, 1147-9.
[4] On Colet's *Aeditio* see C. G. Allen, 'The sources of "Lily's Latin Grammar" ', *The Library*, 5th series, ix (1954), pp. 86-7.
[5] On Lily's works see ibid., p. 87.
[6] For Horman's life see *BRUO*, ii, 963-4.

account.[1] Differences of opinion between Whittinton and Lily led to the outbreak of a pamphlet war in the 1520s, but for all that, Whittinton had more in common with Lily's circle than he did with the grammarians of the past. All alike had ceased to appeal to Alexander and the great men of the thirteenth century for their grammar; instead they took the classical authors as their models: Cicero, Horace, Ovid, Terence and Virgil in particular.

At the same time, during the first two decades of the sixteenth century, the medieval grammars ceased to be printed in England, and must therefore have been dropping out of use in the schools. The three known English editions of the *Ars Minor* of Donatus date from the end of the fifteenth century and the first ten years of the sixteenth.[2] The great *Doctrinale* had first appeared at Oxford in the early days of English printing, but the last of the six known editions came out in 1516.[3] The *Synonyma* and the *Equivoca* ascribed to John of Garland were also issued several times after 1496, but their final appearance was in 1518.[4] The new English grammars took their place, works by Colet, Lily, Linacre, Stanbridge and Whittinton being printed in various editions during the tens and twenties of the sixteenth century. In 1520 the Oxford bookseller John Dorne was disposing of large quantities of the grammars of Stanbridge and Whittinton, as well as works by the continental authors Sulpizio and Valla, and even a few copies of Perotto.[5] These foreign grammarians also appear in the earliest surviving school curricula later in the 1520s. Lorenzo Valla was prescribed for use at Ipswich school in 1528, and Sulpizio at Winchester in 1530. At Eton the works of Johannes Despauterius (died *c.* 1520), *On Versifying*, and of Peter Mosellanus (died 1524), *On Figures*, are mentioned in the same year. The *Copia Verborum* of Erasmus was also in use as an advanced grammar for sixth-form use at Eton and Winchester during this period.[6]

By 1530, however, attempts were being made to introduce uniformity into the teaching of grammar, and this was finally imposed by royal command ten years later.[7] The authorized grammar has usually gone under the name of Lily, but although it incorporated his works, it also drew on

---

[1] For Whittinton's life see *BRUO*, iii, 2039-40, and for his works, H. S. Bennett, 'A check-list of Robert Whittinton's grammars', *The Library*, 5th series, ii (1952), pp. 1-14.

[2] Duff, *Fifteenth-Century English Books*, nos 131-2; *STC*, nos 7015-17.

[3] Duff, *Fifteenth-Century English Books*, nos 22-4; *STC*, nos 315-20.

[4] Duff, *Fifteenth-Century English Books*, nos 153-63; *STC*, nos 11601-17.

[5] F. Madan, op. cit., pp. 73-177 *passim*.

[6] For the sources of early Tudor school curricula see below, p. 114, n 1.

[7] On this subject see also below, pp. 254-8.

the writings of Colet and Linacre from England and on authors such as Despauterius and Melanchthon from abroad.[1] It consisted of two parts. The first, or *Introduction*, printed in 1542, dealt with the eight parts of speech and with elementary syntax, and thus covered the ground of the earlier *Accidence* and *Parvula*. Like them it was in English, but unlike them it abandoned the question and answer procedure for one of direct statement, though some of the phraseology still harks back to the older works. The *Introduction* was followed by the *Institutio Compendiaria totius Grammaticae*, first printed in 1540. This was a lengthy discussion in Latin of all four branches of grammar – orthography, accidence, syntax and prosody. Prose exposition was varied by mnemonic verses, and there was plenty of quotation from classical authors, especially in the section on syntax. The supremacy of this new grammar was destined to last for over two centuries.[2]

Even more revolutionary than these developments in the study of grammar was the great change which befell the literature read in the English schools during the first thirty years of the sixteenth century. Some of the standard medieval readers were still in use when the century opened, to judge from the evidence of printing. The *Liber Parabolarum* is known in three versions from the first decade, and the *Liber Penitencialis* in another three, apparently from the second.[3] The *Eclogue of Theodulus* appeared for the last time in 1515.[4] These venerable works were ceasing to command respect, either for their style or their content, and new authors were adopted in their place. The earliest surviving scheme of reform is the one put forward by Colet in the 1518 statutes of St Paul's.[5] The authors there prescribed for use consisted of a number of fourth- and fifth-century Christian poets, 'that wrote theyre wysdom with clene and chast Latin', such as Juvencus, Lactantius, Proba, Prudentius and Sedulius. Along with these he mentioned two modern authors with approval – Baptista Mantuanus, the Italian Carmelite and author of a popular set of Christian eclogues, and his own friend Erasmus for his *Institution of a Christian Man*. Colet's scheme looks like an attempt to retain the Christian tone of the medieval school readers while moving nearer to the type of classical literature now in fashion. It seems to have had little or

[1] On the authorized grammar and its sources see C. G. Allen, op. cit., pp. 85-100.
[2] A modern edition is *A Shorte Introduction of Grammar*, ed. V. J. Flynn (New York, 1945).
[3] For English editions of the *Liber Parabolarum* see *STC*, nos 252-4, and of the *Liber Penitencialis*, ibid., nos 20079-81.
[4] For English editions of the *Eclogue* see ibid., nos 23940-3.
[5] The statutes of 1518 are printed in Lupton, *Life of Colet*, p. 279.

no influence. Hardly any of the early authors of whom Colet approved were ever published in England, and no later curricula include them.

It was, on the contrary, the pagan classical authors who established themselves as the staple diet of the Tudor schools. This is plain from the earliest detailed timetables which begin to survive from the late 1520s, beginning with those of Eton and Ipswich in 1528.[1] We can see from these how great had been the changes wrought upon the reading programme of the previous centuries. Hardly any of the familiar medieval texts survived in the new curricula except at an elementary level. The basic prayers, of course, such as the Lord's Prayer, and the Creed, which had figured in the medieval primers, continued in use, and an authorized primer preceded by the alphabet was issued by royal command in 1545.[2] The old poem on good manners, *Stans puer ad mensam*, was replaced by newer versions in much the same vein. Sulpizio's poem *Quos decet in mensa*, a similar piece of 128 lines, was in use in the first form at Eton in 1528,[3] while Lily's *Carmen de Moribus* which treats of good conduct in school was prescribed for the second form at Eton in that year, and subsequently gained general currency as an appendix to the first part of the authorized grammar in 1542. Otherwise the *Distichs of Cato* was the most important of the medieval texts to continue in general use; acceptable to the new age as to the old, it was regularly prescribed for the first or second forms of English schools throughout the sixteenth century. But it was the great classical authors who dominated the new curricula, accompanied by one or two modern writers. For elementary reading the fables of Aesop and Lucian's *Dialogues* were most often prescribed, both in Latin translations. For conversation there were the comedies of Terence, and for literary prose the letters of Cicero. The historians usually mentioned were Caesar and Sallust, and the poets included Horace (the *Epistles*), Ovid (the *Metamorphoses*) and Virgil (the *Eclogues* and the *Aeneid*). Cicero also appeared as the author of *De Officiis*, which treats of ethical philosophy. The chief modern works were Mantuan's *Eclogues* and the *Colloquies* of Erasmus. Such were to be the studies of the English schools in the new age.

---

[1] Early Tudor school curricula include Ipswich, 1528 (J. Strype, *Ecclesiastical Memorials*, vol i, part 2 (1829), pp. 139-43); Eton, 1528 (*VCH Sussex*, ii, 417-19); Eton and Winchester, 1530 (*ECD*, pp. 448-51; T. Wright, 'Rules of the free school at Saffron Walden', *Archaeologai*, xxxiv (1852), pp. 37-41); Canterbury, 1541 *ECD*, pp. 465-9); and St Paul's, 1559 (Sir M. McDonnell, *The Annals of St Paul's School* (1959), p. 76).

[2] For the primer see below, p. 258.

[3] *VCH Sussex*, ii, 418. For a modern edition see G. Sulpizio, *Doctrina Mensae*, ed. H. Thomas (1949).

Like all reformers, the grammarians of the New Learning were excessively severe upon their predecessors, being more conscious of the details in which they differed than of the aims they had in common. Many modern historians, themselves educated in the Renaissance tradition, have reproduced their judgements without further thought. But as the last shadows of the New Learning withdraw in our own time, we can look again more clearly and impartially upon the schoolmasters of the middle ages. The loftiness of their motives and the ingenuity of their methods alike deserve more credit than they have received. The poets and statesmen who came out of the Tudor grammar schools are a splendid company, but let us not pass by the institutions, neglected though they be, that educated Roger Bacon, Grosseteste and Wycliffe, or where the love of letters first grew in Chaucer and Langland.

E

Chapter Four

Life in school

The study of the curricula of the medieval grammar schools conveys a good deal about their character and way of life, but it fails to answer all the questions, especially those of an economic and constitutional kind, which we might wish to ask about them. How expensive was education, and for how long did it last? How many staff commanded how large a number of pupils, and by what methods of discipline? More frivolous moments may lead us to think about the recreations and misdemeanours of medieval schoolboys, or about school hours, or even sanitary facilities. Much information about all these things is forthcoming from medieval school statutes, of which the earliest date from about 1300 when the larger and older schools were beginning to codify their rights and traditions. Many more survive from the fifteenth and sixteenth centuries when numerous new endowed schools were being founded.[1] Casual allusions from a wide range of other sources – household accounts, letters, legal and criminal records – provide further material. Medieval schools were not necessarily uniform in their customs and organization, but these sources give us at least an idea of the conditions likely to have been most common.

Let us begin with the problems involved in sending a child to school for the first time. Theories about the age when this should take place only began to be discussed in the early sixteenth century by the educational writers of the northern Renaissance. Most of them followed Quintilian

---

[1] The most valuable school statutes include those of Oxford (1306, before 1350 and before 1380), St Albans (1309), Wotton-under-Edge (1384), Winchester (1400), Newland (1446), Eton (1447), Rotherham (1483), Chichester (1498), Lancaster (1500), St Paul's (1518), Bruton (1520), Rolleston (1524), Manchester (1525), Warrington (1526), Malpas (1528) and Newark (1532). For references see the list of schools below, pp. 295-321.

who had preferred a gradual introduction to knowledge in early child-hood, presupposing the birth of a child into a well-endowed and civilized household. In so far as he and they recognized any age of transition from elementary learning at home to formal studies in a public school, they settled on the age of seven, and we find this taken up by the English writers on education in the period of the Reformation.[1] This very roughly is probably what had already happened in England during the later middle ages. Chaucer's schoolboy martyr was 7 years old when he sat at his primer in the song school, apparently not long after his arrival.[2] After a year or two of song he would have been able to go on to study grammar. Henry V was learning it in 1396 when he was nine.[3] The minimum age of entry to Winchester and Eton was eight, by which time the candidate was expected to be well grounded in reading, song and elementary Latin grammar.[4] In fact, boys seem seldom to have entered Winchester so young, and when after 1472 the age of those admitted to the college is recorded it was generally eleven or twelve, the latter being the maximum age permitted by the statutes.[5] In 1496 an ambitious decree of the Estates of Scotland required all barons and freeholders to set their sons to school at the age of eight or nine.[6] A little later the author of the Magdalen College school *Vulgaria*, writing about 1500, appears to envisage a child leaving his parents for a boarding school at the age of ten.[7] It seems there-fore likely that boys usually set off for grammar school between the ages of nine and twelve, though this probably varied according to circum-stances: the abilities of the pupil, the interest and resources of his parents or patrons and the existence of suitable schools.

Sending a child to school was not something to consider lightly, for it involved expenses of various kinds. Bondmen were the worst off in this respect for they had to pay fines for permission to send their sons to school, to say nothing of the cost of manumitting them so that they could go on to be ordained.[8] Tuition fees on the other hand affected almost

[1] Quintilian, *Institutio Oratoria*, Book I, chapter 1, section 15; see also W. H. Wood-ward, *Erasmus Concerning the Aim and Method of Education* (1904), p. 198, and J. L. Vives, *On Education*, trans. F. Watson (1913), p. cl.
[2] *The Works of Chaucer*, ed. Robinson, p. 161.
[3] C. L. Kingsford, *Henry V* (1923), pp. 14-15.
[4] Kirby, *Annals of Winchester College*, p. 457, *Ancient Laws*, ed. Heywood and Wright, p. 479.
[5] T. F. Kirby, *Winchester Scholars* (1888), pp. 82ff. The conclusion is based on the first 200 scholars whose ages were recorded at their admission.
[6] *The Acts of the Parliaments of Scotland*, vol ii (1814), p. 238.
[7] *A Fifteenth-Century School Book*, ed. Nelson, p. 1.
[8] On this subject see above, pp. 50-1.

everyone. Free places in schools began to appear in the fourteenth century and they were followed in the fifteenth and sixteenth by the foundation of schools offering education entirely free, but such facilities were by no means universal even by the Reformation, when large numbers of children were still being taught for money, especially in the greater towns.[1] School fees cost 4d. a term, or 1s. a year, for the grammar boys at Merton College, Oxford, in 1277, but during the fourteenth century, following a general rise in prices and wages, the Oxford grammar masters to whom they went increased their charges until, by about the 1380s, a university statute forbade them to take more than 8d. a term.[2] Outside Oxford the rate of 8d. a quarter was common during the fifteenth century, although in some places it went up to 10d. or 1s. or even higher.[3]

Although there was likely to be a fee-paying grammar school in any substantial town, pupils from smaller settlements or from the countryside might need to be sent away to school, as would anyone who wished to study under masters of better quality at Oxford or the cathedral schools. This would add the cost of board and lodging to the schoolmaster's bills. Pupils away from home were sometimes accommodated in the master's house; the young Edmund Stonor, for example, boarded with a married schoolmaster in Oxford in about 1380, and Thomasine Percival's school at Week St Mary in Cornwall was reported in 1546 to be a great comfort to the surrounding country, 'for they that list may set their children to board there and have them taught freely'.[4] Private householders also took in boarders. The inhabitants of Ledbury in Herefordshire said in 1548 that they profited greatly from the scholars who came to lodge in their town and whose victuals provided a useful market for the country round.[5] Board and lodging were of course considerably more expensive than

[1] On this subject see below, pp. 215-17.
[2] *The Early Rolls of Merton College, Oxford*, ed. J. R. L. Highfield (Oxford Historical Society, new series, xviii, 1964), pp. 72, 204; *Statuta Antiqua Universitatis Oxon.*, ed. Gibson, p. 170.
[3] Fees of 8d. a quarter are recorded at Nottingham in 1395 (*VCH Notts.*, ii, 216); 12d. at Maldon in 1420 (*VCH Essex*, ii, 516); 8d. at Newland in 1446 (*Reg. Spofford, Hereford*, p. 282); and 10d. later reduced to 8d. at Ipswich in 1477 (*VCH Suffolk*, ii, 326). But higher fees sometimes appear which may disguise other services: 3s. 4d. a quarter for two boys at Croydon in 1394 (Edith Rickert, 'Extracts from a 14th-century account book', *Modern Philology*, xxiv (1926-7), pp. 251-2); 2d. a week at Beccles in 1403-6 (*SME*, p. 210); and 3s. 4d. a quarter at Gloucester in 1410 (*Reports del Case en Ley . . . en le temps . . . de Henry le IV et Henry le V* (London, 1679), sub Hilary Term 11 Henry IV).
[4] *The Stonor Letters and Papers 1290-1483*, ed. C. L. Kingsford, vol i (Camden 3rd series, vol xix, 1919), p. 21; *ESR*, part 2, pp. 25-6.
[5] *ESR*, part 2, p. 93.

tuition fees alone. The cost fluctuated along with the price of food, but its average seems to have changed remarkably little. The 8d. per week paid for the board of the scholars of founder's kin at Merton College in 1277 was the same as the sum allowed for the scholars of Winchester in 1400.[1] Commoners at Winchester in the fifteenth century might pay more – anything from 8d. to 16d. a week – and sums of up to 1s. a week for board at school appear in accounts at different times before the Reformation.[2]

These, although the chief, were not the only expenses of attending school. Clothes which are good enough for the backyard will not do in the more public and formal surroundings of the classroom, and can we doubt that medieval mothers liked their offspring to appear at school to the best advantage? This was certainly the feeling of Henry III when he sent Raulin the son of Master Stephen of Portsmouth to school at Bury St Edmunds in 1255 and provided him with a robe of russet lined with lambskin, a tabard, stockings, a pair of shoes and two pairs of linen garments.[3] Other charges arose from the need of each pupil to provide the materials necessary for his lessons. We shall consider a little later the extent to which books were used in medieval schools but by 1500, if not before, it was quite customary for boys to possess their own copies, and printed versions of the elementary Latin grammars could be purchased for a few pence after this date. Nor was schoolwork confined to reading, and even in the fourteenth century we hear of the writing of exercises and model letters.[4] The grammar boys of Merton College had parchment and ink bought for their use in 1347, as well as wax tablets for taking notes during lectures and disputations.[5] All these materials were still in use in the early Tudor schools. 'Methinkest thou lackest many thynges that is nede for a goode scolar to have,' observes an Oxford master to his pupil in about 1500, 'first a pennar and an ynke horne, and then bookes.' A scholar of the same period describes his equipment thus: 'The last feir my unkle on my fathers syde gave me a pennare and an ynkehorne and my unkle of my mothers syde gave me a penn knyff. Now, and I hade a payre of tabullys [i.e. tablets], I lakkyde nothynge.'[6] The penner was a

[1] Highfield, *Early Rolls*, pp. 72, 201; Kirby, *Annals of Winchester*, p. 487.
[2] Board of 8d. a week is mentioned at Beverley in 1276 (*EYS*, i, 80m); 10d. at Stevenage in 1312 (*VCH Herts.*, ii, 69); 1s. at Croydon in 1394 (*Modern Philology*, xxiv (1926-7), pp. 251-2); 7d. at Beccles in 1403 (*SME*, p. 210); 1s. in Norfolk in 1522 (D. Gurney, 'Household accounts of the Lestranges of Hunstanton', *Archaeologia*, xxv (1834), p. 466); and 9d. at Nottingham in 1532 (*VCH Notts.*, ii, 222).
[3] *CCR 1254-6*, p. 46.
[4] *Statuta Antiqua Universitatis Oxon.*, ed. Gibson, p. 171.
[5] *ECD*, pp. 200-1.
[6] *A Fifteenth-Century School Book,* ed. Nelson, p. 22.

little sheath in which pens were carried, often worn like the inkhorn at the belt. The cost of these accessories was not, it is true, very burdensome; Hugh Willoughby, the Arctic explorer of Elizabeth's reign, had a penner and inkhorn bought for his use in 1526 for only 4d.[1] A further expense might be the provision of lights for dark winter mornings, and John Colet ordered in 1518 that the boys of St Paul's should bring candles of wax, not of tallow, for their own use in class.[2]

With these impedimenta we may imagine the scholar leaving his home or lodging in the early morning to set off for school. The feelings aroused by the occasion cannot now be recaptured, but we can picture the school, prominent in the high street as at Exeter or Salisbury, or in the market place as at Warwick, or, it may be, more secluded down a side street as at Gloucester, poised above a city gate as at Bristol or under the shadow of cathedral walls as at St Paul's. Or away from a town altogether, by a country churchyard in sight of trees and sound of farmyard, like the schools at Ewelme or Newland. On his very first arrival there it was common for the scholar's name to be enrolled for the purpose of record. This custom was established at St Albans in 1339 and it was also in force at Oxford by the 1380s where the grammar masters had to supply lists of their pupils to the university authorities.[3] It was adopted by the methodical Colet who ordered that the children of St Paul's should pay 4d. at their admission for the writing of their names, and it appears in other school statutes of the 1520s.[4] It is a matter for great regret that no such lists of names appear to have survived from medieval times except for those of the scholars of Winchester and Eton.[5]

By entering school the boy also became in some sense a clerk, and therefore subject to the jurisdiction of the ecclesiastical authorities to whose care education in general belonged. At Canterbury, St Albans, and perhaps elsewhere, schoolmasters were privileged at law to deal with cases affecting their scholars, even when these involved laymen outside school.[6] Scholars are indiscriminately described as clerks during the thirteenth and fourteenth centuries, and it is clear that many were in minor orders. The almonry scholars of St Albans, according to statutes promulgated in 1339, had immediately after admission to be shaved with a tonsure after the

---

[1] *Historical MSS Commission, Report on the MSS of Lord Middleton* (1911), p. 383.
[2] Lupton, *Life of Colet*, p. 278.
[3] *Reg. John Whethamstede*, ed. H. T. Riley, ii, 310; *Statuta Antiqua Universitatis Oxon.*, ed. Gibson, p. 173.
[4] Lupton, *Life of Colet*, p. 277.
[5] Kirby, *Winchester Scholars*; Sir W. Sterry, *The Eton College Register, 1441-1698* (1943).
[6] *ECD*, pp. 232-3, 240-3, 252-61.

manner of choristers and to cut their hair short like clerks.[1] Six years later the bishop of Hereford confirmed the first tonsure which a priest named John Pyne had received when he was a boy in Gloucester grammar school.[2] The poll-tax returns for the diocese of Wells in 1377 preserve two lists of scholars, at Glastonbury and Wells, who paid the tax as clergy not as laymen and were therefore clerks in minor orders over the age of fourteen.[3]

The schoolmaster himself, according to circumstances, might be a priest, a clerk of some lesser order or else a married man whose clerical status was ambiguous. He was by far the most important person in the school, the source at once of all knowledge and all authority, the heart which gave the body life. In many places he ruled alone, but if custom was good and the school a large one, an usher was often required to assist him. This was the case both in well-frequented urban schools like Canterbury and Gloucester, and also in the larger endowed schools such as Banbury and Winchester. In a very few schools of ambitious design the staff might even number three. This was necessary when the number of boys was large, as at Eton where the parish clerk was available to help the master and usher in teaching grammar, or at Ipswich where Wolsey provided in 1528 for a master and two ushers, of whom the second was paid less and also acted as keeper of the schoolhouse.[4] It was required too when the curriculum was wider than usual. The two Yorkshire schools founded in the early 1480s by Bishop Stillington at Acaster and by Archbishop Rotherham at Rotherham both supported one master for each of the three arts of grammar, song and writing.[5] At St Paul's, as well as the master and usher of grammar, there was a chaplain who taught the catechism and the articles of the faith.[6] Establishments of this kind were however the exception.

Classes were often large by modern standards. A master who charged 8d. a quarter would have needed to collect a class of forty before he could expect an income of even £5 a year. One or two indications suggest that the fourteenth-century cathedral schools were much larger than this. In 1369 Richard Beckingham, an ecclesiastical lawyer, bequeathed 2d. each to sixty poor clerks of the grammar school of York, 'not being bad boys',

---

[1] *Reg. John Whethamstede*, ii, 315; *ECD*, pp. 296-7.
[2] *Reg. Trillek, Hereford*, ed. J. H. Parry (Canterbury and York Society, viii, 1912), p. 56.
[3] PRO, Exch. KR, Clerical Subsidy Rolls, E 179/4/1 mm 1, 3.
[4] *Ancient Laws*, ed. Heywood and Wright, p. 514; *VCH Suffolk*, ii, 329.
[5] *EYS*, ii, 89-91, 109-111.
[6] Lupton, *Life of Colet*, p. 276.

to pray for his soul, which hints at the full complement of scholars being much larger.[1] Similarly at Wells the thirty-four scholars taxed in 1377 were only the older boys of fourteen or more.[2] When later on endowed schools came to be established, their founders placed heavy burdens on the staff. At Winchester the master and usher presided not only over the seventy scholars on the foundation, but also over the commoners, fixed at ten sons of friends of the college by the founder's statutes of 1400.[3] Nevertheless, the number of commoners increased so rapidly that by 1412 Bishop Beaufort had to complain that between eighty and a hundred outsiders were being accommodated above the statutory number and this, as he quite properly observed, was beyond the master's capacity to teach.[4] Beaufort commanded that the statutes be respected, and the number seems then to have fallen to a more reasonable size, but commoners continued to augment the school throughout the fifteenth and sixteenth centuries. The scholars of Winchester all sat in the single schoolroom and so, whatever auxiliary work was done by the usher, they were all to some extent under the master's eye. The same was true at Eton which, beside its seventy scholars, sixteen choristers and twenty commoners of noble birth, also offered free education to all comers. Since this was coupled with a prohibition against rival schools within ten miles, it is very likely that a number of other boys came to the school every day.[5] At St Paul's Colet was prepared for 153 boys, the number of the miraculous draught of fishes, and the most that could be seated in the schoolroom.[6] As for the lesser schools, we have only the certificates submitted to the chantry commissioners in 1548. These inform us that there were usually 60 to 80 scholars in the grammar school of Chipping Campden, 100 at Worcester in the school of the Trinity Guild, 120 at King's Norton, between 120 and 140 at Crewkerne and Taunton, and so on.[7] But the accuracy of these round numbers is not above suspicion, for the parishioners who drew up the certificates were often intent on justifying the usefulness of their chantry schools and may have exaggerated the figures accordingly.

Many schools were probably much smaller, either through deliberate restriction or lack of demand. We have already noticed that the master of

---

[1] *EYS*, i, 24.
[2] E 179/4/1 m 1.
[3] Kirby, *Annals of Winchester College*, pp. 82, 490.
[4] Ibid., pp. 122-3; Leach, *A History of Winchester College*, pp. 187-93.
[5] Sir H. C. Maxwell-Lyte, *History of Eton College*, 4th ed. (1911), p. 19; *ECD*, pp. 412-415.
[6] Lupton, *Life of Colet*, p. 277.
[7] *ESR*, part 2, sub schools cited.

St Martin's school, Canterbury, was permitted to teach only thirteen grammarians apart from petty scholars learning the elementary subjects.[1] In 1473 the master of Wollaton school in Nottinghamshire agreed to restrict his teaching to twenty-six pupils so as not to encroach on the school of Nottingham near by.[2] At Wotton-under-Edge where there was no restriction the octogenarian inhabitants remembered in 1616 that there had usually been from twenty to thirty boys in the school in the days before the dissolution of the chantries.[3] Smaller still, the private schools maintained by the religious houses for their novices, almonry boys or choristers would have numbered only a dozen or half a dozen souls.

Woodcuts of schools at work often decorate the grammars issued by the early Tudor printers.[4] They show the master presiding from a high chair and grasping a cane or birch in his hand. Beside him stands an unlucky scholar, with open book in his hands, waiting to be catechized, while the rest sit round on their forms. These are mentioned as early as the late twelfth century, and they occur quite naturally as fittings when new schools were built.[5] More careful than the crude illustrations of the contemporary printers is the account by Erasmus of the classroom arrangements at St Paul's in 1521. He describes the schoolroom as a large rectangular chamber, divided into four by means of curtains which could be drawn aside whenever necessary. The first division accommodated the beginners who were learning the catechism, the second was supervised by the under-master and the third by the high-master. The fourth was the school chapel. The seats were arranged in files with gangways between them, sixteen seats to a form, and the head boy of each form sat in a stall of larger size and probably had some authority over his fellows ancillary to that of the masters. Over the chair of the high-master was a statue of the child Jesus as He taught in the Temple, and higher still the image of God the Father was shown speaking the words 'Ipsum audite', 'hear ye Him'.[6]

The hours spent upon the school benches were long, since schoolchildren like their elders rose early to their work and made full use of the

---

[1] See above, p. 69.

[2] *VCH Notts.*, ii, 217.

[3] PRO, Exch. KR, Depositions, E 134/14 James I, Mich., no 28, Gloucester.

[4] For a list consult E. Hodnet, *English Woodcuts* (Bibliographical Society, 1935). Their accuracy should not be taken for granted.

[5] Such as Stratford-upon-Avon, 1427 (*VCH War.*, ii, 330), and Wainfleet, 1484 (*VCH Lincs.*, ii, 484).

[6] *Erasmi Epistolae*, ed. P. S. Allen, vol iv (1922), pp. 517-18; translated in J. H. Lupton, *The Lives of Jean Vitrier . . . and John Colet . . by Erasmus* (1883), pp. 27-8.

E*

hours of daylight. The school statutes of the early Tudor period, which furnish the first full details of the school timetable, show that most boarding schools and day schools alike opened at 6.00 a.m., even in winter. Colet postponed the hour until 7.00 at St Paul's, and this reform was imitated at Manchester in 1525 where allowance had also to be made for the late arrival of those who came from a distance. Lessons then proceeded until 8.00 or 9:00 when there was an intermission of an hour, or sometimes two, for breakfast. Studies were resumed at 10.00 and continued until noon when all broke off for dinner. The longest grind was still to come, since afternoon school usually lasted four hours, from 1.00 till 5.00 or from 2.00 till 6.00. This pattern may be traced in the 1446 statutes of Newland, and is probably characteristic of the later middle ages, as it was to be for long afterwards.[1] Such a working day added up to eight hours, as at Lancaster, or nine and a half, in the case of Newark. Yet the longer hours of daylight in summer often meant an even earlier start – 6.00 a.m. at Manchester, 5.00 at Chichester. The school day at Cuckfield in Sussex, founded in 1528, seems to have lasted a full two hours longer in summer than in winter. But not all educationalists took such a practical view of summertime. At Eton it was a season of greater indulgence when the scholars were allowed a siesta after their dinner and did no work until 4.00, as well as omitting some of their evening studies.[2]

Much of the work of a medieval school must have been carried out aloud, and the presentation of many of the textbooks in question and answer form or in easily memorized verse suggests the ways in which masters and pupils approached the study of grammar. Yet this does not mean that books were not available for use or that their role in teaching was not an important one. Schools, masters and even pupils often possessed their own volumes, even before the invention of printing. The monastic schools were the most fortunate in this respect, for their members could often call on the resources of a large library, with the whole range of grammatical authorities and textbooks, sometimes in more than one copy. Of the secular schools at least three possessed libraries. At St Paul's, long before Colet's foundation, eight choristers were boarded in the cathedral almonry and received a schooling in grammar, either privately or at the cathedral school. During the fourteenth century two of the almoners

---

[1] School statutes which specify school hours include Newland (1446), Chichester (1498), Lancaster (1550), St Paul's (1518), Rolleston (1524), Manchester (1525), Warrington (1526), Cuckfield (1528), Eton (1528-30), Newark (1532) and Winchester (1550). For references see the list of schools, below, pp. 295-321.

[2] Maxwell-Lyte, *History of Eton College*, p. 150.

responsible for looking after these boys bequeathed large collections of books in order to further their education. In 1329 William Tolleshunt left them all his grammar books, including the works of Priscian, Isidore and Hugutio for their use in school, as well as quantities of books on logic, law and medicine which they could borrow if they went on to university.[1] In 1358 William Ravenstone added an even larger collection, comprising forty-three volumes of song, grammar and poetry, both classical and medieval. They included all the major authorities: Priscian, Peter Helias, Hugutio, Alexander and Évrard, often in more than one copy, which left this little group of boys perhaps the best provided with schoolbooks in the whole country.[2]

Winchester College also possessed a library, and an inventory of about 1433 lists nineteen volumes in the grammatical section, as well as five other relevant works elsewhere.[3] Most of the great medieval grammarians were represented. Fifteen of the volumes are mentioned as gifts; the founder himself had deposited Priscian, Hugutio and two copies of the *Catholicon*; two previous schoolmasters had each donated a book, and the rest had come from other friends and alumni of the college. There can be less certainty about the resources of Eton. A library list of 1465 enumerates only five volumes of grammar and three of classical poetry, but this dates from the lowest ebb of the school's fortunes when the college was on the point of being wound up and incorporated with St George's, Windsor. By the early sixteenth century the library resources in general had improved considerably.[4]

These libraries were of course exceptional, but other schools often acquired odd volumes through bequests. John Hanley gave a Priscian to St Albans school before 1310,[5] and Nicholas Pontesbury, subdean of Wells, bequeathed a copy of Hugutio in 1371 to an otherwise unknown school at Wellington, Somerset, for the use of the master there, 'that he and his boys may especially pray for me'.[6] Similarly John Elwyn left all his grammar books to Hedon school in 1465,[7] and Archbishop Rotherham's

---

[1] A. F. Leach, 'St Paul's school before Colet', *Archaeologia*, lxii, part 1 (1910), pp. 220-222.

[2] E. Rickert, 'Chaucer at school', *Modern Philology*, xxix (1932), pp. 257-74.

[3] W. H. Gunner, 'Catalogue of books belonging to the college of St Mary, Winchester', *Archaeological Journal*, xv (1858), pp. 59-74.

[4] M. R. James, 'Chapel inventories', *Etoniana*, xxviii (1928), p. 444. See also R. Birley, 'The history of Eton College Library', *The Library*, 5th series, xi (1956), pp. 231-61.

[5] *Reg. John Whethamstede*, ii, 314; *ECD*, pp. 252-3.

[6] J. Coleman, 'Four Wells wills of the 14th century', *Somerset and Dorset Notes and Queries*, viii (1903), pp. 151-3.

[7] *Testamenta Eboracensia*, ed. J. Raine, vol ii (Surtees Society, xxx, 1855), p. 270.

large bequest of books to Rotherham College in 1498 included an Isidore and a *Catholicon*.[1] These books in their humble way helped to give stability and continuity to schools just as did more expensive donations like buildings, exhibitions and endowments.

For a schoolmaster the essential manuals of his trade were one or two miscellaneous volumes, copied, purchased or inherited, which contained the basic grammars of Alexander or Évrard, the *Sex* or the *Octo Auctores*, with perhaps the master's own commentaries or abridgements, and his *vulgaria* or exercises for translation. Doubtless a country schoolmaster's library began and ended here, but graduate masters and the incumbents of the more important schools may have been better provided. Thomas Romsey, headmaster of Winchester until 1418, possessed an unidentifiable grammar which he presented to the college, while his successor Richard Darcy gave it a copy of the *Grecismus*.[2] John Hamundson, a schoolmaster of York who died in 1472, owned the dictionary of Papias which he bequeathed to his stepson.[3] Just once it is possible to guess at a master's whole resources. John Bracebridge, priest and master of arts, became schoolmaster of Boston in 1390, moving later to greater eminence as headmaster of Lincoln school in 1406. Apart from teaching, his great preoccupation was evidently book collecting, through which he amassed some sixty-six volumes by the end of his life, which suggests him to have been a distinguished and cultivated man. In about 1420 Bracebridge, whom we may suspect to have had strong religious convictions, departed from Lincoln and entered Henry V's new foundation of Syon Abbey as a chaplain to the nuns. Thither he took his books, and there in due course they passed to the convent library: five volumes of philosophy, ten of medicine, forty-six of theology, liturgy and canon law, and five of grammar. The latter included the staple miscellany of tracts and extracts; three important standard works: Priscian *in Majore*, Papias and the *Catholicon*; and lastly a work by Bracebridge himself, also called a *Catholicon*, which seems to have been a general survey of the four parts of grammar. We can hardly doubt that with these resources he well maintained the reputation of Lincoln school in his day.[4]

There are even signs of schoolboys possessing grammatical manuscripts. Brother Edmund, reporting on the young Edmund Stonor at school in

---

[1] *EYS*, ii, 164-5.
[2] *Archaeological Journal*, xv (1858), p. 74.
[3] *EYS*, i, 28
[4] For Bracebridge's life see *BRUO*, i, 239-40, and for his books, Bateson, *Catalogue of the Library of Syon Monastery, passim.*

Oxford in the 1390s, remarks, 'he has the Donatus which I feared was lost'.[1] and short works of this kind may not have been too hard to acquire. A Cato was bought for the boys of Merton College in 1308-9 for 2d., a Donatus for 3d. in 1309-10, and a tattered 'book' of Horace cost only ½d. in 1347-8.[2] Moreover, there survives among the Middleton manuscripts at Nottingham University a larger work which evidently came into the hands of schoolboys during the fifteenth century.[3] It is exactly what one would expect to have met this fate: a thirteenth-century miscellany containing the grammars of Alexander, Évrard and John of Garland, along with the *Sex Auctores*. Most of the contents were out of date by the fifteenth century, but enough of the material remained useful for the book to be relegated to a succession of pupils. Here we find their names inscribed: 'Johannis Wapplode', 'Johannes Cole de Wodyl' and, ungrammatically, 'iste liber constat Radulfe Savage'. Master Savage, who describes himself as 'bonus puer', was apparently the author of various scribbles throughout the book, including the observation 'Willelmus Cayso est pravus puer'.

It was however the invention of printing which really made available a large supply of books for the use of everyone in school. The first grammars to be printed in England, the *Doctrinale* and Anwykyll's *Compendium totius Grammaticae* came out in about 1483, and by 1500 the provision of school textbooks was becoming an important part of the printers' trade.[4] The 1520 account book of the Oxford bookseller John Dorne shows that there was a continuous sale of the grammars of John Stanbridge and Robert Whittinton then in common use. These grammars were usually pamphlets of a few sheets costing only a penny or two apiece, and any schoolboy could have possessed the complete printed works of either master for less than 1s.[5]

The tedium of long hours in school on hard benches was dispelled by liberal use of the rod. Masters faced with controlling very large classes for very long hours hardly expected to keep order by any other means, and their command of the art was as great as their itch to demonstrate it was frequent. The birch was their inseparable companion, and in sixteenth-century Cambridge when the schoolmaster's degree of 'master

[1] *Stonor Letters and Papers*, ed. Kingsford, i, 21.
[2] *ECD*, pp. 220-3, 300-1.
[3] Nottingham University, Middleton MS. Mi LM2; *Historical MSS Commission Report on the MSS of Lord Middleton*, ed. W. H. Stevenson (1911), pp. 212-20.
[4] On the earliest printed grammars see Duff, *Fifteenth-Century English Books*.
[5] F. Madan, 'The daily ledger of John Dorne', *Collectanea I*, ed. C. R. L. Fletcher, (Oxford Historical Society, v, 1885), pp. 172, 175.

of grammar' was conferred, the new graduate demonstrated his prowess by ceremonially flogging 'a shrewd boy', who received 4d. 'for his labour'.[1] Sometimes, however, the urge to chastise led masters into trouble. After the body of John Newshom, one of the Oxford schoolmasters, was found in the River Cherwell by the Petty Pont (now Magdalen Bridge) in December 1301, the coroner's jury reported that while cutting rods to beat his pupils, he had fallen out of a willow tree into the waters and had drowned.[2] In the early 1480s Thomas Fosse, a Bristol schoolmaster, suffered a different kind of woe when an angry parent prosecuted him in the mayor's court for beating and ill-treating his son to the damage of £40![3] Yet in acting thus schoolmasters had no monopoly of cruelty; they merely exercised at school the same authority that parents imposed at home. Beating was socially established everywhere as a proper method of preserving family discipline and inculcating obedience, industry and virtue. In *Piers Plowman* for example, that mirror of fourteenth-century conventions, it is recommended both for scolding or idle wives and for children in general, and is justified both by tradition and by scripture:

> My syre seyde so to me . and so did my dame,
> That the levere childe . the more lore bihoveth,
> And Salamon seide the same . that Sapience made,
>   *Qui parcit virge, odit filium.*
> The Englich of this latyn is . who-so wil it knowe,
> Who-so spareth the sprynge . spilleth his children.[4]

Corporal punishment was therefore a universal discipline, from which not even the highest in the land were free; even royal childhoods throbbed with continual reverberation. In 1424 the 2-year-old Henry VI solemnly granted permission at his council for his nurse to teach him courtesy and manners and to chastise him reasonably from time to time, as the case required. In 1428 he gave similar permission to his tutor, the earl of Warwick. Four years later when Henry was nearly ten, Warwick reported to the council that the king had so grown in stature and in knowledge of his high estate that he more and more resented being chastised, a problem which was likely to increase. Warwick subsequently secured the council's

[1] G. Peacock, *Observations on the Statutes of the University of Cambridge* (1841), appendix, pp. xxx-xxxvii.

[2] *Oxford City Documents 1268-1665*, ed. J. E. Thorold Rogers (Oxford Historical Society, xviii (1891), pp. 161-2).

[3] PRO, Early Chancery Proceedings, C 1/61/390.

[4] Langland, *Piers the Plowman*, ed. Skeat, vol i: A passus v, 32-3; B passus v, 34-41; C passus vi, 137-40.

support for his powers, as well as a promise to stand by him if the king should ever conceive indignation against him on account of his discipline.[1]

By the fifteenth century, however, some educationalists were beginning to be aware that moderation in beating was desirable. Wykeham's 1400 statutes for Winchester, followed at Eton, told the headmaster to punish his pupils in moderation.[2] Thomas Beckington, bishop of Bath and Wells, went much further in his statutes of 1459 for the choristers of Wells Cathedral. There he suggests that boys who refuse to learn their lessons are 'first to be warned kindly, secondly, if they neglect these warnings, sharply to be rebuked, and thirdly, if necessity arise, to be flogged'.[3] This spirit of tolerance achieved wider currency through the writings of the continental educationalists who were influential in sixteenth-century England. Erasmus and Vives, like Beckington, believed that advice and then warnings should precede the use of physical punishment, which they considered only as a last resort. Vives thought that it could not be dispensed with entirely, but Erasmus, though he sanctioned it, admitted in his heart that he deprecated its use, and would rather have removed dull or worthless boys from the school altogether.[4]

To escape, albeit momentarily, from the tedium of the bench and the pains of the rod, schoolboys had recourse to the time-honoured excuses. 'As sone as I am cum into the scole', grumbles the Oxford schoolmaster of 1500, 'this fellow goith to make water and he goyth oute to the comyn drafte. Some after another askith licence that he may go drynke. Another callith upon me that he may have licence to go home. Thies and such other leyth my scholars for excuse oftyntymes that they may be oute of the waye.'[5] It was when going outside to relieve himself that the young Edmund of Abingdon, at school in Oxford towards the end of the twelfth century, miraculously escaped the impact of a large stone which fell from the wall onto his place. He thus survived to become archbishop of Canterbury and to die in an odour of sanctity.[6] Pre-Reformation schools certainly had their privies; that of the school of St Martin-le-Grand in London is

[1] *Proceedings and Ordinances of the Privy Council*, ed. Sir N. H. Nicolas, vol iii (1834), pp. 143, 296-300; vol iv (1835), pp. 134-7.
[2] Kirby, *Annals of Winchester*, p. 485; *Ancient Laws*, ed. Heywood and Wright, pp. 524-5.
[3] *Dean Cosyn and Wells Cathedral Miscellanea*, ed. A. Watkin (Somerset Record Society, lvi, 1941), p. 103.
[4] Erasmus, *Concerning the Aim and Method of Education*, trans. W. H. Woodward, pp. 208-9; J. L. Vives, *On Education*, trans. F. Watson, pp. 117-20.
[5] *A Fifteenth-Century School Book*, ed. Nelson, p. 39.
[6] *Chronicon de Lanercost*, ed. J. Stevenson (Maitland Club, 1839), p. 38.

mentioned in 1360 as in need of repair.[1] Colet's statutes of St Paul's, which probed into almost every aspect of school life, arranged that the boys should go to an appointed place to urinate, and that a poor child of the school should arrange for the residue to be conveyed away from time to time (it was employed for making ammonia by dyers and tanners), receiving the profits in return. 'For other causes if need be', added Colet curtly, 'they shall go to the water side.'[2]

The tedium of the daily round was also varied by religious exercises. Most of those who founded free schools, and not infrequently those who merely gave buildings or other amenities, wanted the pupils to repay their generosity with prayers for their souls. Such prayers were generally said in school soon after arrival, or else before pausing for breakfast, and again after concluding lessons in the afternoon. The arrangements at Newland school, founded in 1446, were fairly typical. At nine the scholars said the psalm *Deus misereatur nobis* with the *paternoster* and *ave*; at five they repeated an intercession to the Virgin followed by the psalm for the dead – *De Profundis* – with another *paternoster* and *ave*, and the collect *Inclina aurem tuam, Domine*.[3] There was generally a solemn obit once a year to commemorate the founder of the school, and occasionally scholars may have been engaged to say prayers for other wellwishers like the Bristol merchant John Gaywood, who arranged in 1471 for a local schoolmaster and his pupils to attend his funeral, and left 8d. to buy them wine for their refreshment afterwards.[4] Or they might take part in the solemn public processions with which the clergy celebrated occasions of joy or offered intercessions in time of trouble. The boys of the three chief London grammar schools and their masters are mentioned walking in the great procession of the city clergy which marked the recovery of the king of France from sickness in 1535.[5]

In London, where there were several schools, public disputations were held regularly by the scholars during the middle ages. William FitzStephen, the biographer of Becket, who wrote his well-known description of the city of London between 1170 and 1183, relates how masters and pupils met together on feast days in the church whose festival it was:

[1] *Calendar of Inquisitions of Miscellaneous*, vol iii (1937), p. 157.
[2] Lupton, *Life of Colet*, p. 279.
[3] *Reg. Spofford, Hereford*, p. 282.
[4] Bristol Archives Office, Great Orphan Book, fo 191v; *The Great Orphan Book*, ed. Wadley, p. 145.
[5] C. L. Kingsford, 'Two London chronicles', *Camden Miscellany XII* (Camden 3rd series, xviii, 1910), p. 11.

6 MEDIEVAL SCHOOLS I

An aerial view of Ewelme, Oxon., showing the church, almshouse and (bottom right) the school, built and endowed by William de la Pole, duke of Suffolk (d. 1450). The movement of charity away from monasteries to schools and almshouses is characteristic of this period.

Here begynneth the shorte Accedence.

7 and 8 *MEDIEVAL SCHOOLS II*

(Above) Outside: the imposi[ng] chapel and grammar school bu[ilt] by William Wainfleet, bishop [of] Winchester (plate 16) at his birt[h]place, Wainfleet, Lincs., in 1484. [In] choosing to honour his birthpla[ce] in this way, the bishop followe[d a] well-established custom. (Left) [In]side: the title page of an ea[rly] Tudor grammar book, showi[ng] a schoolmaster with his bir[ch,] pupils on forms, and the use [of] books in class.

9 A
MEDIEVAL
TOWN AND
ITS SCHOOLS

A sixteenth-century map of Bristol, where Master Robert Londe (plate 10) taught grammar in a chamber above the New Gate (right) beside the castle. A later grammar school was held over the Frome Gate (top) during the 1530s.

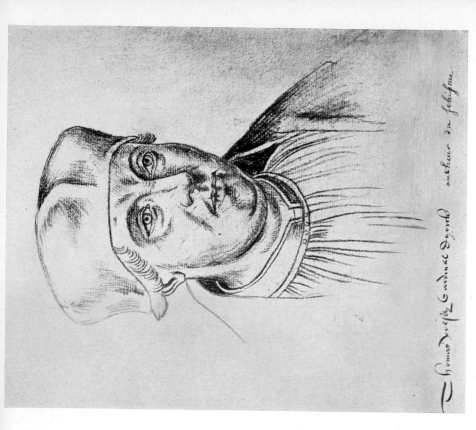

10 *and* 11 *SCHOOLMASTERS*

(Left) the humble Robert Londe (d. 1462), who laboured all his life in Bristol (plates 3 and 9), and (above) the mighty Thomas Wolsey, only briefly a schoolmaster, before rising to become cardinal-archbishop and chancellor

The scholars dispute, some in demonstrative rhetoric, others in dialectic. Some 'hurtle enthymemes', others with greater skill employ perfect syllogisms. Boys of different schools strive against one another in verse or contend concerning the principles of the art of grammar, or the rules governing the use of past and future. There are others who employ the old art of the crossroads in epigrams, rhymes, and metre.[1]

In the 1530s similar gatherings still took place once a year, so we are told by the Elizabethan antiquary John Stow. 'I myself in my youth' he re-called,

> have yearly seen on the eve of St Bartholomew [23 August] the scholars of divers grammar schools repair to the churchyard of St Bartholomew's Priory in Smithfield, where upon a bank boarded about under a tree some one scholar hath stepped up, and there hath apposed and answered, till he were by some better scholar overcome and put down, and then the overcomer taking the place, did like as the first, and in the end the best apposers and answerers had rewards, which I observed not but it made both good schoolmasters, and also good scholars, diligently against such times to prepare themselves for the obtaining of this garland.[2]

Colet however took a different view of these disputations, which he called 'but foolish babbling and loss of time', forbidding his scholars to attend them – a rule which may have been relaxed after his death if we can trust Stow, who remembered that in the 1530s boys came to the ceremony from St Paul's, as well as from Westminster, St Thomas Acon and St Anthony's, 'whereof the last named commonly presented the best scholars and had the prize in those days'.[3]

There were two annual festivals when schoolboys everywhere came into their own and took a chief part in celebrations long sanctioned by custom. On St Nicholas Day or alternatively on Childermas – the feast of the Innocents – a boy-bishop was chosen in all great churches to preside over the religious festivities and to preach a sermon.[4] Schoolchildren seem generally to have been present at the occasion. In Worcester at the end of the thirteenth century the master and his scholars were accustomed to celebrate the feast bearing tapers into the parish church of St Nicholas.[5]

[1] The best translation of FitzStephen's description is by H. E. Butler, appended to F. M. Stenton, *Norman London* (1934), pp. 26-35, especially pp. 27-8.
[2] Stow, *Survey of London*, ed. Kingsford, i, 74.
[3] Lupton, *Life of Colet*, p. 278; Stow, *Survey of London*, ed. Kingsford.
[4] For specimens of such sermons see E. F. Rimbault, 'Two sermons by the Boy Bishop', *Camden Miscellany VII* (Camden Society, new series, xiv, 1875), pp. 1-29.
[5] Leach, *Early Education in Worcester*, pp. 23-6.

At St Paul's, where Childermas was observed, Colet ordered all his pupils to attend the cathedral to hear the boy-bishop preach his sermon and after hearing high mass to offer him each a penny.[1] At Winchester he kept great state in a mitre of cloth of gold given by the founder; a crosier of copper gilt was carried before him, and the solemn proceedings in church concluded with merrymaking in hall, the 'bishop' presenting 20d. in 1406 to a party of mummers who danced before him.[2]

The other great school festival, Shrove Tuesday, was already well-established when William FitzStephen wrote at the end of the twelfth century. On that day, he says,

> boys from the schools bring fighting-cocks to their master, and the whole forenoon is given up to boyish sport; for they have a holiday in the schools that they may watch their cocks do battle. After dinner all the youth of the city goes out into the fields to a much-frequented game of ball. The scholars of each school have their own ball, and almost all the workers of each trade have theirs also in their hands. Elder men, and fathers, and rich citizens come on horseback to watch the contests of their juniors, and after their fashion are young again with the young.[3]

Cock-fighting was general in medieval schools on Shrove Tuesday, the dead bodies being the recognized perquisite of the master, but in the early sixteenth century the custom fell into disfavour among some progressive educationalists. Colet forbade the sport at St Paul's, an example followed at Manchester, but in other more robust communities the Shrove Tuesday battles continued until as late as the nineteenth century.[4]

There were many other holidays during the course of the year besides Shrove Tuesday. Medieval schools often remained in almost continuous session, and the holidays coincided with the great festival days as they occurred. Of Winchester College it has been said that 'the school never closed as a whole in the first few years', although it was possible for the scholars to go home at Christmas, Easter or Whitsuntide.[5] The sixteenth-century curriculum of Eton shows that a whole series of feasts was observed, some commemorating major saints, others local benefactors, and each of these days was to a varying extent a departure from the normal routine. Some were whole holidays while on others a few lessons were given or exercises expected. There were longer holidays at Eton too, some fifteen days at Christmas and twelve at Easter, but the boys still remained

[1] Lupton, *Life of Colet*, p. 278.   [2] Kirby, *Annals of Winchester*, pp. 90-1.
[3] Stenton, *Norman London*, p. 30.   [4] Lupton, *Life of Colet*; *VCH Lancs.*, ii, 584.
[5] Leach, *History of Winchester College*, pp. 179-81.

at school and even pursued some studies. Only after Ascension Day was there an intermission, lasting three weeks until Corpus Christi, when the boys were accustomed to go home to their parents.[1]

The schools of the early Tudor period whose statutes have survived (Bruton, Manchester, Newark, St Paul's and so on) seem also to have continued their work for most of the year, merely observing the greater festivals as holidays. In addition to these, masters desperate to escape from their charges, or at the request of local worthies, sometimes granted extra holidays or 'remedies' as they were called. 'As fare as I can perceyve by my maisters wordes', asserts a perceptive Oxford schoolboy of about 1500, 'he purposeth to go into the contrey for ii or iii days where he woll sport hym and make mery.'[2] Educationalists however warned against granting too many irregular holidays. 'There must be a measure', wrote William Horman in 1519, 'in giving remedies or sporting to children, lest they be weary of going to their book if they have none, or wax slack if they have too many.'[3] Colet forbade the master of St Paul's to grant remedies on pain of a fine of 40s. unless they were requested by the king himself or by an archbishop or bishop in person.[4] Similar prohibitions were made in many of the other new schools in the early Tudor period.

An alternative system was in use at Wotton-under-Edge and imitated at Newland.[5] There holidays were confined to specific periods of the year in the modern fashion, outside which the master was not to cease from keeping school. The holidays lasted for two weeks at Christmas, two at Easter, one at Whitsun and six which began on 1 August and ended on 14 September. The masters did not reap the whole benefit of these holidays, for they had duties as chantry priests which continued all the year round. At Newland the master's own holiday was restricted to a month, later raised to six weeks.

How many years a pupil spent in the grammar school, and until what age, probably varied according to circumstances. For a clerk who aimed to take holy orders, attend a university or enter a religious order five or six years of study were probably necessary. At St Albans in 1339 poor scholars were permitted to stay for up to five years in the almonry of the abbey, as 'this time is enough to become proficient in grammar'.[6] The scholars of Eton and Winchester probably spent six years or more in the

---

[1] Maxwell-Lyte, *History of Eton College*, pp. 145-55.
[2] *A Fifteenth-Century School Book*, ed. Nelson, p. 30.
[3] William Horman, *Vulgaria*, ed. M. R. James (Roxburghe Club, 1926), p. 141.
[4] Lupton, *Life of Colet*, p. 278.
[5] *ECD*, pp. 336-9; *Reg. Spofford, Hereford*, p. 282.
[6] *Reg. John Whethamstede*, ii, 315.

study of grammar from their arrival at the age of eleven or twelve until the statutes obliged them to leave for university on completing their eighteenth year, or in special cases their nineteenth.[1] The age of eighteen was also the upper limit in other schools, such as Wotton-under-Edge (1384) and Rotherham (1483), but many clerical students must have continued to study grammar beyond this age.[2] In the monasteries, novices, who were usually twenty when admitted, spent their first years in the further study of grammar and logic.[3] Candidates for holy orders, who had to be eighteen to be made subdeacons and twenty to be deacons, were often ordained, if the bishop thought them insufficiently learned, on condition that they spend a further year or two at school before taking any higher orders.[4] John Melton, clerk of Mettingham College in Suffolk, was at school at Beccles for six years until 1412 when he was ordained deacon and priest, for which he must have been at least twenty-five.[5] Older still were those unlearned priests who, having somehow slipped through the ordination tests, were detected by the bishop when they came to be admitted to a benefice. There are several cases of such men being told to go off to school again, though we may imagine that they received private tuition rather than endure the indignity of life in a public classroom.[6]

For those who did not aim at a career in the Church, their time at school also varied according to the end in view. At the lower end of the scale a comparatively rapid course in grammar might fit one for a life of trade or business.[7] At the upper end boys of gentle birth, destined for a career in a household or further study at the Inns of Court, may have spent a period at school similar to that of clerks. Thus Hugh Willoughby appears to have been at school at Sutton Coldfield for four years from 1522, before going to Staple Inn in 1526.[8] We find secular youths leaving school at any age from fifteen to twenty. Late schooling of this kind sometimes overlapped with the youthful marriages practised among the propertied classes for business reasons, and more than one gangling youth, squeezed awkwardly onto a school bench, may have had a young wife at home and perhaps even a child.[9]

Considering the large number of people who went to school in the middle ages, we hear remarkably little about their personal experiences

---

[1] Kirby, *Annals of Winchester*, p. 458; *Ancient Laws*, ed. Heywood and Wright, p. 480.
[2] *ECD*, pp. 340-1; *EYS*, ii, 122.   [3] See below, pp. 237-43.
[4] See above, pp. 15-16.   [5] *SME*, p. 210.
[6] See above, pp. 18-19.   [7] See above, p. 77.
[8] *Historical MSS Commission, Report on the MSS of Lord Middleton*, pp. 346, 382-4.
[9] For examples of provision for schooling in marriage settlements see E. Rickert, *Chaucer's World* (1948), p. 55, and *Catalogue of Ancient Deeds*, vol v (1906), A 12603.

there. Interest in biography was of course extremely limited. Lives of the saints were written for edification and the deeds of kings and knights were celebrated, but most people's personal histories perished unrecorded. In any case childhood was the least regarded of all the ages, and was hardly conceived as having any importance in its own right. There was a brief precocious interest in autobiography in the twelfth century. Gerald of Wales tells us of his boyhood at Manorbier and mentions Master Hamo, his tutor at Gloucester.[1] Jocelin of Brakelond records the gratitude of Abbot Samson of Bury St Edmunds to his old schoolmaster, William of Diss.[2] Alexander Neckham recalls with pleasure his earliest studies at St Albans and his student days in Paris.[3] But such revelations cease during the thirteenth century, and for the next 250 years the lack of interest in childhood, and hence in school life, is almost complete. Of almost no great figure of this period do we know the name of the school he attended or the circumstances which first inspired in him a love of learning. No one ever paid tribute to the schoolmasters of Bradwardine, Courtenay or Wykeham, or execrated those who had reared Wycliffe or Peacock. Even Colet and Wolsey have left no details of their schooldays. There is an equal absence of literary interest in the world of school. Chaucer's *Prioress's Tale* is almost alone in describing a schoolboy and a schoolroom, but the episode was already in his sources and it failed to arouse in him the imagination and sympathy which he displayed in describing so many other scenes of English life.[4]

Some of the very few glimpses of schoolboys and their personalities during the later middle ages come in legal records. Not seldom did schoolboys imitate the violence of their fathers, and the older clerks especially tended to get involved in trouble. A brawl at Dunstable in 1274 between the scholars and the townsfolk left many people wounded; one of the townsmen was killed, and an accusation by the dead man's wife led to the flight of Robert the clerk of Sherrington before he could be arrested.[5] On 23 March 1288, when the clerks of Exeter school were making their way home in the afternoon, one of their number, a certain Nyweton, attacked Henna the Jewess in South Street by throwing stones

---

[1] *Giraldi Cambrensis Opera*, ed. J. S. Brewer, 8 vols (Rolls Series, 1861-91), i, 21; iv, 107.
[2] *The Chronicle of Jocelin of Brakelond*, ed. H. E. Butler (1949), p. 44.
[3] Alexander Neckham, *De Naturis Rerum, etc.*, ed. T. Wright (Rolls Series, 1863), p. 503.
[4] C. Brown, *A Study of the Miracle of Our Lady* (Chaucer Society, 2nd series, xlv, 1910), *passim*.
[5] *Annales Monastici*, ed. H. R. Luard, vol iii (Rolls Series, 1866), p. 85.

at her, one of which drew blood and caused her to raise the hue and cry. It is pleasant to record that the city authorities took the case seriously, despite the unpopular status of the plaintiff, and ordered the clerk's arrest.[1] Sometimes these untoward incidents took place in school. Thomas Birchwood, scholar of Canterbury in 1314, confessed to a charge of violently assaulting the vice-monitor, Master Walter.[2] In the following century a Norfolk schoolboy, Robert Barbour, petitioning the chancellor in the early 1460s, recounted how he had gone to Aylsham grammar school with Robert Fayred when, as a result of 'their negligent japing and disport in the said school, the said Robert Fayred was hurt and a long time thereafter died'. At the instance of his enemies, so Barbour complained, he was then indicted, arrested, taken off to the county gaol and disallowed bail to boot. And he no hardened criminal, but a boy of fourteen![3]

From the early sixteenth century there also survive two vignettes of schoolchildren which, while not necessarily typical, preserve enough details to permit some insight into their lives and circumstances. The first is the story of a poor half-crazy priest, Sir Thomas Grey, detained in Wiltshire in 1538 on suspicion of communicating with Rome. A searching examination before six inquisitors elicited the whole story of his life in every detail. He was born in about 1505 at Carlton Husthwaite on the south-western slopes of the Yorkshire moors, the son of a smith. His first schooling was at Topcliffe, seven miles away under a priest named Henry Osgoodby, steward to the earl of Northumberland. Next he was received into the almonry of the nearby Augustinian priory at Newburgh where he stayed for three years, his schoolmaster being Sir John Clerk, and he could remember the visit of the queen of Scots to Newburgh in 1517 after Flodden Field. From there he proceeded to Oxford as a bible-clerk and butler in the Cistercian college, St Bernard's, where he stayed four years and could recall his chamber mates: Mr Byland, Mr Rivers and Mr Buckfast. He then set out on long journeys to Rome, where he was priested, eventually wandering back to England and eking out a living as a chantry priest and hired chaplain until he fell sick. 'It is well proved he has been a lunatic these three or four years', reported Charles Bulkeley, the chief examiner, to Cromwell; 'I cannot perceive that he has any communication with out-

---

[1] Exeter City Archives: Mayor's Court Rolls, 16/17 Edward I m 25d. I owe this reference to the kindness of Mr A. Jackson.
[2] *ECD*, pp. 258-9.
[3] PRO, Early Chancery Proceedings, C 1/27/343.

ward parties.' So saying, the poor suspect whose life history has passed momentarily before our eyes is dismissed for ever.[1]

Another pathetic figure of the same period is 'little Francis', a *protégé* of the ill-fated Edward Stafford, duke of Buckingham, whose story survives among the mass of letters and papers seized by the crown in 1521 on the duke's arrest for treason. We first hear about him in August 1519 when he was staying in the household of the prior of the knights of St John at Clerkenwell, where the prior's chaplain was his tutor and received regular moneys from the duke to maintain him. In November 1519 he was ill with some disease of the head and neck, and payments were made for shaving his head, for a sick girdle and for a white cap to lie in. By the spring of 1520 he was better, and 7d. was paid 'for a hen at Shrovetide, for Francis to sport him with the children'. Writing paper and a pen and inkhorn were purchased for his use indoors, and a bow and arrows, strings, shooting gloves and a brace for his recreation outside. In April, however, he had an ague and was taken off to seek a cure by pilgrimage to St Albans and to the shrine of Master John Schorn at North Marston. The journey was not successful. In May he was suffering again from eruptions on the head and neck, hands and body, which the barber was paid for healing, only to leave him a prey to catarrh and a throat infection. July and August were no better, for they brought him yellow jaundice lasting twenty-four days. Poor Francis! He survived until at least April 1521 when payments to his tutor are recorded, but that is the last we hear of him; he disappears, lost in the ruin which overwhelmed his patron.[2]

The revival of interest in childhood and of efforts to recapture its events and emotions begins in the second half of the fifteenth century. Archbishop Rotherham in his statutes for Rotherham College of 1483 seems to have been the first who went out of his way to recall his childhood: how he was born and brought up in Rotherham and how the chance arrival of a schoolmaster in the town enabled him to begin the studies through which he rose to eminence in later life.[3] Such autobiographical fragments become increasingly common among writers and orators during the course of the sixteenth century. And to the century before the Reformation belong also the first attempts in literature to describe and penetrate the emotions of childhood and of its greatest feature, school life. These attempts do not only deserve attention because of the picture they give of contemporary schoolboys and their behaviour. They are also significant

[1] *LPFD*, xiii, part 2, no 403.
[2] Ibid., iii, part 1, pp. 499-504.
[3] *EYS*, ii, 109-10, 150; *ECD*, pp. 422-5.

as the earliest modern writings about childhood, and they foreshadow the rich literature which in succeeding centuries this subject has inspired.

The origins of the modern literary interest in childhood seem to go back to native English roots as much as to humanist notions coming from abroad. We have already seen how medieval schoolmasters devised *vulgaria* to amuse their pupils by allusions to daily life, and this in itself necessitated a degree of involvement in the minds and interests of those pupils. The most ambitious of the early *vulgaria* was the anonymous collection made at Magdalen College school in about 1500. Its purpose, like that of its predecessors, was primarily grammatical, and it was set out in grammatical order, not in the more attractive form under subjects into which its modern editor has arranged it. The Magdalen *vulgaria* have much to say about schoolboys and their interests, but in one passage in particular the author allowed himself a free rein to describe his feelings, perhaps his memories, about childhood and to point that ever-poignant contrast between the joy and freedom of infancy and the pains and disciplines of school:

The worlde waxeth worse every day, and all is turnede upside down, contrary to th'olde guyse, for all that was to me a pleasure when I was a childe, from iij yere olde to x (for now I go upon the xij yere), while I was undre my father and mothers kepyng, be tornyde now to tormentes and payne. For than I was wont to lye styll abedde tyll it was forth dais, delitynge myselfe in slepe and ease. The sone sent in his beamys at the wyndowes that gave me lyght instede of a candle. O, what a sporte it was every mornynge when the son was upe to take my lusty pleasur betwixte the shetes, to beholde the rofe, the beamys, and the rafters of my chambre, and loke on the clothes that the chambre was hanged with! Ther durste no mann but he were made awake me oute of my slepe upon his owne hede while me list to slepe. At my wyll I arose with intreatese, and whan th'appetite of rest went his way by his owne accorde, than I awoke and callede whom me list to lay my gere redy to me. My brekefaste was brought to my beddys side as ofte as me liste to call therfor, and so many tymes I was first fedde or I were cledde. So I hade many pleasurs mo besides thes, wherof sum be forgoten, sum I do remembre well, but I have no leysure to reherce them nowe.

But nowe the worlde rennyth upon another whele, for nowe at fyve of the clocke by the monelyght I most go to my booke and lete slepe and slouthe alon, and yff oure maister hape to awake us, he bryngeth a rode stede of a candle. Now I leve pleasurs that I hade sumtyme. Here is nought els preferryde but monyshynge and strypys. Brekfastes that were sumtyme brought at my biddynge is dryven oute of contrey and never shall cum agayne. I wolde tell more of my mysfortunes, but thoughe I have leysure to say, yet I have no pleasure, for the reherse of them makyth my mynde more hevy. I sech all the ways I can to lyve ons at myn ease, that I myght rise and go to bede when me liste oute of the fere of betynge.[1]

This, the earliest, yet stands as one of the most successful treatments of the great themes of childhood's glory and of the growing boy's first intimations of mortality. It is the archetype of every modern author who has written with joy of his own childhood and has recalled the anguish and tumult of his first boarding school.

There also survive from the end of the middle ages some songs of school life which appear to be the work of adults and hence exhibit the same new interest in childhood and in penetrating its emotions. The earliest comes from a fifteenth-century grammatical miscellany now at Lincoln Cathedral, where it lies for ever imprisoned between the *Accentarius* and the *Dictionarius* of John of Garland. No wonder it cries out with frustration, the frustration of the schoolboy driven almost beyond endurance by the hard benches, the endless grammatical hexameters and the relentless incursions of the usher:

> Wenest thu, huscher, with thi coyntyse,
> Iche day beten us on this wyse,
>   As thu wer lord of toun?
> We had levur scole for-sake
> And ilche of us an-other crafte take,
>   Then long to be in thi bandoun.

Could we but get him outside, by the millstones or near the crab tree with its crop of small, hard apples:

> But wolde god that we myth ones
> Cache the at the mulne stones,
>   Or at the crabbe tre –
> We schuld leve in the such a probeyt
> For that thu hast us don and seyd
>   That alle thi kyn suld rwe the.[2]

[1] *A Fifteenth-Century School Book*, ed. Nelson, p. 1. The capitals and punctuation have been modernized.
[2] Lincoln Cathedral, MS 132 fo 100; printed in R. H. Robbins, *Secular Lyrics of the XIVth and XVth Centuries*, 2nd ed. (1955), pp. 105, 265.

But we are powerless. The energy with which the song begins fails to survive to the end, and when all emotion has subsided we are still in school, still at his mercy.

A second poem of about 1500 is much less realistic. It is a moral piece in alternating lines of Latin and English, the rather unexceptional confession of a naughty schoolboy: his late arrival at school, his idleness when there, his disregard for his parents' trouble on his behalf.[1] Only the last verse is a surprise: bonhomie instead of repentance, let us enjoy ourselves nevertheless:

> Ffelo be gladde and make gud chere,
> *Dolentes cum tripudijs,*[2]
> Ffor all men schall nott thryfe to here
> *Que exhibentur studijs.*[3]

Is it not the first flight of a young Falstaff?

The mood of optimism is seen at its best in a third piece, which the London grocer Richard Hill copied down into his commonplace book in the early sixteenth century. This is another schoolboy's tale of woe, but through it all there runs a vein of cheerful impudence unconquered by the hardest blows. This boy is as loth as anyone to rise at 6.00 on a Monday morning; he gets to school late, and meets the wrathful pedagogue:

> 'Where hast thou be, thow sory ladde?'
> 'Milked dukkes, my moder badde',

for which piece of sauce he gets his posterior peppered so hard that it stings like fennel seeds. But though he reflects 'much sorrow have he for his deeds', he is incapable of our first boy's bitterness, and back in his place his mind begins to revolve glorious, impossible revenges:

> I wold my master were a watt,
> And my boke a wyld catt,
> And a brase of grehowndes in his toppe;
> I wold be glad for to se that!

The vision grows in the imagination:

---

[1] London, BM, MS Add. 14,997 fo 44v; printed in K. Hammerle, 'Verstreute me. und frühne. Lyrik', *Archiv für neueren Sprachen*, clxvi (1934), pp. 203-4.
[2] 'Weeping with jubilation.'
[3] 'Who are kept at studies.'

I wold my master were an hare,
And all his bokes howndes were,
And I myself a joly hontere;
To blow my horn I wold not spare,
For if he were dede I wold not care![1]

The imagination seems to leap the schoolroom walls; the chase goes on through woods and pastures new. School is not for ever, and the world waits outside.

[1] R. L. Greene, *A Selection of English Carols* (1962), pp. 145-6, 241-2.

Chapter Five

Patrons and schoolmasters

We have now seen something of the life and studies of the medieval English schools, and this raises further questions: who was responsible for supervising their work, and who was involved in teaching in them? Education in the middle ages, and indeed for long afterwards, belonged to the spiritual not the secular sphere of life, and naturally came under the care of the ecclesiastical authorities. It is sometimes assumed that the medieval Church exercised a positive control over school education, yet further experience suggests that in England, at least, the authorities showed very little interest in schools compared with the attention they gave to religious houses and parish churches. How evident this is from reading the surviving acts of councils, popes and bishops. The councils of the twelfth and thirteenth centuries, both general and provincial, provide scarcely half a dozen pieces of legislation concerning schools. The popes of the twelfth century were not unaware of the importance of education, and in later times they were often concerned with university affairs or with legislating for the better education of the religious orders. But the humbler English grammar schools rarely caught their attention. The papal registers of the fourteenth and fifteenth centuries show only two or three examples of papal intervention in English school education, and then only in response to local initiative.[1]

Much the same can be said of the English bishops from the Conquest to the Reformation. They cannot be accused of indifference to education; many were active in fostering individual schools and providing endowments to facilitate their work. Bishops were always willing to respond to appeals for help from schools whose rights and privileges stood in need

[1] See for example *Calendar of Papal Letters*, v, 300, 542; viii, 348-9.

of protection. Yet at the same time they gave little attention to supervising what was taught in schools, and who taught it. The councils and synods of the thirteenth century, for example, at which the English bishops tried to regulate nearly every aspect of ecclesiastical life, hardly ever touched on schools, schoolmasters, scholars or their problems. It was a rare bishop who, like Alexander Stavensby, bishop of Coventry and Lichfield from 1224 to 1238, bothered to remind those concerned to appoint learned and virtuous men to the schools of the diocese.[1] Similarly in the fourteenth century John Grandisson, bishop of Exeter, was apparently alone in concerning himself in 1357 with the teaching methods of the school-masters of the south-west, when he ordered that boys should be made to construe and understand the basic elements of the faith before being taken on to read Latin poetry.[2] In the fifteenth century, an example of episcopal intervention in the diocese of Norwich, where we find the borough authorities of Ipswich in 1477 establishing a scale of fees to be charged by the local schoolmaster 'according to the assessment of the lord bishop of Norwich', is equally uncommon.[3]

Such examples of episcopal intervention are therefore the exception rather than the rule. The English ecclesiastical authorities, untroubled by heresy until the 1380s, seem to have taken the orthodoxy of the school curriculum for granted and to have been complacent about its quality. Only the appearance of the Lollards caused something in the way of second thoughts. When in 1408 Archbishop Arundel issued constitutions for the province of Canterbury with the intention of promoting reform and discouraging heresy, he included one which prohibited school-masters from teaching their pupils anything about the faith or the sacra-ments against the determination of the Church, or allowing their pupils to hold disputations concerning matters of faith.[4] But there is nothing to show that a closer supervision of schools and their masters resulted from this. Not until the Reformation was well advanced did the role of school-masters become so crucial to the authorities that they were made subject to a system of licensing and supervision like that to which the parish clergy had long been accustomed. But before the Reformation the place of the schools within the English ecclesiastical system was taken for granted, and hardly any conscious effort was made to keep them under control.

If nobody bothered overmuch about the curricula and effectiveness of schools in general, the appointment of schoolmasters was quite another matter and one which aroused a good deal of interest. As early as the

[1] *Councils & Synods*, i, 211.
[2] *ECD*, pp. 314-17, and above, p. 62.
[3] Ibid., pp. 422-3; *VCH Suffolk*, ii, 326.
[4] *ECD*, pp. 394-5; *Concilia*, iii, 317.

twelfth century, attempts were being made to regulate the methods by which schoolmasters were appointed. Thus Pope Alexander III (1159-81), writing apparently to the bishop of Winchester, ordered that no one should exact money in return for granting a licence to teach, and that if anyone failed to appoint a schoolmaster for that reason, the bishop should do so instead.[1] In 1179 the Lateran council also prohibited anyone from selling the licence to teach, and this was repeated in England by the council of London in 1200.[2] An earlier English council, at Westminster in 1138, had already forbidden schoolmasters to sublet their schools to others for money.[3] The legislation of Alexander III and the Lateran council was included in the *Decretals* published by Gregory IX in 1234, and thus became part of the corpus of canon law for the rest of the middle ages. Its purpose was evidently to facilitate the growth of schools by freeing them from at least one possible financial burden. The legisation makes clear that a right to appoint or license schoolmasters already existed by the twelfth century, but it does not tell us who exercised the right, and this is the next question to consider.

The English bishops, as the chief local executives of the Church, might be expected to have claimed or acquired rights of appointing and licensing the schoolmasters in their dioceses. Yet although most of them did exercise such rights occasionally, there is little sign that any diocesan ever tried to secure a monopoly of educational appointments. The only clear case of a bishop claiming to appoint all the schoolmasters in his diocese comes not from England but from Wales, where in 1488 Bishop Pavy of St Davids, when collating a schoolmaster to Haverfordwest, asserted that the sole power of conferring the grammar schools of the cathedral city and the diocese belonged to him both by right and custom.[4] In England the only suggestion of episcopal patronage over local schools in general comes from the diocese of Norwich where in the fourteenth and fifteenth centuries we find the bishops appointing masters not only in the episcopal towns of Norwich and Thetford, but in other country towns and villages, with some of which they had little or no ties of lordship.[5] In England

[1] *Corpus Juris Canonici*, ed. E. Friedberg, vol ii, cols 768-70: Decretal V tit. v cap. ii-iii; *ECD*, pp. 118-19.

[2] Decretal V tit. v cap. i; *ECD*, pp. 122-3.

[3] *Concilia*, i, 506, 415; *ECD*, pp. 138-9, 96-7.

[4] *Episcopal Registers of St Davids 1397-1518*, ed. R. F. Isaacson, vol ii (Cymmrodorion Society, 1917), pp. 524-5.

[5] e.g. Blofield (1350), Fincham (1432), Harleston (1433), Shipden (1455), Shouldham (1462), Sparham (1408) and Thornage (1474). Some of these places were the centres of rural deaneries, and the distribution of schools in medieval Norfolk suggests that a system of ruridecanal schools may have existed, at least in outline.

generally, however, bishops exercised the right of nominating school-masters in only one or two places in each diocese. The bishops of six of the eight monastic sees appointed the masters of their cathedral cities.[1] Otherwise we find them only making appointments in places where they had some special lordship, such as the archbishop of Canterbury possessed at Hadleigh in Suffolk, the bishop of Durham at Hexham and the bishop of Exeter at Crediton.[2]

If bishops themselves did not claim a general right of licensing and appointing masters, it might be thought that they passed on the duty to their subordinates: the chancellors of their cathedrals and the archdeacons of their dioceses. The chancellors of the English secular cathedrals had themselves originated as schoolmasters, and although by the thirteenth century they had all relinquished to a deputy the menial work of teaching grammar, they remained under the obligation of lecturing to the local clergy on theology and canon law, and thus retained an interest in local education.[3] The chancellors of the nine English secular cathedrals, with the exception of Exeter, certainly appointed the schoolmasters of their respective cathedral cities from at least the thirteenth century onwards. But in only two or three places do they appear to have claimed and won a wider jurisdiction over other local schools. At Lincoln it was recognized by 1236 that the chancellor had the right to appoint to all the schools in Lincolnshire except for those upon the prebendal estates of his fellow canons.[4] Likewise the chancellor of York possessed, certainly by 1307 and probably long before, a similar power over every grammar school within the territorial jurisdiction of the chapter, which included places as far away as Doncaster and Guisborough.[5] Similar control was exercised at Southwell Minster, which was a cathedral in all but name, and one of the three lesser seats of the archbishop of York. There the prebendary of Normanton who acted as chancellor claimed by 1238 the right to collate schoolmasters throughout Nottinghamshire, even to towns as important as Newark and Nottingham.[6] But apart from these three examples, there is no sign that the other chancellors ever claimed, let alone exercised, the power of appointing schoolmasters outside the cathedral cities themselves.

[1] i.e. Canterbury, Carlisle, Durham, Ely, Norwich and Winchester. There is no evidence about Rochester, and Worcester was an exception.
[2] *VCH Suffolk*, ii, 325; *Reg. Romeyn, York*, ed. W. Brown, vol ii (Surtees Society, cxxviii, 1917), p. 78; *Reg. Brantyngham, Exeter*, i, 378-9.
[3] On the office of chancellor see also above, pp. 80-1, and below, pp. 173-4.
[4] *VCH Lincs.*, ii, 422.
[5] Edwards, *English Secular Cathedrals*, pp. 196-7; *EYS*, i, 22.
[6] *VCH Notts*, ii, 183.

Archdeacons too appear to have nominated schoolmasters in only a few places. They did so in two cathedral cities – Exeter and Worcester – but not apparently elsewhere in those dioceses.[1] At Cambridge the archdeacon of Ely managed to retain a jurisdiction over the local schools for long after the development of the university. In 1276 his right was recognized of appointing a deputy, the master of glomery, generally a university graduate, to supervise the grammar schools of the town and to judge cases affecting their pupils which did not involve the scholars of the university itself.[2] At Oxford, which shook off the local ecclesiastical jurisdiction earlier than Cambridge, the archdeacon appears not to have possessed such rights, and the Oxford grammar masters were appointed and supervised by the chancellor of the university. It is however interesting to note that the archdeacon of Oxford was present in 1306 when statutes were passed by the university regulating its grammar schools.[3] The remaining examples of archidiaconal control of schools and their masters relate to peculiar jurisdictions. At St Albans in 1309 the monastic archdeacon gave various privileges to the local grammar school, though it is not certain if he appointed its masters.[4] And in the north the archdeacon of Richmond, who ruled with almost episcopal authority over his vast, remote archdeaconry, is found appointing schoolmasters both in Preston and in Richmond towards the end of the fourteenth century.[5] But once again, these examples seem to be exceptional rather than normal, and there is no sign of any general custom that archdeacons should appoint schoolmasters throughout their jurisdictions.

The conclusion is therefore inescapable that while the English ecclesiastical authorities possessed a certain amount of educational patronage, they did not monopolize it to the exclusion of others. In most places the right to appoint or license schoolmasters lay in private hands, and it belonged to a wide variety of people. Sometimes it was claimed by the lord of the manor or borough where the school was held. Baldwin earl of Devon who died in 1262 possessed the township of Plympton 'with the advowson of the schools'.[6] John of Gaunt and Henry IV, in 1372 and 1400 respectively, appointed schoolmasters at Higham Ferrers because it was a borough

[1] H. L. Parry, *The Founding of Exeter School* (1913), pp. 7-9; *VCH Worcs.*, iv, 477-8.
[2] *Vetus Liber Archidiaconi Eliensis*, ed. C. L. Feltoe and E. H. Minns (Cantab. Antiquarian Society Publications, xlviii, 1917), pp. 202, 289-91.
[3] *Statuta Antiqua Universitatis Oxon.*, ed. Gibson, pp. 20-3, 169-74.
[4] *VCH Herts.*, ii, 52.
[5] A. Hamilton Thompson, 'The registers of the archdeaconry of Richmond, 1361-1442', *Yorks. Archaeological Journal*, xxv (1919), pp. 192, 196, 200.
[6] *Calendar of Inquisitions Post Mortem*, vol i (1904), p. 174.

PATRONS OF ENGLISH SCHOOLS 1066–1400

◊ Bishops
▢ Secular clergy (A = Archdeacon; C = Chancellor)
■ Augustinian Canons
● Benedictines
C Cistercians
× Laymen

F

belonging to their duchy of Lancaster.[1] Similarly, the monks of Bury St Edmunds claimed the nomination of schoolmasters not only in their town of Bury but in Beccles, Botesdale and Mildenhall, which were manors belonging to the abbey.[2] In other places the patronage of the school belonged to the local religious house through a donation from the king or a lay magnate, of which a number were made in the twelfth century when the regular clergy still enjoyed a high reputation for their learning. In this way the monks of Eye gained possession of the schools of Dunwich, the canons of Gloucester and Huntingdon exercised control over education in their respective towns, and there are other examples.[3] Such monasteries thus came to possess an interest in public education at an early date.

The right to appoint or license schoolmasters in a particular place constituted an advowson very much like that of a parish church, and shared some of the same characteristics. Educational, like ecclesiastical, patronage lay in various hands, mostly clerical but in a few cases secular as well. It too might pass into the king's hands as a consequence of wardship or regalian right. Canon law had forbidden the taking of money for a licence to teach, but the right to grant licences did not cease to be attractive. The local schoolmaster was a useful figure to have in one's sphere of influence; moreover, he taught for fees and his office therefore had a monetary value, worth seeking and worth bestowing. So we find patrons of schools taking as much care to preserve and enforce their rights as did patrons of parish churches. As early as the reign of Henry I the canons of Huntingdon were calling on their diocesan, the bishop of Lincoln, for help against 'adulterine' schools which threatened their own rights of appointment.[4] Likewise in the early fourteenth century the chancellor of Beverley Minster strove to prevent unauthorized teaching in the towns of Beverley, Dalton and Kelk, which lay under his jurisdiction.[5] The Cistercian monks of Beaulieu went to law in 1343 to defend their rights over the school of Faringdon in Berkshire.[6] In Gloucester the two local houses of Austin

---

[1] *John of Gaunt's Register, 1372-1376*, ed. S. Armitage-Smith, vol i (Camden 3rd series, xx, 1911), pp. 103-4; *ECD*, pp. 372-5.
[2] *VCH Suffolk*, ii, 307; Sylvia L. Thrupp, 'Replacement-rates in late medieval English population', *Economic History Review*, 2nd series, xviii (1965), p. 113.
[3] *VCH Suffolk*, ii, 303; *VCH Gloucs.*, ii, 315; *VCH Hunts.*, ii, 108.
[4] Mary Bateson, 'The Huntingdon song school', *English Historical Review*, xviii (1903), pp. 712-13.
[5] *EYS*, i, 80m-82, 87-9, 92.
[6] *Registrum Brevium*, 4th ed. (London, 1687), fo 35. On this occasion the king claimed the case as belonging to the crown, like disputes over the advowsons of churches.

canons, the priories of Lanthony and St Oswald's, each claimed the sole privilege of appointing schoolmasters, and they fought two great legal battles over the matter at the end of the thirteenth century and again at the end of the fourteenth, both of which resulted in the victory of Lanthony.[1] As late as 1513 its canons thought it worth while to invoke the aid of the bishop of Worcester against new infringements of their rights.[2] But the evidence for the patronage of schools comes largely from the charters by which it was granted or recognized in the twelfth and early thirteenth centuries, and it is by no means certain that patrons were able to keep a firm hold on their rights until the Reformation.

This mass of rights and jurisdictions, both restricted and extensive, both clerical and lay, clearly failed to make up a coherent system for the appointment of schoolmasters and the supervision of their work. Only in a few places, such as the counties of Lincoln and Nottingham already mentioned, did control become largely centralized in the hands of a single ecclesiastical dignitary. Elsewhere this tendency does not seem to have been effective. Thus in Norfolk in 1240 the master of the cathedral school of Norwich tried but failed to prove his authority over the grammar school of Rudham, some twenty-five miles to the west. The Austin canons of Coxford Priory, the lords of the manor, resisted his claim that none could keep school there without his licence, and won their case in the bishop's court.[3] Here, as in most of the English counties, local patrons held on to their rights. Even so, it is unlikely that the patronage of schools was ever as universal and effective as was the patronage of parish churches. The absence for a large number of towns where schools existed of any records of educational patronage may mean that none was ever claimed, still less enforced. There were other places too where the right of appointing schoolmasters was maintained only with difficulty, as in London. There the patrons of the authorized schools waged a long and never wholly successful battle against illegal schoolmasters who flourished on the considerable demand for education in the metropolis.[4]

Such were the patrons of the English schools in the thirteenth and

[1] On the thirteenth-century disputes between Lanthony and St Oswald's see A. Hamilton Thompson, 'The jurisdiction of the archbishops of York in Gloucestershire', *Transactions of the Bristol and Gloucs. Archaeological Society*, xliii (1921), pp. 85-180. On those of the late fourteenth century there are many deeds in the Lanthony Cartulary (PRO, Chancery Masters' Exhibits, C 115), vols A 3, 4, 6, 7 *passim*.
[2] Worcs. Record Office, Reg. S. de Gigli, folios 202v-3; *VCH Gloucs.*, ii, 319.
[3] H. W. Saunders, 'A history of Coxford Priory', *Norfolk Archaeology*, xvii (1910), pp. 311, 343.
[4] On the schools of London see below, pp. 169, 210-13

fourteenth centuries, and the disputes into which their patronage led them. During the fifteenth and sixteenth centuries they were joined by many more. This was the period when endowed schools first began to be founded by private benefactors to provide free education for all who sought it. Like the older schools these new ones needed patrons to appoint masters when necessary, and in some cases to administer the school endowments as well. Sometimes the patronage remained with the lay family or the guild responsible for the foundation; at other times it was made over to some corporation: a religious house, borough council, city company or group of lay feoffees. These new foundations will be described elsewhere; their effect was to widen the selection of people with an interest in education, and to strengthen the share of the laity in what had been in the thirteenth century predominantly a concern of the clergy.[1]

Apart from their appointment of masters, we know little of the part which patrons played in the life of their schools. Doubtless their intervention was sometimes necessary to discipline or remove an unworthy master, though the only patrons to have left records of such action are bishops and cathedral chapters. Thus in about 1350-2 the chapter of Salisbury secured the dismissal of the cathedral schoolmaster, Henry Nugge, who was said not to be teaching regularly, and in 1429 the bishop of Worcester deprived one Sir Richard of the mastership of the city school there on account of his idleness, negligence and vicious conduct.[2] On rarer occasions schools may have needed the protection of the patron against enemies. When in 1559 an allegation was made that the grammar school of Wotton-under-Edge was a concealed chantry and liable for confiscation, the patron, Sir John Berkeley, took up the case and 'by his means the same was stopped'.[3]

We can now turn to the schoolmasters themselves. As so often in medieval times it is far easier to describe the office than the kind of men by whom it was occupied. Something can be gathered of the way in which schoolmasters were appointed, the qualifications demanded of them, the duties assigned to them and the stipends they received. The biographies of schoolmasters on the other hand are always slender and often nonexistent. At best they tell us little more than who was a graduate and who not; who a priest and who a clerk. The individual almost always eludes

[1] On this subject see below, pp. 205-6.
[2] Edwards, *English Secular Cathedrals*, pp. 195-6; Leach, *Early Education in Worcester*, pp. 76-7.
[3] *VCH Gloucs.*, ii, 403.

our attention; his triumphs and his reputation have not survived him. Only for John Leland does the praise of his contemporaries still faintly ring along the centuries – 'flos grammaticorum'.

Until the middle of the fourteenth century the appointment of masters of arts appears to have been customary in many of the best schools. Such, at least, was the case at Hereford, Lincoln, London and York among the English cathedrals.[1] At Oxford too the university statutes of the early fourteenth century assume that the masters of grammar schools will usually be masters of arts, and school teaching was evidently so popular among the regent masters of the university that they had to be forbidden to keep grammar schools for more than three years.[2] By the middle of the fourteenth century, however, there are signs of a shortage of graduates willing to become schoolmasters. In 1351 the chapter of Lincoln granted the city grammar school to a clerk named John Muscham who evidently lacked the master's degree, because the condition was made that 'if a master of arts should come and ask for the school he should be admitted, since by custom the teaching of the school belongs to an MA'.[3] Again, at York in 1368 the chancellor noted that since the last mortality, or plague, because of the shortness of the term of appointment and the scarcity of masters of arts, none had cared till then to teach in the cathedral school. He therefore appointed Master John of York, who was so qualified, to teach not for the customary period of three or five years, but until he had obtained another benefice.[4] Similar developments appear at Oxford. The university statutes of the later fourteenth century now provide for the admission of schoolmasters who are not MAs if they have the testimony of a grammar master who is one, but if there is none such in Oxford, the testimony of two other good men of the university will suffice. This decline in the qualifications of the Oxford teachers is particularly significant when compared with the decline in standards noted by Dr R. W. Hunt in the grammatical writings produced in fourteenth-century Oxford.[5]

Perhaps for this reason the later middle ages saw the introduction at both English universities of qualifications for schoolmasters less difficult

[1] *Statutes of Lincoln Cathedral*, ed. H. Bradshaw and C. Wordsworth, vol ii (1897), p. 71 [for Hereford]; *VCH Lincs.*, ii, 423; A. F. Leach, 'St Paul's school before Colet', *Archaeologia*, lxii, part 1 (1910), p. 217; *EYS*, i, 13.
[2] *Statuta Antiqua Universitatis Oxon.*, ed. Gibson, pp. 20-3.
[3] *VCH Lincs.*, ii, 423.
[4] *EYS*, i, 23.
[5] *Statuta Antiqua Universitatis Oxon.*, ed. Gibson, p. 170; Hunt in *Studies Presented to Daniel Callus*, pp. 185-7.

to achieve than the degrees in arts. At Oxford we saw how the chancellor exercised the right to examine and to license anyone who wished to practise as a grammar master in the city.[1] By the fifteenth century, if not before, this licence became regarded as a useful qualification by school-masters from elsewhere who did not possess a proper degree, since it carried with it the approbation of the university authorities. Consequently we find such masters coming up to Oxford and asking for the chancellor's licence to teach grammar simply for the honour to be gained thereby, and without any intention of teaching in Oxford. The practice was still common in the early sixteenth century, and the surviving registers of the university record some forty-eight supplications and admissions between 1509 and 1536, almost all concerning schoolmasters who lacked degrees in arts.[2] They came up to Oxford, recounted the number of years they had taught or studied grammar, and asked for a licence to teach. In return they were required to perform some token exercises: sometimes to lecture in public on a book of Cicero or Sallust, sometimes merely to compose a number of verses in praise of the university. Only rarely were they subjected to an examination. Although strictly speaking the chancellor merely conferred a licence, this was generally regarded by the recipients and even by the university as a degree. It is referred to more than once as a *gradus*, and one candidate who sought it in 1514 explained that he had been promised a post in a free school, for which he needed to be a graduate.[3] Those who held the licence were usually styled 'master of grammar' or 'master in grammar', although occasionally the term 'bachelor of grammar' was used, perhaps in view of the limited qualifica-tions and humble status of the 'graduate'. As the sixteenth century wore on, the number of bachelors and masters of arts willing to teach in schools again increased and made the lesser qualification redundant. A mere four or five admissions are recorded after 1536, the last of all occurring in 1568.

At Cambridge where the chancellor had never issued licences to teach, the demand for a special qualification in grammar was met by establishing a proper degree course by statute, apparently in about 1385.[4] A candidate

[1] See above, p. 46.
[2] Oxford University Archives, Regg. G and H *passim*; *Reg. Univ. Oxon.*, i (1885), pp. 38-269 *passim*. Mr W. Mitchell kindly supplied me with transcripts of the original entries.
[3] Oxford University Archives, Reg. G fo 238v; *Reg. Univ. Oxon.*, i, 93, sub Thomas Hatton.
[4] M. B. Hackett, *The Original Statutes of Cambridge University* (1970), pp. 130-1, 265-6.

for the Cambridge degree of 'master of grammar' was expected to have taken part in three public disputations and to have delivered thirteen lectures on Priscian's *Constructions*. Three masters deputed by the university had also to attest to his ability, knowledge and standing. After being admitted to the degree, he had to spend a year of regency or further teaching in which he gave more lectures on Priscian *in Majore* and a further three on poetry in the manner of Priscian upon Virgil.[1] The course continued in operation during the fifteenth century, and the foundation of Godshouse by William Bingham in 1439 was intended to give support to some of those engaged upon it.[2] Some fifty supplications and admissions in grammar are recorded between 1500 and 1548, although by this period the Cambridge degree tended to be awarded as at Oxford, not for exercises carried out at the university, but to schoolmasters from elsewhere in need of a qualification. The custom fell into disuse at Cambridge at much the same time as at Oxford, and the last recorded graduation in grammar took place there in 1548.[3]

What qualifications were usual among the schoolmasters of medieval England? Some of those at the cathedral schools continued to be MAs after the mid-fourteenth century, but others were admitted who were only bachelors of arts, masters of grammar or had not even graduated at all. The masters who taught for fees in the other towns are so shadowy that it is impossible even to guess at the proportions of graduates and non-graduates among them. But with regard to the endowed schools which were founded between the 1380s and the Reformation we can speak with more confidence. Very few of the founders of these schools explicitly stated that their masters should be graduates. Even at Winchester William Wykeham in his statutes of 1400 asked merely that the head-master have teaching experience, and Henry VI repeated this at Eton in 1447, adding however that he should be an MA 'if possible'.[4] Most other founders demanded nothing more than honesty of morals and a competent knowledge of grammar, and only a handful of them

---

[1] *Documents Relating to the University and Colleges of Cambridge* (1852), i, 374. 'Priscian on Virgil' presumably refers to Priscian's 'Partitiones Duodecim Versuum Aeneidos Principalium' (*Grammatici Latini*, ed. H. Keil (1857-70), iii, 459-515). I am as usual indebted to Dr R. W. Hunt for this suggestion.
[2] On Godshouse see below, pp. 221-2.
[3] *Cambridge University Grace Book Γ*, ed. W. G. Searle (1908), pp. xxxi-iii; *Grace Book Δ*, ed. J. Venn (1910), pp. 1, 48.
[4] Kirby, *Annals of Winchester College*, pp. 484-5; *Ancient Laws*, ed. Heywood and Wright, p. 524.

attempted to restrict the master's place to graduates or men with teaching experience.[1]

The leading endowed schools such as Eton, Magdalen, St Paul's and Winchester nevertheless had little difficulty in attracting graduates, and nearly all their masters before the Reformation were entitled to wear the hood as well as the gown. Elsewhere graduates were less common. In the three counties of Worcestershire, Gloucestershire and Somerset, for example, some sixteen endowed schools existed between 1384 and 1540, forty-eight of whose masters can be identified during this period. Fourteen of these are definitely graduates and half of them can be traced to Oxford. Another seven were sometimes styled 'master', but their graduate status is doubtful, and the rest had no degree. If only a minority therefore were graduates, it is nevertheless of interest that endowed schools in small towns and even in the country could attract university men to teach there for a few years before going on to a cure of souls.

There was some movement too between the schools and the universities. When the canons of Lanthony Priory granted the schoolmastership of Gloucester to John Hamelyn in 1396, the contract provided for his wishing to leave the school for a year to study at a university.[2] Maurice Plank, appointed master of Wisbech grammar school in 1407, was similarly granted permission by the bishop of Ely to study at Cambridge for two years, so long as he appointed an usher to teach in his absence.[3] The registers of both the universities in the early sixteenth century supply many instances of schoolmasters who were taking time off from their charges to read for a degree. Sometimes they merely asked to be admitted to the degree in grammar as a formality, but on occasion they supplicated for the higher degrees in arts and their teaching experience, or their responsibilities in their schools, earned them a dispensation from some of the requirements. Thus in 1505 Richard Church, BA, was permitted to count the three years he had spent as a schoolmaster in Canterbury towards the requirements of the MA, and similarly in 1510 Thomas

---

[1] The exceptions include Sevenoaks (1432) where the master is to be a BA (*ECD*, pp. 400-3); Wye (1447) 'an M. Gram. or other graduate' (Wye College, Statutes, folios 10v-11); Macclesfield (1502) 'a graduate' (D. Wilmot, *A Short History of the Grammar School of Macclesfield* (1910), p. 11); Blisworth (*c.* 1505) 'a graduate of Oxford' (*VCH Northants.*, ii, 229); Cromer (*c.* 1505) 'an M.A.' (W. K. Jordan, *The Charities of London* (1960), pp. 221-2); Farnworth (*c.* 1507) 'an M.A., B.A., or M. Gram.' (*VCH Lancs.*, ii, 589); and Malpas (1528) 'a graduate' (Anon., 'Malpas grammar school', *Transactions of Historic Society of Lancs. and Cheshire*, lxv (1913), p. 199).
[2] PRO, C 115, vol A 7 fo 187.
[3] *Ely Diocesan Remembrancer*, no 191 (1901), p. 67 *recte* 75; Ely Reg. Fordham fo 204.

Stanbridge, supplicating for the BA, was given a dispensation in view of his being a schoolmaster at Banbury.[1]

That schoolmasters should be in holy orders was never a general rule, and those who worked only for fees in the town schools and had no other duties were indifferently priests, clerks or laymen. The clergy had the advantage of increasing their salaries by undertaking ecclesiastical duties, the laity that of a wife to look after the boys who frequently boarded in the master's house. Several of the most famous grammarians of medieval Oxford, like John Cornwall and John Leland, were married men. On the local scale we find that of twenty-five schoolmasters recorded as working for fees in the three counties already mentioned between 1280 and 1540, seven were described as chaplains, priests or *domini* and a further six as clerks. The remainder may have been laymen, though in this as in so much else it is hard to be certain.

At the secular cathedral schools the masters were usually clerics, for although their schools might be held away from the close and in the city, they were generally assigned a stall in the choir and even charged with choral duties. It was to their advantage to frequent the cathedral when obits were held, for the sake of the payments which were made on these occasions, and sometimes the master was allowed to augment his salary by serving one of the cathedral chantries, or even by undertaking the duties of a vicar-choral.[2] Nevertheless, we find that three of the masters at York in the later fifteenth century were married men, and masters who were not in major orders appear to have been acceptable at St Paul's as well, even before Colet refounded the school in 1510.[3] Most of the new endowed schools which appeared in the fifteenth century also had a sacerdotal character which made it necessary or desirable for their incumbents to be in priests' orders. Either they were attached to colleges of secular priests, one of whom was responsible for teaching a grammar school, or else they were chantries founded to provide intercessions for the founder as well as education. In that case the master had a daily mass to celebrate as well as a class to teach. Almost none of the new schools of the fifteenth century was founded as a school alone. The often quoted foundation by William Sevenoaks of a school at Sevenoaks in 1432, whose master was by no means to be in holy orders, is one of the rare exceptions.[4]

[1] *Reg. Univ. Oxon.*, i, 292, 70.
[2] *VCH Yorks.*, i, 420; *VCH Lincs.*, ii, 427; *Valor Ecclesiasticus*, vol i (1810), pp. 127-8 [for Wells].
[3] *EYS*, i, 28; *Archaeologia*, lxii, part 1 (1910), p. 203.
[4] *ECD*, pp. 398-403.

F*

However, in larger foundations like Winchester and Eton where the spiritual duties were otherwise assigned and where the schoolmasters had only to teach, the traditional indifference to their status was maintained. Wykeham made no ruling on the subject, and Henry VI merely said that his master and usher should not be married; indeed he forbade the latter to be in holy orders.[1] Archbishop Rotherham for his college at Rotherham founded in 1483 only preferred the grammar master to be a priest if possible, and the first incumbent, John Bocking, was in fact a married man.[2] So was John Anwykyll, the first master of Magdalen College school in the 1480s.[3] Colet's indifference when he founded St Paul's as to whether the master was married, single or in orders, provided he was a good Latinist, was not therefore new; it came in the same tradition.[4] Moreover, in the early sixteenth century it ceased to be customary for the founders of the smaller schools to make them chantries as well and to give the schoolmaster priest's duties. Founders of schools such as Nottingham (1512), Winchcombe (1521) and Manchester (1525) threw open the masterships to priests or others and contented themselves with prayers of intercession in school instead of masses by the master.[5] Of course, many priests continued to hold office in these schools; the first master of Nottingham had previously been a parish priest, and in 1535 the master of Winchcombe served a chantry on his own account.[6] The clerical schoolmaster was to be a familiar figure for centuries. But in 1548 came the dissolution of the chantries, and the chantry schools which survived this process became secularized. Thereafter there remained few schools whose masters were clerics of necessity.

How lucrative was the schoolmaster's profession? In the case of those who worked for fees in the towns it is difficult to be certain. The scale of their charges however suggests that with a class of seventy or eighty pupils, masters could make about £10 a year, and the sum may have been increased by gratuities and the profits of taking in scholars to board.[7] Not all of this was clear profit, for the master had often to hire a building for his teaching, sometimes even from the patrons who had appointed him. At Coventry the monks of the cathedral priory rented out the schoolhouse for 20s. a year, while at Exeter and Gloucester the sum was

[1] *Ancient Laws*, ed. Heywood and Wright, pp. 524-5.
[2] *EYS*, ii, 115, 141-2.
[3] *BRUO*, i, 39.
[4] Lupton, *Life of Colet*, p. 272.
[5] *VCH Notts.*, ii, 220; PRO, Exch. Land Rev., LR 6/29/2; *VCH Lancs.*, ii, 583.
[6] *VCH Notts.*, ii, 221; *LPFD*, viii, no 171.
[7] On the subject of fees see above, pp. 117-18, 121.

24s.[1] The masters of the cathedral schools were also largely self-supporting. While some of the secular chapters may have paid them small salaries (at Wells they got only 2 marks a year), they lived on the whole by taking fees as did the masters in towns elsewhere. Indeed they were sometimes expected to make financial contributions to the chapter. At York the vice-chancellor claimed the sum of 20s. a year from the grammar school,[2] and at Salisbury the school furnished the sum of one mark for the obit of a former chancellor, but by 1448 the chapter had agreed to suspend the payment as long as the school was satisfactorily conducted.[3] At Wells too the schoolmaster was charged in 1410 with an annual payment of 1s. to the chapel of St Mary.[4] With a few exceptions, the monastic cathedral schools seem not to have become free until they were refounded by Henry VIII in the early 1540s, and the secular cathedral schools not until Edward VI's government issued injunctions to that effect in 1547.[5]

In the new endowed schools, on the other hand, masters were paid regular salaries in return for teaching all or some of their pupils gratis. Wykeham set a good standard in 1400 by providing £10 a year for the headmaster of Winchester, with commons to the value of 1s. a week, a chamber which he shared with his usher and one of the chaplains, and an annual livery of cloth worth about 17s.[6] Henry VI's plans for Eton were more ambitious and, since he intended that the master should be a graduate, he offered a salary of £16 as well as commons and cloth and a chamber for the master's sole use. In fact, the vicissitudes suffered by the college and its endowments after Henry's deposition reduced the salary to £10, which was still a generous sum.[7] Yet these rewards were dwarfed by the arrangements which Colet made for St Paul's in 1518. He offered his 'high-master' a mark a week, which in a year would have amounted to more than £34, over twice what his counterpart at Winchester could possibly have made, who, indeed, was worse off than Colet's second or 'sur-master' whose allowance was exactly half that of his superior's. It is true that the high-master did not receive commons, but he was assigned a house of

[1] *VCH War.*, ii, 319; Exeter Cathedral Library Dean and Chapter MSS, no 2228; PRO, C 115 (The Lanthony Cartulary), vol A 7 fo 187.
[2] *EYS*, i, 13, 20.
[3] Dora H. Robertson, 'Notes on the buildings in the city and close of Salisbury' *Wilts. Archaeological and Natural History Magazine*, xlviii (1939), pp. 1-30.
[4] *Historical MSS Commission, Tenth Report, Wells Cathedral MSS*, i, 441.
[5] On this subject see below, pp. 263-6, 275.
[6] Kirby, *Annals of Winchester College*, pp. 486, 497, 499, 510.
[7] *Ancient Laws*, ed. Heywood and Wright, pp. 527, 548, 550, 576; Maxwell-Lyte, *History of Eton College*, p. 65.

very ample proportions and the usual livery of cloth each year, while his deputy had also a suitable lodging.[1]

Such generous salaries as these were exceptional and Wykeham's rate of £10 a year, without however the offer of board as well, was adopted in most of the new free grammar schools which came into being during the fifteenth and early sixteenth centuries. As well as the salary a house or chamber was usually provided, often beside or above the schoolroom. The master either received his salary from trustees or administered the endowments himself. Sometimes, as at Wotton-under-Edge and Newland in Gloucestershire, he had to exhibit the scholars supported on the foundation and keep the lands and possessions of the school in good order; the Wotton master is recorded holding a court for his tenants.[2] The endowed schoolmasters were also obliged to pay subsidies, like the beneficed clergy, and after 1534 they suffered the additional burden of annates and tenths, the taxes equivalent to the whole of the first year's income and a tenth of it in subsequent years, which all incumbents of benefices had now to pay to the king. In 1536 a bill was introduced into parliament on a Cornish initiative to remove these charges from educational foundations, but it failed to gain approval.[3] Endowed schools continued to be so burdened until annates and tenths were relinquished by Mary in 1555, Edward VI having granted exemptions for one or two of the foundations he made. When Elizabeth reappropriated annates and tenths in 1559, schoolmasters were at last officially excused from such payments.[4]

Schoolmasters employed in religious houses or private households probably received much the same as their colleagues in the £10 grammar schools. When the larger abbeys retained a layman or a secular priest to teach the younger monks or the boys of the almonry, they generally gave him board and lodging, fuel, a gown and further wages of anything between £2 and £6. In the great households of the laity, masters seem to have received similar rewards. The grammar master of the royal household under Edward IV received food, fuel, light, clothing and wages of 4d. a day or else £3 6s. 8d. for the whole year.[5] In the earl of Northumberland's household in 1511 he had bread, beer, fuel and £5 per annum.[6] Sixteenth-

---

[1] Lupton, *Life of Colet*, pp. 273-4.
[2] PRO, Exch. KR Depositions, E 134/14 James I, Mich. no 28, Gloucester.
[3] PRO, State Papers, SP 1/104 pp 151-4; *LPFD*, x, 461.
[4] *Statutes of the Realm*, iv, part 1, 364.
[5] A. R. Myers, *The Household of Edward IV* (1959), pp. 137-8.
[6] *The Household . . . of the Fifth Earl of Northumberland*, ed. T. Percy (1905), pp. 44, 47, 51, 97.

century writers were often scornful of the wages given to schoolmasters in the households of the great. In 1531 Sir Thomas Elyot complained that when gentlemen 'hiare a schole maister to teche in their houses, they chiefly enquire with howe small a salary he will be contented, and never do inserche howe moche good lernynge he hath, and howe amonge well lerned men he is therin estemed, usinge therin lasse diligence than in takynge servantes'.[1] Roger Ascham, writing in the 1560s, declared that the gentry took more care to discover a good groom than a learned man to teach their children, gladly giving the groom a stipend of 200 crowns a year, while loth to offer the schoolmaster 200s.[2]

These criticisms were typical of the mid-sixteenth century when, as Hugh Latimer pointed out, £10 a year was hardly enough to allow a man to buy himself books or give drink to his neighbours.[3] Besides, education was more highly valued than before, and it was thought proper to attract men of the highest standard into the teaching profession. The new writers on education therefore condemned the old £10 salary as inadequate in an age of rising prices. 'Ther be in this realme many well lerned', declared Elyot, 'whiche if the name of a schole maister were nat so moche had in contempte, and also if theyr labours with abundant salaries mought be requited, were righte sufficient and able to induce their herers to excellent lernynge.'[4] A year or two later Thomas Starkey put into the mouth of Reginald Pole the statement that it would not be amiss to unite two or three of the small £10 schools to make one good one, supporting an excellent master.[5] When in 1547 Edward VI ordered all cathedrals to keep a free school, he fixed the master's salary at £13 6s. 8d. with a house, while the usher got half as much and a chamber.[6] In the new foundations of his reign there was a tendency for salaries to rise, but no uniform standard was adopted, and while in some places £20 was fixed upon, in others the old £10 was considered quite enough.

But there is no sign that such salaries were felt to be insufficient in the fifteenth century before the rise in prices. The endowed schools, as we have seen, attracted a fair proportion of graduates and do not seem to have

---

[1] Elyot, *The Boke Named the Gouernour*, ed. Croft, i, 113.
[2] Roger Ascham, *The Schoolmaster*, ed. J. A. Giles (1864), p. 104.
[3] Hugh Latimer, *First Sermon Preached Before King Edward VI* (8 March 1549). He gives 12 or 14 marks as inadequate for a priest's stipend.
[4] Elyot, *The Boke Named the Gouernour*, ed. Croft, i, 165.
[5] T. Starkey, *A Dialogue between Pole and Lupset*, ed. Kathleen M. Burton (1948), p. 181.
[6] *Visitation Articles and Injunctions of the Period of the Reformation, 1536-1575*, ed. W. H. Frere and W. M. Kennedy, vol ii (Alcuin Club Collections, xiv-xvi, 1910), p. 139.

suffered from an undue turnover of staff. Endowed schoolmasters with £10 a year were also better off than most chantry priests. The stipends of the chantries in Gloucestershire recorded in 1548, omitting those which were vacant and hence perhaps too poor to support an incumbent, fell mostly between £7 and £5, although not a few were lower still. Only four chantry priests in the county were receiving more than £8 a year. In Somerset too the commonest incomes ranged between £5 and £8, only eleven priests being paid salaries above this rate.

Yet the endowed schools in turn fell below the incomes of the majority of rectories and vicarages, and not a few schoolmasters, tiring of the labours of the schoolroom or in quest of higher preferment, managed at length to obtain a cure of souls. Thus Robert Lyster, retained by the monks of Evesham as their schoolmaster in 1524, was presented by them to the nearby rectory of Willersey two years later, and when they engaged William Scollowe to teach for them in 1538 they stipulated that he should give six months' notice if he wanted to resign to take up another benefice.[1] Of the forty-eight masters known to have served in the endowed schools of Worcestershire, Gloucestershire and Somerset between the 1380s and 1540, fourteen are recorded as moving on to rectories and vicarages, though none of them ever secured high office. Contrariwise at least five of the forty-eight were men who had held cures of souls before they began to teach. Such exchanges remind us that the clerical schoolmasters differed little in standing and qualifications from the middle ranks of the beneficed clergy.

Dedicated schoolmasters there certainly were, men who spent most of their lives in the profession. John Paradise was schoolmaster of Wotton-under-Edge for nearly thirty years between 1427 and 1456, and one of his successors, Robert Coldwell, resigned in about 1552 after more than forty. Some pedagogues laboured on well after the usual age of retirement. Thomas Guyldesburgh had been a schoolmaster in Chichester for more than thirty years when he got himself imprisoned for debt during the 1460s, and sent a piteous plea to the chancellor for his release, declaring that he was over eighty, 'right corpulent, and hath a malady in his leg that he may neither well ride nor go'.[2] Another octogenarian schoolmaster was John Ree who was still teaching the grammar school at Rock in Worcestershire in 1561 when he was over eighty, and his career stretched back for at least twenty-five years.[3] Others however moved from school

[1] *Reg. Univ. Oxon.*, i, 114; Worcs. Record Office, Reg. J. Ghinucci, fo 26v; PRO, Exch. Augm., Misc. Books E 315/101, folios 36v-7.
[2] PRO, Early Chancery Proceedings, C 1/27/371; *VCH Sussex*, ii, 401.
[3] *ESR*, part 2, pp. 271-2; PRO, Exch. Land Revenue, LR 6/115/1-3.

to school, trying to rise up the scale to the more prestigious establishments like Eton and Winchester. Thomas Romsey, schoolmaster of Winchester between 1394 and 1418, had previously taught at Chichester, and his successor Richard Darcy had been usher of Gloucester. When Darcy resigned in 1424 there were several candidates for his place, among whom another schoolmaster of Gloucester, Richard Davy, rode over to Winchester for interview, but the successful applicant was Thomas Alwyn who had been teaching at Newport Pagnell in Buckinghamshire. Alwyn had a very varied career, for he spent only six years at Winchester before going back to the country, this time apparently to a school at Leighton Buzzard, whence in 1441 he returned once more to Wykeham's college.[1]

Naturally the teaching profession, which has always attracted rogues and villains, had a fair number of both in medieval times when chicanery was less restrained and manners more violent. There was Master Henry, schoolmaster of Huntingdon in 1255, whose under-master Robert was an overt evildoer with his greyhounds to the venison of the forest of Huntingdon, with Henry's connivance, or so it was said. Both men were arrested when the foresters discovered a buck, a haunch of venison and a greyhound in their house, but being clerks they probably escaped.[2] There was Reginald, schoolmaster of Norham, who joined in an affray in the parish church of Auckland in 1302 in which a monk of Durham who had come to deliver a legal judgement was beaten up and dragged out of the church by the feet.[3] There was John Oxford, usher of Clare school in 1381, indicted for taking part in the Peasants' Revolt, or rather in the riots and robberies which accompanied its course in Suffolk.[4] And there was the violent John Martyn, schoolmaster of the parish of St Michael-at-the-North-Gate in Oxford, who on Sunday 9 August 1450 gathered a number of his scholars in St Michael's church at the time of high mass, so that if the priest attempted to read a sentence of excommunication against him, the assembled scholars could snatch the sentence from the priest's hands and drag him out of the pulpit. When Martyn was committed to prison for a breach of the peace, a number of his scholars tried to break in to rescue him during the night, but this insurrection, says the record thankfully, was peaceably put down by divine will. Martyn was obliged to make satisfaction to those he had wronged and to enter into a bond of £5 to

[1] *BRUO*, i, 29.
[2] *Select Pleas of the Forest*, ed. G. J. Turner, (Selden Society, xiii, 1901), p. 21.
[3] Durham Dean and Chapter Muniments, Priory Reg. I part 2 fo 80v.
[4] E. Powell, *The Rising in East Anglia in 1381* (1896), p. 62.

observe good behaviour. Did he forfeit it, we wonder, when less than three years later he was again in trouble for helping two reverend chaplains to attack the house of an Oxford citizen, breaking open his doors, beating him up and doing other damage against the peace of the king and the university?[1]

How little can now be recovered of the lives and qualities of the medieval English schoolmasters the preceding survey will have made clear. As a profession schoolmasters attracted little attention from their contemporaries and they hardly figure at all in medieval literature. Not until the sixteenth century do we get a considered judgement upon them, but then it comes from the educational writers of the New Learning and is a far from favourable one. Sir Thomas Elyot bewails in 1531 how few are qualified to give instruction to children:

> Lorde god, howe many good and clene wittes of children be nowe a dayes perisshed by ignorant schole maistres. Howe litle substancial doctrine is apprehended by the feweness of good gramariens? Not withstanding I knowe that there be some well lerned, which have taught, and also do teache, but god knoweth a fewe, and they with small effecte, having therto no comforte.[2]

Thomas More was hardly less severe when he reminded his readers two years later 'howe, in our owne time, of al that taught grammer in England not one understode the latine tong'.[3] Before we take these criticisms too seriously we must remember that Elyot and More belonged to an age of reformers to whom the old medieval grammar, the medieval school authors and the masters who had expounded them deserved nothing but contempt. A more practical assessment of the early Tudor schoolmasters may have been that of the chantry certificates of 1548. As we turn over the pages in which the abilities of chantry priests and schoolmasters are recorded, we find a few deserving of blame, it is true, but most of them judged to be learned and of honest conversation.[4] We know too little of the lives of the medieval schoolmasters to dismiss their abilities with contempt, and the impression where it is clearer is usually more favourable. In William Wainfleet a schoolmaster rose to wear the episcopal mitre, and

---

[1] *Registrum Cancellarii*, ed. H. E. Salter, vol i (Oxford Historical Society, xciii, 1932), pp. 212, 324.
[2] Elyot, *The Boke Named the Gouernour*, ed. Croft, i, 163.
[3] 'The second part of the confutation of Tyndale' (1533), in *The Workes of Sir Thomas More . . . in the Englysh Tonge* (London, 1557), p. 723.
[4] See the reports in *ESR* part 2, *passim*.

in Wolsey's case the cardinal's hat; both men were chancellors of England. A schoolmaster of St Albans was one of the earliest English printers; the author of the Magdalen College *Vulgaria* produced a minor classic of English literature; and in Robert Henryson a schoolmaster of Dunfermline was united with a poet of originality and importance.

Historical developments

Chapter Six

The schools from the twelfth century to 1400

It is in the twelfth century that the modern history of English education may well be said to begin. This is not to imply any deprecation of the schools of Anglo-Saxon England, nor even to suggest that continuity with the past was broken by the Norman Conquest. Schools had long existed in the monasteries and in some great households, and were long to do so, but the twelfth century saw, if not the beginning, the significant expansion of education in England, with the springing up of large numbers of public, secular schools in the cities and towns of the kingdom.[1] Unlike the schools of the monasteries and households they were public and open to any who could afford the expenses of attending them. They are thus the direct ancestors of modern schools, and the development of their institutions can be studied through each successive century, a process which through lack of evidence is much harder to trace backwards into the Saxon past. The very fact that significant quantities of educational source material begin to survive from the twelfth century onwards suggests something of a new era, and certainly makes this a suitable point to begin writing a history. In the next two chapters we shall attempt three tasks. The first is to describe the extent of education in England from the twelfth century to the fifteenth, in so far as it is illustrated by the number and distribution of schools. The second is to examine the constitutional history of the schools and to show in what ways their institutions developed. The third is to suggest some of the connections which existed between education and society in this period, especially with regard to

[1] For the definition of these terms see above, pp. 59-60.

the patronage and benefactions which the schools attracted from the men and women of these times.

It was around the English cathedrals that the earliest and most important of the twelfth-century schools grew up. Such places, as we noted in a previous chapter, were particularly favourable to the growth of education:[1] they were diocesan centres, the residence and resort of large numbers of priests and clerks, the seat of the bishop, his household and his administration. A good school was essential to train the ministers needed for the cathedral, the administrators desired by the bishop, and the parish clergy of the area who, if perfection was to be sought, required to be well schooled in grammar, theology and canon law so that they might properly minister to the souls in their care. Schoolmasters therefore appear in most or all of the seventeen English cathedral cities between the Conquest and the end of the twelfth century. The circumstances of this depended upon whether the local cathedral had a chapter of secular canons or was staffed by monks. In nearly all the former cases the schoolmaster was admitted to be a member of the cathedral chapter.[2] At York the arrangement dates back to the Conqueror's first archbishop, Thomas of Bayeux, who reigned from 1070 to 1100.[3] At Salisbury it can be traced to his contemporary St Osmund, whose constitutions of 1090 for his cathedral clergy mention an officer called the *archiscola*. Osmund only specified his duties as arranging the lesson rota in church and writing letters for the chapter, but it seems likely that he was also intended to teach or supervise the school. The first known incumbents of the office in the early twelfth century were indeed referred to as schoolmasters.[4] Likewise at St Paul's Cathedral, London, Master Durand the *scholasticus* appears in 1102, and his successor Master Hugh was actually entitled schoolmaster when he was instituted between 1111 and 1127.[5] Similar masters were added to the chapters of nearly all the remaining secular cathedrals during the twelfth century. But when the cathedral was monastic, it was clearly impossible for the schoolmaster, a secular priest or clerk, to become a member of the chapter, and other arrangements had to be made. Archbishop Lanfranc at Canterbury entrusted the school of the city between 1077 and 1087 to the

---

[1] See above, p. 79.
[2] The standard work on the secular cathedrals and their schools is Edwards, *English Secular Cathedrals*, pp. 176-205.
[3] Hugh the Chantor, *The History of the Church of York, 1066-1127*, ed. C. Johnson (1961), p. 11.
[4] Edwards, *English Secular Cathedrals*, pp. 181-2.
[5] J. Le Neve, *Fasti Ecclesiae Anglicanae, 1066-1300*, ed. Diane E. Greenway, vol i (1968), p. 25.

care of the secular canons of St Gregory's outside the north gate of the city.[1] Later, however, both at Canterbury and in most of the other monastic cathedral cities it was normal for the schoolmaster to be appointed and supervised by the bishop, but in other respects to remain a lonely figure, unattached to the cathedral and teaching his school independently of it in the city.

London, as well as being the largest of the cathedral cities, far out-distanced every other town throughout the middle ages in wealth, popu-lation and importance as a place of resort. It is not therefore surprising to find that, besides the cathedral school of St Paul's already mentioned, two other recognized schools had already come into existence by the middle of the twelfth century, pointing to a greater demand for education than could be satisfied by the cathedral school alone. Between 1134 and 1141 when the see of London was vacant, Henry of Blois, bishop of Winchester, addressed a letter to the clerical authorities in the city ordering them to proceed against anyone who might teach in London without the licence of the schoolmaster of St Paul's, except for those who kept the schools of St Mary Arches and St Martin-le-Grand. The latter two churches were privileged places outside the jurisdiction of the diocese of London, the one being a peculiar of the archbishop of Canterbury and the other a royal free chapel. The policy expressed by Henry of Blois, of restricting the number of schools in London to three, continued to be upheld until the middle of the fifteenth century, and random references attest to the continuity of the authorized schools throughout this period. It is likely however that other schools existed from time to time. William FitzStephen, writing in the late twelfth century, observed that besides the privileged schools other people were sometimes permitted to teach as a personal favour or on account of their learning. Moreover, the denunciation of unlawful schoolmasters by the bishop of Winchester, repeated by other authorities in 1394 and 1446, suggests that despite the regulations certain masters did attempt from time to time to set up illegal schools for their own profit and that of the public.[2]

Next to London and the other cathedral cities, nearly all of them places of note, there were a number of other important centres: the county towns, the major ports and the larger centres of commerce and resort

[1] *Cartulary of the Priory of St Gregory, Canterbury*, ed. Audrey M. Woodcock (Camden third series, lxxxviii, 1956), pp. 1-3.
[2] On the early schools of London see *Early Charters of St Paul's*, ed. Marion Gibbs (Camden third series, lviii, 1939), pp. 215-19, and A. F. Leach. 'St Paul's school before Colet', *Archaeologia*, lxii, part 1 (1910), pp. 191-238.

inland, about thirty in number. Schools had already begun to appear in one or two of them, such as Dunwich and Pontefract, by the opening of the twelfth century, and under Henry I (1100-35) others are mentioned at Dunstable, Gloucester, Huntingdon, Oxford, Reading, St Albans and Warwick.[1] By Henry II's reign (1154-89) there are also notices of schools in Bedford, Bury St Edmunds, Colchester, Derby and Northampton. With the coming of the thirteenth century the list grows longer, for not only do most of the twelfth-century schools provide further proof of their continuing existence, but the names of several more important towns can be added. Schools appear in Bristol, Leicester and Shrewsbury in the first half of the century, and in Cambridge, Dover, Guildford, Lancaster, Nottingham and Stamford in the second half. It is not clear whether there was really a further expansion of education in the thirteenth century, or whether the appearance of new schools is simply related to the more extensive source material of this period, but the result is to suggest that at least half the important towns of thirteenth-century England (apart from the cathedral cities) can supply evidence for the existence of a school.

At the same time schools begin to appear in the smaller towns: those which throve around a port or market, or enjoyed the possession of a castle or an important church. There are indeed stray references to schools in such places even in the twelfth century. Reginald of Durham's collection of the miracles of St Cuthbert, made after 1170, casually mentions two examples from the north of England, in what we might suppose to have been wilder parts: a reading school at Yarm in Yorkshire in the 1130s, and a school kept by a secular priest in the parish church of Norham on the English side of the Tweed.[2] But it is in the thirteenth century that the spreading of education into the smaller towns can be seen most clearly. In Yorkshire, for example, there are references to seven, besides the cathedral school at York: Beverley, Guisborough, Hedon, Helmsley, Malton, Pontefract and Wakefield.[3] In the west of England schools appear in such places as Bridgwater, Bridport, Cirencester, Malmesbury, Plympton, Shaftesbury, Taunton and Wotton-under-Edge. Some of these places were only very small boroughs; others, like Awre near Gloucester, Kinoulton near Nottingham and Rudham in Norfolk, were nothing more than villages. Adding these instances to those of schools in the larger

---

[1] Most of the references to twelfth-century schools are in *ECD*, but the texts, translations and dating of the documents there printed are all frequently in need of revision. See also the list of schools below, pp. 295-321.

[2] *Reginaldi Dunelmensis Libellus*, ed. J. Raine (Surtees Society, i, 1835), pp. 34, 149-50.

[3] For references to these schools, and to those which follow, see the list of schools below, pp. 295-321.

Scale: 0 25 50 75 100 125 Miles

Hexham

Carlisle
Cockermouth
Durham

Guisborough

Helmsley

Lancaster
Clitheroe
Malton

YORK

Beverley
Hedon

Wakefield
Pontefract

Chesterfield
Louth

Newark
LINCOLN

Shrewsbury
Nottingham
Kinoulton

Stamford
Rudham
Taverham
Norwich

LICHFIELD
Leicester
Beccles

Ludlow
NORTHAMPTON
Huntingdon
Mildenhall

Worcester
Bury
St Edmunds

Stratford
CAMBRIDGE

HEREFORD
Colchester

Gloucester
Dunstable

Awre
OXFORD
St Albans

Cirencester
Berkhamsted

Wotton
Malmesbury
Reading

Bristol
Marlborough
LONDON

WELLS
Canterbury

Bridgwater
SALISBURY
Guildford
Dover

Taunton
Winchester
Lewes
Battle

Shaftesbury
Arundel

EXETER
Bridport
CHICHESTER

Plympton

ENGLISH SCHOOLS IN THE THIRTEENTH CENTURY

● Schools
■ Schools and places of higher studies

towns, it is possible to make a total of over sixty locations in England during the thirteenth century. The distribution, as the map suggests, is remarkably even over the whole country, and is by no means confined to the lowland zone. The picture is the more impressive when it is remembered how casual are references to schools in the record sources, and how few even of these both survive and are known.

This reminds us of an important point. The instances of places where schools are recorded are merely examples; they cannot represent the whole extent of the facilities for education available in the twelfth or thirteenth centuries. There are no characteristic records of education in medieval England to give the historian the same confidence with which he turns to enumerating manors, boroughs or parish churches. Schools and their masters appear only by chance in a variety of records both secular and ecclesiastical, and even towns which still boast ample medieval archives or dioceses where conscientious bishops and registrars left records of their work have rarely much to tell of their schools. Some important towns – Chester and Coventry, Newcastle and Southampton – are completely absent from our lists at present; others, such as Bedford and Warwick, appear in the twelfth century but not in the thirteenth. These lacunae are primarily due to the shortcomings of the record material, and it would be quite unsafe to infer that the missing towns lacked the educational resources possessed by others of similar size, wealth and character.

As to what subjects were taught in these early schools it is difficult to be precise, since the charters and deeds from which in most cases their existence is deduced talk merely of 'schools' and 'schoolmasters' without revealing their kind. The word 'school' was applied indiscriminately to every kind of institution, even the most elementary, and it is quite possible that the schools which occur in some small towns and villages, like the example at Yarm, taught only reading and song. Those in most of the cities and towns however, by analogy with later centuries when more is known about their activities, probably taught both song and grammar. Higher studies were certainly available at the secular cathedrals, and in a few other important towns. Lincoln and Exeter, for example, possessed important schools of theology and law in the twelfth century, while Hereford was well known for natural science.[1] Alexander, prior of Canon's Ashby in Northamptonshire, writing a little before 1200, declared that there were many teachers of theology in England at that time, so that 'almost every city' had one, and he specially singled out the two examples

[1] Edwards, *English Secular Cathedrals*, pp. 185-92.

nearest to him: Northampton and Oxford.[1] While Oxford and Cambridge were the only towns apart from the cathedral cities where institutions of higher study developed successfully, one or two other places, notably Northampton and Stamford, came near to having similar institutions in the thirteenth and fourteenth centuries.[2]

More can be said about the constitutions of the early schools than about their curricula. In this respect let us begin with the cathedral schools, since they form a well-defined group whose constitutional development was both precocious and comparatively well documented. We have seen how the secular cathedrals came to include a schoolmaster in their chapters after the Conquest. It was not long before his office began to attract endowments which gave its occupant an assured income. At London, Bishop Richard de Belmeis I granted the tithes of two estates to his schoolmaster in about 1127, and further tithes were added by one of his successors, Richard FitzNeal, in the 1190s.[3] At Salisbury, in about 1139, King Stephen appropriated the church of Odiham in Hampshire for the support of the schoolmaster, while at York, Archbishop Roger (1154-1181), arranged for an annual payment of £5 to the school out of the clerical taxation levied on the diocese.[4] During the twelfth century, however, the secular cathedral schoolmaster in nearly every case developed into a dignitary with more important functions than keeping a school, at least a grammar school. He acquired other duties as secretary to the chapter, keeper of its seal and supervisor of its library, which both increased his status and occupied his time. He retained an interest in teaching, but at the more advanced level of giving occasional lectures on theology or canon law to the local clergy. The main teaching work, that of grammar, he relinquished to a deputy. To mark his more exalted rank and duties he acquired the new title of 'chancellor', and the old one of 'schoolmaster' passed to the deputy who taught the grammar school. This process was probably in train by the middle of the twelfth century. The first use of the term 'chancellor' is found at Lincoln in about 1148, and it had spread to all the remaining secular cathedrals by 1225.[5] By the 1230s and 40s,

[1] R. W. Hunt, 'English learning in the late twelfth century', *Transactions of the Royal Historical Society*, 4th series, xix (1936), p. 20.
[2] H. G. Richardson, 'The schools of Northampton in the twelfth century', *English Historical Review*, lvi (1941), pp. 595-605; *VCH Lincs.*, ii, 468-74.
[3] Marion Gibbs, op. cit., pp. 216-19.
[4] *Charters and Documents of Salisbury*, ed. W. R. Jones and W. D. Macray (Rolls Series, 1891), pp. 8-9; *EYS*, i, 13-14.
[5] On the development of the office of chancellor see Edwards, *English Secular Cathedrals*, pp. 176-85.

references to chancellors and schoolmasters as separate officers show that the division of functions was then complete.[1]

At the turn of the twelfth and thirteenth centuries the cathedral schools became the subject of legislation by the Church – the only important occasion in the later middle ages when an attempt was made to provide a network of secular schools over the whole of Western Christendom. The Lateran council of 1179 ordered each cathedral to maintain a schoolmaster and to give him a competent benefice so that he might teach the clerks of the cathedral and other poor scholars for nothing.[2] This decree was repeated and amplified by the second Lateran council of 1215 to the effect that schoolmasters, now specified as teaching grammar, should be maintained in every cathedral and in other churches where sufficient resources existed. Moreover, each metropolitan (or archiepiscopal) cathedral was also to support a theologian able to lecture on the holy scriptures and other matters pertaining to the cure of souls. Both masters, the theologian and the grammarian, were to be given prebends in the cathedrals concerned in order to provide them with salaries.[3]

In England the Lateran decrees were followed in spirit rather than according to the letter. The provision of lecturers in theology, according to the decrees, was only necessary at Canterbury (a monastic cathedral) and York. In fact, theological lecturers were maintained and provided with prebends at all the secular cathedrals in the later middle ages, in circumstances which have already been noted.[4] With regard to the provision of grammar schools, however, the English cathedrals did less than the Lateran decrees had intended. Not that the cathedral grammar schools died out; they remained well frequented, and in almost every case survived until the Reformation in a flourishing condition. Several have continued without intermission until the present day.[5] But in medieval times they were far more rudimentary and far less 'cathedralian' in character than they became after the Reformation. True, where the cathedral was secular the master was appointed by the chancellor (except at Exeter), and often rented the schoolhouse from the chapter. He was usually assigned a stall in the choir and expected to teach the choristers and the older clerks of the second form. But he became primarily the schoolmaster of the city

---

[1] e.g. at Chichester, 1232 (*VCH Sussex*, ii, 400); Wells, *c.* 1235 (*Historical MSS Commission, Wells Cathedral*, vol i (1907), p. 35; Lincoln, 1246 (*VCH Lincs.*, ii, 422).
[2] J. D. Mansi, *Sacrorum Consiliorum Collectio*, vol xxii (1778, reprinted 1961), cols 227-8.
[3] Ibid., cols 999-1000.
[4] See above, pp. 79-86.
[5] In the thirteenth century, references can be found to grammar schools in all the cathedral cities except for Ely and Rochester.

rather than of the cathedral. His school was called the 'general school', the 'high school' or the 'school of the city', and only rarely the 'school of the cathedral'. In most cases it lay away from the close in the city proper, and its masters were sometimes married men, as were three of those at York towards the end of the fifteenth century.[1] The dissociation of the school from the cathedral was even more marked when the chapter was monastic, as at Canterbury or Winchester. There the schoolmaster, appointed by the bishop and not by a member of the chapter, had no stall, might well be married and also carried on his work in the city rather than in the precincts.

Moreover, the cathedral grammar masters never secured that 'competent benefice' which the Lateran councils had prescribed for them, and so their teaching was never wholly free. Although the original schoolmasters of the secular cathedrals had acquired endowments in the twelfth century, these naturally passed to the chancellors into whom those schoolmasters developed. The later grammar masters sometimes received a very small salary from the chapter, but their frequent obligation to pay rent for the schoolhouse or an annual levy to the chapter, together with one or two direct references to fees, show that in most of the secular cathedral schools the master's main source of income came from his pupils.[2] In the monastic cathedral cities the masters had never acquired endowments and, with no dependence on the chapter, must have lived entirely upon what their pupils brought them. Apart from the four or five cathedral schools which became endowed during the fifteenth century as a result of local initiatives, the rest continued to take fees as a matter of course until the Reformation.[3]

The only recipients of free education at the secular cathedrals were the choristers, and they constituted a class apart from other scholars. In most places they numbered between ten and fourteen in the later middle ages, and received free board, lodging and schooling in return for their services in choir.[4] They were most commonly organized in a separate house under a master who either himself or through deputies trained them in song and taught them reading and some grammar; in some cases they may have studied the latter with the city grammar master. But in general they formed a small and secluded body; only at Lincoln did the choristers' school show signs of growth which made it at one stage likely to rival the grammar school of the city. There the choristers had acquired a special grammar master of their own by 1390, and in 1407 he secured

---

[1] *EYS*, i, 28.   [2] See above, p. 157.   [3] See below pp. 214-15.
[4] On the choristers of the secular cathedrals see Edwards, *English Secular Cathedrals*, pp. 307-17.

permission to teach relatives of the canons and other boys dependent upon them. This threatened the livelihood of the city schoolmaster and aroused the concern not only of his patron, the chancellor, but of the mayor and citizens as well, and a formal agreement had to be made to define the exact rights of both schools. The choristers' grammar master was allowed to keep the gains he had made: commoners dwelling with the choristers, relatives of canons and vicars-choral, and the boys of their households. But all others, whether from within or without the close, were henceforth to go without exception to the city grammar school.[1]

The Lateran council of 1215 had ordered the keeping of free schools not only in the cathedrals but in other great churches which could bear the cost and, whether or not in response to this decree, we certainly do find grammar schools associated with some of the larger collegiate churches during the thirteenth and fourteenth centuries. In northern England they appear in the three great minsters of the diocese of York: Beverley, where the school had already existed in the twelfth century; Southwell, where it occurs in 1313; and Ripon, where it is mentioned in 1348.[2] In the south the royal collegiate chapel in Hastings Castle had canons responsible for teaching grammar and song in the twelfth century, while at Warwick, where the local school was given into the charge of the canons of St Mary's during Henry I's reign, the schoolmaster appears as an integral member of the college in the early fourteenth century.[3] That every collegiate church included a grammar school during this period is, however, unlikely and we should resist the temptation to infer its existence without explicit evidence.[4] In many of these churches the canons or prebendaries were not resident, and the vicars-choral engaged merely in their duties in the choir. Some colleges of great antiquity like Westbury-on-Trym and Wimborne Minster probably had no grammar school until these were provided by special benefactions in the second half of the fifteenth century. As for the colleges that did have schools in earlier times, references to the rent of the schoolhouse and the payment of fees show that these schools like those of

[1] *VCH Lincs.*, ii, 424-6.

[2] For Beverley see *EYS*, i, 80c-m; for Southwell, *Reg. Greenfield, York*, ed. W. Brown and A. Hamilton Thompson, vol iv (Surtees Society, clii, 1938), p. 137; and for Ripon, *EYS*, i, 141.

[3] For Hastings see *ECD*, pp. 68-9; for Warwick, ibid., pp. 58-9, 86-9, 272-7, and *VCH War.*, ii, 299-301.

[4] This was the assumption generally but incorrectly made by A. F. Leach, especially in *SME*, pp. 115, 166, a point to which A. G. Little drew attention in his review in *English Historical Review*, xxx (1915), pp. 525-9.

the cathedrals were not free, and that only the choristers, if such existed, were likely to have got their education for nothing.[1]

Next to be considered are the other early schools, those which we find in the English towns and villages of the twelfth and thirteenth centuries. It seems likely that these schools were at first very informal. A master sought out a town to which clerks resorted so that he might live by teaching them; clerks flocked to any place where a master was at work. The continuity of such schools must often have depended upon the uncertain coincidence of a number of factors. A succession of qualified masters had to be willing to work in a town where the demand for education was sufficient to give them a competent livelihood. It is possible to imagine many things which would have imperilled the existence of such schools: bad masters, public indifference, poverty or plague. At Oxford, where we are fairly well supplied with information, we know that local disturbances sent the scholars fleeing elsewhere on several occasions: to Cambridge and Reading in 1209, to Northampton and Salisbury in 1238 and again to Northampton in 1263. The last great migration, the Stamford one, occurred as late as 1334. Elsewhere many other migrations probably took place more silently, after the death or resignation of the master around whom the scholars had gathered.

Yet from their earliest days in the twelfth century, the English schools were also beginning to acquire privileges and possessions which facilitated their work and made their continuity much more certain. In this respect the early appearance of patrons claiming the right to appoint school-masters was important. It may have seemed irksome at first when some religious house or local lord attempted to exercise control over the masters who wished to teach in a particular place. But once the ecclesiastical councils of the twelfth century had established that no fees should be exacted for licensing schoolmasters, the presence of a patron could be an advantage. Here was an authority which could deal with rivals who imperilled the master's livelihood by drawing away his pupils, and which was at hand to replace the master when he retired or died. We do not know how much those who claimed the patronage of schools actually exerted themselves in appointing good schoolmasters, but it is likely that the king and the lay lords had this in mind when they granted control of schools to local religious houses. In the well-documented case of the abbey of St Albans, the importance of the patron is apparent. When the school of the town became vacant in the time of Abbot Richard (1097-1119), he invited

[1] Thus at Beverley fees are mentioned in 1312, but the choristers were to be taught grammar for nothing (*EYS*, i, 94-5; *ECD*, pp. 270-3).

a clerk named Geoffrey of Maine to come from France and teach it. Geoffrey was late in arriving and found when he did that the abbot had entrusted the school to another master, but he was promised the next vacancy and supported himself in the meanwhile by teaching in the neighbouring town of Dunstable.[1] Later in the century Alexander Neckham, afterwards to be a famous scholar, also taught the school at Dunstable until he was able to negotiate for appointment to St Albans with Abbot Warren (1183-95). This provided the abbot with the chance to make a witty reply: 'si bonus es, venias (if you are good, you may come); si Nequam, nequaquam (but if not, by no means)'![1]

Second in importance to the possession of a patron was the acquisition of facilities for the school to do its work. Already by the twelfth century the schools were beginning to attract benefactions: permanent buildings for their accommodation, exhibitions of food or money to support their scholars and even books for use in class. The list of such benefactions forms one of the most interesting themes of the history of education in the later middle ages, and indeed of the social history of the period as well. For the benefactors who helped to make the schools more stable and effective thereby demonstrated the growing interest of society in the work which the schools were doing. At first the gifts and legacies were small; in the twelfth and even the thirteenth centuries the amount of charity received by the schools was minimal compared with the lavish endowments being given to houses of monks and regular canons. But as the interest in monasticism declined, so that in the schools increased, and a time was to come when education replaced the monastic life as a major charitable preoccupation of the pious and the wealthy.

One of the most essential of a school's requirements was a permanent schoolhouse, and it was also one of the earliest forms of benefaction. At Derby the schoolhouse was the gift of Walkelin of Derby and his wife Goda, who gave their own dwelling-house between 1161 and 1182 to accommodate the scholars of Derby rent free, the hall being used for the school and the master and scholars living in the chambers.[2] At Bury St Edmunds Abbot Samson bought some stone buildings in the town before 1193 and gave them for the use of the schoolmaster, also without charge, so that the poor clerks who studied there might be relieved of the contributions they had previously paid towards renting the school.[3] At Wells it

[1] *Gesta Abbatum Monasterii Sancti Albani*, ed. H. T. Riley, vol i (Rolls Series, 1867), pp. 72-3, 196.
[2] *The Cartulary of Darley Abbey*, ed. R. R. Darlington (1945), i, 80-1.
[3] *Chronicle of Jocelin of Brakelond*, ed. Butler, p. 45; *VCH Suffolk*, ii, 307-8.

was one of the canons, Roger of Chewton, who in about 1235 conveyed houses in the city to the chancellor of the cathedral for the use of the school. They were to be let out to the schoolmaster, who had to pay the existing rent charges, keep the buildings in repair and lead his pupils every day before school broke up in a prayer for the souls of Roger and his parents.[1] Similarly at St Albans another clerk, Master Richard of Naundes, gave the schoolhouse in the 1280s on condition that the master should teach sixteen of the poorest scholars for nothing in lieu of rent.[2] Other schools were to acquire their buildings in similar ways during the fourteenth and fifteenth centuries.

For the scholars who gathered at these schools, often living away from home with inadequate resources, food was another basic preoccupation. 'We scholars of Lincoln', writes Thomas of Holland in 1222 to Master Ralph de Nevill, the newly appointed chancellor of England, 'never find venison for sale, nor does anyone give it to us. You, being established in great power and enjoying your lord's favour, could easily satisfy a friend in such a thing, and it would be glorious to me if, through your bounty, I could set something so rare on the table for my companions.'[3] Such gifts, if indeed they were made, must have been unusual, but in many places local arrangements were made for supplying poor scholars with at least their basic food. At Norwich Bishop Suffield who founded the hospital of St Giles in 1246 for the relief of the poor and sick provided that seven poor scholars should be chosen from Norwich school to receive board at the hospital during school terms, being changed for others when they had mastered their studies.[4] At Pontefract we hear in 1267 that the hospital of St Nicholas was bound to distribute forty loaves each week to the scholars of Pontefract school.[5] Similar doles were given out by hospitals at Bridgwater and Winchester.[6] They were also provided by monasteries. At Worcester in about 1290 the schoolmaster was entitled to claim a maundy of food each week from the prior for one of his clerks, in return for teaching the monks' relatives and others maintained by the priory out of charity.[7] At St Albans too it was recorded in about 1310 how certain abbots in the past had granted 28 loaves a week for distribution by

[1] *Historical MSS Commission, MSS of Wells Cathedral*, vol i (1907), p. 35.
[2] *ECD*, pp. 252-3; *VCH Herts.*, ii, 49-50.
[3] PRO, Ancient Correspondence, SC 1/6/13; W. H. Blaauw, 'Letters to Ralph de Nevill', *Sussex Archaeological Collections*, iii (1850), p. 38.
[4] *VCH Norfolk*, ii, 442-3.
[5] *EYS*, ii, 3-4.
[6] *Reg. Drokensford, Wells*, p. 268; *VCH Hants.*, ii, 255.
[7] Leach, *Early Education in Worcester* (Worcs. Historical Society, xxix, 1913), pp. 22-3.

G

the schoolmaster to his poor scholars.[1] Later still in 1342 Bishop Grandisson of Exeter, when carrying out reforms at Launceston Priory in Cornwall, ordered the monks to invite poor scholars apt for learning to partake of the daily refection in their hall.[2]

Alongside the mere distribution of food there soon developed the provision of regular exhibitions, either in the form of money or of board and lodging, which would bear a larger proportion of a scholar's expenses. In England during the thirteenth century widespread efforts were made by the episcopate to reserve for scholars the office of *aquebaiulus* or holy-water clerk in the parish church, which carried with it the duty of assisting in the parish services on Sundays and festivals in return for small emoluments, and left the rest of the week free for attendance at school. 'The benefice of holy water', observed the bishop of Exeter in 1287, 'was originally instituted so that poor clerks could be found to school from its profits.'[3] He was one of several diocesans who ordered that the office should be so employed, at least in the churches near to the schools of the cathedral city and the 'castles' of the diocese, meaning apparently the important towns possessing both castle and school.[4] That these commands were not without effect is shown by instances when bishops ordered them to be observed in particular churches. Thus in 1280 Archbishop Pecham arranged for two clerks in the parish church of Bakewell in Derbyshire to attend school on weekdays, and Bishop Hazleshaw of Bath and Wells made the same provision for the parish clerk of Kingsbury Episcopi in 1307.[5] Hazelshaw's successor, John Droxford, ordered the removal of the holy-water clerk of Chedzoy near Bridgwater in 1318 because he was not literate or tonsured, and installed another who was properly qualified.[6] The custom of giving the clerk's place to a scholar continued until at least the mid-fourteenth century. At Torksey in Lincolnshire the borough customs of about 1345 relate that the parishioners shall choose the clerk and find him to school with their alms.[7] In 1369 William Wykeham, bishop of Winchester, who had noticed that married men and men unschooled had recently been given the office of holy-water clerk in the churches once reserved for scholars, repeated the ordinance of one of his predecessors on the subject.[8] Despite this intervention, however,

---

[1] *ECD*, pp. 252-3. [2] *Reg. Grandisson, Exeter*, ii, 955.
[3] *Councils and Synods*, ii, 1026-7.
[4] Ibid., i, 174, 211, 309, 407, 514, 606, 713.
[5] Dugdale, *Monasticon*, vi, part 3, 1246; *Reg. Bekynton, Wells*, i, 82.
[6] *Reg. Drokensford, Wells*, p. 13.
[7] *Borough Customs*, ed. Mary Bateson, vol ii (Selden Society, xxi, 1906), p. 212.
[8] *Reg. Wykeham, Winchester*, ii, 75-6.

the tendency seems to have grown after 1400 for the office of clerk to become a long-term appointment, often held by older men, and it may be that the foundation of free schools and of other kinds of exhibitions came in time to make the original reservation for scholars unnecessary.[1]

The official measures taken to assist poor scholars were seconded by a number of private benefactions which also sought to provide deserving boys with adequate exhibitions. One of the earliest was that of Master Simon of Farlington, archdeacon of Durham during the reign of King John, who purchased the manor of Kyo near Durham and conveyed it to the cathedral priory there for the support of three scholars of Durham school. They were to be chosen by the schoolmaster each day and sent to the almoner who was bound to provide them with food, drink and beds in the almonry house. Unfortunately, however, the archdeacon died before the conveyance had been completed, and his brother Henry not only entered upon the property but granted it in 1226 for quite different purposes of charity to the hospital of the Trinity at Gateshead. A satisfactory compromise was at length arranged by Bishop Poore of Durham (1228-37), so that the hospital retained the manor but agreed to pay half the income to the three scholars in the cathedral almonry, and this amounted to 40s. a year.[2]

At Carlisle exhibitions for poor scholars were provided by Ralph Ireton, bishop from 1280 until 1292, out of the wealthy rectory of Dalston which lay near his palace, Rose Castle, four and a half miles south of the cathedral city. By an ordinance of 1285 he divided the rectory into three portions: one for the vicar of the parish, the second for the archdeacon and the third for the maintenance of twelve poor scholars chosen by the bishop and studying in the city of Carlisle. The new arrangements came into effect, and in 1291 the scholars were receiving £16 a year out of the rectory. But then came disaster. The bishop died in March 1292 and the king, who had the right of filling vacant benefices while the see was unoccupied, immediately tried to appoint one of his clerks to the rectory of Dalston which he supposed to be vacant. It then became clear that a division of the benefice had been made without the necessary royal approval, and the king overruled it. He ordered his nominee to be given possession and the other parties including the scholars lost their rights. Bishop

[1] See the examples in Heath, *The English Parish Clergy on the Eve of the Reformation*, pp. 19-20.
[2] *ECD*, pp. 124-7. The date of *c.* 1190 there suggested for the original benefaction is almost certainly too early.

Ireton's benefaction thus came to nothing, but that does not destroy the originality of his scheme, which was unusual for the time and gives him an honourable niche in the history of the period.[1]

When we reach the fourteenth century the provision of exhibitions for poor scholars increases in both number and scale, as more great men divert their wealth to promote the study of grammar and to assist those engaged upon it. One of the most successful foundations of this period was made at Exeter by another bishop, John Grandisson, who tells us however that he was merely putting into effect the intentions of his predecessor, Walter Stapledon, who ruled from 1308 to 1326. Stapledon is best remembered as the founder in 1314 of Exeter College, Oxford, to accommodate thirteen scholars from Devon and Cornwall reading the university arts course. After he had founded a house for educating scholars in logic at Oxford, says Grandisson,

> he diligently fixed the affection of his heart towards the support of boys studying grammar and being educated in life and morals, and therefore he acquired three acres of glebe in the village of Yarnscombe in our diocese and the advowson of the church, and obtained a special licence to appropriate the same to the master and brethren of the hospital of St John the Baptist within the east gate of the city of Exeter for the support of boys studying and being instructed as aforesaid.

But in 1326, during the disturbances which followed the overthrow of Edward II, the good bishop lost his life at the hands of a London mob, and it was left to his successor to complete the foundation he had planned. As arranged by Grandisson in 1332 there were to be not more than twelve scholars. The master of the city grammar school of Exeter was to choose up to two candidates from each of the four archdeaconries of the diocese, of whom one or two were to be taken if possible from Yarnscombe itself, where the endowments of the exhibitions lay. Three were to be nominated by the dean and chapter of Exeter from among the choristers whose voices had broken, and one by the Columbers family, lords of Yarnscombe. They were to be accommodated for five years in the hospital of St John and provided with lodging, straw for their beds, pottage and 5d. a week apiece to buy extra food. They had a tutor (*sciolus*) to watch over them, who was to be a priest if such could be found, but though he taught them manners and helped with their grammar,

---

[1] J. Wilson, 'Peculiar ordination of a Cumberland benefice', *Scottish Historical Review*, v (1907-8), pp. 297-303; *Taxatio Ecclesiastica* (Record Commission, 1802), pp. 318-19; *CCR 1288-96*, pp. 263-4.

their formal education was had at the city grammar school under the general schoolmaster. The foundation was to have a long life of over 200 years before disappearing at the Reformation.[1]

Exhibitions were also founded at Lincoln cathedral. There in 1347 Sir Bartholomew Burghersh endowed a chantry in the chapel of St Katherine for five priests to pray by the tombs of his father and brother. Finding that the generous endowment produced a surplus of £10 beyond what was needed to support the priests, the dean and chapter decided in 1349 to add six boys to the foundation. They were to be aged eight or thereabouts when admitted, knowing their Donatus or elementary grammar, and able to sing. They were to remain for eight years, to be removed at sixteen, and to proceed in due course to the priesthood. They got board, lodging, clothing and received their education at the city grammar school. In return they assisted in the services of the chantry and read to the chaplains at meals. The success of the Burghersh scholarships led John Buckingham, bishop of Lincoln, to institute a similar scheme of his own in 1388. He founded the Buckingham chantry in the cathedral for two priests and two clerks, the latter being boys between the ages of seven and sixteen, whose life and duties imitated those of the Burghersh scholars in almost every respect. The Buckingham funds diminished as time went on, and in 1489 the two clerks were reduced to one. Otherwise both foundations continued to support their scholars, who even survived the Reformation which swept away the chantries themselves.[2]

The last of the fourteenth-century exhibitions which we shall notice is also the most curious. The 'college' of Bredgar near Sittingbourne in Kent was founded in 1392 by a group of local clerks and laymen led by Master Robert Bredgar, for a chaplain and two scholars. The chaplain was only a chantry priest and did not teach; the scholars were admitted at 7 years old, one of them being chosen from the founder's kin and the other from the three local parishes where lay the college lands. They were to pass their time in the study of 'reading, song, grammar and the other liberal sciences', which may have meant going away if Bredgar had no school. When the scholars had acquired a reasonable facility in composing and construing their grammar, they were allowed to assist the chaplain in saying the divine office. They were then permitted to finish their studies by going to university, provided they did not hold their scholarships after

[1] For Stapeldon's biography see *BRUO*, iii, 1764-5, and the introduction to *Reg. Stapeldon, Exeter*. The ordinance of 1332 is in *Reg. Grandisson, Exeter*, ii, 666-9.
[2] *VCH Lincs.*, ii, 427-9.

the age of twenty-five. The registers of the archbishops of Canterbury, which record the institutions and resignations of the scholars, also show them going on to take priests' orders and settling down as the incumbents of neighbouring parish churches. Bredgar thus provides an unusual example of scholarships based in the countryside rather than at one of the major centres of learning.[1]

All the foundations which we have rehearsed did something to subsidize the costs of education, and thereby helped to bring it within the reach of more of the poor and deserving. They concentrated upon relieving the day-to-day expenses of food and lodging because, in an age when it was still common for scholars to seek their education far from home, the cost of bed and board at 8d. a week was a far greater burden to bear than the comparatively small fees of 4d. and 8d. a quarter usually charged by schoolmasters. Perhaps for this reason the earliest benefactors of education gave little attention to subsidizing the cost of tuition itself. One of the few places where this was done was at Bury St Edmunds, where in 1193 Abbot Samson, who had already provided the town with a schoolhouse, arranged for an annual pension of £2 to be paid to the schoolmaster of Bury out of the church of Wetherden. The master could not of course live on this sum alone, but subsequently he seems to have been expected to teach forty poor clerks for nothing on account of the endowment.[2] A similar arrangement has already been noticed at St Albans, where sixteen poor scholars received a free education after the 1280s.[3]

The complete endowment of a schoolmaster to teach grammar for nothing was also achieved during the thirteenth century, in a form which was to be widely imitated during later times. The first free schools were associated with the new fashion for founding colleges of secular clergy, which itself requires some explanation. As the thirteenth century wore on, interest in establishing houses of monks, friars and nuns began gradually to diminish; indeed after 1300 it practically ceased. Instead the endowment of new houses of secular clergy came into vogue. Some were university colleges, designed to maintain their members in the study of arts or theology. Others lay in the country and were staffed by chantry priests who sang the divine office each day and celebrated masses for the souls of the founder and his relatives. Both kinds of college frequently maintained

---

[1] For the history of Bredgar College see *VCH Kent*, ii, 230. The statutes are in *Literae Cantuarienses*, ed. J. B. Sheppard, vol iii (Rolls Series, 1889), pp. 15-21. See also *Reg. Chichele, Canterbury*, vol iv, index, sub Bredgar.
[2] *The Chronicle of Jocelin of Brakelond*, ed. Butler, p. 95; *VCH Suffolk*, ii, 308, 312.
[3] *VCH Herts.*, ii, 49-50.

boys and clerks either out of charity or to assist in the daily services, and arrangements had then to be made for schooling them.[1]

The first collegiate foundation which both included a number of boy scholars and provided a master to teach them appears to have been Merton College, Oxford, founded by Walter of Merton, chancellor of England, in 1264. His college was chiefly intended as an academic community of university scholars who had taken their BA and wanted to continue studying for the higher degrees in arts, theology or law. But the founder's statutes of 1270 also included provision for the education of up to thirteen of his relatives, who would be boys studying grammar, with a status lower than undergraduates, and the college was to maintain a grammar master to teach them, to whom even the fellows were urged to go 'without a blush' to improve their knowledge. By the 1270s the college was also maintaining twelve poor 'secondary scholars', a benefaction apparently intended by Richard earl of Cornwall, king of the Romans, but put into effect by Merton himself. They too appear to have been boys learning grammar rather than undergraduates. But the grammatical side of the college did not flourish. The secondaries vanished away after the middle of the fourteenth century, and the boys of founder's kin were sent out to a professional master in the town rather than having one of their own. They themselves disappear from the records after 1460.[2]

The provision for grammar boys at Merton was imitated at some other of the early university colleges: Peterhouse and Clare in Cambridge, and most notably at the Queen's College, Oxford, founded in 1341 by Robert of Eglesfield, chaplain to the queen of Edward III. His foundation provided not only for an academic establishment of a provost and twelve fellows, but for a large group of poor boys, 'rather less in number than twice that of the fellows', and in any case not more than seventy-two of them. They were to be selected from the places where the college had property at the age of fourteen or less. They were to be instructed in plainsong and grammar, before going on to the undergraduate studies of logic and the rest of the arts course. Two clerks were to be retained to teach them song, and a grammarian and an artist for the other subjects. They were thus intended to begin as schoolboys and to end as undergraduates. But as Dr A. B. Cobban has pointed out, in no case did the study of grammar in these early colleges ever develop to a significant

[1] On the development of the secular colleges see Thompson, *The English Clergy and their Organization*, pp. 132-60.
[2] *The Early Rolls of Merton College*, ed. J. R. L. Highfield (Oxford Historical Society, new series, xviii, 1964), pp. 69-73.

extent; it remained a project rather than a reality, a low priority stillborn through inadequate resources. At Queen's, for example, the number of boys was never large – there were only four in 1415 – and they went outside the college for their instruction, their schoolmaster being the famous grammarian John Leland in the early fifteenth century.[1]

Much more successful was the college school founded by John Grandisson, bishop of Exeter, at Ottery St Mary in Devon in 1338. Born in Herefordshire in 1292 of an important family of Swiss origin, he studied at Oxford and Paris before commencing his long episcopate at Exeter which lasted from 1327 until his death in 1369.[2] As well as being an indefatigable administrator and a notable benefactor of his large and remote diocese, he displayed an interest in schools unusual for the time. We have already seen how in 1332 he put into execution Walter Stapledon's benefaction for the scholars of Exeter; how in 1342 he arranged for the feeding of poor scholars at Launceston Priory; and how in 1357 he issued general instructions for the schoolmasters of his diocese.[3] It is therefore less surprising that the secular college which he founded himself should have included a grammar school when such an addition was still uncommon. The college of Ottery St Mary was founded in 1338 for eight canons, eleven priests and chaplains, twelve clerks and eight choristers, and to this extent was no different except in size from the many other chantry colleges of the period. Where it differed was in the addition of a grammar master to teach the choristers at a salary of 2 marks, 'besides the emoluments of the school'. This suggests that the master, while primarily intended for the benefit of the inmates of the college, was also envisaged as teaching outsiders for money. Certainly this was the eventual outcome; the college supported a succession of schoolmasters, and when dissolved by Henry VIII in 1545, the king established a new grammar school to fill the place of the old.[4]

The next collegiate foundation of this period to have included a grammar school appears to have been Cobham in Kent, established by John Lord Cobham in 1362 for a master and five chaplains; clerks and choristers being added later. Whether one of the chaplains was originally intended to teach grammar is not certain, but in 1383 work was carried

[1] A. B. Cobban, *The King's Hall, Cambridge* (1969), pp. 50-2; J. R. Magrath, *The Queen's College, Oxford* (1921), i, 45-9, 141-2.
[2] For Grandisson's biography see *BRUO*, ii, 800-1, and the introduction to the third volume of *Reg. Grandisson, Exeter*.
[3] See above, pp. 182, 180, 143 respectively.
[4] For the statutes of Ottery see J. N. Dalton, *The Collegiate Church of Ottery St Mary* (1917), especially pp. 93, 98 and 100.

out on 'the college and schoolhouse of Cobham' and in 1389 the bishop of Rochester, sanctioning the addition of two clerks to the foundation, ordered that they study letters 'in the school with the other scholars in so far as they are able'.[1]

These early attempts at endowing grammar schools are interesting, but they pale into insignificance before William Wykeham's great foundation of Winchester College. Here for the first time arose an endowed school not only greater than any hitherto attempted, but of a size, wealth and importance able to stand comparison with any of the other ecclesiastical foundations of the century, academic or devotional. The founder, who was born in 1328 and died in 1404, rose from comparatively humble origins to become bishop of Winchester and chancellor of England, his lifetime of service to the crown and his enjoyment of high preferment enabling him to amass a considerable fortune.[2] This he expended in founding the two great colleges at Winchester and Oxford, but whereas his New College at Oxford had at least been preceded by Merton, Queen's and the other colleges already established there, nothing quite like Winchester had yet been planned anywhere. Like Ottery and Cobham it was partly a secular college for the celebration of the divine office by a warden and ten fellows all in priest's orders. But the study of grammar, instead of being merely incidental to the life of the community, at Winchester became its main purpose. There were to be seventy scholars of grammar under a master and usher – far more than any previous founder had conceived, except perhaps for Robert of Eglesfield in his wilder dreams. They were to be aged between eight and twelve at their first admission, competent in reading, song and the grammar of Donatus, and were to stay in the college until qualified to proceed to university, but not beyond the age of eighteen. In due course they could go on to the sister college at Oxford, which had the same complement of seventy scholars, there to read the arts course, to graduate and at last to enter the ranks of the clergy.

Winchester College was not open to the public at large. Apart from the scholars, a small number of commoners were to be admitted, sons of friends of the college who paid for themselves, but it was not intended to offer education to anyone else, either freely or for fees. The scholarships

---

[1] P. J. Tester, 'Notes on the medieval chantry college at Cobham', *Archaeologia Cantiana*, lxxix (1964), p. 119; J. Thorpe, *Registrum Roffense* (1769), p. 237. Leach (*SME*, p. 203) declares that the original foundation of Cobham included a grammar master, but I have been unable to trace his source.

[2] For Wykeham's biography see G. H. Moberly, *Life of William of Wykeham*, 2nd ed. (1893).

G*

themselves were confined to carefully specified classes of people. The first preference was to be given to the founder's relatives and their descendants, and the second to the inhabitants of the places where the lands of the two colleges were situated. Next came candidates from ten counties in a given order, which were chiefly those containing the college lands, and last of all, if there were any places left, came the inhabitants of the rest of England. We have met similar restrictions in the scholarships at Bredgar, Exeter, and the Queen's College, Oxford, and far from being quaint or eccentric they reflect the obligations of family and lordship which formed the main strength of medieval society. The founder's chief obligation was to his family, the more so because he had diverted to the college the wealth which they might have expected to inherit. Likewise, as a landlord exacting rents and services from its tenants, the college had equal responsibilities to them as their lord: to protect and patronize them, and in consequence to give their children priority of admission to its scholarships. Moreover, this method of selecting candidates was amply vindicated by its success. It gave the best education that the times could afford to large numbers of children who might otherwise have attended country grammar schools with poorer facilities, or else no school at all. The majority of them passed through Winchester, crowded the lecture rooms of Oxford, mastered its studies and went on to occupy some of the highest offices and the best benefices in the land. Seven of those who entered Winchester before 1500 became diocesan bishops, and a further three became archbishops: Henry Chicheley and William Warham at Canterbury, and Hugh Ing at Dublin.[1]

Yet although Winchester attained lasting eminence as one of the greatest English schools, it was too ambitious and expensive a project to find many imitators. It took the resources of a king or a cardinal to equal Winchester, and by the Reformation only two other such foundations had been made: that of Henry VI at Eton in 1440 and that of Thomas Wolsey at Ipswich in 1528. The archetype of the endowed schools of later times was not so much Winchester as a humbler foundation contemporary with it. This was the free grammar school of Wotton-under-Edge in

---

[1] For the foundation charter (1382) and the statutes (1400) of Winchester, see Kirby, *Annals of Winchester College*. Lists of wardens, fellows and scholars are given in the same author's *Winchester Scholars*. For the history of the college see Kirby's *Annals*, Leach's *History of Winchester College*, and his article in *VCH Hants.*, ii, 261ff.

The Wykehamist bishops were Thomas Beckington (Wells), Thomas Jane (Norwich), John Kingscote (Carlisle), William Knight (Wells), Richard Mayhew (Hereford), John Russell (Lincoln) and Robert Sherborne (Chichester). In addition Hugh Pavy (St Davids) may have been a commoner. For their biographies see *BRUO*, *passim*.

Gloucestershire, founded by Lady Katherine Berkeley in June 1384, less than two years after the publication of Wykeham's charter for Winchester. The foundress was the widow of twenty years' standing of a previous Lord Berkeley and Wotton was her dower residence, but though her retirement there may have given her time to reflect on the usefulness of such a charity, it is unlikely to have been simply a personal inspiration, or a new idea suggested suddenly by the foundation of Winchester. The Berkeleys were great patrons of religion and even of scholarship, and a few years later Katherine's stepson, the reigning Lord Berkeley, was to employ John Trevisa to translate into English the two standard Latin works by Englishmen on history and science. Moreover, Wotton had possessed a grammar school as far back as the end of the thirteenth century, and in 1347, nearly two years after Katherine's marriage into the Berkeley family, an attempt, which apparently failed, had been made to establish a free school in the borough. Whatever Wykeham's influence, the school at Wotton, as might be expected of so contemporaneous a foundation, had also some independent origins.[1]

The school had some resemblances to Winchester, on the smaller scale dictated by less ambitious plans and smaller resources. The foundation supported a schoolmaster and only two poor scholars receiving free board, lodging and education. The master, who was to be in priest's orders, had two functions. He was to sing daily masses for the souls of the foundress and her relatives, and to teach grammar gratis to the two scholars and to anyone else who should come to him. Of these two offices the educational was intended to take precedence over the liturgical, and the official title of the foundation was the 'House of Scholars of Wotton'. The offer of free instruction to all comers was a novel departure from Winchester, but an example to be widely followed in later times. Indeed Wotton includes most of the basic features of the smaller endowed schools which were founded from then until the 1510s. It supports a master who is also a chantry priest, it is dedicated to providing free education to outsiders rather than boarding its own foundationers, and its connections are with the immediate locality which it serves, rather than with a larger area as at Winchester and Eton. With the foundation of Wotton and Winchester in the 1380s the formative period of the endowed grammar schools is over. Two kinds of institutions have now appeared.

[1] On Wotton and the previous history of its school see E. S. Lindley, *Wotton under Edge* (1962), especially, p. 224, and *CPR 1348-50*, p. 268. For the Berkeley family see J. Smyth, *The Lives of the Berkeleys*, ed. Sir J. Maclean, 3 vols (1883-5), and on Lady Katherine in particular, i, 346-7. Extracts from the foundation statutes of Wotton (1384) are printed in *ECD*, pp. 330-41.

There is the college school, maintained by some but not all of the secular colleges incidentally to their other activities, and there is the chantry school, a small foundation centred around a single priest-schoolmaster. In the following centuries it remains only to increase and multiply these institutions.

We can now review the extent of the facilities for education in fourteenth-century England at the time that all these new foundations were taking effect. The foremost schools of the day were undoubtedly those of Oxford, where scholars flocked to learn grammar and the techniques of business, quite apart from the undergraduates properly speaking who came to read the arts course. The university authorities claimed jurisdiction over the grammar schools and their scholars, and gave much time to supervising them. Masters, whether graduates or not, had to be admitted to teach by the chancellor, and by 1306 two regent masters of arts were being appointed for a year at a time to supervise the grammar schools. University statutes which regulated the conduct of the schools and gave advice on teaching methods suggest that several masters were usually working at one and the same time. Although there was something of a decline in the standard of teaching during the fourteenth century, the Oxford masters in general enjoyed a high reputation, and two of them – John Cornwall (*fl.* 1344-9) and John Leland (d. 1433) – exercised considerable influence over the members of their profession elsewhere.[1]

The evidence for the other towns and cities is much as it was in the thirteenth century. London continued to possess its three ancient schools, and there are indications that other masters were also at work there.[2] Grammar schools are mentioned in all but three of the other cathedral cities,[3] and, depending on their accidental appearance in record sources, in a selection of the other important towns. But there are considerably more traces than hitherto of schools in the smaller country towns, though as before it is hard to say whether this represents a real increase over the previous century or is merely related to more plentiful source materials. To take only one area as an example, in the three north-eastern counties of Lincoln, Nottingham and York, some thirty-three schools can be traced at one time or another during the fourteenth century, compared with only thirteen in the previous 100 years. Twenty-five of these are specifically

---

[1] On the fourteenth-century Oxford schools and their masters see Hunt in *Studies Presented to Daniel Callus!* pp. 163-93, *VCH Oxon.*, iii, 40-3, and also above p. 95.

[2] e.g. in 1392 Richard Exton appears teaching a grammar school near the Crutched Friars (*Calendar of Plea and Memoranda Rolls of London 1381-1412*, ed. A. H. Thomas (1932), p. 182).

[3] In all, that is, except Durham, Ely and Rochester.

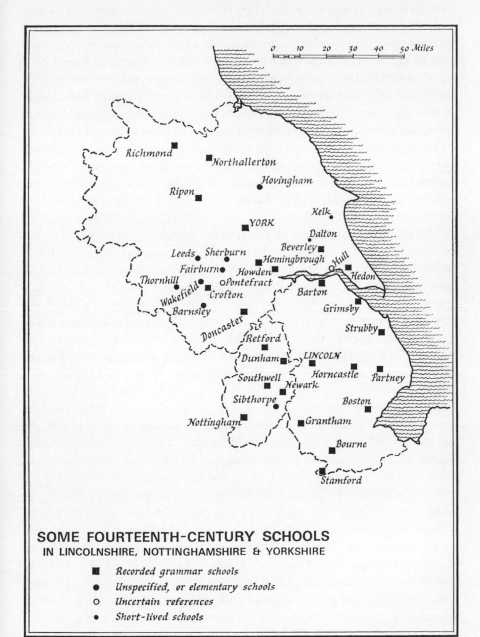

SOME FOURTEENTH-CENTURY SCHOOLS
IN LINCOLNSHIRE, NOTTINGHAMSHIRE & YORKSHIRE

- ■ *Recorded grammar schools*
- ● *Unspecified, or elementary schools*
- ○ *Uncertain references*
- • *Short-lived schools*

described as grammar schools.[1] They occur not only in the county towns, cathedral cities, and most of the other local centres, but also in several villages, and are particularly evident in Nottinghamshire and the southern part of the West Riding. The records are still too sparse to reveal how many of these schools were open in any single year, and perhaps in some cases they were only short-lived. But some had certainly established their permanence beyond doubt, and successive references suggest that an intending schoolboy in Holderness could have gone either to Hedon or to Beverley at any time during the fourteenth century, just as his counterpart in Nottinghamshire could probably have chosen between Newark, Nottingham and Southwell. This region of the country is in no sense unique, and close study will probably reveal similar numbers of schools in other areas.

The history of education in the fourteenth century in so far as it has been recorded was almost entirely one of progress: of new schools appearing and new benefactions of all kinds. The apathy and hostility to learning which it is reasonable to suppose also existed has left few traces. Yet such traces there are, and they are particularly evident in the last thirty years of the century: an age which, vexed with unpopular governments, social unrest and anticlericalism, saw unusual strains and turmoils in English society. Even education did not entirely escape the strife and cynicism of the times. In the Peasants' Revolt of 1381 Thomas Walsingham, the chronicler of St Albans, would have us believe that the rebels forced schoolmasters to swear to give up teaching children grammar.[2] At Cambridge the rising was accompanied by an attack on the university archives. A bonfire of documents was made in the market square and an old woman named Margery Starre tossed the ashes to the winds, crying 'Away with the learning of the clerks, away with it!'[3]

The defenders of the established order could be equally hostile to education for social reasons if they thought it allowed the children of villeins and others of ignoble birth to rise in the Church to wealth and power above their station. In the parliament of 1391 the Commons, themselves gentry and prosperous burgesses, petitioned the king to forbid 'neifs' or villeins from putting their children to school 'to advance them by clergy, and this in maintenance and saving of the honour of all freemen of the realm'.[4] The king however returned a non-committal

[1] See the map on p. 191.
[2] *Chronicon Angliae*, ed. E. M. Thompson (Rolls Series, 1874), p. 308.
[3] *VCH Cambs.*, iii, 11.
[4] *Rotuli Parliamentorum*, iii, 294.

answer and nothing was done. This kind of prejudice against the rise of the low-born through education seems to have been quite widespread. It was not merely a defensive gesture by the governing class, for it was held equally by radical critics of society who all upheld the traditional social order and denounced breaches in it. The author of *Pierce the Ploughmans Crede*, a violent piece of anticlericalism composed in the 1390s, attacked it with great bitterness:

> Now mot ich soutere his sone setten to schole,
> And ich a beggers brol on the booke lerne,
> And worth to a writere and with a lorde dwelle,
> Other falsly to a frere the fend for to serven!
> So of that beggers brol a bychop schal worthen,
> Among the peres of the lond prese to sitten.[1]

Even in the fifteenth century there is more than one example of a family being disparaged by its enemies for having allegedly risen from lowly birth to wealth and rank by means of education. The Pastons of Norfolk and the Hodys of Somerset were both victims of such slanders.[2] But it would only be proper to end on a more hopeful note. Education may have encountered prejudice, but in the end it was the support it attracted that prevailed: the patronage of Grandisson, the wealth of Wykeham and the more modest contributions of so many others. And in that most popular of poems, *Piers Plowman*, the relief of poor scholars takes its place with the other worthy charities which drive devils from the deathbed and give the soul easy passage to the joy of the saints.[3]

[1] *Pierce the Ploughmans Crede*, ed. W. W. Skeat (EETS, 1867), lines 744-9. Compare *Piers Plowman*, ed. Skeat (1886), vol i: C text passus vi, lines 63-7.
[2] *Paston Letters and Papers of the Fifteenth Century*, ed. Davis, vol i, pp. xli-ii; H. C. Maxwell-Lyte, 'The Hody Family', *Somerset and Dorset Notes and Queries*, xviii (1925), pp. 127-9.
[3] Langland, *Piers Plowman*, ed. Skeat, vol i: A text passus viii, 28-34; B text passus vii, 26-31; C text passus x, 30-5.

Chapter Seven

The schools from 1400 to 1530

The fourteenth century had seen the origin of the endowed schools; in the fifteenth they became at last a widespread and popular form of charity. It is here, and not in the age of the Reformation, that the great movement really begins by which during five centuries hundreds of private benefactors founded hundreds of endowed schools all over England, and thus effected one of the principal achievements of English civilization. It is no longer necessary or possible to give individual attention to all the new schools as they appear; henceforth they form a class of their own, whose general characteristics we shall now attempt to distinguish one by one.

As in the fourteenth century, many of the new grammar schools formed part of larger colleges of secular priests, the foundation of which continued to be popular among the great. Their purpose was still principally devotional rather than educational – the endowment of priests to sing the divine office and celebrate the mass – but it became increasingly common for the foundation to include masters of grammar and song. Sometimes these masters were intended merely for the benefit of the clerks and choristers on the foundation. Thus at Fotheringhay in Northamptonshire, Edward duke of York erected in 1411 a large college for a master, twelve chaplains, eight clerks and thirteen choristers. The statutes, which date from about 1415, order one of the chaplains to teach grammar to the choristers and one of the clerks to train them in song, an arrangement that was still in force when the college was dissolved in 1548.[1] In other places

[1] A. Hamilton Thompson, 'The statutes of the collegiate church of Fotheringhay', *Archaeological Journal*, 2nd series, xxv (1918), especially, p. 272. For the history of the college and school see *VCH Northants.*, ii, 223-4, and *ESR*, part 2, pp. 153-4.

however the grammar master was also available to teach boys from outside, as at Tong in Shropshire, where a college was founded in 1410 by Isabel, the widow of Sir Fulk Pembridge, lord of a number of manors in Shropshire, Staffordshire and elsewhere. The statutes which she issued in 1411 provided for an establishment of five chaplains, two clerks, thirteen poor and a grammar school. Once more the teaching of grammar was entrusted to one of the chaplains, but here he instructed not only the ministers of the college but other poor youths of the place or from the neighbouring villages.[1]

The foundation of colleges with grammar schools, some private and some public, continued throughout the fifteenth century and well into the sixteenth; indeed as late as the early 1540s Henry VIII was establishing secular colleges at Thornton and Burton-on-Trent, both of which included grammar schools.[2] But if schools in colleges become increasingly common, they were never universal. Some founders continued to provide merely for the divine office; others who were preoccupied with poverty rather than education added an almshouse to the college instead of a school. In such places clerks or choristers in need of instruction may have been sent away for it, as at Mettingham College in Suffolk, two of whose clerks were taught by the schoolmaster of the nearby town of Beccles in 1403-4.[3]

In any case only a minority of the new schools were those in the colleges. Few save the most wealthy had the resources to endow whole communities of clerks and chaplains, and most of the interest in education in the fifteenth century found expression in the cheaper and more modest foundation of chantry schools like that which we have already noticed at Wotton in 1384. The association of chantries and schools may require some explanation. Education was a growing interest of the age, but it was still eclipsed by the popularity of the mass, that most supreme of all rites, the sacrifice of Christ's body at which efficacious intercessions might be made for the health of the living and the relief of the dead. The founder of the school thus stood to gain spiritual benefits of a powerful and effective kind if he made the master a priest whose daily masses would include perpetual intercessions for his soul. How the duty of saying mass and the canonical hours was adapted to the demands of the school timetable is hard to say; still, the best testimony to the success of the combination of school and chantry is the large number of such foundations made during the fifteenth century, many by men of great learning and experience.

[1] *CPR 1408-13*, p. 280; Dugdale, *Monasticon*, vi, part 3, 1401, 1407.
[2] On these schools see below, p. 267.
[3] *VCH Suffolk*, ii, 337.

Indeed, it is curious how not only the schoolmasters of chantries but also those maintained by guilds and monasteries were almost always expected to be priests and given liturgical duties to perform. Hardly anyone seems to have thought of founding a mere school whose master would be simply a schoolmaster.[1] It was not until the early years of Henry VIII's reign that the association of schools and chantries began to go out of fashion. As we have already noticed, the founders of schools like Nottingham (1513), Winchcombe (1521) and Manchester (1525) made no provision for a chantry.[2] They seem to have regarded the foundation of a school as an end in itself, and were content to have prayers recited for their souls by the pupils in class, rather than offered by a priest in the canon of the mass; consequently the mastership of these schools was thrown open to priests or laymen indifferently. The fashion gradually spread, and in 1548 the association of schools and chantries was finally broken with the forcible dissolution of the latter by the Protestant government of Edward VI.

Most of the chantry schools provided free education to all comers, rather than giving exhibitions of board and lodging. Some however charged fees. This was the case at Newland in Gloucestershire, founded by Joan the widow of Robert Greyndour in 1445. The chantry priest received £12 a year, out of which he had to pay a clerk, and was also allowed to take fees at the rate of 4d. from those learning the abc and psalter, and 8d. from the grammarians.[3] Other founders reckoned to provide free education merely for the poor, Thus Richard Felaw, merchant of Ipswich, who endowed the school there in 1483, envisaged the master as teaching freely only the children of those with lands and tenements worth less than 20s. a year, or whose goods were under the value of £20.[4] Similarly at Liverpool John Crosse, a prosperous London rector, gave lands in 1515 to support a priest 'to keep a grammar school and take his advantage from all the children except those whose names be Crosse, and poor children that have no succour'.[5] Other such examples are not uncommon.

The first of the chantry schools, as we have seen, was probably Wotton-under-Edge in 1384, but in the decades immediately following, the number of similar foundations was not large. It has been overestimated, because of the belief that any chantry founded in the fourteenth or fifteenth century whose incumbent appears teaching a school at the survey of chantries in 1548 must necessarily have been founded for that purpose.

---

[1] For an exception see above, p. 155. [2] See above, p. 156.
[3] *Reg. Spofford, Hereford*, p. 282. [4] *VCH Suffolk*, ii, 327. [5] *VCH Lancs.*, ii, 593.

In fact, the teaching of grammar in many chantries was a later innovation by the patron or the incumbent, which frequently took place only in the early sixteenth century. Even when in 1548 witnesses insist that a chantry was founded to include a free school it is not always safe to believe them. They could be misinformed as well as dishonest, and in 1548 there were great incentives to prove chantries schools and thereby secure their continuance. Unless there is early evidence that a chantry was founded as a school or came to include one, it will be wise not to anticipate the existence of schools which are first recorded in 1548. Consequently, until the educational history of every English county has been thoroughly investigated, the precise rate at which new foundations were made must remain uncertain. But it seems to have been small until the 1440s, most decades apparently producing only two or three new schools. It was in 1440 that Henry VI marked his arrival at manhood by taking the first steps towards the setting up of Eton College, and the king's enthusiasm for education, which certainly spread to his councillors, may well have excited wider imitation. At least thirteen schools were endowed between 1430 and 1450, after which the impetus weakened for a time, perhaps because of the civil disorders which darkened the closing years of Henry's reign. There seems however to have been a steady revival of interest during the last third of the century, and by the early 1500s the number of new foundations had reached a dozen a decade, rising to over two dozen in the 1520s.

Who could afford to endow these schools? While those in the colleges were almost entirely due to prelates and wealthy lay magnates, the cost of founding a chantry school (or even a school alone) was comparatively small, and came within the resources of a much larger range of people. In the first place it involved the purchase or setting aside of as much land or rent as would secure an annual income of £10, which was the maximum salary normally enjoyed by schoolmasters before the Reformation. This, at twenty times the annual income (the usual purchase price), would cost £200. Then there was the fee for securing the king's licence to amortize the property, that is, to grant it for perpetual ecclesiastical use. This came to £20 in the case of Wotton in 1384, and £35 in that of Newland in 1445.[1] Lastly a curtilage and dwelling-house for the chantry priest with accommodation for the school as well would add at least another £20 or £30. The endowment of a chantry school cost more than that of a mere chantry, whose priests were usually paid less, but in turn it was probably less expensive than that of an almshouse or hospital where a number of souls

[1] *CPR 1381-5*, pp. 413-14; *CPR 1441-6*, p. 388.

had to be maintained.[1] The founders of schools in the fifteenth and sixteenth centuries therefore ranged from the king through bishops and lords down to the more affluent clergy, gentlemen and burgesses. Beyond them, as we shall see, groups of townspeople and yeomen of lowlier degree were also involved through managing such guilds and parish chantries as came to support schools. These founders we shall now review in order, pausing to admire some of their works, and beginning with the king.

Henry VI was not the first English monarch to interest himself in education, for Edward II had endowed the King's Hall in Cambridge and Henry V had projected a college at Oxford, but none of his predecessors seems to have got as far as founding a public grammar school. Henry was still only eighteen when he began the foundation of Eton College in the summer of 1440, choosing a site just half a mile away from Windsor, his birthplace and residence, from whose very walls he would be able to witness the building of his college and watch over it when it was finished. As planned in the foundation charter of 11 October 1440, Eton was to be a secular college with school and almshouse attached, similar to many other foundations which the great magnates of the kingdom had made and were making. There were to be a provost, ten fellows, four clerks and six choristers to undertake the divine office, an almshouse for twenty-five poor men, and twenty-five poor scholars receiving board and lodging with a master to instruct them.[2] The schoolmaster was also to teach grammar for nothing to anyone else who came to him, and since in 1446 Henry prohibited other schools within ten miles of Eton, it is clear that he intended his school to serve the locality, as well as the counties where it held lands after the manner of Winchester.[3] In the following February, 1441, the king issued a foundation charter for a college at Cambridge to be called the King's College of St Nicholas, for a rector and twelve scholars, no explicit connection with Eton being stated.[4] Henry's two colleges were at first modestly conceived, and fell somewhat short of Wykeham's great double foundation, having much more in common with the collegiate churches and university colleges of the earlier fifteenth century.

Henry's ambitions however grew with the years that followed. He

[1] Winchcombe school (Gloucs.) in 1521 was in fact founded from an endowment intended, but insufficient, for an almshouse (PRO, Exch. Land Rev., LR 6/29/2; *VCH Gloucs.*, ii, 421).

[2] Dugdale, *Monasticon*, vi, part 3, 1434-5. For the early history of Eton see Maxwell-Lyte, *History of Eton College*, especially chapters 1-4.

[3] *ECD*, pp. 412-15.

[4] *CPR 1436-41*, pp. 521-3.

visited Winchester College in July 1441, secured the services of its head-master, William Wainfleet, whom he afterwards made provost of Eton, and began to augment his colleges so as to equal and even surpass those that Wykeham had made. In 1443 he issued statutes for Eton and also revised the foundation of King's, but the Eton statutes as they survive are in fact later, dating from 1447. They show a considerable augmentation both of the liturgical and the educational sides of the college. Ten chaplains were added to the resources of the chapel; the clerks were raised from four to ten and the choristers from six to sixteen. The school was magnified to the size of Winchester, with seventy poor scholars and an usher to assist the master. As at Winchester the scholars were chosen first from natives of the parishes in which either King's or Eton held property, second from natives of particular counties, in this case Buckingham and Cambridge, and last from the rest of the kingdom. Up to twenty commoners were also to be admitted to study with them, and free teaching continued to be offered to all comers. King's College was remodelled in turn on the lines of Wykeham's Oxford foundation. In 1443 Henry stated that he had long since determined that the scholars of Eton should proceed to King's when sufficiently instructed in grammar. In 1445 he secured papal approval for an establishment of a provost and seventy scholars, and in the following year formally refounded the college by letters patent and act of parliament.[1]

Despite the founder's generosity, the history of Eton in the fifteenth century was to be a troubled one. While Henry VI remained king it flourished; the college was lavishly endowed with lands and privileges, and the full complement of scholars was reached as early as 1447. After Henry's overthrow in 1461, however, an act of parliament nullified all the grants made by the three Lancastrian kings, and the hold of the college on its estates became uncertain. The new king, Edward IV, did not look favourably on his enemy's foundation, and granted many of its lands to the nearby college of St George in Windsor Castle. In 1463 he secured a papal bull annexing Eton to St George's, and although this never became effective, the college revenues fell sharply, the number of scholars had to be reduced and the stipends of the teaching staff to be cut by a third. Only very gradually did the college by its own efforts and those of its influential friends win favours from the king and the restoration of some of its old endowments. By 1485 with the accession of Henry VII the continuity of the college was no longer in doubt, but the damage of the

[1] For the statutes of Eton and King's see *Ancient Laws*, ed. Heywood and Wright. The early Eton scholars are listed by Sir W. Sterry, *The Eton College Register 1441-1698* (1943).

Yorkist period left its mark. The masters' salaries remained less than the founder had intended, and it has been doubted whether even in the early sixteenth century there remained a full complement of scholars. Even so, Eton remains a noble and important foundation, standing supreme with Winchester in wealth and resources above all the other grammar schools of the fourteenth and fifteenth centuries.

Among the king's subjects who imitated his patronage of schools, the bishops as always were prominent. Of the ecclesiastics who assisted Henry in the foundation of Eton and King's, several of whom he promoted to sees, at least five busied themselves in educational schemes of their own. William Alnwick, bishop of Lincoln and diocesan of Eton during the foundation of the college, was himself a co-founder of the grammar school of Alnwick, Northumberland, in 1448.[1] Thomas Beckington, the king's secretary, later bishop of Bath and Wells, published in 1459 a most careful and enlightened set of statutes for the education of his cathedral choristers, as well as building them a new schoolroom over the cloisters.[2] William Wainfleet, second provost of Eton and subsequently bishop of Winchester, founded two grammar schools: one as part of his great college of St Mary Magdalen in Oxford, and another at his birthplace, Wainfleet in Lincolnshire.[3] John Chedworth, second provost of King's until promoted to be bishop of Lincoln, was the founder of the school at Cirencester in his native county of Gloucester.[4] John Carpenter, another of Henry's Eton agents and afterwards bishop of Worcester, had a hand in no less than four new educational projects. He was master of St Anthony's Hospital, London, in 1441 when the diocesan bishop sanctioned the appropriation of a parish church to endow a free grammar school there. In his diocese of Worcester he was responsible for establishing the free public libraries at Worcester and Bristol, together with a new grammar school for his college of Westbury-on-Trym in 1463.[5] These are only five among the company of bishops who endowed

---

[1] *CPR 1446-52*, p. 170. For Alnwick's life see *BRUC*, p. 11.

[2] *Dean Cosyn and Wells Cathedral Miscellany*, ed. Dom A. Watkin (Somerset Record Society, lvi, 1941), pp. 98-109. For Beckington's life see *BRUO*, i, 157-9; for his care of education in his diocese see above, p. 19.

[3] Stanier, *History of Magdalen College school, Oxford*, pp. 1-9; *VCH Lincs.*, ii, 483-4. For Wainfleet's life see *BRUO*, iii, 2001-3.

[4] *Valor Ecclesiasticus*, vol ii (1814), p. 447. For Chedworth's life see *BRUO*, i, 401-2.

[5] On Carpenter see *BRUO*, i, 360-1, and R. M. Haines, 'Aspects of the episcopate of John Carpenter', *Journal of Ecclesiastical History*, xix (1968), pp. 11-40. For St Anthony's see *CPR 1436-41*, p. 238, and *SME*, p. 261; for Westbury, Worcs. Record Office, Reg. Carpenter, i, fo 183v. The libraries at Bristol and Worcester are discussed above, pp. 84-5.

school after school in the century before the Reformation. Nor were the lesser clergy far behind. William Sponne, archdeacon of Norfolk, gives us Towcester school, Northamptonshire, in 1448; John Combe, canon of Exeter, endowed Crewkerne school at his birthplace in Somerset in 1499 and his fellow countryman John Edmunds, chancellor of St Paul's, was one of three men of Bruton who founded the free school there in 1520.[1]

At least one other great clerk, Thomas Wolsey, demands some attention as the founder of a school, both because of his own importance and the unusual scale of his plans. Wolsey, born at Ipswich and educated at Magdalen College, was for a short time master of its grammar school in the winter of 1497-8, and like Wainfleet he succeeded in rising from the master's chair to the episcopal bench.[2] When in the 1520s Wolsey reached the summit of his power as a cardinal, papal legate, archbishop of York and chancellor of England, possessing enormous wealth and unparalleled influence, he turned his mind to educational schemes of a grandeur appropriate to his dignity and ambition. His chief project was the great Cardinal College at Oxford, begun in 1525, but – like Wykeham and Henry VI before him – he intended also to found a grammar school or rather, as one already existed in Ipswich, to endow and enlarge it on a more magnificent scale.[3] At Ipswich, therefore, in the summer of 1528 he began the foundation of a second Cardinal College on a scale seen hitherto only at Winchester and Eton. The college was to include priests engaged in the divine office, and an almshouse as well as a school. To discharge the services there were to be a dean, twelve fellows, eight clerks and eight choristers, while the school was to consist of fifty scholars receiving board and lodging, with a master and two ushers to rule them. As at Eton free instruction was also to be given to all comers. On 1 September Wolsey drew up a detailed curriculum for the school, based on the use of the new grammars of Colet and Lily, and on the reading of classical Latin authors. By the following January the headmaster could write that the school was proceeding well, the boys of good intelligence and the numbers rapidly increasing. But in 1530 came Wolsey's fall, and the seizure and closure of the college by the king followed soon afterwards. The school survived, for it had existed independently before the college and had endowments of its own, but Wolsey's great attempt to make it a

[1] *VCH Northants.*, ii, 225-7; *VCH Som.*, ii, 448-9, 453.
[2] For Wolsey's career see *BRUO*, iii, 2077-80.
[3] In the 1520s Wolsey also contemplated founding a school at Tonbridge in Kent (*LPFD*, iv, part 1, nos 1459, 1470-1).

rival to Eton and Winchester came to nothing only two years after its first beginning.[1]

The lay nobility and great magnates also figure as founders of schools, their wealth and wide connections naturally leading them to add the patronage of education to their many other charitable and religious activities. Walter Lord Hungerford, treasurer of England and steward of the king's household who died in 1447, began the building of an almshouse and grammar school in his lordship of Heytesbury in Wiltshire and bequeathed lands for their support, though the bequest was not carried out until 1472.[2] His younger contemporary, William de la Pole, duke of Suffolk, who figures chiefly as the able and unpopular statesman of the 1440s, deserves also to be remembered as one who assisted the king in founding Eton and who erected a grammar school and almshouse on his own account at Ewelme in Oxfordshire where his palace lay.[3] In the early sixteenth century a group of several peers with educational interests can be discerned centring on the family of Stanley. The second wife of Thomas Stanley, first earl of Derby, was Lady Margaret Beaufort who, as well as founding the famous professorships of divinity in the two universities, was the authoress of the grammar school of Wimborne in Dorset, begun in 1497 but not completed until 1511 after her death.[4] Derby's grandson and heir by his first wife, Thomas the second earl, contributed in his turn to the endowment of a school at Blackburn in 1514, reserving the nomination of the master to himself and his heirs.[5] His uncle Edward Stanley, Lord Monteagle, the first earl's younger son by his first wife and hence stepson to the Lady Margaret, also projected a school though he did not live to found it. In his will of 1523 he requested that his wealth be used to endow a school at Hornby near Lancaster. The endowment was never made, though Monteagle's son and heir later maintained a schoolmaster there at his own expense.[6] Yet one of the executors, in whom the testator had placed especial trust, was Thomas Lord Darcy, himself the founder of the grammar school of Whitkirk in

---

[1] For the history of Wolsey's college see *VCH Suffolk*, ii, 142-4, 328-31, and for its curriculum, J. Strype, *Ecclesiastical Memorials* (1829), i, 139-43.

[2] R. C. Hoare, *The Modern History of Wiltshire: Heytesbury* (1824), i, part 2, p. 102; *VCH Wilts.*, iii, 337-8.

[3] Maxwell-Lyte, *History of Eton College*, pp. 11-13, 18, 35, 37, etc.; *Historical MSS Commission, Ninth Report* (1913), part 1, pp. 216-22; *VCH Oxon.*, i, 470.

[4] *CPR 1494-1509*, p. 79; J. Hutchins, *History of Dorset*, 3rd ed. (1868), iii, 191-2.

[5] W. K. Jordan, *The Social Institutions of Lancashire* (Chetham Society, 3rd series, xi, 1962), pp. 35-6.

[6] Ibid., pp. 37-8.

Yorkshire.[1] So much interest in schools among such a small circle can hardly have been accidental, and considering the equal wealth and enlightenment of many other noble families at this time it is unlikely to have been unique.

Almost every region of the country provides examples of the foundation of schools by laymen and women of lesser rank. They include members of well-established county families, like Joan Greyndour of Clearwell in Gloucestershire, foundress of Newland in 1445, or Sir Thomas Boteler of Bewsey, Lancashire, who willed the grammar school of Warrington in 1520.[2] There are landowners who had made their way as lawyers, such as David Holbach and Humphrey Coningsby, founders respectively of the schools at Oswestry in Shropshire (*c.* 1423) and Rock in Worcestershire (1513).[3] There are royal servants, county figures in their own right, like John Ferriby, controller of the household of Henry VI, and his contemporary Thomas Gloucester, receiver-general of the duchy of Cornwall, who both projected schools in their native county of Gloucestershire: the one at Chipping Campden (*c.* 1443) and the other at Gloucester, planned in 1446 but never carried out.[4] The great London merchants are also well represented. Besides William Sevenoaks the grocer, whose foundation at Sevenoaks in 1432 has been noticed in a previous chapter, there are the mercer John Abbot who founded the school of Farthinghoe in Northamptonshire in 1443, and the goldsmith Edmund Shaw who erected his school at Stockport in Cheshire in 1487.[5] The following century sees a multiplicity of foundations by such men. Nor were the burgesses of provincial towns slow to follow their example. One, Richard Felaw, merchant, bailiff and parliamentary burgess of Ipswich, has already been mentioned as the benefactor of its grammar school in 1483. Another, Vincent Tehy, merchant and mayor of Southampton, was involved in a scheme for founding schools in the island of Jersey in 1496.[6] They too were but the vanguard of a large company.

[1] *Complete Peerage*, ix, 113-15; *LPFD*, iii, part 2, no 2915.

[2] *CPR 1441-6*, p. 388; *VCH Lancs.*, ii, 601.

[3] Mrs Bulkeley-Owen, 'The founder and first trustees of Oswestry grammar school', *Transactions of the Salop Archaeological and Natural History Society*, 3rd series, iv (1904), pp. 185-216; *LPFD*, i, part 2, p. 934 no 53.

[4] For Ferriby see *Reg. Chichele, Canterbury*, ii, 577-8, 652. The account in *VCH Gloucs.*, ii, 417-18, is incorrect. For Gloucester and his bequest see London, Lambeth Palace Library, Reg. J. Stafford, folios 146v-7, and *Calendar of Records of the Corporation of Gloucester*, ed. W. H. Stevenson (1893), no 1134.

[5] For Farthinghoe see *ECD*, pp. 414-17; for Shaw and Stockport, B. Varley, *History of Stockport Grammar School*, 2nd ed. (1957), especially pp. 1-30.

[6] *VCH Suffolk*, ii, 327; *CPR 1494-1509*, p. 83.

As well as the endowment of schools by individual merchants and burgesses, the fifteenth century provides interesting examples of educational patronage by urban communities in general. Town corporations began to exert themselves to defend and improve their local schools. In 1407 the mayor and citizens of Lincoln took some interest in the threat of the new choristers' grammar school to the livelihood of the city schoolmaster, and appeared as parties to the treaty between the dignitaries of the chapter which settled the dispute. Later on the treaty, with its definition of the rights of the city master, was carefully entered up in the city records.[1] At Coventry the corporation took the initiative in inviting a schoolmaster to the city in 1425, and in 1439 they sent the mayor and six of the council to remonstrate with the prior of the cathedral against imposing a monopoly of education in the city, urging the right of any citizen to put his child to school where he pleased.[2] In other places, however, the town council imposed its own restrictions on teaching, with the idea of creating an attractive post for a recognized schoolmaster without fear of rivals. Thus at Ipswich it was ordered in 1477 that the grammar schoolmaster should have jurisdiction over all scholars, and in 1482 the council made an order about the fees he could charge.[3] Similarly at Bridgnorth in 1503 the council of the twenty-four burgesses ordered that no priests should teach children on their own account once the schoolmaster had come, but that every child should resort to the common school.[4] Lastly there is at least one example of a town council arranging for the endowment of its school. In 1478 the mayor and burgesses of Appleby granted three chantries in their patronage to a single chaplain who covenanted, while he held them, to keep a grammar school, taking fees according to the ancient custom of the school. By 1548, if not before, this had become a free school.[5]

Sometimes the maintenance of the town schoolmaster was borne by a religious guild or brotherhood, representing burgesses both prominent and less prominent in the community. Such guilds had long existed in the towns for the purpose of supporting chantry priests or performing works of charity, and the fifteenth century provides several signs of their developing interest in education. Not that we ought to exaggerate the number of guild schools before 1500. Although the chantry commissioners of 1548

---

[1] *VCH Lincs.*, ii, 426.
[2] *The Coventry Leet Book*, ed. M. D. Harris, part 1 (EETS, 1907) pp. 101, 118, 190.
[3] *ECD*, pp. 422-4; *VCH Suffolk*, ii, 325-6.   [4] *ECD*, p. 439.
[5] *SME*, pp. 268-9; J. Nicolson and R. Burn, *History and Antiquities of Westmorland and Cumberland* (1778), i, 329.

noted many schoolmasters supported by such guilds, the antiquity of these arrangements, like those of the chantries, is often impossible to discover. It has too frequently been assigned to the fifteenth century when the opening years of the sixteenth would be more likely. Contemporary references to guild schools are none too common before 1500. There is of course the well-known example of Stratford-upon-Avon, where the schoolmaster was already teaching in a house belonging to the guild of St John the Baptist and the Holy Cross by 1413. In 1426-7 the guild paid nearly £10 to build a new schoolhouse and finally, at some date before 1482, Master Thomas Joliffe, a wealthy local priest, gave an endowment to make the school free. The master was henceforth to be one of the five priests on the guild establishment; he was to have a chamber in the guild-hall and celebrate mass in its chapel.[1] At Chipping Norton in Oxfordshire a grammar school appears as one of the primary objects of the guild of the Holy Trinity which the vicar and four of his parishioners were licensed to found in 1450.[2] In 1506 there are references to the maintenance of school-masters by the guilds of St Mary the Virgin at Boston, and of the Holy Trinity at Wisbech.[3] The following decades were probably responsible for the appearance of several more.

There was a similar growth of interest in schools among the yeomanry of the countryside. The chantry commissioners of 1548 encountered lands in many parishes given by sundry benefactors unknown for educational uses, and sometimes the existence of a free school may have been due to several small donations, too small to preserve the names of the contri-butors for posterity. Thus in 1521 John Hall of Lewes bequeathed 6s. 8d. a year out of his lands 'to the brotherhood of Billingshurst [Sussex] for the term of twenty years if the said free school proceed and be kept, or else not'.[4] As the popularity of education increased, it is also likely that in parishes where a collection of lands had grown up to support a chantry priest, the inhabitants resolved to apply the endowment to a school or to add education to the priest's duties. Such decisions by lesser men are just as interesting as those of the great, but they have rarely left any trace of time or circumstance.

The involvement of laymen of all ranks from king to commons in the foundation and endowment of schools during the fifteenth century constitutes a major development in the history of English education, so much more is it apparent after 1400 than in the centuries before. Nor did the connection cease once the initial bequests had been made. All the new

[1] *VCH War.*, ii, 329-32.
[3] *VCH Lincs.*, ii, 451; *VCH Cambs.*, ii, 327.
[2] *CPR 1446-52*, p. 402.
[4] *VCH Sussex*, ii, 398.

endowed schools required patrons who would appoint and supervise the succession of schoolmasters, and pay them their salaries too if the masters were not trusted to administer the endowments by themselves. Again, compared with the relatively small number of lay patrons of whom we hear in the thirteenth and fourteenth centuries, there is a considerable increase in the fifteenth and sixteenth. Sometimes the patronage of the new school remained with the local family who had first endowed it: thus the Berkeleys of Beverstone appointed the schoolmasters of Wotton-under-Edge while the Greyndour family and their heirs the Baynhams did the same at Newland near by. Sometimes the responsibility was given to a group of local feoffees, of which there are early examples in David Holbach's school at Oswestry and John Ferriby's at Chipping Campden. London merchants naturally tended to place their foundations in the care of the city companies to which they belonged: thus John Abbot's school at Farthinghoe was entrusted to his Mercers' Company, and Edmund Shaw's at Stockport to his, the goldsmiths. By the early sixteenth century borough corporations were also becoming involved: Agnes Mellers chose the corporation of Nottingham to supervise the free school which she founded there in 1512, and Joan Cook did the same at Gloucester in 1540. In each case the lady's late husband had been a prominent burgess and mayor.[1]

Despite these developments, it would be foolish to underestimate the share of the clergy in the foundation and government of the new schools, and to see the increasing involvement of the laity as necessarily antisacerdotal, or carried out at the expense of the ancient clerical interest in education. Rather the clergy shared in what was a general growth of interest. Not only did they themselves found schools, as we have seen, but they were also trusted to govern them though usually, it is true, by founders also clerical. Monasteries appear as patrons because as undying corporations they were able to fulfil the necessary duties of patronage just as well as the city companies or borough corporations. Thus the Benedictines of Winchcombe came to control the endowments of the fifteenth-century grammar school at Cirencester and the school founded at Winchcombe itself in 1521.[2] The Austin canons of Bruton and the Benedictine abbot of Faversham were also entrusted with the public schools established there in 1520 and 1527 respectively.[3] The regular clergy came thus to have more

[1] *VCH Notts.*, ii, 220; *VCH Gloucs.*, ii, 344.
[2] *Valor Ecclesiasticus*, ii, 447; *VCH Gloucs.*, ii, 421.
[3] *VCH Somerset*, ii, 448-9; W. K. Jordan, 'Social institutions in Kent, 1480-1660', *Archaeologia Cantiana*, lxxv (1961), p. 72.

interests in education than the instruction of their own brethren and dependents would have entailed. The century before the Reformation also provides the first examples of school patronage by university colleges. Magdalen was of course responsible for its founder's two grammar schools at Oxford and Wainfleet; Childrey in Berkshire – willed in 1526 – was put under the government of Queen's, and Sedbergh school in Yorkshire, founded in the following year, under that of St John's College, Cambridge.[1] And if the monastic patrons disappeared in the course of the 1530s, the university colleges came to take an increasing share in the government of schools as the sixteenth century wore on.

The endowed schools were of course only the most prominent and expensive benefactions of the age, and many humbler gifts – buildings, books and bursaries – were also made to the schools during this period. Thus in 1484 Robert Harset, clothmaker of Long Melford in Suffolk, bequeathed his house to be used as a school, and in about 1490 Isabel Hyet, a lady of the forest of Dean, left land worth some 10s. a year for the support of the poor scholars of Newland.[2] Wills, which begin to survive in large numbers after the end of the fourteenth century, provide many examples of bequests to support 'scholars', either of schools or universities, and being frequently made only upon the deathbed, record merely a part of the educational charity which many people must have dispensed in the course of their lives. Edmund Dudley, minister of Henry VII, was urging the needs of poor scholars in the early sixteenth century just as Langland had done in the late fourteenth: 'Let not to departe with some of your sylver to comfortt and relief poore schollers, and especiall suche as be willing and apt to lerne which lack exhibicion: let them have what is necessarie . . . for a better Chauntree shall ye never founde.'[3] Casual alms of this kind have rarely been recorded, but the household accounts of Sir Henry Willoughby of Middleton in Warwickshire in the 1520s do show how the knight dealt out pennies to poor scholars as well as the larger gifts he made to his neighbours' sons as they set off for school or university.[4]

It is now appropriate to review the facilities for education in England between 1400 and 1530, in this age of increasing benefactions. The pre-eminent schools for most of this period continued to be those of Oxford.

[1] *VCH Berks.*, ii, 275-6; *EYS*, ii, 291.
[2] *VCH Suffolk*, ii, 340; Sir J. Maclean, 'Chantry certificates, Gloucestershire', *Transactions of the Bristol and Gloucs. Archaeological Society*, viii (1883-4), p. 293.
[3] Dudley, *The Tree of the Commonwealth*, ed. D. M. Brodie (1948), p. 63.
[4] *Historical MSS Commission, Report on the MSS of Lord Middleton* (1911), especially pp. 334, 338, 346, 364, etc.

The leading master there in the early fifteenth century, John Leland who died in 1433, was praised by his followers as 'the flower of grammarians', and his grammatical treatises circulated further afield than those of any of his contemporaries.[1] There were still several grammar schools at Oxford in the 1440s, as appears from a list of all the university halls and their specialities compiled by John Rous, the Warwickshire antiquary.[2] By this time the house where Leland taught, called Peckwater Inn, had become a community of lawyers, but five other halls were mentioned as places where grammar was still studied: Tackley Inn, Ing Hall, Lyon Hall, White Hall and Cuthbert Hall, and for the first three there is indeed independent evidence of their tenancy by grammar masters during the middle years of the century. To these halls may be added at least one other, St Hugh's, a dependency of St Edmund Hall, which appears as a grammar school in 1458.[3] But in the second half of the century the teaching of grammar at Oxford seems to have been in decline, either as part of the general recession suffered by the university or because of the increasing competition of good local schools. The grammar halls already mentioned disappear from the records one by one, and in 1492 the two masters of arts deputed by the university to supervise the schools were said to have no work to do.[4] This decline was only arrested by the opening of Magdalen College school in about 1480, which gave Oxford for the first time a free grammar school. There a succession of graduate masters held forth, some of whom – John Anwykyll, John Stanbridge and Thomas Wolsey – were men of considerable learning and ability. Stanbridge, as we have already seen, was the leading English schoolmaster of his time, and his grammatical writings and adaptations for children were the first to have a wide currency in print, while his pupil in the school, Robert Whittinton, became in his turn one of the most notable practitioners of the next generation.[5] With these masters Oxford maintained its reputation as the leading centre of school education into the early sixteenth century.

Events at Cambridge seem broadly to have followed the Oxford pattern. Until the middle of the fifteenth century there were still feepaying

[1] On Leland see above, pp. 95-6.
[2] A. Wood, *City of Oxford*, ed. A. Clark, vol i (Oxford Historical Society, xv, 1889), pp. 638-41. On the fifteenth-century Oxford grammar schools in general see *VCH Oxon.*, iii, 40-3.
[3] A. B. Emden, *An Oxford Hall in Medieval Times* (1927), pp. 173-7.
[4] *Statuta Antiqua Universitatis Oxon.*, ed. Gibson, p. 300.
[5] On Magdalen School see Stanier, *A History of Magdalen College School, Oxford*. The biographies of the early masters are in *BRUO* and in J. R. Bloxam, *The Register of St Mary Magdalen College, Oxford*, vol iii (1863).

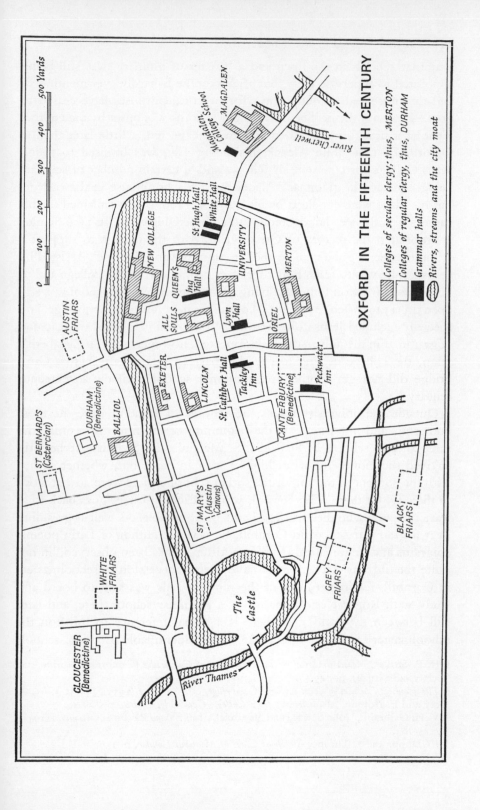

OXFORD IN THE FIFTEENTH CENTURY

Colleges of secular clergy: thus, MERTON
Colleges of regular clergy: thus, DURHAM
Grammar halls
Rivers, streams and the city moat

500 Yards

0   100   200   300   400   500

CLOUCESTER
(Benedictine)

WHITE
FRIARS

ST BERNARD'S
(Cistercian)

AUSTIN
FRIARS

DURHAM
(Benedictine)

BALLIOL

ST MARY'S
(Austin
Canons)

The Castle

River Thames

GREY
FRIARS

BLACK
FRIARS

EXETER

LINCOLN

St Cuthbert Hall

Tackley
Inn

CANTERBURY
(Benedictine)

Peckwater
Inn

NEW COLLEGE

ALL
SOULS

QUEEN'S

Ing
Hall

Lyon
Hall

UNIVERSITY

ORIEL

MERTON

St Hugh Hall

White Hall

Magdalen School

College MAGDALEN

River Cherwell

grammar schools in the town and a 'master of glomery' was still being appointed to supervise them, but after 1500 he is hardly ever mentioned, and the office and its duties must for practical purposes have ceased to exist.[1] Here too the decline of the older schools was offset by the endowment of a new foundation – as might be expected, a little later than at Oxford. In 1496 John Alcock, bishop of Ely, was licensed to found Jesus College for a master, six fellows and 'a certain number of scholars being educated in grammar'. Alcock built a schoolhouse in the college, but his plans were cut short by his death in 1500, and it remained for his successor in the see, James Stanley, to complete his work. In 1506 Stanley appropriated the rectory of Great Shelford to the college to support a schoolmaster, 'a good man, learned in grammar and rhetoric'. Assisted by an usher, he was to teach four choristers maintained by the college and to give free instruction to boys coming from elsewhere. The school was still open in 1549 when the king's commissioners visited Cambridge and specially excluded Jesus College from their injunctions against the teaching of grammar in the university. It disappeared, however, early in Elizabeth's reign, the college ceasing to pay the masters' salaries after 1567. Cambridge did not get another free grammar school until the seventeenth century.[2]

Outside the university towns the schools of London were the most numerous and important. At the beginning of the fifteenth century the three ancient schools of St Paul's, St Martin's and St Mary Arches still enjoyed the monopoly of teaching at least in name but, whether or not with the consent of the authorities, other schoolmasters were now at work in the city. Of these John Seward, whose teaching career goes back to at least 1404 and who died in 1435, is the most notable. As well as presiding over a grammar school in Cornhill, he was the author of Latin poems, epigrams and grammatical treatises, written, it has been observed, 'in not quite the old way'.[3] There must have been a succession of schoolmasters in Cornhill, for in 1419 one of the king's wards was sent to board and study with Roger Keston, master of a grammar school there, and later still between 1439 and 1441 there is a casual reference to 'Morton the schoolmaster's son, in Cornhill'.[4] Other identifiable London schools

---

[1] H. P. Stokes, *Medieval Hostels of the University of Cambridge* (Cambridge Antiquarian Society, xlix, 1924), pp. 49-57.

[2] *The Earliest Statutes of Jesus College, Cambridge*, ed. A. Gray (1935), pp. 31-3, 61; A. Gray and F. Brittain, *A History of Jesus College, Cambridge* (1960), pp. 30-2.

[3] V. H. Galbraith, 'John Seward and his circle', *Medieval and Renaissance Studies*, i (1943), pp. 85-104.

[4] *ECD*, pp. 396-7; Thrupp, *Merchant Class of Medieval London*, p. 156.

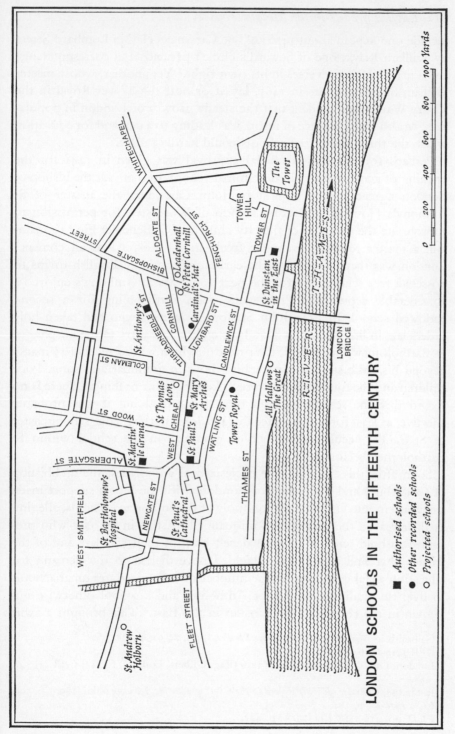

LONDON SCHOOLS IN THE FIFTEENTH CENTURY

■ *Authorised schools*

● *Other recorded schools*

○ *Projected schools*

H

include one kept in about 1410 at 'The Cardinal's Hat' in Lombard Street by William Relyk, one of Seward's circle of friends and correspondents, and a maker of Latin verses in his own right.[1] Yet another, whose master William Shipton occurs in 1465, lay at or near the Tower Royal in the Vintry Ward.[2] It is evident that the steady growth of London in population, wealth and as a place of resort was leading to a demand for education which the three authorized schools could hardly satisfy.

Perhaps for this reason official approval was given in 1441 for the opening of another authorized grammar school. In that year the bishop of London agreed to the request of John Carpenter, the master of St Anthony's Hospital and future bishop of Worcester, for permission to appropriate the revenues of the city church of St Benedict Fink to maintain a master teaching grammar freely in the hospital to all comers.[3] London was therefore one of the earliest of the large English towns to possess a free school, and for the next 100 years St Anthony's enjoyed a considerable reputation. Plans were soon forthcoming for a second endowed school. In 1444 John Stafford, a layman who had taken holy orders late in life, bequeathed lands to endow a chantry in the hospital of St Bartholomew, Smithfield, the priest of which was to receive 2½ marks beyond his basic stipend for teaching boys in grammar and song. Poor children and the founder's kin were to be taught for nothing.[4] There is no record that the scheme secured official approval but it was probably effective, at least for a time, since in 1476 John Barkby, later schoolmaster of St Paul's, occurs as 'teacher of grammar in the school within St Bartholomew's Hospital.[5]

Soon after this, in 1446, the ecclesiastical authorities, the archbishop of Canterbury and the bishop of London, with the king's support made a new attempt to enforce the monopoly of the authorized schools, alleging as their reason the presence of unqualified masters in the city who presumed to hold schools 'in great deceit both of their scholars and of the friends that find them'. They yielded nevertheless to the demand for education as far as increasing the number of authorized grammar schools to five: the traditional three, St Anthony's and a school otherwise unknown in the church of St Dunstan in the East.[6] This brought a swift

[1] Galbraith in *Medieval and Renaissance Studies*, i, pp. 89-91, 104.
[2] *CPR 1452-61*, p. 285.
[3] London, Guildhall Library, MS 9531/6 (Reg. Gilbert, London) fo 183; *CPR 1436-41*, p. 238.
[4] R. Sharpe, *Calendar of Wills Proved in the Court of Husting, London*, vol ii (1890), p. 508.
[5] *CCR 1476-85*, p. 28.
[6] *ECD*, pp. 416-18; *CPR 1441-6*, p. 432.

protest from four prominent city rectors: William Lichfield of All Hallows the Great, Gilbert Worthington of St Andrew Holborn, John Coote of St Peter Cornhill and John Neel of St Mary Colechurch and master of the hospital of St Thomas of Acon. In a petition to the House of Commons in 1447 they drew attention to the superfluity of young people in London needing education, not only those born in the city but those who came from elsewhere, 'some for lack of schoolmasters in their own country . . . and some for the great alms-giving of lords, merchants and others, the which is in London more plenteously done than in many other places of this realm'. This, they declared, required an appropriate number of schools and masters in London, and not a monopoly 'for the singular avail of two or three persons. . . . For where there is a great number of learners and few teachers, and all the learners be compelled to go to the same few teachers and to none others, the masters wax rich in money and the learners poor in cunning, as experience only sheweth.' The four rectors therefore asked permission each to appoint a grammar master in their parishes, removals and reappointments to be made by them and their successors, in other words to establish four more grammar schools in the capital. The king's response to this was not unfavourable: let it be done as it is desired, provided it be done with the advice of the bishop of London or the archbishop of Canterbury.[1] Whether or not these dignitaries raised objections we do not know, but none of the projected schools occurs in later times, except for that in the hospital of St Thomas of Acon, which was certainly in existence in 1535 and may well have sprung from the original petition.[2]

Attempts continued to be made to improve the educational facilities of the capital. In 1459 that 'honourable and famous merchant' Simon Eyre, draper and sometime lord mayor of the city, died leaving a huge fortune of which 5,000 marks alone were designed for charitable purposes. In particular he gave £2,000 to the Drapers' Company to establish a secular college of a master, five priests, six clerks and two choristers at Leadenhall in Cornhill, as well as a master and usher to keep a grammar school and other masters to teach writing and song. For some reason, however, the great bequest was never applied in this form, and Eyre's grammar school did not come into being.[3] It remained for Dr John Colet half a century later to provide London with a magnificent foundation on the scale of

[1] *Rotuli Parliamentorum*, v, 137.
[2] C. L. Kingsford, 'Two London chronicles', *Camden Miscellany XII* (Camden third series, xviii, 1910), p. 11.
[3] Stow, *Survey of London*, ed. Kingsford, i, 154.

which Eyre had dreamed, when in 1509 he began to refound the ancient cathedral school of St Paul's as a free grammar school endowed with his own money. Colet's ambitious plans are deservedly famous and hardly need retelling here. His school maintained a 'high' or head-master and a 'sur' or second-master, with a chaplain to assist them, and offered salaries twice as high as anywhere else to attract men of the greatest talent. The first high-master was William Lily, a grammarian of note, who had studied in Italy and was well up in the latest techniques of Renaissance education. Free instruction was offered to 153 boys and new grammars were specially commissioned for their lessons. The success of St Paul's was immediate, and three of the pupils of Lily alone – Anthony Denny, Edward North and William Paget – were destined to become the councillors of Henry VIII and Edward VI.[1]

The state of education in early Tudor London after the events rehearsed above remains something of a mystery. The appearance of new foundations is balanced by the obscurity and possible disappearance after 1450 of the old schools of St Martin's and St Mary Arches. The number of private schools is always hard to judge. On the eve of the Reformation there were still only three pre-eminent London schools, as there had been a century before, but consisting now of St Anthony's, St Paul's and St Thomas of Acon. That the first two at least were free marked something of an improvement. But the great expansion of education in London was to take place during and after the Reformation with the foundation of such important schools as Westminster (1540), Christ's Hospital (1552) and Merchant Taylors' (1561).

Of the other important English towns seventeen were cathedral cities, and in all save Rochester the ancient schools may still be traced during the fifteenth century. Moreover, three of these schools had been made free by 1500, thus anticipating the achievement most often associated with Colet and St Paul's. As early as 1414 Thomas Langley, bishop of Durham, founded a chantry of two priests in his cathedral church: one to teach grammar and the other song, receiving poor scholars 'freely, for the love of God, if they or their parents have humbly asked for this', but taking, from those who were willing to pay, the moderate fees accustomed to be charged in other schools. Their salaries, £2 at first, were raised to £10 in 1440, and the schools survived to be incorporated in the new cathedral foundation made by Henry VIII in 1541.[2] At Lichfield Bishop William

---

[1] See Lupton, *Life of Colet*; M. F. J. McDonnell, *The History of St Paul's School* (1909) and his *Annals of St Paul's School* (1959).
[2] *VCH Durham*, i, 371-5.

Smith, in a reform very characteristic of the period, remodelled the decayed hospital of St John the Baptist in 1495 and established in it an almshouse and a master and usher charged with teaching grammar freely to all scholars whatsoever.[1] At Chichester the cathedral school was endowed, also at the bishop's instance, in 1498. In that year Bishop Edward Story appropriated the prebend of Highley to the school, drew up new statutes for its conduct and made it free to all comers.[2] Colet therefore had recent precedents when he began the similar task of making St Paul's into a free school. In the remaining period before the Reformation one further school in a cathedral city, that of Worcester, appears to have become endowed. At some date between 1504 and 1532, the city school came to be maintained by the guild of the Trinity, which paid one or two masters who probably taught at least some children for nothing. The guild was not a wealthy one; by 1538 the school had become a heavy burden and soon afterwards it was wholly abandoned. Overshadowed by the new cathedral school founded in 1541 by Henry VIII, the guild school was nevertheless revived in 1547 and again in 1561 and has come down to modern times as the Worcester Royal Grammar School.[3]

With regard to the other places of note – the shire towns and greater centres of commerce – the evidence is almost as unsatisfactory as in former times. In some towns, such as Boston, Bristol, Coventry, Gloucester and Nottingham, there are fairly frequent allusions to schools and their masters during the fifteenth century, but in others, of which Newcastle, Plymouth and Southampton are examples, no schools have yet been found. Once more this is primarily due to the shortcomings of source material or to lack of research, rather than a clear sign that these towns lacked the educational facilities possessed by others of similar size and wealth. Very gradually during the period 1400-1530 some of the larger towns came to have endowed schools of their own. The foundation of the free school of Lancaster was begun in 1469, though not completed until 1500; at Hull the foundation began in 1479 and at Ipswich in 1483. In the early sixteenth century others were added at Guildford, Nottingham, Lewes and a few other places, but they were still rare when the Reformation began, and most of the large towns did not get their free schools until the middle of the sixteenth century. Until then they still depended on the labours of individual masters working for fees.

[1] *VCH Staffs.*, iii, 281; Lichfield Diocesan Registry, BA 1/13 (Reg. W. Smith) folios 148-51v; R. Churton, *Lives of William Smyth and Sir Richard Sutton* (1800), pp. 79-82.
[2] *VCH Sussex*, ii, 402-4.
[3] *VCH Worcs.*, iv, 478-9.

ENDOWED SCHOOLS
FOUNDED IN ENGLAND 1330–1530
AND OPEN TO THE PUBLIC

○ *Reading and song schools*

◑ *Reading or song and grammar schools*

● *Grammar schools (some probably also teaching reading or song)*

□◨■ *Similar schools attached to colleges of secular clergy*

0 25 50 75 100 125 *Miles*

Alnwick

Durham

Appleby
Brough
Sedburgh
Hornby
Lancaster
St Michael-on-Wyre
Pocklington
Broughton Blackburn Acaster
Leyland Middleton Hull
Liverpool Bolton Whitkirk
Stockport Manchester Royston
Warrington Rotherham
Macclesfield
Malpas Newark Tattershall Wainfleet
Farnworth Sibthorpe Boston
Oswestry Rolleston Nottingham Grantham Cromer
Tong Lichfield King's Lynn
Wolverhampton Wisbech Aylsham
Rock Brington Aldwinkle
Warwick Higham Ferrers
Stratford Fawsley Cambridge Ipswich
Worcester Ch. Campden Blisworth
Evesham Banbury Towcester Saffron Walden Sudbury
Winchcombe Farthinghoe Houghton Earls Colne
Newland Chipping Norton Berkhamsted
Cirencester Oxford Waltham-stow
Wotton-under-Edge Ewelme
Westbury-on-Trym Childrey Faversham
Lambourn Eton LONDON Wye
Heytesbury Reading Sevenoaks
Bruton Guildford Cuckfield
Crewkerne Winchester Lewes
Ottery Wimborne Chichester
Week St Mary Milton Abbas

It was rather the smaller towns and a few fortunate villages which first benefited from the establishment of free schools. This was because most donors felt impelled to patronize the places of their birth, or where their lordships lay, rather than the large towns where they made their money. Thus in Gloucestershire the earliest endowed schools were founded not in Bristol or Gloucester, but in lesser towns like Chipping Campden, Cirencester, Westbury-on-Trym, Winchcombe, Wotton-under-Edge and in Newland which was only a village. Not all these places had been without schoolmasters before, but the new endowed schools certainly brought stability. Their patrons and endowments existed to supply a constant succession of adequate schoolmasters, whose pupils could always be sure of getting their education, often at no cost to themselves. Not that the distribution of the early endowed schools was very regular, or in many counties very dense. While Gloucestershire had six by 1530, its larger neighbour Somerset had only two. In Lancashire there were as many as twelve by that date, while in Norfolk which was bigger and more populous there were only three. Smaller or more remote counties such as Cambridge or Cornwall had only one or two, but still there was hardly a single English shire without at least one when the Reformation began. Moreover, schoolmasters continued to teach for money in the smaller towns and even in the occasional village, especially in counties where not many new schools had been endowed. We have already seen how the fifteenth-century bishops of Norwich appointed schoolmasters both in Norwich and Thetford, and in a number of lesser towns and villages: Fincham, Harleston, Shipden, Shouldham, Sparham and Thornage. None of these places was very large, yet there is no sign that the schools concerned were endowed ones.[1]

Another source of education was to be found in the great households of the king, the bishops and the lay magnates, who frequently maintained schoolmasters to teach their own children and to instruct the other wards, clerks and choristers who might be living with them. Education in the royal household can be traced back to at least the early fourteenth century. Here there were two main groups of teachable boys: the children of the chapel royal, and the noble youths who were either in the king's wardship or came to be trained as 'henchmen', or pages. The children of the chapel received a musical education in the first instance, but they were not merely choristers, nor were they turned away when their voices had broken. That they were also able to learn grammar is evident from the promotion of many of them to study at university at the king's expense. In 1317

[1] See above, p. 144.

Edward II founded the first royal university college, the King's Hall, Cambridge, its original nucleus consisting of a royal clerk to act as master and twelve children of the chapel who were to follow the arts course. Throughout the fourteenth and fifteenth centuries a proportion of children proceeded either to the King's Hall or to other royal foundations in the two universities.[1] Exactly what arrangements were made for their tuition in grammar is not certain until 1401 when a chaplain named John Bagby was retained to teach them at a salary of £5 a year.[2]

The fully developed system of education in the royal household is clearly discernible by the middle of the fifteenth century from the *Liber Reges Capelle* of *c.* 1449 and the *Black Book of the Household* which dates from between 1467 and 1477.[3] The children of the chapel, reckoned at ten by the former and eight by the latter, learned plainsong and polyphony from a song schoolmaster who was also charged with teaching them good manners. The king's henchmen or pages of honour, numbering six or more as the king might please, were tutored by the master of the henchmen, a squire of the household, who schooled them in deportment, riding and feats of arms. Both groups of boys received instruction from a grammar master, who might or might not be a priest, and was to be skilled in poetry and grammatical rules. His services were also available to the poor clerks of the king's almonry and to other men and children of the court desirous to learn his art. The names of these 'schoolmasters of the henchmen', as they were usually called, do not seem to be extant before the 1520s. The earliest of whom we know was a certain Francis Philip who probably held the post by 1521. He had studied at Oxford but owing to poverty went down without taking his MA.[4] In December 1523 he appears as the ringleader in a curious plot involving other members of the royal household which aimed at seizing a consignment of taxation on its way to London in order to raise men and to capture Kenilworth Castle, or so it was said. After the discovery of the plot Philip inevitably suffered a traitor's death at Tyburn, a strange conclusion for an up-and-coming young schoolmaster.[5] His successor, Robert Whittinton, who was in

---

[1] Cobban, *The King's Hall, Cambridge*, pp. 60-3, where the whole subject is explained most clearly.
[2] J. H. Wylie, *History of England under Henry IV*, vol ii (1894), p. 487; vol iv (1898), p. 208.
[3] *Liber Reges Capelle*, ed. W. Ullmann (Henry Bradshaw Society, xcii, 1961), p. 57; A. R. Myers, *The Household of Edward IV* (1959), pp. 126-7, 136-8.
[4] Oxford, Bodleian, University Archives, Reg G folios 271, 274, Reg H fo 72; *Reg. Univ. Oxon.*, ed. Boase, i, 98.
[5] Edward Hall, *Chronicle Containing the History of England* (1809), p. 673.

office by 1528, cut a much more respectable figure, with a teaching career stretching back to 1501 and a number of popular textbooks to his credit. That his services were valued is shown by his salary, which at £20 was twice as much as most schoolmasters earned.[1] Whittinton retired at Christmas 1538 and was succeeded by Ralph Stannowe, an MA of Cambridge.[2]

The royal interest in education was reflected in many other great households. Private tuition is mentioned in a house in Coventry as early as 1318.[3] William Lord Ros, who made his will in 1413, arranged that the chaplain who sang for his soul should also teach grammar to his children, and the Luttrells of Dunster had a John Scolemaystre staying in their household for ten weeks in 1424.[4] Records of schools both in ecclesiastical and in lay households become increasingly common after the accession of Henry VII. Archbishop Morton's boys at Lambeth Palace were fortunate to be taught by John Holt – later appointed tutor to the prince of Wales – whose elementary Latin grammar *Lac Puerorum* was composed for their use.[5] Morton's contemporary Thomas Langton, bishop of Winchester from 1493 to 1501, also kept a school for the boys of his household, and the humanist writer Richard Pace who was one of their number has recorded the delight with which the bishop heard his scholars repeat in the evening what their teacher had told them during the day.[6] Among the laity Henry Percy, fifth earl of Northumberland, had a schoolmaster in his household by 1511 and Edward Stafford, the last of the ill-fated dukes of Buckingham, had one in 1521 for his wards and henchmen.[7] Thomas Grey, second marquess of Dorset, mentioned Henry Brooke, 'schoolmaster to my son Henry', in his will of 1530.[8] Not that the sons of the nobility were always educated in their own households. Thomas Grey himself and his two brothers have already been noticed

[1] For Whittinton in the royal household see *Trevelyan Papers*, ed. J. P. Collier, vol i (Camden Society, lxvii, 1857), p. 143; *LPFD*, xiii, part 2, no 1280, fo 9b etc. For his biography see *BRUO*, iii, 2039-40.
[2] *LPFD*, xiv, part 2, no 781 fo 64b.
[3] *The Liber Albus of the Priory of Worcester*, ed. J. M. Wilson (Worcs. Historical Society, xxxiii, 1919), p. 65 no 801.
[4] *Reg. Chichele, Canterbury*, ii, 23-4; H. C. Maxwell-Lyte, *History of Dunster* (1909), i, p. 101.
[5] John Holt, *Lac Puerorum* (c. 1496), sig. A i.5; for his career see *BRUO*, ii, 953-4, and also above, p. 110.
[6] Richard Pace, *De Fructu* (Basel, 1517), p. 28.
[7] *Regulations and Establishment of the Household of the Fifth Earl of Northumberland*, ed. T. Percy (1770), p. 44; *LPFD*, iii, part 1, p. 500.
[8] *Testamenta Vetusta*, ed. N. H. Nicolas (1826), ii, 652.

H*

attending Magdalen College school, where they were tutored by Thomas Wolsey.[1] Knights and gentlemen of lesser means sometimes made use of local schools. In the 1530s, Hugh Willoughby, who later explored the Arctic and was the second son of Sir Henry Willoughby of Middleton, went to school in the nearby town of Sutton Coldfield, while Nicholas son of Sir Thomas Lestrange of Hunstanton was also sent away to school, possibly at North Elmham.[2]

That some of the parish clergy also engaged in teaching has already been suggested in an earlier chapter, such teaching being usually in the elementary subjects, reading and song.[3] There are however a few indications that their range sometimes extended to include grammar as well. Rectors of parish churches occasionally gave tuition to those of their brother clergy whom the bishop found insufficiently learned to receive ordination or institution to a benefice.[4] A few parish priests may have taught grammar to secular boys as well. John Broke, a malter of Braughing in Hertfordshire, claimed to have learnt some grammar from the parish chaplain there, one Sir John, in the late 1460s.[5] The rector of Bilborough in Nottinghamshire who sued a youth in 1506 for twelve weeks' board and schooling was probably a teacher of grammar, for he afterwards became schoolmaster of Nottingham.[6] Two years later Richard Alkborough, rector of Burrough in Leicestershire, had ten scholars living with him – boys of leading county families such as Ashby, Skeffington and Villiers. He too became a professional grammar master later on.[7] Yet that teaching of a high level was common among the parish clergy or in any sense expected of them is doubtful. Teaching grammar is not mentioned in the popular manuals which treated of a priest's duties, nor did the failure to do so ever excite the wrath of the radical critics who so freely attacked all the other shortcomings of clerical life. Not until the Reforma-

---

[1] George Cavendish, *The Life and Death of Cardinal Wolsey*, ed. R. S. Sylvester (EETS, 1959), p. 5, and above, pp. 35-6.

[2] *Report on MSS of Lord Middleton*, pp. 346, 352, 359; D. Gurney, 'Household accounts of the Lestranges of Hunstanton', *Archaeologia*, xxv (1834), p. 466.

[3] See above, pp. 66-7.

[4] Compare examples from Devon, 1312 (*Reg. Stapeldon, Exeter*, p. 268), and Somerset, 1462-3 (*Reg. Bekynton, Wells*, i, 372-3; ii, 540). The rector in the latter case was subsequently, and perhaps formerly, a schoolmaster.

[5] Heath, *The English Parish Clergy on the Eve of the Reformation*, p. 208, dated from R. Clutterbuck, *History of the County of Herts.*, iii (1827), p. 156.

[6] *VCH Notts.*, ii, 221-2.

[7] Oxford, Brasenose College, Principal Yate's Book (1668), pp. 97-8. Alkborough was grammar master at Higham Ferrers in 1526 (*A Subsidy Collected in the Diocese of Lincoln, 1526*, ed. H. E. Salter (Oxford Historical Society, lxiii, 1909), p. 131).

tion were concerted attempts made by the convocation of Canterbury and some of the bishops to get the parish clergy to employ themselves in teaching boys the alphabet, reading, song or grammar.[1]

If the fifteenth century seems to us a period of educational progress, and of the endowment of schools on an unprecedented scale, some contemporaries thought otherwise. Shortly before 1439, on the eve of the foundation of Eton and the other new schools of the 1440s, William Bingham, rector of St John Zachary in London, in a petition to Henry VI drew a most unfavourable picture of the facilities available in the kingdom for learning grammar.[2] He asked the king to consider the lack of grammar school masters in the realm, which was likely to hinder the recruitment of the clergy and thereby to impair the whole clerical estate. He had found of late, he said, that east of the road from 'Hampton' (probably Hampton-on-Thames) to Coventry, and thence northwards to Ripon, seventy schools or more were empty which had all been occupied within the last fifty years, all because of the great scarcity of masters. This he ascribed to the decline of the study of grammar in the universities, because no endowments had yet been provided to support those who studied it there, as there had been for all the other liberal arts. Bingham was not alone in these views. Of the four London rectors who petitioned for more schools in the capital in 1447, two were his friends: John Coote and Gilbert Worthington; so it is not surprising that their petition also calls to mind 'the great number of grammar schools that sometime were in diverse parts of this realm, besides those that were in London, and how few be in these days'.[3]

Bingham's own petition concluded with proposals to found a house in the university of Cambridge to support twenty-four scholars of grammar with a priest to govern them, and for this he needed the king's patronage and support. The response was favourable. Royal permission was granted to proceed with the foundation and some modest properties formerly belonging to the alien priories were made over to provide an endowment. In 1448 the king's charter of foundation was issued, naming Henry as founder and Bingham as second founder. The college, which was named Godshouse, was governed by a proctor or master, and its statutes provided for twenty-five undergraduate scholars who were to read sophistry and logic and 'the subtler and deeper parts of grammar' such as Priscian,

---

[1] See below, pp. 254-6.
[2] *ECD*, pp. 402-3; A. H. Lloyd, *Early History of Christ's College, Cambridge* (1934), pp. 356-7.
[3] *Rotuli Parliamentorum*, v, 137.

Virgil and other poets, as well as the science of metre. When in due course they had qualified to take the university degree of master of grammar, they were liable to be called on to go and teach grammar anywhere in England that a grammar school had been built during the last forty years and where there was a suitable salary or livelihood for the master. In this way Bingham's scholars were to supply the want of schoolmasters which he had noticed in the 1430s.

In the event, however, Godshouse remained a much smaller foundation than Bingham had wished for. It seems unlikely ever to have supported more than a master, a lecturer and four scholars at any one time, and while some of the latter certainly took degrees in grammar, none has yet been traced to a school elsewhere. The college survived in this state until 1505 when a refoundation was carried out by Lady Margaret Beaufort who gave new endowments and renamed the house Christ's College. The fellows and scholars of the new foundation were intended to follow the usual arts course, but there still remained places for six who were to study grammar and go forth as chance required to teach their art in other parts of the kingdom.[1]

Even after the great advances made in founding new schools in the second half of the fifteenth century, there is still at least one dissenting voice to cast doubt upon the achievements of the age. This time the critic is Edmund Dudley, Henry VII's councillor, in the treatise on government which he wrote in prison in the Tower of London in 1509-10, shortly before his execution by Henry VIII. Perhaps being 'in worldly vexation and troubled with the sorrowful and bitter remembrance of death' helped to colour his surprisingly gloomy account of the state of education in his day:

> Loke well upon your two unyversyties, howe famouse thei have ben and in what condicion thei be now. Wheare be your famouse men that were wont to reade dyvinytie in every cathedrall churche and in other great monasteries? Where be the good and substanciall scollers of gramer that have ben kept in this realme before this tyme; not only in every good towne and citie and in other places, but also in all abbeyes, priories and collages, in prelates howses and often tymes in houses of men of honor of the temporaltie.[2]

---

[1] For Bingham and his college see A. H. Lloyd, *The Early History of Christ's College, Cambridge*, especially pp. 379ff. The statutes of Godshouse and Christ's are printed in *The Early Statutes of Christ's College, Cambridge* ed. H. Rackham (1927).
[2] Dudley, *The Tree of the Commonwealth*, p. 62.

These words from a man of some education and much experience call for our respectful attention, but their accuracy is not hard to question. The decline of the universities was a well-worn theme even among academics, yet it must be set beside the colleges, scholarships and lectureships which were founded in increasing numbers in the fifteenth century. The lecturing duties of cathedral chancellors were not entirely forgotten, and education in the monastic almonries, secular colleges and private households seems if anything to have been increasing. Dudley's belief in the decline of the grammar schools is interesting as a sequel to Bingham's, but it would not have been easy for him to prove the existence in former times of all the schools which he believed to have disappeared. Yet in the awareness of a problem and the desire for improvement, Dudley, like Bingham, provides yet another sign of the growing interest in education during the century before the Reformation.

Chapter Eight

The religious orders and education

Our inquiries so far have been limited to the developments among the secular schools in England during the middle ages. Of all the educational institutions which existed the secular schools were the most populous and catered for the largest groups among the educated public: the secular clergy and the laity. Their importance is undeniable, yet it is not the whole story. Besides the seculars and the laity there were the religious orders, by no means insignificant in numbers, which at their peak in the late thirteenth and early fourteenth centuries contained no less than 17,000 souls. As their members all lived in varying degrees of discipline and seclusion, it was difficult for them to attend the public schools, besides which the special ends towards which their lives were directed often called for special kinds of education. Hence the religious orders came to possess their own schools, which though less populous than the schools of the world were no less ambitious in their work and useful in their effect. More than this, the religious in many places came to acquire educational interests outside their own communities and to offer facilities for learning not only to their own members but to seculars as well. For all these reasons they demand our attention, and to them we must now turn.

In the twelfth century the age in which English education had been dominated by the Benedictine monasteries was just drawing to a close.[1] Previously in the almost complete absence of secular schools the monasteries had been obliged to arrange for the education of prospective recruits from early childhood. They had received young boys or 'oblates' whom their

[1] On the monasteries and education in the eleventh and twelfth centuries see M. C. Knowles, *The Monastic Order in England*, 2nd ed. (1963), to which the following paragraphs are much indebted.

parents offered at a tender age, and boarded and schooled them so that they might live in the monastery and make their profession as monks when they grew up. This system is still visible in the constitutions issued by Archbishop Lanfranc for the cathedral priory of Christ Church, Canterbury, in the 1070s or 80s. When children were to be offered as oblates, they were brought by their parents already tonsured into the monastery church at the time of mass. After the gospel, the child bore the bread and wine necessary for the eucharist and offered it to the celebrant priest. Then the parents took the child to the altar and wrapped his hands in the altar cloth, as a token of his dedication. They promised the abbot that they would not cause the child to abandon the monastic life, and their promise had also to be written down and witnessed. The abbot then did off the child's cloak and put on a monk's cowl, after which he was taken away to be shaven and clad in full monastic dress.[1]

Some other details of the life of the oblates can be gathered from Lanfranc's constitutions. They were under the supervision of the 'master of the children', a discreet monk, assisted by other masters. They lived in the monastery and had their own chapter meetings as the monks did, for the punishment of misdemeanours. They attended many of the divine offices in the monastery church and sang antiphons when necessary. They learned reading and practised chant. When they grew up they made their profession as monks. By the twelfth century, however, the practice of child oblation was dying. It was becoming unnecessary in that with the increasing number of secular schools, boys could be educated in the world and join a religious order, if they developed the vocation to do so, when they grew up. The last recorded examples of the practice in the English Benedictine houses belong to the mid-twelfth century. Meanwhile an order against receiving boys under the age of fifteen had already been issued in 1134 by the new reformed order of monks, the Cistercians, and this was raised to eighteen in 1175.[2] In 1168 the monks of St Augustine's, Canterbury, who disapproved of the practice, procured a papal decree that no one should be received as a novice until he was eighteen.[3] After 1215 the canon law of the western Church discouraged the entry of children into the religious orders under the age of fourteen.[4]

[1] *The Monastic Constitutions of Lanfranc*, ed. M. C. Knowles (1951), pp. 110-11, *et passim*.
[2] *Statuta Capitulorum Generalium Ordinis Cisterciensis*, ed. J. M. Canivez, vol i (1933), pp. 31, 84.
[3] *Historiae Anglicanae Scriptores X*, ed. R. Twysden (1652), col 1815.
[4] *Corpus Juris Canonici*, ed. E. Friedberg, vol ii (1881), col 571.

In addition to the reception of oblates, the twelfth-century monasteries sometimes gave education to other boys who either did not become monks or were never intended to do so. In 1149 Geoffrey of Quarrington gave his son Ralph to be brought up for seven years in Ramsey Abbey.[1] At about the same time Gerald of Wales, the famous ecclesiastic and historian, went to school in the abbey of St Peter at Gloucester under Master Hamo, whom he described as 'a most learned man'.[2] His own subsequent career was not that of a monk, but of a secular clerk. And in the 1170s Queen Eleanor of Aquitaine sent a child whom she had found abandoned in the highway to be brought up at Abingdon Abbey, where we are told that he studied letters.[3] But here too the rise of secular schools in the twelfth century makes it unlikely that many secular boys received instruction in the monasteries, and the recorded instances are indeed few. Already the amount of schooling offered by the monks to outsiders was small: not negligible, nor without value, but additional rather than central to the facilities for education generally available.

The religious scene changed dramatically with the rise of the friars under their first founders, Francis and Dominic, at the beginning of the thirteenth century. The friars represented a new development, quite different from the older kind of monasticism. They had their convents, their common life and their daily office like the monks, but in other respects they differed markedly. First and foremost, they were not to remain confined within the walls of their communities, but to go out into the world: to preach, to minister to the souls of the laity and to perform works of mercy. Second, they were far more strictly bound than any monks to a life of poverty, having no endowments to support them and living almost entirely from alms – hence their name of mendicants, or beggars. Third and most relevant to our subject, they were zealous pursuers of learning, who developed effective systems by which all their members could acquire a competent degree of knowledge and the most talented receive the best education that the times allowed. This emphasis on education was not of course a luxury; it was absolutely essential to the efficient execution of their pastoral role, as Humbert of Romans, master-general of the Dominican order who died in 1277, explained very clearly: 'Study is not the end of the Order, but it is exceedingly necessary to

---

[1] *Chronicon Abbatiae Rameseiensis*, ed. W. D. Macray (Rolls Series, 1886), pp. 268-9.
[2] *Giraldi Cambrensis Opera*, ed. J. S. Brewer, vol iv (Rolls Series, 1873), p. 107.
[3] *Materials for the History of Thomas Becket*, ed. J. C. Robertson, vol i (Rolls Series, 1875), p. 213.

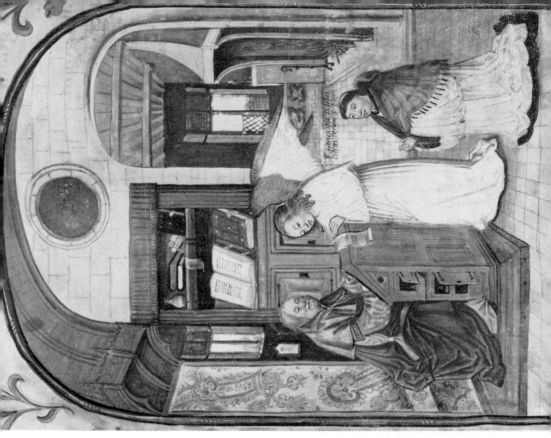

12 *and* 13
*BENEFACTORS OF
SCHOOLS: I–THE
CLERGY*

(Right) Richard FitzJames
(d. 1522), bishop of London,
founder of Bruton grammar
school; (far right) his dean,
John Colet (d. 1519),
refounder of St Paul's
school. Though bitter
enemies, they agreed in
their love for education.

14 BENEFACTORS
OF SCHOOLS:
II–THE NOBILITY
AND GENTRY

Lady Katherine Berkeley
(d. 1385), who founded the
first chantry grammar
school at Wotton-under-
Edge, Gloucs., in 1384. She
lies by her second husband,
Thomas Lord Berkeley.

15 *BENEFACTORS OF SCHOOLS:*
III–THE MERCHANT CLASS

John Cook (d. 1528), mercer and mayor of Gloucester, and his wife
Joan (d. 1546), founders of the Crypt school, Gloucester.

16 *THE EDUCATIONAL ACHIEVEMENT* of fifteenth-century England is typified by William Wainfleet, the first schoolmaster of the English Renaissance to rise to heights of wealth and power, and himself the founder of schools at Oxford and Wainfleet (plate 7). His guardian angel offers up his coat of arms and that of his greatest achievement – Magdalen College.

secure its ends, namely preaching and the salvation of souls, for without study we can do neither.'[1] The emphasis on study was a particular characteristic of Dominic and his followers, and in the early days it did not find acceptance everywhere, but as the thirteenth century passed all the mendicant orders began to realize the benefits of learning and the perils of neglecting it, so that all in time dedicated themselves to following the Dominican ideal.

Four great orders of friars organized themselves in the first half of the thirteenth century. The Dominicans were the earliest to reach England in 1221, and the Franciscans followed three years later. They were the two larger orders, the Dominicans having some fifty-three houses by the fourteenth century, a number they maintained until the Reformation, and the Franciscans having fifty-seven, rising to about sixty in the early sixteenth century. The first Carmelites came in about 1240 and the Augustinians in 1249 and their resources were slightly smaller. There were usually thirty-seven Carmelite houses in the later middle ages, and thirty-three Augustinian. In point of numbers the friars reached their peak of about 5,000 in the early fourteenth century, but this fell by as much as a half immediately after the Black Death, rising slowly again to 3,000 in the fifteenth and early sixteenth centuries. Very roughly the friars formed a quarter of the population of the religious orders at most periods during the later middle ages.[2]

One of the special characteristics of the friars was their readiness to take boys into their order after this had fallen out of favour with the monks. The Dominicans indeed fixed the entry to the novitiate at eighteen in their constitutions of 1228, but this was not necessarily observed in later times, and some of the other orders reduced the age considerably.[3] The Franciscan constitutions of 1280 decided on eighteen as well, but they also permitted boys to be received from the age of fifteen in exceptional cases. In 1316 they lowered the age of entry to the canonical minimum of fourteen, and nine years later it became possible for even younger children to enter the order if their parents offered them, though they were not to be fully professed until they were fifteen.[4] The Augustinians in 1290 fixed on the

[1] Humbert de Romans, *Opera*, ed. J. J. Berthier, vol ii (1889), p. 41.
[2] On these statistics see further M. C. Knowles and R. N. Hadcock, *Medieval Religious Houses: England and Wales*, 2nd ed. (1971), pp. 212-50, 492-4.
[3] *Archiv für Litteratur- und Kirchengeschichte des Mittelalters*, ed. P. H. Denifle and F. Ehrle, vol i (1885), p. 202.
[4] P. M. Bihl, 'Statuta generalia ordinis edita', *Archivum Franciscanum Historicum*, xxxiv (1941), p. 39; A. Carlini, 'Constitutiones generales ordinis fratrum minorum anno 1316', ibid., iv (1911), pp. 277, 527.

age of fourteen, but sixty years later they made it eleven, and after 1385 younger boys could also be accepted.[1] These practices caused some scandal, and in 1357 the friars' great enemy Richard FitzRalph, archbishop of Armagh, accused them of enticing boys into their orders when they would never have been able to attract grown men, quoting a specific instance of a man whose son had been 'abducted' by the friars of Oxford before he was thirteen.[2] Shortly after this the university authorities at Oxford passed a statute prohibiting the friars there from receiving converts who were less than eighteen, but the friars fought back and in 1366 the statute was rescinded in parliament after an appeal.[3] In 1402 another attempt was made to restrict the reception of boys, this time by a petition from the House of Commons that the age of entry should be raised to twenty-one, but the crown responded more cautiously and merely issued a statute reaffirming the canonical age of fourteen as the minimum, while still permitting parents who so wished to put their children with the friars at an earlier age.[4] Boys continued to enter the orders, and the fifteenth century provides more than one example of entry at the age of ten or eleven.[5]

The Dominicans, whose constitutions of 1228 are the earliest, were not specific about the qualifications for entry into the order, candidates being merely examined 'in morals and knowledge'.[6] In view of the youth of some of those admitted it is very likely that many novices needed instruction in grammar, and Roger Bacon said as much in 1271 when he claimed that 'many thousands' entered the Franciscan and Dominican orders who could read neither the psalter nor Donatus.[7] Grammar schools of some kind must have existed within the order, for in 1328 the Dominican general chapter ordered that no one should be permitted to learn logic until he was proficient in grammar.[8] In 1520 Clement Guadel of the convent of Yarm in Yorkshire was allowed to attend grammar school while he was a friar there, and in 1538 the Dominicans of London had a

---

[1] F. Roth, *The English Austin Friars, 1249-1538* (1966), pp. 136-7.

[2] J. R. H. Moorman, *The Grey Friars in Cambridge, 1225-1538* (1952), pp. 107-8.

[3] *Statuta Antiqua Universitatis Oxon.*, ed. Gibson, pp. 164-5; *Rotuli Parliamentorum*, ii, 290.

[4] Ibid., iii, 502.

[5] J. R. H. Moorman, op. cit., pp. 106-13; F. Roth, *Sources for a History of the English Austin Friars* (reprinted from *Augustiniana*, viii-xi, 1958-61), pp. 266, 385. For a Carmelite instance see PRO, C 1/4/104.

[6] *Archiv für Litteratur*, i, 202.

[7] Bacon, *Opera Inedita*, ed. J. S. Brewer (Rolls Series, 1859), p. 426.

[8] *Monumenta Ordinis Fratrum Praedicatorum Historica*, ed. B. M. Reichert, vol iv (1899), p. 179.

grammar master in their house who was maintained at the expense of the Goldsmiths' Company.[1]

The chief object of the Dominican studies however was theology, and it dominated all their legislation on the subject of study and learning.[2] Very early on in the history of the order, in the constitutions of 1228, it was laid down that no house should be without a teacher, the subject of whose lectures would appear to have been elementary practical theology, suitable for preparing the friars for their preaching and pastoral work. The Dominicans originally discouraged the study of the arts. The 1228 constitutions declared that students should not study the books of the 'Gentiles' and philosophers, though they might look into them occasionally. They were not to learn secular sciences nor those which were called the 'liberal arts' without a special dispensation from the authorities of the order.[3] But it soon became clear that if theology was to be properly studied at anything more than an elementary level, it involved the mastery of logic and philosophy. In 1259, therefore, the Dominican general chapter ordered that each province should have a centre for the study of the arts, where the young men might receive instruction.[4] And by the end of the century the order was beginning to evolve a coherent scheme of education by which its more talented members could be prepared for study in the universities. The general chapter of 1297 laid down that residence in the order for two years and instruction in song and the divine office should precede the study of arts.[5] In 1305 the general chapter at Genoa set out the order of studies as follows. No one was to study logic unless he had passed two years in the order. After three years of logic, he could progress to natural philosophy, after two years of which he could go on to hear lectures on the *Sentences* of Peter Lombard, the chief textbook of theology then in use. A student who had made progress in logic and philosophy and had heard the *Sentences* for two years might go on to a *studium generale*, which meant a centre of advanced study open to friars of the order everywhere, which might or might not be in a university town.[6] In 1309 it was further provided that a year should be passed in hearing lectures on the Bible before going on to the *studium*

---

[1] *VCH Yorks.*, iii, 282; *LPFD*, xiii, part 2, no 809.
[2] The following paragraphs on the Dominicans are based mainly on A. G. Little, 'Educational organisation of the mendicant friars in England', *Transactions of the Royal Historical Society*, new series, viii (1894), pp. 49-70.
[3] *Archiv für Litteratur*, i, 222.
[4] *Monumenta Ord. Frat. Praed.*, vol iii (1898), p. 99.
[5] Ibid., iii, 285.
[6] Ibid., iv, 12-13.

generale.[1] With such preparations the Dominican students would be well grounded to study theology at the highest level, in a university if necessary.

These higher studies in logic, philosophy and theology would not have been available at every Dominican convent, but at a smaller number of centres in each province of the order. In 1335 the general chapter commanded each province (of which England was one) to maintain two centres for the study of arts, two for natural philosophy and two for theology.[2] This minimum was probably exceeded in England, but the subject is rather unclear. The study of the arts or logic is however mentioned at Glasgow in 1476 and at Oxford in 1505, while philosophy was apparently studied at King's Lynn in 1397. Towards the end of the fourteenth century there are indications that the higher study of theology was pursued at several English convents: Guildford, Ipswich, Lincoln, Newcastle-on-Tyne, Norwich and Thetford, as well as at London in 1475.[3] Lastly there were the *studia generalia* at Paris and Oxford, and later Cambridge, where the Dominicans had established houses. At this level study in the order was truly international, foreign students being received at English houses, and English friars of distinction crossing the Channel to read theology at Paris and elsewhere.[4]

The organization of studies among the Franciscans is badly obscured by lack of records, but it was clearly well established by the middle of the thirteenth century.[5] The first historian of the order in England, Thomas of Eccleston, tells us that by 1254 there were thirty lecturers solemnly disputing in the English houses, and three or four who lectured without disputation. Moreover the minister of the English province, William of Nottingham, had assigned students in the universities to succeed these lecturers on their death or removal. The study of arts had not developed in the order at this time, and these were clearly theological lectures: the students at the universities pursuing the subject at an advanced level and doubtless expounding it in a more elementary way in the convents. Eccleston mentions five places to which lecturers went from Oxford: Bristol, Canterbury, Hereford, Leicester and London, and there are

---

[1] *Monumenta Ord. Frat. Praed.*, iv, 38.
[2] Ibid., p. 229.
[3] *Transactions of the Royal Historical Society*, new series, viii (1894), pp. 51-6.
[4] For instances of foreign friars in English Dominican houses see A. B. Emden, *A Survey of Dominicans in England, 1268-1538* (1967), pp. 22-7.
[5] This section is chiefly based on A. G. Little, *Studies in English Franciscan History* (1917), pp. 158-73, and on his article in *Transactions of the Royal Historical Society*, new series, viii (1894), pp. 63-7.

references to other schools at Gloucester, Northampton and Norwich at this time.[1]

It is probable that the Franciscans developed a course of studies broadly similar to the Dominicans'. In 1292 their general chapter ordered each province to provide centres for the study of arts in which the young members of the order might be instructed.[2] In 1421 another decree prescribed that friars must have lectured on arts and philosophy for seven years and on the *Sentences* for at least one year before proceeding to take the degree of DD in a university.[3] While nothing is known of the siting of the Franciscan schools of grammar, logic or philosophy, seven centres of the higher study of theology are mentioned in England in 1336: Coventry, Exeter, London, Norwich, Stamford and York. These convents fall each into one of the seven 'custodies' or divisions of the English province, and it is probable that each served the other houses in its custody.[4] From there the student friars could progress to study theology at a *studium generale* such as Paris or Oxford, these being international to the whole order, as was usual among all the friars.

The educational arrangements of the Augustinians followed much the same pattern.[5] The young friars of the order, after a year's novitiate in which they learned the divine office, were eligible to be sent to grammar school. A decree of the general chapter in 1315 ordered each province to set aside two houses for the study of grammar, and the presence of fourteen boys at Thetford in 1424 and sixteen at Lynn in 1446 makes it likely that these houses at least supported such schools. Next the students could pass to the schools of logic and philosophy, which were ordered to be established in each province in 1326, either in one or in two places. In England three of these schools are mentioned, corresponding to three of the four districts or 'limits' into which the province was divided. Friars from the limit of Cambridge would have attended Norwich for this purpose, those from Lincoln, Leicester, and those from Oxford, Bristol. After at least three years in such a school one could go on to a *studium generale*, of which there were three kinds in the order. The province possessed its own *studia generalia* for its own friars, and once again these corresponded to the limits: Lynn for Cambridge, Stamford for Lincoln, and London for Oxford. Two other advanced schools at York and

[1] *Monumenta Franciscana*, ed. J. S. Brewer, vol i (Rolls Series, 1858), pp. 38-9, 319; *CCR 1242-7*, p. 447; *CCR 1256-9*, p. 241.

[2] *Archiv für Litteratur*, vol vi (1892), p. 64.

[3] *Transactions of the Royal Historical Society*, new series, viii (1894), p. 65.

[4] Ibid., pp. 68-9.

[5] On this subject see Roth, *The English Austin Friars*, pp. 140-77.

Lincoln were called *studia concursoria*, but their exact nature is unknown. Lastly the schools at Oxford and Cambridge ranked as *studia generalia* of the whole order, to which friars from all over Europe might be sent to study, but only after they had passed three years in the *studia generalia* of their provinces. All three grades of *studia generalia* were concerned with the study of theology, but logic and philosophy could also be pursued there.

The Carmelite constitutions issued in 1324 ordered that places should be provided in each province for the education of the friars in grammar, logic, philosophy and theology.[1] Traces of these study centres can be found in England, where Hitchin and Maldon are known to have had schools of grammar and logic, while philosophy was studied at Winchester and theology at Coventry, London and Stamford.[2] Higher than these schools were the *studia generalia* where theology and philosophy could be studied, and to which all the provinces in the order might send their friars. Curiously enough the constitutions of 1324 mention London as the English *studium generale*, but later on Oxford and Cambridge seem to have taken its place. In 1396 we hear that England was divided into four districts centred on London, Norwich, Oxford and York, each of which sent an equal number of friars to the universities. And in the following year Pope Boniface IX ordered that the length of time spent in studying arts should be seven years and for theology another seven, after which three years must be spent lecturing upon the *Sentences* and one upon the Bible before taking the doctorate of divinity.[3]

Clearly all four orders of friars developed highly organized systems for educating their brethren in the later middle ages. This leads us to ask if they extended their facilities to others, opening their grammar schools to other boys than the oblates and novices, and admitting secular clerks to their lecture rooms. The evidence unfortunately is not conclusive. In 1497 the Augustinian general chapter specifically forbade its members to keep schools of grammar and song to which seculars might have access.[4] But the willingness of the friars to receive young children suggests that they sometimes offered to educate them with a view to their becoming novices later on, and that those who never developed a vocation went forth into the world having had an education at the friars' expense. Such a boy may have been John Gaunte of Tickhill in Yorkshire who recalled in 1568, when giving evidence in a tithe dispute, that from about 1502 when he

[1] *Monumenta Historica Carmelitana*, ed. B. Zimmerman, vol i (1905), p. 60.
[2] M. C. Knowles, *The Religious Orders in England*, vol ii (1961), pp. 144-5.
[3] *Calendar of Papal Letters*, v, 1, 19-20.
[4] Roth, *The English Austin Friars*, p. 177.

was four until the age of fifteen, he had 'learned in the schools in the friars of Tickhill', who were Augustinians, and had then left and been set to husbandry or farming.[1] A similar case is that of Henry Triplett who told an Oxford church court in 1579 that sixty years earlier when he was fourteen he had gone to school at the Dominican priory in the city; this lasted however for only a year, and in later life he became a glover.[2] A third example, also from the Tudor period, suggests a friar acting as a private tutor in a lay household. Writing to Cromwell in 1533, John Coppledyke, a Lincolnshire gentleman, tried unsuccessfully to intercede for an Augustinian friar who was being transferred to London from one of the local houses of the order. Coppledyke praised the friar's diligence in teaching his children and added, 'such another, to my mind, of his conversation and kindness and good disposition in my house, shall be very hard for me to get'.[3]

There are also a few indications that older students were sometimes admitted to the friars' lectures, at least in the thirteenth century. The Dominican constitutions of 1228 make a distinction between public and private lectures, and the general chapter of the Franciscans in 1292 forbade seculars to be admitted to lectures on law and medicine, as if implying that there was no difficulty for them to attend those on theology. The presence of secular clerks in the classrooms of the mendicant orders is well attested on the continent, and is likely therefore to have been found in England too, at least on occasion.[4]

Meanwhile what was the interest in education among the older religious orders – the monks and the regular canons? There were two great orders of monks in England after the twelfth century – the black or Benedictines and the white or Cistercians. Of these the black monks were the more numerous, with over 200 houses and 3,800 members in the thirteenth and early fourteenth centuries (excluding small cells), while the Cistercians occupied about 75 houses and had some 2,100 members.[5] After the disappearance of child oblation in the twelfth century, entry to the monastic life was always made in adulthood, the age of twenty being generally accepted as the minimum for the aspiring novice. By this time candidates for the novitiate had probably already followed some kind of course at a secular school, and some attention seems to have been given to ensuring

[1] *Select XVIth Century Causes in Tithe*, ed. J. S. Purvis (Yorks. Archaeological Society Record Series, cxiv, 1947), pp. 108-9.
[2] Oxford, Bodleian, University Archives, Hyp. B 2 (not paginated, but *circa* fo 78).
[3] *LPFD*, vi, no 1270.
[4] See the references in A. G. Little, *Studies in English Franciscan History*, pp. 168-72, not all of which seem as conclusive as he suggested.
[5] For more detailed statistics see Knowles and Hadcock, op. cit., pp. 489-90.

that they were literate before they were admitted. Bishop Walpole's injunctions for Ely in 1300 declared that scholars or clerks seeking to be admitted as monks were to be received 'if literate and otherwise fit'.[1] Archbishop Winchelsey, when visiting Gloucester Abbey in the following year, ordered that candidates for admission should be examined for their knowledge of letters and song.[2] The monks of Christ Church, Canterbury, in 1324 refused admission to an inexperienced clerk named Edmund Basing and advised him to go away to learn reading, song and grammar before presenting himself again.[3] After being admitted to a monastery a candidate passed a year as a novice in which he received from a senior monk instruction of a practical rather than an intellectual nature. He was taught how to behave and how to perform the menial services demanded in church and cloister; he received instruction in the rule of his order, and he began to learn the material of the liturgy which in due course he would have to recite.

The minimum literary qualifications demanded of monks in the thirteenth century were thus that they should be able to read, sing, and perform the liturgy correctly, and no doubt many communities aimed at little more. But the success of the friars in developing a system of local schools and invading the universities was very probably responsible for stimulating in the older orders of monks and canons a sense of their deficiencies and a desire to improve their educational standards. By the middle of the thirteenth century the first attempts were being made by both the black monks and the white to improve the facilities for study in their orders. In 1245 the general chapter of the Cistercian order, which met at Cîteaux, urged that every abbey should have facilities for study if possible, and that there should be at least one place in each province (of which England was one) where theology could be studied all the year round.[4] Two years later the general chapter of the English Benedictine houses in the province of Canterbury made a similar pronouncement that a lecture in theology or canon law should be established in each abbey or priory where the resources permitted, to be read either by a religious or a secular person.[5] This early legislation both of the white and the black monks was tentative rather than decisive, and it is by no means certain how far it was carried

[1] S. J. A. Evans, 'Ely chapter ordinances', *Camden Miscellany XVII* (Camden third series, lxiv, 1940), p. 14.
[2] *Historia et Cartularium Monasterii Gloucs.*, ed. W. H. Hart, vol i (Rolls Series, 1863), pp. lxxxiv-v.
[3] *Literae Cantuarienses*, ed. J. B. Sheppard, vol i (Rolls Series, 1887), pp. 126-7.
[4] *Stat. Ord. Cist.*, ed. Canivez, vol ii (1934), pp. 289-90.
[5] *Chapters of the English Black Monks*, ed. W. A. Pantin, vol i (Camden third series, xlv, 1931), pp. 27-8.

out. However, the impulse towards improvement did not die away, but grew stronger as the years passed and the successes of the friars and the seculars at the universities became ever more apparent. In 1275 the cathedral priory of Christ Church, Canterbury, always a house with high standards, instituted a lecturer in theology, who in the absence of trained monks was a friar, William Everal, a point which caused much misgiving to the monastic chronicler. 'This', he grumbled, 'was unheard of in former times, and what will be the result of this lecture and school the future will show, since novelties produce quarrels.'[1] But two years later the Benedictine chapter of the southern province decided that the time had come to establish a centre at Oxford to which brethren from any house of the order might be sent to study, the chapter making the significant comment, 'so that study may cause our religion to flourish again'.[2] In order to pay for the scheme a rate was levied on each house, but the disagreements this caused held up the venture, and in the meantime the white monks got in ahead of the black. In 1280 Edmund earl of Cornwall came to an agreement with the Cistercian general chapter to found a monastery at Oxford to which the monks could go for study, and this foundation opened in the western suburbs of the city in the following year as Rewley Abbey. It was the first settlement of any of the regular clergy at an English university.[3]

The difficulty of co-ordinating a large number of disunited and autonomous houses continued to delay the Benedictines for several more years. In 1283 Sir John Giffard of Brimpsfield in Gloucestershire provided the site for a college, also in the west of Oxford, but by 1288 still nothing had been done, and the leaders of the order summoning their colleagues to a new general chapter reminded them of 'how much reproach we have borne in the past for not erecting a house at Oxford for the students of our order, while the Cistercians from the same region as ours have built their place of study like prudent and honest men whom the Lord has blessed'.[4] However, by 1291 the first Benedictine scholars appear to have arrived at Oxford, and in 1298 the study centre of the black monks, Gloucester College, was at last formally established.[5] It very much reflected the auto-

[1] *The Historical Works of Gervase of Canterbury*, ed. W. Stubbs, vol ii (Rolls Series 1880), p. 281.
[2] Pantin, *Chapters*, i, 75.
[3] On Rewley Abbey see *VCH Oxon.*, ii, 81-3, and *Stat. Ord. Cist.*, ed. Canivez, vol iii (1935), pp. 200, 217.
[4] Pantin, *Chapters*, i, 127.
[5] On its early history see V. H. Galbraith, 'Some new documents about Gloucester College', *Snappe's Formulary*, ed. H. E. Salter (Oxford Historical Society, lxxx, 1924), pp. 337-86b.

nomous nature of the Benedictine houses in that while it had a prior as supervisor and a common hall and chapel, the chambers were built and maintained by several different houses which accommodated their own monks there or rented them out to others. Furthermore, two of the greatest Benedictine houses came ultimately to have their own colleges at Oxford. As early as 1286, before Gloucester College was properly open, the monks of Durham Cathedral had begun to buy land in Oxford for a house for their own students, and this was eventually established as Durham College.[1] Then in 1331 the cathedral priory of Christ Church, Canterbury, opened a hall for four monks which Archbishop Islip endowed as Canterbury College in 1363.[2] At much the same time John Crowden, prior of Ely (1321-41), opened Ely Hostel at Cambridge for those of his house who wished to study there, and this also provided accommodation for monks from elsewhere.[3]

William Broc of Gloucester Abbey, the first Benedictine to attain the doctorate of divinity at Oxford, took his degree in 1298 to the great rejoicing of his order – five abbots and many priors, monks, clerks and gentlemen attending the festivities held to mark the occasion.[4] Others followed him, both of the white and the black monks, and it soon became possible for the Oxford graduates to return home and begin lecturing on theology to their brethren. Worcester Priory in particular was able to lend its graduate monks to the other houses of the order, as well as using them at home. Thus John of St Germans went off to lecture at St Augustine's, Canterbury, from 1308 to 1310, and Ranulf Calthorpe was lecturing at Ramsey in 1318 when he was recalled to Worcester to take the place of the convent's own lecturer, Richard Bromwich.[5]

As well as the two great orders of monks, there were a large number of religious houses in England belonging to the three orders of canons regular – the black or Augustinians, the white or Premonstratensians and the Gilbertines. Of these the Augustinians with about 208 houses and about 2,700 canons at the peak period ranked second in numbers only to the Benedictines, but their role in the educational revival is much more obscure, and it is not until 1325 that an ordinance of their general chapter survives ordering that scholars from the order be sent to the 'schools',

[1] H. E. D. Blakiston, 'Some Durham college rolls', *Collectanea III*, ed. M. Burrows (Oxford Historical Society, xxxii, 1896), pp. 6-7.
[2] *VCH Oxon.*, ii, 68.
[3] J. Bentham, *History and Antiquities of Ely Cathedral*, 2nd ed. (1812), p. 20.
[4] *BRUO*, i, 272.
[5] On St Germans see *BRUO*, iii, 1626; on Calthorpe, ibid., i, 340-1; and on Bromwich, ibid., i, 277-8.

which evidently means the universities.[1] The Premonstratensians are not known to have made any general arrangements for education in England, although individual canons certainly studied at university during the fifteenth century.[2] It is surprisingly the modest order of the Gilbertines with only 24 houses and perhaps 250 inmates which seems first among the regular canons to have developed a strong interest in education. In 1290 their chief house, the priory of Sempringham in Lincolnshire, received a papal licence to appoint a discreet and learned doctor of theology to teach the brethren in that subject.[3] At the same time the convent was negotiating to acquire a site in Cambridge for a house of study, and this opened in 1291 as the priory of St Edmund, the students of which, we are told, were assiduous in attending lectures and disputations.[4] Finally in 1301 a Lincolnshire rector, Master Robert Luttrell, granted Sempringham a site in Stamford which though not recognized as a university town was nevertheless an important centre for the study of both grammar and theology. This site was used to build a third house of study which, according to the bishop of Lincoln who confirmed the grant in 1303, was to provide a place for scholars of the order to study philosophy and theology. Its subsequent history however is not clear.[5]

Thus the second half of the thirteenth century and the first half of the fourteenth saw nearly all the great orders of monks and canons develop an interest in education with a view to fostering the study of theology among their members. At first the impetus for improvement came from within the orders themselves without any stimulus from outside other than the educational successes of the friars and the secular clergy. Then in the first half of the fourteenth century the papacy took a hand and sought by the promulgation of canon law to rationalize and enforce the policies which the religious themselves had begun. The first of these papal pronouncements on the education of the regular clergy was the decree *Ne in Agro* issued by Pope Clement V at the general council of Vienne in 1311. That an opportune way might not be lacking for monks to make progress in learning, every monastery where the resources sufficed for the purpose was to maintain a suitable master to instruct the brethren in the elementary branches of learning.[6] Here was the first sign of a new concern

---

[1] *Chapters of the Augustinian Canons*, ed. H. E. Salter (Oxford Historical Society, lxxiv, 1922), p. 13.
[2] H. M. Colvin, *The White Canons in England* (1951), pp. 320-3.
[3] *Calendar of Papal Letters*, i, 516.
[4] Ibid., p. 514; *VCH Cambs.*, ii, 254-6.
[5] *CPR 1301-7*, p. 6; Dugdale, *Monasticon*, vi, part 2, 947-8.
[6] *Corpus Juris Canonici*, ed. E. Friedberg, vol ii (1881), cols 1166-8.

with grounding monks in grammar and logic as well as the theology with which their own legislation had been chiefly concerned. This papal legislation was carried a good deal further by one of Clement's successors, Benedict XII, a Cistercian monk who reigned at Avignon from 1334 until 1342 and made himself something of a reputation as a reformer of the clergy. During his pontificate Benedict issued three great reforming constitutions for the three largest monastic orders: *Fulgens sicut Stella* for the Cistercians in 1335, *Summi Magistri* for the Benedictines in 1336 and *Ad Decorem Ecclesiae* for the Augustinian canons in 1339. The question of education occupies no little space in all three of them.[1]

Benedict XII's educational policies centred on two points: the provision of a schoolmaster in each monastery to teach grammar and logic to the monks, and the further education of the best pupils at university in the study of theology or canon law. Thus the Benedictine and Augustinian constitutions demand that each monastery shall maintain a schoolmaster to instruct the monks in the 'primitive sciences', that is, grammar, logic and philosophy. The master could be either a member of the order or another religious or a secular. If a secular, he was to receive board, clothing and a salary of not more than 20 *livres tournois*, or about £3 6s. 8d. in the English currency of that day. If a member of the order, he was only entitled to 10 *livres tournois* along with his food and clothing. Secular *students* however were not to be admitted to these monastic schools. Curiously, there was no corresponding provision for schoolmasters in the Cistercian constitutions of 1335, but this does not mean that the white monks were wanting in this respect, for only recently in 1331 the general chapter of their own order had commanded that communities of forty monks or more should maintain a lecturer to instruct the younger brethren in grammar and logic, and that houses of smaller size should either maintain a lecturer or send their monks to a larger house which possessed one.[2]

After the monks and canons had been instructed in the elementary branches of learning, they were to go on to the study of theology and canon law or, in the case of the Cistercians, theology alone. The arrangements for the Cistercians reflected their strongly centralized organization which transcended national frontiers. There were to be five local centres of higher study in Western Europe, and one international one at Paris.

---

[1] These are printed in C. Cocquelines, *Bullarum Privilegiorum ac Diplomatum Romanorum Pontificum Collectio*, vol iii, part 2 (1741), pp. 203-13, 214-20, 264-86, respectively.

[2] *Stat. Ord. Cist.*, ed. Canivez, iii, 392-3. For indications of the size of the English Cistercian houses at this time, see Knowles and Hadcock, *Medieval Religious Houses: England and Wales*, pp. 110-28.

Every monastery of over forty monks was to send two of them to study theology at Paris, and each with over thirty was to send one. Houses of between eighteen and thirty monks were to send one of them to the local centre of higher study, which in the case of the British Isles was to be Oxford. The Benedictine and Augustinian constitutions did not provide for an international study centre. For them it was enough that each monastery with twenty inmates or more should send one to university, the place being unspecified. As our main purpose is to describe only the local facilities for education in each monastery, we will here take leave of the subject of monks and canons at the universities. We have already noticed the establishment of colleges for the black and white monks at Oxford in the 1280s, and for the black monks at Cambridge by the 1330s. The Augustinian houses however, though they individually sent canons to study at Oxford during the fourteenth century, did not succeed in opening a college, dedicated to St Mary, until the 1430s.[1] We may also note that the Cistercians moved their house of study from Rewley to a new college of St Bernard in 1437.[2] Oxford remained the chief university centre of the three large orders in England; at Cambridge apart from the Gilbertines only the Benedictines established themselves, where in 1428 they acquired land to build a new hostel for their students, later known as Buckingham College.[3]

The educational legislation of Benedict XII continued in force in England until the 1530s. It now remains to be seen how the cloister schools for the monks functioned during this period. In Benedictine houses the school was usually located in the western alley of the cloisters, and the arrangements at Durham as they were on the eve of the Reformation in the 1530s have been well described by the anonymous author of the *Rites of Durham* who set down his reminiscences of the old priory in 1593.

In the west side of the cloister, on the south side of the cloister door, a little distant from the said door, there is a strong house called the treasure-house. . . . Over against the said treasure-house door, there was a fair great stall of wainscot where the novices did sit and learn, and also the master of the novices had a pretty stall or seat of wainscot on the south side of the treasure-house door over against the stall where the

---

[1] Evangeline Evans, 'St Mary's College in Oxford for Austin canons', *Oxfordshire Archaeological Society Report* (1928), pp. 367-91.
[2] W. H. Stevenson and H. E. Salter, *The Early History of St John's College, Oxford* (Oxford Historical Society, new series, i, 1939), pp. 3-110.
[3] *VCH Cambs.*, ii, 312. But at least two Benedictine houses near Cambridge – Bury and Norwich – had an Oxford connection (*VCH Oxon.*, iii, 303).

novices did sit and look on their books, and there did sit and teach the novices both forenoon and afternoon. And also there were no strangers nor any other persons suffered to molest or trouble any of the said novices or monks in their 'carols' [or enclosures], they being studying on their books within the cloister, for there was a porter appointed to keep the cloister door for the same use and purpose.[1]

The number of novices in such a school must have varied, but even in the largest houses there can never have been many. Nine are mentioned at Winchester in 1460, but in 1496 they had been reduced to four, and in 1533 there was only one. Some years there were none at all.[2] At Durham there are said to have been usually six.[3] They were under the general care of the master of the novices, a senior monk, but he was not necessarily their schoolmaster since the English monasteries, following the constitutions of Pope Benedict, sometimes retained a secular priest to teach them. If the schoolmaster was a monk, he was either chosen from among the seniors (at Durham 'one of the oldest monks that was learned was appointed to be their tutor') or was a younger man just down from university. Thus in 1503 Bishop Redman of Ely visiting the Premonstratensian abbey of West Dereham summoned one of the canons, Robert Walton, from Cambridge, appointed him subprior and told him to teach his brethren diligently.[4] At Evesham in the 1530s Robert Joseph was in his early thirties when, having been recalled from Oxford, he became schoolmaster of the novices.[5] Often, however, the house preferred to retain a secular priest, and at Winchester there was a succession of these from 1495 until the dissolution. In 1495 Peter Druett, MA, was appointed to teach grammar at a salary of £4 and in 1510 William Parkhouse, MA, BMed, to teach dialectic for £6, as well as being medical adviser to the convent. The last of these masters, John Pottinger, who took up office in 1538, was not a graduate but had studied at New College, Oxford, before leaving to get married, and had since been usher in Wykeham's college at Winchester.[6] A large number of other such appointments show that the greater monasteries did not avoid retaining seculars, but rather sought the services of graduates of a good standard to educate their novices.

[1] *The Rites of Durham*, ed. J. T. Fowler (Surtees Society, cvii, 1902), pp. 84-5.
[2] *VCH Hants.*, ii, 257.
[3] *The Rites of Durham*, ed. Fowler, pp. 96-7.
[4] F. A. Gasquet, *Collectanea Anglo-Premonstratensia*, vol iii (Camden third series, xii, 1906), p. 224.
[5] *The Letter Book of Robert Joseph*, ed. H. Aveling and W. A. Pantin (Oxford Historical Society, new series, xix, 1967), p. xiv.
[6] *VCH Hants.*, ii, 258-9, where for 'Porthouse' read 'Parkhouse'.

The papal legislation had ordered that the convent schoolmaster, whether a monk or a secular, should be paid by the house, but this was not always the case. Often indeed the master did receive a salary, as the examples from Winchester demonstrate, and even a senior monk was entitled to one. A solemn indenture survives from 1532 in which the prior of Bath appointed John Pitt, one of the senior monks, to the office of schoolmaster in the priory at an annual stipend of £4.[1] Sometimes the master's expenses were paid by a benefactor from outside. In 1519 the earl of Northumberland was paying £6 13s. 4d. for the wages of the schoolmaster of Alnwick Priory, a house of white canons.[2] In 1527 John Cole, warden of All Souls College, Oxford, actually endowed a schoolmaster in Faversham to teach grammar to the novices of the abbey there as well as to secular boys from the town outside.[3] Sometimes, strange though it may seem, the monks themselves were expected to pay their master's fees. In the later middle ages the custom grew up in many English monasteries that instead of dispensing clothes and other necessary gear from a central store, the monks should be given a *peculium* or allowance to buy such things as and when they were needed. In some places the novice or junior monk was expected to pay his master out of this *peculium* as if he had been a secular boy in a secular school. This had its disadvantages. At the Augustinian priory of Kyme in Lincolnshire in 1440 there were only two student canons and the senior brother who taught them refused to discharge his office adequately because they could only afford to pay him 20d. a quarter.[4] Yet Bishop Alnwick who visited Newnham in Bedfordshire, another Augustinian house, in 1442, finding the canons 'unlettered and almost witless', not only ordered the provision of a schoolmaster but sanctioned his support by his pupils as well as by the house.[5] We hear of similar payments too in Benedictine houses: at Ely in 1448 and at Glastonbury in 1538 on the very eve of the dissolution.[6]

The curriculum of the cloister school consisted ideally as we have seen

---

[1] PRO, Exch. Augm. Misc. Books, E 315/103, fo 128-v.

[2] C. J. Bates, 'The border holds of Northumberland', *Archaeologia Aeliana*, new series, xiv (1891), pp. 424-5.

[3] W. K. Jordan, 'Social institutions in Kent, 1480-1660', *Archaeologia Cantiana*, lxxv (1961), p. 72.

[4] *Visitations of Religious Houses in the Diocese of Lincoln, 1420-1449*, ed. A. Hamilton Thompson (Lincoln Record Society, vii, xiv, xxi, 1914-29), ii, 171-2.

[5] Ibid., iii, 237-8.

[6] For Ely see S. J. A. Evans, 'Ely almonry boys and choristers in the later middle ages', *Studies Presented to Sir Hilary Jenkinson*, pp. 157-8; and for Glastonbury, *Dean Cosyn and Wells Cathedral Miscellany*, ed. A. Watkin (Somerset Record Society, lvi, 1941), pp. 159-61.

of grammar, logic and philosophy, and there are scattered references to all these subjects being taught in practice during the later middle ages. At Durham we are told that the novices went daily to school for seven years. Anyone who showed himself apt for learning was picked out and sent away to the convent's house at Oxford to study theology.[1] For those who could not go to university the more conscientious houses continued to provide lectures on theology within their own walls, and sometimes also on canon law. At Christ Church, Canterbury, William Gillingham, doctor of theology, lectured in the 1380s, and Richard Godmersham, doctor of canon law, likewise in the early fifteenth century.[2] Thornton Abbey in Lincolnshire had also a lecturer in canon law at this time.[3] In the same tradition came the attempts of Richard Kidderminster, abbot of Winchcombe from 1488 to 1525, to make his abbey a model of study and learning. He tells us that in his time two bachelors of theology lectured daily, one on the Old Testament and the other on the New, while he himself held forth twice a week on the master of the *Sentences*.[4] The last burst of monastic lecturing came after 1535 at the command, strangely enough, of Henry VIII who ordered all religious houses to provide a daily lesson of holy scripture lasting one hour, which all the brethren were to attend – part of the curious policy of reforming the monasteries which was so soon overtaken by the decision to destroy them.[5]

But while some houses like Durham in the 1530s seem to have faithfully carried out the papal decrees, the same could not be said of many others. Time and again bishops who visited monasteries in the fifteenth and sixteenth centuries found that teaching was either being given inadequately or not at all, and that the religious in consequence were ignorant and incapable. Some houses were persistent offenders. The Augustinian priory of Canons Ashby in Northamptonshire housed a dozen canons in the fifteenth century. When Bishop Gray of Lincoln visited there in about 1432 he ordered that someone should be assigned to teach the novices and younger canons in the elementary branches of learning. Yet at the next visitation in 1442 one of the brethren complained of the lack of a teacher of grammar, and Canons Ashby again lacked a schoolmaster in 1520 when a

[1] *The Rites of Durham*, ed. Fowler, pp. 96-7.
[2] W. G. Searle, *Christ Church, Canterbury* (Cambridge Antiquarian Society Publications, xxxiv, 1902), pp. 182, 184.
[3] *Lincoln Visitations, 1420-1449*, iii, 373-82.
[4] On both Winchcombe and monastic education generally see W. A. Pantin, 'Abbot Kidderminster and monastic studies', *Downside Review*, xlvii (1929), pp. 199-211.
[5] *Concilia*, iii, 790-1.

later visitor had to arrange for one to be appointed.[1] Nor were the greater abbeys and priories always much better. Deficiencies in the teaching arrangements were noted at Tewkesbury in 1378, Winchester in 1387, at Durham in the same period, Peterborough in 1432 and Christ Church, Canterbury, in 1511 – to name but a few.[2] While these shortcomings cannot be excused, it is easy to see how they came about. Few monasteries were lucky enough to have a continuous stream of recruits, and in most of them the arrival of a novice once every few years would have called for *ad hoc* arrangements. It would not have been hard to put off making them and be thus caught out at the next visitation. Still, visitors did something to check these faults and right up to the Reformation the indolence of the religious was being countered by the vigilance of the authorities. The reforming convocation of Canterbury in 1529 ordered the enforcement of the decree *Ne in Agro*, and Thomas Cromwell's visitors inquired whether novices had a master to teach them grammar and good letters as late as 1535.[3]

The educational concerns of the English monasteries did not stop at their own brethren. Many religious houses during the later middle ages supported a number of secular boys and youths within their walls who received board, lodging and often education too in the monastic almonry. The earliest examples of these almonry boys are found in Benedictine houses in the thirteenth century. At Guisborough in Yorkshire in 1266-8 a teacher is mentioned instructing the poor boys supported in the house out of charity.[4] At Worcester in 1290 the schoolmaster of the city was responsible for teaching the relatives of the monks and others boarded in the almonry of the cathedral priory.[5] In 1299 the archbishop of Canterbury ordered the almoner of Rochester to feed and maintain poor scholars in the almonry according to the ancient custom.[6] In the fourteenth century references to almonry boys in the greater houses of the black monks become common. They first appear at Ely in 1314, at Christ Church, Canterbury, in 1320, at St Albans in 1339, at Reading in 1345, at

[1] *Lincoln Visitations, 1420-1449*, i, 32; ii, 45; *Lincoln Visitations, 1517-1531*, ed. A. Hamilton Thompson (Lincoln Record Society, xxxiii, xxxv-vii, 1940-7), ii, 99.
[2] Worcester, Worcs. Record Office, Reg. Wakefield, fo 132v (Tewkesbury); *VCH Hants.*, ii, 258 (Winchester); Pantin, *Chapters*, iii, 83 (Durham); *Lincoln Visitations, 1420-1449*, i, 102 (Peterborough); *ECD*, pp. 444-5 (Canterbury).
[3] *Concilia*, iii, 723, 788.
[4] C. R. Cheney, 'Letters of William Wickwane, chancellor of York', *English Historical Review*, xlvii (1932), pp. 629, 633.
[5] Leach, *Early Education in Worcester*, pp. 22-3.
[6] *Reg. Winchelsey, Canterbury*, ed. Rose Graham, vol ii (Canterbury and York Society, lii, 1956), p. 841.

I

Durham in 1352 and at Westminster in 1355. It was probably in this century that they reached their zenith in numbers, there being twenty-three at Ely in 1329, twenty-eight at Westminster in 1386, and as many as thirty-nine 'clerks of the school' at Glastonbury in 1377.[1] Later on the numbers seem to have fallen, and between twelve and fourteen became common in the larger establishments, with only a handful in such of the smaller houses as maintained them. The examples of almonry boys so far given have all related to the houses of the Benedictines, but the institution did spread to the other two large orders. There are several allusions to them in the Augustinian houses of the fifteenth century, and among the Cistercians the abbeys of Forde in Dorset and Furness in Lancashire are known to have possessed them by the 1530s.[2]

Who were these almonry boys, and why did the monasteries bother to maintain them? They seem often to have been relatives of the monks, and at Ely in 1314 it was provided that no monk should nominate a boy more often than once every four years so that all the brethren should have an equal share of the patronage.[3] At Furness in the 1530s, the children of the abbey tenants were also apparently eligible for entry.[4] Once again, the best picture of their life in the monastery comes from the description of Durham on the eve of the Reformation:

> There were certain poor children, called the children of the almonry, who only were maintained with learning and relieved with the alms and benefactions of the whole house, having their meat and drink in a loft on the north side of the abbey gates. . . . The which loft had a long porch over the stairhead, slated over, and at either side of the said porch or entry there was a stair to go up to it, and a stable underneath the said almonry or loft, having a door and an entry in under the stairhead to go into the stable. . . . And also the meat and drink that the aforesaid poor children had was the meat that the master of the novices and the novices left and reserved, and was carried in at a door adjoining to the great kitchen window into a little vault in the west end of the

[1] For Ely see *Camden Miscellany XII*, pp. 38-9, and *Studies Presented to Sir Hilary Jenkinson*, pp. 155-63. For Canterbury, *Literae Cantuarienses*, ed. J. B. Sheppard, vol i (Rolls Series, 1887), pp. 444-5. For St Albans, *ECD*, pp. 296-7. For Westminster, ibid., pp. 306-15. For Reading, *VCH Berks.*, ii, 247. For Durham, *Durham Account Rolls*, ed. J. T. Fowler, vol i (Surtees Society, xcix, 1898), pp. 207ff. For Glastonbury, PRO, Exch. K. R., Clerical Subsidy Rolls, E 179/4/1 m 3.
[2] *Lincoln Visitations, passim*; G. Oliver, *Monasticon Dioecesis Exoniensis* (1846), pp. 340-1 (for Forde); T. West, *The Antiquities of Furness*, 3rd ed. (1822), p. 195.
[3] *Camden Miscellany XII*, pp. 38-9.
[4] West, *Antiquities of Furness*, p. 195.

frater house like unto a pantry, called the covey, which had a man that kept it called the clerk of the covey, and had a window within it, where one or two of the children did receive their meat and drink of the said clerk, out of the covey or pantry window so called, and the said children did carry it to the almonry or loft. Which clerk did wait upon them every meal and to see that they kept good order.[1]

The chief duty of the almonry boys was to assist those of the monks who were in priest's orders to say their daily masses at the side altars of the church, acting as servers and saying the liturgical responses. Naturally this involved educating them, for illiterate clerks were worse than useless. At Durham in the 1380s where they were only semi-literate, they could not say the *Confiteor* or the *Misereatur* and were so unprepared to carry out their office that they hindered and delayed the monks from saying their masses.[2] While reading and song might have sufficed for this work, the almonry boys were generally taught grammar as well. Sometimes they had their own grammar master inside the monastery, who was frequently the same secular priest that taught the brethren. In other places they were sent out to the schools of the town, as was the practice at Worcester in 1290, at St Albans around 1330 and at St Oswald's, Gloucester, in 1400.[3] The length of time they spent in the almonry was fixed at not more than four years at Ely in 1314, and up to five at St Albans in 1339 since 'this time is enough for becoming proficient in grammar'.[4] The boys frequently went on to be monks or canons in the house which had nursed them. Bishop Gray ordered the monks of Bradwell Priory, Buckinghamshire, in 1431-2 to maintain teachable children who in the course of time might be admitted as brethren of the house, and in 1468 the chronicler of Christ Church, Canterbury, recorded the admission of four new monks from the almonry school.[5] At Furness the boys were either chosen as monks or provided to lay offices in the service of the abbey.[6]

In addition to the almonry boys, many of the larger Benedictine and Augustinian houses maintained and educated a number of singing boys and youths to assist in the liturgy of the church.[7] At Norwich in the

---

[1] *The Rites of Durham*, ed. Fowler, pp. 91-2.
[2] Pantin, *Chapters*, iii, 83.
[3] Leach, *Early Education in Worcester*, pp. 22-3; *ECD*, pp. 298-9; PRO, Chancery Masters' Exhibits, C 115 (Lanthony Cartulary), vol A 7 fo 207.
[4] *Camden Miscellany XII*, pp. 38-9; *ECD*, pp. 296-7.
[5] *Lincoln Visitations, 1420-1449*, i, 23; Searle, *Christ Church, Canterbury*, p. 106.
[6] West, *Antiquities of Furness*, p. 195.
[7] On this subject in general see F. Ll. Harrison, *Music in Medieval Britain*, 2nd ed. (1963), especially pp. 38-45.

thirteenth century it was customary for a boy to begin the litany on the vigil of St John the Baptist, and to introduce an antiphon on the feast of All Saints and the commemoration of All Souls on the following day.[1] At the visitation of Durham in the 1380s it was observed that there had formerly been clerks singing in harmony (*organum*) and helping the monks with the treble chant, but that now there was none, to the great nuisance and tedium of the brethren singing in choir.[2] However, the assistance of clerks and boys in the monks' own services was much less common than their employment to sing a special daily mass with elaborate musical settings in the Lady chapel or the nave to the honour of the Virgin. This was a characteristic development of the later middle ages. 'Clerks of the chapel', that is to say older youths or men singing in the Lady chapel, appear at Worcester in 1393 when there were three of them, and boys of the chapel are mentioned two years later. Their numbers are not recorded until 1481 when there were four boys, rising to eight after 1486.[3] At Winchester the prior and convent appointed John Dyer in 1402 to attend the daily mass of the Virgin and to teach singing to four boys. As at Worcester, the number of these boys had risen to eight by 1482, and this number was maintained until the Reformation.[4] At Durham Bishop Langley, who endowed a public grammar school and song school in 1414, arranged that the song schoolmaster should take part in singing the mass of the Virgin together with a competent number of his scholars. By 1448, however, the monks were appointing their own song schoolmasters, charged with teaching the monks and eight secular boys as well as attending the daily mass of the Virgin.[5] As the fifteenth century continues, references to the boys of the chapel and their masters occur in more and more of the larger Benedictine houses, most of which probably supported such boys by the 1530s, as well as in some of the Augustinian communities. Cirencester and Lanthony in Gloucestershire both had such boys just before their dissolution.[6]

As before, there comes from Durham a faithful description of the arrangements in the song school on the eve of the Reformation:

---

[1] *The Customary of Norwich*, ed. J. B. L. Tolhurst (Henry Bradshaw Society., lxxxii, 1948), pp. 135, 187, 76.

[2] Pantin, *Chapters*, iii, 84.

[3] I. Atkins, *The Early Organists of Worcester* (Worcs. Historical Society, xxxii, 1918), pp. 7ff.

[4] *VCH Hants.*, ii, 259-60.

[5] *VCH Durham*, i, 372; *Historia Dunelmensis Scriptores Tres*, ed. J. Raine (Surtees Society, ix, 1839), appendix, pp. cccxv-vii.

[6] For Cirencester see PRO, Exch. Augm. Misc. Books, E 315/94, folios 159v-61, and for Lanthony, E 315/93, folios 231v-2.

There was in the centory garth in under the south end of the church . . . betwixt two pillars adjoining to the nine-altar door, a song school builded to teach six children to sing for the maintenance of God's divine service in the abbey church, which children had their meat and their drink of the house's cost among the children of the almonry. Which said school . . . was very finely boarded within round about a man's height about the walls, and a long desk from one end of the school to the other to lay their books upon, and all the floor boarded in underfoot for warmness, and long forms set fast in the ground for the children to sit on. And the place where the master did sit and teach was all close boarded both behind and of either side, for warmness.[1]

The numbers of the boys of the chapel, as the examples suggest, were always small and four, eight or ten were most common. Their master, generally called the 'master of the children' or the 'master of the boys', was a secular clerk, often of high musical abilities. He supervised the singing arrangements for the Lady mass and for other special occasions, played the organ in the monastery church when necessary and instructed the boys in music. Something can be gathered of their studies in the document appointing Thomas Foderley as cantor of Durham in 1496, which bound him to teach them to play the organ and to sing plain chant, prick note or noted music, and various kinds of polyphony: faburden, descant, swarenote and counter. In return for this he received a salary of £10.[2]

Clearly this musical curriculum was a good deal more advanced than the studies of the elementary song schools, and the children of the chapel went far towards being specialized students of music. Generally there is no mention of them learning grammar, and it may be significant that when Gloucester Abbey appointed John Tucke in 1513 as master of both grammar and song, he had to teach grammar to the younger brethren and the boys of the almonry, but song alone to the five or six boys of the chapel.[3] However, in one or two instances by the 1530s these boys had come to be given lessons in grammar as well. At Winchester in 1538 the convent schoolmaster, John Pottinger, taught them grammar along with the monks and the almonry boys, and at Cirencester in the same year Henry Edmunds was appointed master of the children and told that when they were sufficiently instructed in pricksong, he was to teach them their Latin accidence.[4]

[1] *The Rites of Durham*, ed. Fowler, pp. 62-3.
[2] *Historia Dunelmensis Scriptores Tres*, appendix, p. ccclxxxvi.
[3] *Hist. Cart. Mon. Gloucs.*, ed. W. H. Hart, vol iii (Rolls Series, 1867), pp. 290-1.
[4] *VCH Hants.*, ii, 259; PRO, E 315/94, folios 159v-61.

The last group of lay children who occasionally appear in the monasteries were the private boarders, sons of the patron or of the neighbouring gentry, who received a gentle upbringing in the abbot's household. It is possible that they had access to the schoolmaster of the almonry boys: in 1266-8 John Blaby, a landowner in the North Riding of Yorkshire, was permitted to send his two sons to Guisborough Priory to study under the master who taught the poor boys there.[1] In other cases the boys may have brought their own private tutor with them, like the three young gentlemen who lived with their schoolmaster in Woburn Abbey in 1538.[2]

So much for the educational concerns inside the religious houses of medieval England. Yet in many cases their interests in education did not stop at the convent walls. Their wealth and privileges inexorably forced their attention away from a secluded life to the concerns of the world – the educational no less than the economic or political. We have already noticed how from the twelfth century onwards the monks of Bury and St Albans had claimed the right to appoint schoolmasters in the towns and manors under their lordship. In other places, such as Bedford, Derby and Gloucester, monks or canons had been given rights of educational patronage by private benefactors. The instances in which religious houses went to law to protect these rights testify to the value they attached to them.[3] Moreover, at least three monasteries came to subsidize very considerably the education in the towns over which they presided. Abbot Samson of Bury, as we saw before, gave a schoolhouse to the scholars of the town towards the end of the twelfth century and followed it up by arranging for an annual payment of £2 to the schoolmaster out of the church of Wetherden, on condition that he taught forty poor scholars for nothing.[4] This arrangement was still in operation in the fifteenth century when, in 1444, Robert Farceux was appointed master of the grammar school of Bury with £2 from Wetherden, an extra 13s. 4d., a gown and board and lodging in the abbey for himself and his clerk.[5] It is highly probable, though we are not told so, that in return for these emoluments his school was partially, if not wholly, free.

At Evesham it was presented in 1548 that ever since the reign of Edward III the abbots of the great Benedictine monastery there had paid the sum of £10 with meat and drink to a schoolmaster for keeping a free

---

[1] *English Historical Review*, xlvii (1932), pp. 629, 633.
[2] *LPFD*, xiii, part 1, p. 361.
[3] On this subject see above, pp. 148-9.
[4] See also above, p. 184.
[5] *VCH Suffolk*, ii, 312.

grammar school in the town of Evesham.[1] This assertion may hold a grain of truth, in that the schoolmasters of Evesham in the 1530s were also chaplains of the carnary chapel, founded by Abbot Boys who reigned from 1345 to 1367. More probably the free school dated from 1462 when the abbey was permitted to appropriate the parish church of Eyford, a deserted village in the Cotswolds, to provide a grammar master for the novices and other boys in the monastery at a salary of £10, a facility which could easily have become extended to the town itself.[2] But it is not until 1538, on the very eve of the downfall, that we have direct evidence of the free school which the abbey was keeping. In that year the monks appointed William Scollowe, BA, as schoolmaster with £10 a year and the house next to the school in the town in return for celebrating mass in the carnary chapel and teaching the scholars who came to him without charge.[3] So Evesham provides one clear example of an abbey keeping a free grammar school for the benefit of the locality. The other comes from Reading and is of the same period. There the schoolmaster of the town before the Reformation was Leonard Cox, a graduate of both universities and a well-known exponent of the New Learning in school, who dedicated his *Arte or Crafte of Rhetoryke* to Abbot Faringdon of Reading in 1524. Although in the preface to this book Cox described himself as master of the grammar school founded by the abbot's predecessors in the town of Reading, it was not until 1539, just before the abbey was dissolved, that he received a formal indenture of appointment, probably to safeguard his interests for the future. This granted him the school and schoolhouse and a salary of £10 a year for teaching grammar and poetry to those who resorted to him, and shows that Reading Abbey like Evesham provided the people of the town with a free school.[4] In these three examples of Bury, Evesham and Reading, and there were perhaps a few others, we see the monasteries dispensing education freely to the public, as they were once erroneously thought to have done all over the country.[5]

It might well be asked at this point how the study of grammar in the religious houses related to that which was taught in the world outside. Was the standard of teaching as high as that in the secular schools, and

[1] *ESR*, part 2, pp. 272-3.
[2] Worcester, Worcs. Record Office, Reg. Carpenter, i, fo 186v.
[3] PRO, Exch. Augm. Misc. Books, E 315/101, folios 36v-7.
[4] Salisbury, Diocesan Record Office, Chartularium Redingense, fo 32; *VCH Berks.*, ii, 70.
[5] There are also ambiguous references to monastic schools, which may have been public, at Burton-upon-Trent (PRO, E 315/105, fo 12); Christchurch, Hants. (PRO, SP 1/132, pp. 221-2); and Leicester (*Lincoln Visitations, 1420-1449*, ii, 208).

were the monasteries in the mainstream of educational development in England? With regard to the greater houses the answer to both questions is certainly 'yes'. The list of monks who are found teaching the cloister schools includes several who were university men, and the secular chaplains employed to teach were of comparable standing and quality to those in the world outside. It was not indeed unknown for such school-masters to move from a secular to a monastic school, and vice versa. Those who taught and studied in the greater religious houses frequently had access to good libraries. The surviving catalogues of the Benedictine houses at Canterbury and Dover and of Augustinian communities such as Lanthony and Leicester show larger holdings of the standard gram-marians and poets than were likely to have been available at any but a very few of the secular schools.[1] And if nearly all the leading writers on grammar in medieval England were seculars, every schoolboy had reason to be grateful to the anonymous Dominican friar of King's Lynn who completed in 1440 the *Promptorium Parvulorum*, the first English to Latin dictionary.[2]

In these circumstances the curricula of the monastic schools are not likely to have varied greatly from those in the world outside. A gram-matical miscellany used in the cloister school of Christ Church, Canterbury, at the end of the fifteenth century contains the material one would expect to find: English and Latin vocabularies, English *vulgaria* for translation into Latin based on local life and proverbs and a transcript of the *Grecismus* of Évrard of Béthune.[3] Soon after this the New Learning began to reach the religious houses, at much the same time that it penetrated the secular grammar schools. The library catalogue of Syon Abbey in Middle-sex, drawn up between 1504 and 1526, shows the works of the fashionable new continental grammarians like Perotto, Sulpizio and Valla shouldering those of the great medieval authors.[4] Further to the west, the letter book of Robert Joseph, monk of Evesham, which covers the years 1530-2, reveals the New Learning already well established in the cloister school of an ancient Benedictine abbey. Joseph was sent from Evesham in about 1523 to study at Oxford and was recalled to the abbey in 1529, being soon

[1] M. R. James, *The Ancient Libraries of Canterbury and Dover* (1903), pp. 355ff, 413ff; T. W. Williams, 'Gloucestershire medieval libraries', *Transactions of the Bristol and Gloucs. Archaeological Society*, xxxi (1908), pp. 157, 160; M. R. James, 'Catalogue of the library of Leicester Abbey', *Leics. Archaeological Society Transactions*, xix (1935-7), p. 134, xxi (1939-41), pp. 9-13.

[2] See above, p. 97.

[3] BM, MS Harley 1587, described in F. A. Gasquet, *The Old English Bible and other Essays*, 2nd ed. (1908), pp. 225-46.

[4] Bateson, *Catalogue of the Library of Syon Monastery*, pp. 1-77.

afterwards appointed schoolmaster to the novices. His studies had given him a good acquaintance with the rediscovered classical authors and the new literary fashions of the day, which he lost no time in imparting to his pupils. The lecture on the *Eunuchus* of Terence with which he began his work is preserved among his letters, and so is another, on a poem by Baptista Mantuanus in praise of St Catherine.[1]

The importance of the schools of the religious orders in medieval England cannot be doubted. In the first place they were responsible for the further education of large numbers of friars, monks and canons in grammar, arts and theology. The facilities they offered were to a large extent developed by their own spontaneous efforts in the thirteenth century. It is difficult to sum up briefly the quality of the education those facilities provided, but if it often sank low in the smaller monastic communities through the negligence recorded in episcopal visitations, it equally rose to the high level of competence shown in the greater monasteries and with the friars, where many a worthy career began that later ended in the mastery of theology at Oxford and Cambridge. Secondly, a large number of seculars received their education in the schools of the religious orders, and though the contribution of each house was small, the aggregate over the whole country must have run into many hundreds. The almonry schools of the greater abbeys in particular, with their free board and lodging and their graduate masters, are surely impressive less for their limitations than for the fact that they existed at all, and on such a generous scale.

[1] *The Letter Book of Robert Joseph*, ed. Aveling and Pantin, pp. xiv, 56-9, 124-7.

1*

Chapter Nine

The schools under Henry VIII

We have now surveyed the educational institutions characteristic of the middle ages – the schools of cities and towns, of chantries, colleges and the religious orders. We have seen something of their life and studies, and the interest they aroused in their time. It now remains to discover how and when the 'medieval' era of education in England came to an end. In one sense this had happened by 1520, by which time the old school curriculum was rapidly changing into that of the Renaissance.[1] As institutions, however, the medieval schools did not undergo significant change until the 1530s and 40s, as a consequence of the Reformation, which swept away the religious houses and the chantries, with considerable implications for a large number of schools dependent upon them. To this period we shall now turn, to investigate the effects of the Reformation upon English education for good or ill, to pursue the fate of the institutions whose origins we have traced, and by contrast to observe what new ideas and policies were emerging to dominate the age.

During the fourteenth and fifteenth centuries there had been a growing interest in education at every level of society, marked especially by the founding of scholarships and ultimately of free schools. This interest, rather than undergoing significant change, increased in the sixteenth century and the Tudor patrons of education largely repeated and amplified the work of their fifteenth-century predecessors. What was new in the sixteenth century was not that education attracted private charity, but that it became a subject of public policy, a matter of concern to the spiritual power, and even more surprisingly to the civil power as well. In the middle ages neither Church nor crown had given much thought to the

[1] On this subject see above, p. 106.

schools. The clerical authorities, whether popes, councils or bishops, took
comparatively little trouble to legislate about education or to supervise it.
The crown became involved with schools and their masters only on the
rare occasions when they fell within its secular jurisdiction. But in the
sixteenth century both the crown and the Church became concerned far
more than ever before with the organization and work of the schools, and
this was the case not only in England but all over Europe. This involvement was due partly to educational and partly to religious reasons. Great
men, both clerical and lay, educated in the New Learning, convinced of
the superiority of a new kind of grammar and literature over old and dis-
credited ones, were anxious to modernize the curricula of the schools,
raise the standard of their work and make them generally more effective.
There was in fact a strong interest in education for its own sake, and this
was seconded by equally strong religious motives. The sixteenth century
saw a great religious revival, of which the two Reformations, the Protestant
and the Catholic, were both aspects. There was a greater determination
than before to improve the standard of religious life and to build a more
truly Christian society. This meant educating the clergy so that their work
of celebrating divine service, preaching and pastoral care might be better
discharged. It also meant educating the laity, primarily in the elements of
the faith but also in literacy, so that they might reform and elevate themselves by the reading of good works. All this led to a greater interest in
what the schools were doing. Unfortunately this age of reform was also
an age of conflict, when the reformers were more conscious of their
differences than their similarities. To secure the triumph of the reformed
faith, which at different times and in different countries might be Catholic,
Lutheran, Calvinist or Anglican, it was necessary to make sure of the
schools, where the loyalties of future generations were to be formed.
Ecclesiastical authorities, whether fighting heresy or conservatism, could
no longer take the religious content of education for granted as they had
done in medieval times, while the crown, conscious of the political
dangers of religious nonconformity, was equally concerned to promote
uniformity in the schools. For these reasons the sixteenth century saw
more attempts than before to legislate for education, to supervise schoolmasters, to control their work and to introduce a desirable uniformity into
their classrooms.

It was thus no accident that the anticipation of the Protestant Reformation by Wycliffe and the Lollards was accompanied by the first attempts of
the leaders of the English Church to control the religious activities of the
schools. The constitutions issued by Archbishop Arundel for the province

of Canterbury against the Lollards in 1408 included an order that masters and others who taught boys in arts, grammar or the elementary subjects should not teach anything concerning the catholic faith or the sacraments against what had been determined by the Church. Nor might they allow disputations by their scholars about these matters in public or private, on pain of severe punishment.[1] This order was reproduced in the standard commentary of the fifteenth century on English canon law, William Lyndwood's *Provinciale*, but there is nothing to show that at this time it resulted in any more stringent supervision of the schools.[2] By the 1520s, however, the still Catholic English Church was threatened by heresy far more dangerous than Lollardy, as the first breath of Lutheranism came in from the continent and began to inspire supporters in England. Faced with new heresies and conscious of the need for reform within the Church, the clerical authorities began slowly to respond. In November 1529 a new convocation of the Canterbury province met at St Paul's to consider ecclesiastical reform and to take measures against heresy, and the decrees finally approved on 22 March 1530 included three which aimed at improving and regulating the education being offered in the country. First, with regard to the regular clergy, the convocation repeated the long-standing decree of Pope Clement V, *Ne in agro*, that each religious house should have an instructor in grammar, and that those of the religious who proved apt in letters should be sent to study at university. Second, a new injunction was passed for the secular clergy, ordering all rectors, vicars and chantry priests to employ themselves, when not engaged in divine service, in study, prayer, preaching or instructing boys in the alphabet, reading, song or grammar. Third, the council turned to the school-masters themselves and ordered them to begin by teaching the boys entrusted to them a simple summary of the faith and of what to do and avoid, but to refrain from giving them books to read which might corrupt their minds or their faith.[3] These injunctions were by no means revolutionary ones, but they do indicate a greater interest in education than had been shown by any English church council since 1408, and they presage the greater legislation on education which was to come later.

The last and most significant action of the convocation of 1530 was its attempt to promote the use of a single form of grammar in every school throughout the country. Hitherto there had been no uniformity in

---

[1] *Concilia*, iii, 317; *ECD*, pp. 394-5.
[2] William Lyndwood, *Provinciale*, Lib. V tit. 4; (ed. 1679), pp. 282-4.
[3] *Concilia*, iii, 722-3, 726.

teaching. Schoolbooks had been until recently available only in manuscript and the traditional grammar course, though broadly similar everywhere, had been modified in detail by each schoolmaster as he thought fit. But after 1500 the mass production of printed grammars and texts made it possible to overcome the isolation of the individual masters, and it became reasonable to impose a single treatise of grammar which would be available everywhere. As it was, several new grammars were in print by the 1520s and promised to perpetuate the differences between the teaching of grammar in one school and another. The works ascribed to John Stanbridge were in use at several prominent schools, but Colet had produced a treatise of his own for St Paul's, and this was adopted by Wolsey with some additions for his new college at Ipswich in 1528. The grammar of a third master, Robert Whittinton, was frequently printed in the 1520s and was evidently popular as well.

The imposition of a standard form of grammar by the ecclesiastical authorities seems to have been in prospect by 1525 since the revised statutes of Manchester grammar school, issued in that year, adopted the grammar of Stanbridge, or any other form which 'in time to come shall be ordained universally throughout all the province of Canterbury'.[1] The project may also have been in the mind of Cardinal Wolsey, himself an ex-schoolmaster, and as papal legate the supreme ecclesiastical authority in England. In 1529 Peter Treveris the Southwark printer issued what he claimed as an authorized grammar, which was actually the Pauline treatise of John Colet and William Lily with Wolsey's revisions for Ipswich. The Latin title of Treveris's edition may be translated, 'The rudiments of grammar and the method of teaching, not merely of the school of Ipswich, happily established by the most reverend Lord Thomas, Cardinal of York, but also prescribed for all the other schools in the whole of England.'[2] Despite this claim, however, no previous prescription is known which could justify the authority claimed in the title, and the adoption of a standard grammar remained to be discussed in the convocation at St Paul's in March 1530. In its decree on the subject, convocation complained that because of the disruption of schools by plague or the death of the master, it often happened that a boy who had begun his grammar under one teacher was obliged to go to another, who used different methods of teaching, so that many who studied grammar found it difficult to make progress. It was therefore decided that a uniform method of teaching

[1] *VCH Lancs.*, ii, 583.
[2] V. J. Flynn, 'The grammatical writings of William Lily', *Papers of the Bibliographical Society of America*, xxxvii (1943), p. 95; *STC*, 25944-7.

grammar should be established throughout the whole province within a year. During that time the archbishop of Canterbury, together with four bishops, four abbots and four archdeacons, representing the orders of the clergy in convocation, were to choose a suitable grammar and prescribe it for general use. The names of this committee are unknown and its deliberations for the moment came to nothing.[1]

During the 1530s a few of the English bishops attempted some modest educational reforms in their dioceses in the spirit of the decrees of 1530. Hugh Latimer, bishop of Worcester, visiting his clergy in 1537 ordered the chantry priests to instruct the children of their parishes to read English, 'so that thereby they may the better learn how to believe, how to pray, and how to live to God's pleasure'. Nicholas Shaxton in 1538 and Edmund Bonner in 1542, in their respective dioceses of Salisbury and London, exhorted all the secular clergy, not only the chantry priests, to teach their parishioners' children to read English, taking moderate payment.[2] But by this time ecclesiastical policy, and hence educational policy, was no longer the independent concern of the clergy. In 1534 Henry VIII effectively destroyed papal supremacy over the English Church and subjected it to a far more real and rigorous supremacy of his own. His first act as supreme head of the Church was to order the publication of his new title by parish priests to their congregations and by schoolmasters to their pupils, an ominous sign of the power he now held over them.[3] Two years later he appointed commissioners to carry out a visitation of the whole country and issued injunctions for them to transmit to the clergy. The tenth injunction sought to impose an obligation on all wealthy clerics to give charity to poor scholars, 'to the intent that learned men may hereafter spring the more'. For every £100 of his income, a beneficed cleric was to support one scholar at university or at a grammar school, 'which after they have profited in good learning, may be partners of their patrons' cure and charge . . . or may, when need shall be, otherwise profit the commonwealth with their counsel and wisdom'.[4] It was not new for the clergy to raise up scholars to succeed them. Thomas Gascoigne, the Oxford theologian, wrote in the middle of the fifteenth century that he had known a rector who found twenty youths to school from the profits of a single church, all of whom became priests, and other examples of this kind of

[1] *Concilia*, iii, 722-3.
[2] *Visitation Articles and Injunctions of the period of the Reformation*, ed. W. H. Frere (Alcuin Club, xiv-vi, 1910), ii, 17, 56, 85.
[3] P. L. Hughes and J. F. Larkin, *Tudor Royal Proclamations*, vol i (1964), p. 231.
[4] *Visitation Articles and Injunctions*, ii, 10-11.

patronage are not uncommon.[1] But under Henry the first attempt was made to make this duty statutory, and similar measures were enforced in varying degrees under all his children.[2]

More important still, the king took up the project of the uniform Latin grammar, which he successfully carried out with the publication of the *Institutio compendiaria totius grammaticae* in 1540 (old style). The preface to this work described how the king had noticed the diversity with which grammar was taught in different schools, and had appointed certain learned men to compile a clear and short grammar based on the best authors. The names of these men are not known, but they drew up a grammar based partly on the earlier works of William Lily, high-master of St Paul's school from 1512 to 1522, with additions and modifications from other well-esteemed grammarians of the early sixteenth century. The text, in Latin, was an advanced treatment of the rules and irregularities of grammar, and the complexities of syntax and prosody. The published version of 1540 carried the king's authority, and expressly forbade the use of any other grammar in school; consequently the works of Stanbridge and Whittinton did not appear in print after this date. Two years later in 1542 (old style) an elementary grammar was also issued by the king's command, entitled *An Introduction of the Eyght Partes of Speche*, based like the other on Lily's works, amended to include material from other sources. This consisted of a brief discussion in English of the eight parts of speech, their accidence and the simpler constructions, and children were intended to progress from it to the more detailed treatment of grammar in the *Institutio*. The *Introduction* was also authorized for general use, and after 1542 the two grammars were usually published together, though they long retained the character of separate works.[3]

The authorized grammar proved to be very successful. It was founded on an author of worth and popularity, revised and augmented by learned men according to the best opinions and practices of the day, briefly and plainly set forth. As usually printed in the sixteenth century, beginning with the alphabet, following with a catechism in Latin and English, and giving the texts in turn of the *Introduction* and *Institutio*, it provided a

[1] Gascoigne, *Loci e Libro Veritatum*, ed. J. Thorold Rogers (1881), p. 112. For specific examples see *BRUO*, i, 323, sub Richard de Bury; *Reg. Bekynton, Wells*, i, 60-1; and *Testamenta Vetusta*, ed. N. H. Nicolas (1826), pp. 564, 569.

[2] For an example of this obligation being observed in 1548 see *Historical MSS Commission, Reports on Various Collections*, vol vii (1914), p. 49.

[3] On the authorized grammar see above, pp. 112-13 and also the useful article by C. G. Allen, 'The sources of Lily's Latin Grammar', *The Library*, 5th series, ix (1954), pp. 85-100.

textbook for every stage of the school curriculum. It continued to be prescribed and enforced by Edward VI, Mary and Elizabeth, and went on being used in revised versions for three centuries, the very last edition appearing as late as 1858. In 1545 the king supplemented the grammar with a uniform 'primer' or collection of prayers for use in school, which replaced the many different collections which had circulated since the fourteenth century. The primer was in English, but when pupils had gained sufficient knowledge of Latin they had the option of using a Latin version. The primer was more affected by the religious vacillations of the following reigns than was the grammar, and by 1549 alterations to it were already being made.[1]

The immediate effect upon the schools of royal supremacy over the Church was thus the imposition of a uniform grammar. But the period 1536-40 in which the crown intervened in education for the first time also saw the destruction of the religious orders and the confiscation of their property, beginning with the closure of the smaller monasteries in the summer of 1536 and ending with the surrender of Waltham, the last of the abbeys, on 23 March 1540. We have already described the educational facilities with which the religious orders were involved; they formed only a part of the general facilities for education available in England, but that part was by no means negligible. The dissolution of the monasteries and friaries meant in the first place the end of the cloister schools which many of them had maintained for the last 200 years or more. There were still nearly 10,000 monks, friars and regular canons in the early sixteenth century, most of whom had followed a curriculum in these schools varying in content from song and grammar to philosophy and theology. During their history the cloister schools had been the nurseries of saints and statesmen, of theologians and historians, and had made their own valuable contribution to the English culture of the middle ages. They had opened their doors to the New Learning in the sixteenth century no less than the secular schools, and in the new age of faith they might have done much, but instead they were utterly swept away. Their fate was shared by the almonry schools kept in most of the greater houses for the secular clerks and choristers needed for services, and the poor boys sustained out of charity. These schools were small by secular standards, of rarely more than a dozen boys and often less, but put together over the whole country they must have provided education for several hundred people. Yet they too did not survive the closure of their houses.

What then of the masters and boys maintained in these schools, whom

[1] *Concilia*, iii, 875; *Statutes of the Realm*, iv, 111.

the dissolutions left stranded? The boys do not seem to have been eligible for compensation, but the masters were, for the crown did feel a strong duty towards the adult inmates of the religious houses, and not only the monks but their secular officers and servants were eligible for pensions. The procedure was for the officers concerned to sue in the court of augmentations, the body set up by the crown to administer monastic property, bringing evidence of the salaries they had enjoyed while the abbeys still stood. They were then awarded pensions in compensation. William Tyler, MA and secular priest, who had taught grammar in the almonry of Forde Abbey in Dorset since 1537, is typical of the men retained by the larger houses to teach the almonry boys and often the novices as well. His stipend had included board, lodging, an annual gown and £3 6s. 8d. a year, and for this he received a pension of £3.[1] John Pitt on the other hand, formerly subprior of Bath Abbey, was the kind of senior monk who had taught the novices in the cloister school, to which he had been appointed in 1532 at a salary of £4. This secured him a pension of £4 for life, in addition to the £9 which he also received as an ex-monk.[2]

The other kinds of schools with which the monasteries had been involved were secular establishments taught by secular masters and open to the public, but under the governance and control of the religious houses. They fell into two groups, both small in numbers. First there were some ancient schools which had grown up in towns dominated by a great abbey, like Bury, Evesham, Reading and St Albans, over which the abbey had extended protection and patronage. The monks appointed the master, owned the schoolhouse, and in the first three places at least, provided free education by paying the master's stipend. Next there were a few endowed schools of private foundation over which religious houses had been made trustees, responsible for appointing masters and paying them from the endowments. These included schools at Bruton, Cirencester, Farnworth, Faversham and Winchcombe, as well as Lewes where the local prior merely appointed the master. There was no general attempt at the dissolution of the monasteries to save the public schools associated with them, as there was to be when the chantries were dissolved in 1548, and the fates of these schools varied widely, depending on local factors rather than on crown

[1] Exeter, City Archives, DD 22783; G. Oliver, *Monasticon Dioecesis Exoniensis* (1846), pp. 340-1.
[2] PRO, Exch. Augm. Misc. Books, E 315/103, fo 128-v. The decree and order books of the Augmentation Office provide information on a few monastic schoolmasters, but by no means all; the grant to Tyler for example was never enrolled in the Augmentation records, nor doubtless many others.

policy. Of the ancient abbey schools, two continued without difficulty. At Reading the schoolmaster, Leonard Cox, was a well-known grammarian and in 1541 the king specially confirmed his office as schoolmaster of Reading, his tenure of the schoolhouse and his annual stipend of £10 with arrears back to Michaelmas 1539 when he had last been paid by the abbey.[1] At Evesham the master did not even suffer a temporary withdrawal of his wages, but the new receiver appointed to administer the abbey lands went on paying him until he had secured an official confirmation of his position from the court of augmentations in 1542.[2] At Bury and St Albans, however, the fate of the schools is more obscure and local education may or may not have been disrupted until the re-establishment of St Albans school by a private benefactor in 1549, and of Bury by the king in 1550.[3]

The schools in the second group suffered a variety of fates. At Ciren-cester the grammar school came to an end soon after the dissolution of its trustees, the monks of Winchcombe, and apparently no school was kept in the town until in 1545 the inhabitants, 'driven thereunto of great necessity', converted one of the chantries in the parish church to support a schoolmaster. Thereafter a school again existed in the town, but with an endowment of only £7, less than the £10 which the masters had enjoyed before the Reformation.[4] At Faversham the free school also came to an end along with the abbey, though if the last schoolmaster can be trusted, this was the result of dishonesty on the abbot's part.[5] The schoolmaster of Bruton did sue for his rights before the court of augmentations, which in justice ought to have respected the separate foundation of which he was incumbent and sent him back to his old duties with his old stipend. Instead of this the court, which may or may not have been deliberately misled, chose to regard him as one of the officers of the abbey with a personal life interest and not only awarded him a pension but exonerated him from teaching the free school in future. To the great indignation of the people of Bruton, the free school came to an end, and by 1549 the pensioned master seems to have given up teaching altogether, for he was accused of turning the schoolroom into a malthouse. The school was only rescued after the local inhabitants had twice petitioned the crown, and in 1550 the government of Edward VI at last restored the old endowments and made a new foundation, after an interregnum which had lasted for

---

[1] *VCH Berks.*, ii, 251.
[2] PRO, Ministers' Accounts, SC 6 Henry VIII/4054 fo 7; E 315/101, fo 36v.
[3] *VCH Herts.*, ii, 56-7; *VCH Suffolk*, ii, 312-13.
[4] *ESR*, part 2, pp. 84-5.
[5] W. K. Jordan, 'Social institutions in Kent, 1480-1660', *Archaeologia Cantiana*, lxxv (1961), p. 72; Bodleian, MS DD All Souls c 180, no 1.

ten years.¹ At Winchcombe things almost went the same way, for the court of augmentations treated its master too as if he were just another officer of the abbey, gave him a pension and permitted him to cease from teaching gratis. But for reasons now obscure this decree was never put into effect. The local receiver of the abbey lands appears paying the school-master his regular salary of £10 in 1542 with arrears to 1539, and the school continued its existence with the loss of only its schoolhouse.² Farnworth school was even more fortunate; the court respected the endowment which had been in the keeping of the priory of Launde and the annual income continued to be paid.³ At Lewes, where the prior had only nominated the master, the school endowments were administered by lay feoffees and never even fell within the scope of the dissolutions, though in 1548 when the mastership was vacant there was a little delay in getting a new incumbent appointed.⁴

The fate of the monasteries was shared by those of the hospitals which were staffed by brethren living under a rule and so, despite their charitable work, were also in a sense religious houses. Some of these also had educational concerns – indeed some of the earliest benefactions for poor scholars in the thirteenth and fourteenth centuries had been established in hospitals and were still in existence. Thus the hospital of St John the Baptist at Bridgwater, which had bound itself in 1298 to maintain thirteen poor scholars attending grammar school in the town, still maintained them in 1535.⁵ Of the thirteen boys studying grammar whom Bishop Grandisson had established in the hospital of the same name at Exeter in 1332, nine were still supported there in 1535,⁶ while at St Leonard's, York, a benefaction of ancient origin still maintained twelve clerks and choristers studying grammar and song.⁷ These foundations surrendered to the king in 1539 and their scholars, like the almonry boys in the monasteries, ceased to be maintained. The one public school associated with a hospital seems to have fared better. The history of the grammar school of St Thomas of Acon in London is very obscure; its

¹ PRO, Exch. Augm. Misc. Books, E 315/101, fo 122v; *Somerset Chantries*, ed. E. Green (Somerset Record Society, ii, 1888), pp. 131-2; E. H. Fairbrother, 'The foundation of Bruton school', *Somerset and Dorset Notes and Queries*, xii (1911), pp. 49-52; *CPR 1549-51*, pp. 191-2.
² E 315/101, fo 152; SC Henry 6 VIII/1243, fo 68.
³ W. K. Jordan, *The Social Institutions of Lancashire, 1480-1660* (Chetham Society, 3rd series, xi, 1962), p. 33.
⁴ *VCH Sussex*, ii, 413-14.
⁵ *Valor Ecclesiasticus*, vol i (1810), pp. 208-9.
⁶ Ibid., vol ii (1814), p. 314, and see above, pp. 182-3.
⁷ Ibid., vol v (1825), p. 18.

foundation was sanctioned in 1447 and it is mentioned in 1535, but its precise connection with the hospital of the same name is uncertain. The hospital was surrendered to the crown in 1538, but when the premises and possessions were sold off to the London Company of Mercers in 1542, it was on condition that they kept a free grammar school in perpetuity, of one master teaching twenty-five children at a salary of £10. It certainly looks as though the school had been attached to the hospital before 1538, and that the crown was desirous of having it continued.[1]

Still, it would be unjust to characterize the effects of the Henrician Reformation upon education as merely negative, and to conclude that the crown carried through the dissolution of religious houses merely for its own personal gain. In one sense the seizure of the monasteries was part of the process of reforming and improving the Church, and there was a widespread hope that some monastic endowments might be applied to the support of education, and other charities. Writing to Henry VIII in 1536, Thomas Starkey, man of letters and chaplain to the king, had suggested that the monasteries might be turned into 'common schools for the education of youth in virtue and religion, out of the which you may pick men apt to be ordained bishops and prelates'.[2] By the autumn of 1538 rumours were in the air that some abbeys at least were to be converted into colleges of secular priests engaged in preaching, teaching and hospitality. The monks of Evesham immediately wrote to Thomas Cromwell to ask that their house might be one of those which the king proposed to alter into educational establishments, while Bishop Latimer put in a plea on behalf of Great Malvern as a place to be converted for teaching, preaching, study and housekeeping, and asked, 'shall we not see two or three in each shire changed to such a remedy?'[3] In the event none of the houses for which intercession was made gained any respite, and it was not until the spring of 1539 that the crown made clear its intentions. On 23 May 1539 a bill was hurriedly passed through both houses of parliament in a single day, authorizing the king to establish a number of new bishoprics, cathedrals and collegiate churches. The preamble to the bill, drafted by the king himself, declared an intention of diverting resources which had hitherto sustained 'the slothful and ungodly life' of those 'which have borne the name of religious folk' to the support of charities 'whereby

---

[1] J. Watney, 'Mercers' School', *London and Middx. Archaeological Transactions*, new series, i (1905), pp. 120-4, and also above, p. 213.
[2] *England in the Reign of Henry VIII*, ed. S. J. H. Herrtage (EETS, 1878), p. lvi.
[3] For these and other similar requests see *LPFD*, xiii, part 2, nos 306, 866, 1036; xiv, part 1, no 183.

God's word might be the better set forth, children brought up in learning, clerks nourished in the universities, old servants decayed to have livings, almshouses for poor folk to be sustained in, readers of Greek, Hebrew and Latin to have good stipend, daily alms to be administered, mending of highways, exhibitions for ministers of the church'.[1] The king evidently intended to utilize the buildings of some of the great monasteries to house these new cathedrals and colleges, providing prebends in them for some of the ex-religious and attaching to them a number of useful charities, including grammar schools, for the benefit of the public.

To begin with, the schemes of the king and his advisers were ambitious ones. As well as seven monastic cathedrals which needed to be re-established, Henry thought in terms of a large number of new dioceses, cathedrals and schools – far more than were in fact to be forthcoming in the end. A memorandum in the king's own handwriting which probably belongs to the spring or summer of 1539 proposed thirteen new cathedrals, all on the sites of former abbeys and priories, and as many as eighteen were considered at one time or another.[2] In the autumn of 1539 detailed lists were drafted of the deans, prebendaries and other ministers needed in each foundation, and the cost involved. The schemes were lavish, particularly in their provisions for education. Each cathedral was to have a choir of from six to ten boys, with a master to teach them, and a grammar school for the study of Latin, Greek and in some cases even Hebrew. Each school was to have a number of foundation scholars, varying from twenty to sixty, all of whom would receive free board, lodging and clothing. Teaching was to be done by a master and usher, with the generous salaries of £20 and £10, and it is very probable that they were also intended to instruct outsiders. Lastly there was to be provision for the higher studies. Most of the new cathedrals were to have from four to twenty exhibitions to the universities, as well as a reader in divinity to give lectures locally. But the three most important foundations in the scheme – Canterbury, Westminster and Durham – were to become almost miniature universities, with readers in Greek, Hebrew, Latin, civil law and physic.[3]

On 27 November 1539 Cromwell sent a copy of the draft scheme for Canterbury to Archbishop Cranmer for his comments. These were only moderately approving, for although Cranmer conceded that 'it will be a very substantial and godly foundation', he had several criticisms of detail.

[1] T. Wright, *The Suppression of the Monasteries* (Camden Society, xxvi, 1843), pp. 262-3; *Statutes of the Realm*, iii, 728; *Journals of the House of Lords*, i, 112.
[2] Wright, op. cit., pp. 263-4.
[3] H. Cole, *Henry VIII's Scheme of Bishopricks* (1838), pp. 1-28.

The prebendaries he thought were quite unnecessary: 'commonly a prebendary is neither a learner nor teacher but a good viander'. As for the five readers, he could not see that they would have any audience, 'for as for your prebendaries, they cannot attend to apply [themselves to] lectures, for making of good cheer. And as for your sixty children in grammar, their master and their usher be daily otherwise occupied in the rudiments of grammar.' Far better, he suggested, to do away with the prebendaries and establish in their stead 'twenty divines at £10 apiece, like as it is appointed to be at Oxford and Cambridge; and forty students in the tongues, and sciences, and French, to have ten marks apiece; for if such a number be not there resident, to what intent should so many readers be there? And surely it were great pity that so many good lectures should be read in vain.'[1]

Perhaps it was Cranmer's criticisms that led to the drawing up of more modest plans for the establishments of the new cathedrals. This second scheme proposed to concentrate the readerships at the two universities, where they were later established as regius chairs, and left only one reader in divinity at each cathedral, rather like the chancellors of medieval times. The university exhibitions were severely reduced in number, and some cathedrals were not to have them at all. The grammar schools were now left as the main educational features of the cathedrals, but in some cases even they were modified to do away with the usher and the foundation scholars.[2] The final step seems to have been to reduce the number of new cathedrals from the twenty proposed in the second scheme. This may have been due to Cromwell, one of whose memoranda in the summer of 1539 includes a note 'to diminish some of the bishoprics'.[3] The final result was the refoundation of seven old monastic cathedrals – Canterbury, Carlisle, Durham, Ely, Rochester, Winchester and Worcester – and six new foundations, all on the site of former abbeys – Bristol, Chester, Gloucester, Oxford (Osney), Peterborough and Westminster.

Foundation charters were issued for the new cathedrals between 1540 and 1542, but it was not until 1544 that a commission was appointed to draw up statutes for their governance. The commissioners included Nicholas Heath, bishop of Worcester, George Day, bishop of Hereford, and Richard Cox, archdeacon of Ely, of whom the first two were later to suffer in the cause of Catholicism and the latter in that of Protestantism.

---

[1] *Miscellaneous Writings and Letters of Thomas Cranmer*, ed. J. E. Cox (Parker Society, 1846), pp. 396-8.
[2] H. Cole, op. cit., pp. 28-74.
[3] *LPFD*, xiv, part 2, nos 424, 427, 430.

The statutes they drafted were sent out to most of the cathedrals in the summer of 1544, but they were not closely related to the earlier schemes of 1539, nor were they even uniform among themselves.[1] They ranged from the still comparatively lavish arrangements at Canterbury and Westminster down to the very modest ones thought suitable for Bristol and Carlisle. In most cases, however, provision was made for a master 'learned in Greek and Latin', with a stipend of between £13 and £20, and an usher 'learned in Latin'. They were to give free instruction to all comers and their conduct and curricula were prescribed in great detail. There were also a number of foundation scholars, varying from fifty at Canterbury to eighteen at Durham. These scholars, who were normally expected to stay at school for four or five years, received board and lodging worth 4 or 5 marks a year, as well as free education. At first provision was also made for exhibitions from the cathedrals to the universities, these again ranging in number from twenty-six at Canterbury to four at Rochester. The exhibitions, however, did not survive for long and by the end of the reign they had been abolished, the cathedral chapters being obliged to return the endowments to the crown.[2] The lectureships in divinity never appeared at all.

The scheme for cathedral schools which was finally put into effect had many anomalies. The three smallest cathedrals, Bristol, Gloucester and Carlisle, were treated poorly, and never had foundation scholars or university exhibitions. At Durham the king incorporated into his foundation the older grammar school endowed by Bishop Langley in the early fifteenth century.[3] At Oxford the cathedral school was of only brief duration. As first founded in 1542 the see of Oxford was established in the abbey of Osney in the western suburbs of the city, and at this time the cathedral appears to have included the usual grammar school.[4] Then in 1546 the king began founding his new college of Christ Church in the university, and transferred to it the cathedral chapter from Osney. The plans for the joint foundation drawn up in October 1546 did include a grammar school with a master, usher and forty scholars, but this was never effective. When the college opened in January 1547 shortly before the king's death,

[1] *The Statutes of the Cathedral Church of Durham*, ed. A. Hamilton Thompson (Surtees Society, cxliii, 1929), pp. xxxviiiff, a good discussion of the Henrician cathedral foundations with specimens of the foundation charters and statutes. For Canterbury see also *ECD*, pp. 452-69.

[2] e.g. *LPFD*, xx, part 1, no 400.

[3] *VCH Durham*, i, 374-5.

[4] As appears from a survey taken after the removal of the see from Osney (*Hearne's Collections*, ed. H. E. Salter, vol x (Oxford Historical Society, lxvii, 1915), pp. 29-31).

the resources intended for the school were diverted instead to support forty undergraduate scholars, and the cathedral-college was thereafter concerned only with the higher studies.[1] Nor was a school founded at Winchester where Henry, who allowed Wykeham's college to remain intact, probably thought another foundation superfluous. The seventy scholars of the college approximated to those of the other Henrician cathedrals, for which they were indeed the original model, and although Wykeham's college had not been planned as a public school for the neighbourhood, there are signs that in the sixteenth century local boys were being admitted as commoners, so that even in this the foundation resembled Henry's other schools to a degree.[2] Norwich too was omitted from the plans throughout. This old monastic cathedral had surrendered to the crown earlier than the rest, in April 1538, and had been immediately re-established with a dean and prebendaries, but without a cathedral school. Not until 1547 was this omission remedied by the government of Edward VI, and then the free school which they founded was put under the control of the city and housed away from the cathedral with which it had little connection.[3]

Henry VIII's cathedral schools were the latest version of an already ancient institution the origins of which went back to the twelfth century, and most of the schools he refounded have lasted until the present day. In one or two cases there was complete continuity with the medieval school, as at Canterbury and Durham where the old schoolmasters were re-appointed to the new foundation.[4] But compared with the cathedral schools of the middle ages there were two obvious differences in Henry's creations. The schoolmasters became more closely associated with the cathedrals than before. Their appointment lay with the dean and chapter; they dined in the common hall, while it was kept up, with the other ministers of the church; and they usually lodged and taught in the cathedral precincts. Moreover, the education they offered now became free, thus carrying further a reform already introduced at four or five places before the 1530s, and which was finally to be extended to every cathedral in 1547.[5]

The cathedral schools were not however the whole of the king's some-

[1] H. L. Thompson, *Christ Church* (University of Oxford College Histories, 1900), pp. 272-4.
[2] *VCH Hants.*, ii, 273-4.
[3] *CPR 1547-8*, p. 13.
[4] C. E. Woodruff and H. J. Cape, *Schola Regia Cantuariensis* (1908), p. 56; *VCH Durham*, i, 374-5.
[5] See below, p. 275.

what erratic educational achievement. At the time he was projecting cathedrals, he was also thinking in terms of some additional secular colleges on old monastic sites. Two of these were ultimately founded at Burton-on-Trent in 1541 and at Thornton, Lincolnshire, in the following year, and both establishments included free grammar schools. The king changed his mind and suppressed Burton in 1545, but Thornton school survived and at the dissolution of the college by Edward VI in 1548 was continued by order of the crown.[1] The last of Henry's college schools was at Cambridge. Here in 1546 he began the magnificent new foundation of Trinity College, formed by amalgamating the two ancient colleges of the King's Hall and Michaelhouse. As at Christ Church, Oxford, the initial plans included not merely an establishment of university scholars but a grammar school as well, consisting of a master, usher and forty children boarded on the foundation. Unlike Christ Church, the Trinity school did come into operation for a short time. The foundation charter issued on 19 December 1546, though it dealt mainly with the provost and sixty fellows, also alluded to 'boys or pupils in the grammar school of the college'. The school appears to have opened in 1547 with six boys, but the full complement of forty was reached in the following year, and it was only the visitation of the university by Edward VI's commissioners in 1549 that brought its life to an untimely end. The policy of the crown had changed by this time, and was now to suppress the study of grammar in the universities so that they might better concentrate on the higher studies, injunctions to this effect being delivered at Cambridge in July 1549. An exception was made for the school at Jesus College, but the Trinity grammar school was closed down and its endowments were diverted, as the Christ Church ones had been, to support undergraduates. So neither university town secured a Henrician grammar school in the end.[2]

Henry VIII also had a hand in at least two other new schools of the 1540s. In 1541 he permitted William Barlow, bishop of St Davids, to convert some of the endowments of the college of Abergwili in his diocese towards founding Christ's College, Brecon, for the maintenance of a master, usher and twenty foundation scholars, which proved to be a most useful benefaction for the wild countryside in which it lay.[3] And in 1545 he sold to John Hales, a Coventry man and one of the officials of the chancery, the site and lands of the hospital of St John the Baptist in

[1] *LPFD*, xvi, no 1135(9); xvii, no 71(8); xxi part 1, no 321; *ESR*, part 2, pp. 134-5.
[2] W. W. Rouse Ball, *Cambridge Notes*, 2nd ed. (1921), pp. 13-14; C. H. Cooper, *Annals of Cambridge*, vol ii (1843), p. 32. The schoolmaster was the ex-schoolmaster of Burton!
[3] *LPFD*, xvi, no 503(30); *ESR*, part 2, pp. 316-18.

Coventry at a very advantageous price, on condition that he founded a free grammar school there to be called King Henry VIII's School, Coventry.[1] It does not necessarily follow from this that other founders of schools got church property from the crown at a cheap rate. Joan Cook of Gloucester, who bought some of the lands of Lanthony Priory to endow the Crypt school at Gloucester in 1539, got a grant after Bishop Latimer had interceded in her favour, but she paid the usual purchase price of twenty times the annual value.[2]

It was not long after the dissolution of the monasteries before the king began to cast covetous eyes upon the secular colleges which had hitherto escaped suppression. One by one during the 1540s the colleges surrendered themselves and their property into the king's hands, but the process was not complete when Henry VIII died in January 1547, and several colleges remained to be dealt with by the Chantry Act of Edward VI later that year. The last of them were not finally extinguished until the summer of 1548. Here it will be convenient to consider the whole question of the dissolution of the colleges in both reigns, and the effect which this episode of the Reformation had upon English education. Although by no means all the secular colleges possessed schools, many had come to do so during the previous two centuries, and these schools were of two kinds. Some were grammar schools for the ministers of the college: the choristers, clerks and occasionally perhaps even the chaplains. The 1415 statutes of Fotheringhay, as we have seen, had provided for thirteen choristers and masters to teach them song and grammar.[3] Similarly at Rushworth College in Norfolk Lady Anne Wingfield had established a grammar master in 1490 to teach the five poor boys of her foundation and eight other children.[4] In other places, however, the college schools were open to outsiders as well. This was so at one or two ancient colleges such as Southwell and Warwick, and at a number of the fourteenth- and fifteenth-century foundations: Acaster, Higham Ferrers, Ottery St Mary, Rotherham, Tattershall, Tong, Westbury-on-Trym and Wye, to name the most obvious examples.

None of the schools meant only for the college inmates survived the surrender of their houses either under Henry VIII or Edward VI, and like the almonry schools of the monasteries they simply disappeared.

[1] *LPFD*, xx, part 1, no 1335 (38-9).
[2] *LPFD*, xiii, part 1, no 1179; R. Austin, *The Crypt School Gloucester* (1939), pp. 29, 145-6.
[3] See above, p. 194; *VCH Northants.*, ii, 223-4.
[4] E. K. Bennet, 'The college of Rushworth', *Norfolk Archaeology*, x (1888), pp. 367-71, 375.

Those which were public grammar schools on the other hand were in most cases preserved. There seem to have been only two or three exceptions to this rule. At Westbury-on-Trym near Bristol, the school, founded by John Carpenter in 1463, did not outlive the surrender of the college in 1543, but the king had opened a new cathedral school in Bristol itself in the previous year, and this may have made Westbury seem redundant.[1] The school at Burton-on-Trent was also closed along with the college in 1545, but both were after all very recent foundations. The college school at Tong, established in 1410 for the benefit of the children of the neighbourhood, may have been a third casualty, but even in this case we cannot be sure that it was still extant when the college was dissolved in 1546.[2]

In most cases, however, the college grammar schools remained in being. At Higham Ferrers, where Archbishop Chicheley's college surrendered in 1542, the buildings and estates were granted out to Robert Dacres, one of the king's councillors, but only on condition that he maintained two chaplains, thirteen bedesmen and a competent schoolmaster in Higham, the latter to be nominated by the crown and to receive £10 a year.[3] Exactly the same happened at Wye, the foundation of another archbishop, John Kemp, which surrendered to the king in 1545. When later that year the college and its possessions were granted to the queen's secretary, Walter Buckler, it was once again on condition that he maintain a sufficient schoolmaster to teach a free grammar school at a salary of £13 6s. 8d.[4] Tattershall grammar school also survived the dissolution of the college, for it is mentioned as existing at the beginning of Elizabeth's reign.[5] In two other places Henry himself erected foundations to replace the old college schools. In May 1545 he granted the college of St Mary, Warwick, to the burgesses of the town and gave them the responsibility of maintaining a free grammar school called 'the king's new school of Warwick', the master to be appointed by the crown and to receive a house and the usual £10 a year.[6] Later in the same year at Ottery St Mary, where the college had just been surrendered, the king made over the site of the college to a corporation of four of the inhabitants, and re-established the collegiate school as 'the king's new grammar school of Ottery St Mary',

[1] *VCH Gloucs.*, ii, 108, 379.
[2] For Tong see above, p. 195, and *LPFD*, xxi, part 2, no 199(30).
[3] Ibid., xviii, part 1, no 474(27).
[4] E. Hasted, *History of Kent* (1778-99), iii, 174.
[5] *Historical MSS Commission, Report on the MSS of Lord De Lisle and Dudley*, vol i (1925), p. 202.
[6] *LPFD*, xx, part 1, no 846(41).

with a £10 schoolmaster teaching grammar to all comers.[1] To these new foundations one other may perhaps be added. It is not certain that the ancient college of Crediton had maintained a public grammar school before its surrender in 1545, but it is highly suggestive that in 1547, just after Henry VIII's death and probably at his initiative, a corporation of governors of the church was established exactly as at Ottery, charged with maintaining the same kind of free grammar school. It seems quite possible that this too was the continuation of an older school, rather than just a new benefaction.[2]

It must now be clear that although Henry VIII cannot be accused of indifference to the effects on education of the secularization of religious property, his remedies were erratic and lacked uniformity. The *ad hoc* arrangements for schools contrast strikingly with the broader view of education taken by the government of Edward VI when the chantries were dissolved in 1548. The total effects of Henry's policies, such as they were, may be summarized as follows. In the first place the suppression of all the monasteries and friaries, and of a great many colleges and hospitals, involved the disappearance of all the education which they had provided for their own members and dependants. Individually such schools were small; collectively they benefited many hundreds of people, and they had made a valuable contribution to English culture in their day. The effect of the dissolutions upon public secular schools is less easy to summarize, so difficult is it to make an exact list of those dependent upon the religious houses before their fall. Eighteen schools however, dependent to some extent upon the houses seized by Henry VIII, have been mentioned in the preceding pages, apart from the king's own foundations. Eleven of these survived his reign without much difficulty,[3] one (Bruton) was temporarily extinguished and three came to an end altogether.[4] The history of the other three is obscure.[5] So much for the king's debit account. We can credit him on the other hand with endowing twelve permanent grammar schools in the cathedral cities and at Thornton, as well as his share in at least two other benefactions. His foundations also provided more than 250 scholarships and over 100 places for choristers. The educational effects of the dissolutions were thus very similar to the religious ones: the destruction of one area of education resulted in improvements in another area,

---

[1] Ibid., xx, part 2, no 1068(45).
[2] *CPR 1547-8*, pp. 43-4.
[3] i.e. Evesham, Farnworth, Higham Ferrers, Lewes, London (St Thomas Acon), Ottery, Reading, Tattershall, Warwick, Winchcombe and Wye.
[4] i.e. Cirencester, Faversham and Westbury-on-Trym.
[5] i.e. Bury St Edmunds, St Albans and Tong.

but on a much smaller scale, the crown having taken the opportunity to benefit itself. Nevertheless it is important to see this balance of destruction and improvement in perspective. The schools just mentioned formed only a part of the national system of education. The schools of the chantries and the secular cathedrals, the growing number of independent endowed schools, the still numerous masters who taught for private gain, all continued their work through Henry's reign, largely unaffected by the dissolutions. Here, as in so many other ways, royal actions failed to affect Tudor society as a whole.

Chapter Ten

The schools from Edward VI to Elizabeth

In 1545 Henry VIII, having swallowed the monasteries and most of the secular colleges, turned his attention towards the chantries and religious guilds. He himself died having scarcely begun the task of seizing them, but his work was continued after his death by the government of his son, Edward VI, and successfully completed in 1548. Like the dissolution of the religious houses, that of the chantries and guilds was to have considerable implications for education. During the fifteenth century, and until as late as the 1510s, it had been customary when endowing a new school to make it a chantry as well, and the schoolmaster a chantry priest praying for the founder's soul. Many of these dual foundations still existed in 1545. Not a few of the other chantries and guilds, though originally founded merely to support divine services or to do other works of charity, had come to maintain schools as well during the early sixteenth century, at the initiative of their patrons and governors. And there were yet others where the priests were not expected to teach but did so voluntarily in order to increase their often meagre stipends. The seizure of all these foundations thus involved a large number of local schools as well.

At the same time, the educational importance of the chantries and guilds ought not to be exaggerated. It is often assumed that on the chantry legislation hung the fate of most of the education then provided in England, but this is by no means true. Those chantries which supported a school or where the priest was a teacher were not only a minority among their own kind; they were also a minority among all the schools which existed in the 1540s. Even in the fifteenth century some grammar schools had been endowed without the addition of a chantry, such as Sevenoaks and Magdalen College school, Oxford. Their number grew rapidly after about

272

1510, and by 1530 the omission of the chantry when founding a school was all but universal. Most of the schools of recent foundation, as well as those which Henry VIII had established in the cathedrals, were thus entirely unaffected by the suppression of the chantries. So were the even larger number of feepaying schools, which in many places still provided the only education available. The guild and chantry schools, like those of the monasteries and colleges, were but a part of the national supply of education, and this should not be forgotten.

It was on 15 December 1545 that the 'bill for the dissolution of chantries, colleges and free chapels' was read for the first time in the House of Lords, where it passed without dissent only two days later; it was a little longer in the Commons, but there too it went through all its stages within a week, and was ready for the royal assent on 23 December.[1] The first motive of the crown in securing the act was to prevent unauthorized seizures and alienations of chantry lands in imitation of its own expropriation of church property. The preamble to the act declared that many founders and incumbents of chantries had already entered upon the lands or made alienations of the endowments, an assertion for which there is indeed some evidence.[2] It was therefore provided in the act that all colleges, chantries, hospitals and guilds which had been illegally dissolved within the last ten years should revert to the crown. But the act was also represented as a measure of reform. In many places, it declared, where chantries, hospitals and guilds had been founded to give alms to the poor and to perform other charitable deeds, the governors and incumbents did not rule their properties or employ the revenues according to the virtuous intentions of the founders, 'and for that the king's highness . . . intendeth to have the premises used and exercised to a more godly and virtuous purpose', Henry was given power during his lifetime to appoint commissioners under the great seal to enter upon the chantries and their possessions, and vest them in the king.

The first Chantry Act thus gives the impression that the chantries are to be reformed rather than merely confiscated by the crown. This impression was reinforced by the speech which Henry VIII is said to have made to parliament on Christmas Eve 1545, the last time he ever addressed the assembly:

I cannot a little rejoice when I consider the perfect trust and sure confidence with which you, without my desire or request [sic], have

---

[1] *Statutes of the Realm*, iii, 988-93; *Journals of the House of Lords*, i, 274-6.
[2] *Yorkshire Chantry Surveys*, ed. W. Page, vol i (Surtees Society, xci, 1894), pp. x-xi.

committed to my order and disposition all chantries, colleges, and hospitals. Surely if I, contrary to your expectation, should suffer the ministers of the Church to decay, or learning (which is so great a jewel) to be diminished, or poor and miserable people to be unrelieved, you might say that I were no lover of the public wealth nor yet one that feared God. Doubt not, I pray you, but your expectation shall be served more godly and goodly than you will wish or desire, as hereafter you shall plainly perceive.[1]

The king appointed commissioners to make a survey of the chantries on 14 February 1546. There were twenty-four commissions, to each of which was allocated a county or a pair of adjoining ones. Each commission was headed by the diocesan bishop, and included between four and fourteen other members, chiefly officers of the court of augmentations or of the other departments of government – men experienced in the problems of surveying and administering religious property.[2] Much of the work probably fell on the local receivers and stewards of crown lands who were in many cases included on the commissions for the sake of their intimate knowledge of local affairs. The commissioners began by sending injunctions to the clergy and churchwardens of each parish. The latter were ordered to inquire how many chantries, hospitals, free chapels, guilds and stipendiary priests were maintained in their parish, as well as the names of the founders, the purpose of the foundations and how the revenues were now being employed. They were to ascertain the annual revenues of the endowments and the value of the plate, jewels, ornaments and other goods belonging to each foundation. They were to make a certificate of all these things and bring it before the commissioners at an appointed time and place, together with any documents relevant to the inquiry. From the certificates of each parish, enrolments were made county by county, and these form the first, or Henrician, series of chantry certificates.[3]

A little more than a year after the passing of the Chantry Act, however, it lapsed by reason of the king's death on 28 January 1547. By that time only two or three chantries had been seized by the king, and only one of these, at Aldwinkle in Northamptonshire, founded to maintain a song school, had any connection with education. As we shall see, the crown, though conscious of the need to foster the study of grammar, was

[1] Abridged from Edward Hall, *Chronicle Containing the History of England* (1809), pp. 864-5.
[2] For the commissions and their members see *LPFD*, xxi, part 1, no 302(30).
[3] For the injunctions see *Concilia*, iii, 875-6. The surviving certificates are in PRO, Exch. Augms., E 301, and most of the educational entries are in *ESR*, part 2.

indifferent to the fate of elementary schools.[1] The king's death reprieved the chantries, but not for long. The new government of Edward VI headed by Edward Seymour, duke of Somerset, soon made clear its Protestant sympathies, and began to prepare a further reformation of the Church on Protestant lines. During the summer of 1547 royal commissioners visited each diocese, and issued injunctions to the clergy which mostly repeated the educational policies of Henry VIII's reign. The old king's primer and grammar were prescribed for use in the schools, incumbents of benefices worth over £100 a year were ordered to maintain a scholar at school or university and chantry priests were urged to teach children to read and write and bring them up in good manners. The king's commissioners also visited the cathedrals, and here they found scope for new educational reforms. Although Henry VIII had endowed free grammar schools at seven of the old monastic cathedrals and at his six new cathedral foundations, this reform had not extended to the ancient secular cathedrals, of which only Chichester, Lichfield and London possessed free schools. The other six cathedral cities had only a master teaching for fees in the city, whose connection with the chapter was often tenuous. The injunctions of 1547 therefore commanded that every cathedral lacking a free grammar school should provide one out of its common lands and revenues, with a master receiving £13 6s. 8d. and a house rent free, and an usher getting half as much and a chamber. In the case of choristers whose voices had broken and who were no longer eligible to stay in the choristers' school, the chapters were to give them exhibitions of £3 6s. 8d. for five years to support them at a grammar school.[2]

The first parliament of Edward VI's reign met on 4 November 1547 and it saw the first steps towards the creation of a Protestant religious settlement, with an act permitting communion in both kinds, and with the repeal of the medieval heresy laws. These measures were accompanied by a new chantry bill. Unlike that of Henry VIII which had mentioned only the abuses in the chantries, the new bill took a thoroughly Protestant line in attacking the institution itself and castigating those who trusted in 'vain opinions of purgatory and masses satisfactory' rather than in 'their very true and perfect salvation through the death of Jesus Christ'. To the Protestant reformers, the chantries were not only useless but pernicious,

---

[1] For a list of chantries dissolved under the act of 1546 see *ESR*, part 1, pp. 64-5. For Aldwinkle see *ECD*, pp. 434-5 and *ESR*, part 2, p. 146. Two colleges, Tong and St Edmund's, Salisbury, both with educational connections, were surrendered to the crown during 1546, but it is difficult to associate them with the Chantry Act because surrenders of colleges had been going on independently since the early 1540s.

[2] *Visitation Articles and Injunctions*, ii, 121-2, 129, 138-9.

K

and must be swept away altogether. The new bill therefore proposed to convert all the endowments of prayers for the dead to 'good and godly uses, as in erecting of grammar schools . . . the further augmenting of the universities, and better provision for the poor and needy'. The effect of the bill was that all colleges, chantries and free chapels which had maintained a priest in perpetuity within the last five years should be vested in the crown, as well as religious (but not craft) guilds and their possessions. The king was to appoint new commissioners to make another survey of all colleges, chantries and guilds. In cases where a grammar school or a preacher had been maintained by ordinance of the foundation since the previous Michaelmas, lands were to be assigned from the foundation to maintain the school or preacher for ever. Where the foundation was also a parish church, arrangements were also to be made to endow a vicarage in order to provide for the cure of souls. The commissioners were to carry out their survey within a year, and the bill was to take effect from the following Easter (1 April 1548). But certain foundations were specially exempted from it: the universities, including the chantries within them, the colleges of Windsor, Eton and Winchester, and the cathedrals, though not in the latter case their chantries.[1]

The impression given by the second chantry bill was one of reforming an obsolete institution while preserving and improving the charitable services associated with it. Endowments already supporting grammar schools and preachers would be preserved, while new resources would be made available for other grammar schools, for the universities and for the support of the poor. Public opinion, however, was by no means convinced of the good intentions of the bill, and its passage through parliament was not easy. In the House of Lords it was at first opposed not only by the conservative bishops but by Archbishop Cranmer himself. When it went to the House of Commons on 15 December it aroused considerable opposition on account of the proposed confiscation of the lands of religious guilds, which in some towns had maintained parish churches as well as public works, which were not included among the charities safeguarded by the bill. The opposition was led by the burgesses of King's Lynn and Coventry, who laboured so successfully that the privy councillors who sat in the Commons feared that not only might the clause on the guilds be thrown out but the whole bill be put in jeopardy in view of the approaching date for the prorogation of parliament. A compromise had therefore to be arranged with the burgesses of the two towns who were promised, on their agreeing to drop their objections, that the king would make them a

[1] *Statutes of the Realm*, iv, part 1, 24-33.

special grant of the guild lands in question, a promise which was later carried out. After this it was possible to present the bill again, and it was passed by the House of Commons on 22 December.[1]

On 14 February 1548 an entirely new set of commissioners were appointed to survey the chantries. This was partly made necessary by the different circumstances of the Edwardian Chantry Act. All chantries were now to be confiscated, grammar schools and preachers to be safeguarded and all dispossessed incumbents to be pensioned. In addition, the government took the opportunity to seize the endowments of church lights, which had been forbidden to be used, except on the altar, in the summer of 1547.[2] As before, there were twenty-four commissions, made up of between five and thirteen members, eight or nine being the most common number. Each commission dealt with one county, or with two in which case the members divided up to carry out the survey, and each county did in fact receive separate treatment. Only a few of the commissioners of 1546 were reappointed, and the bishops were almost entirely absent, but as in 1546 most of the new members were officers of the court of augmentations or the other departments of the central government.[3] In 1547, just before Henry died, the court of augmentations had been entirely reconstituted. The crown lands in each county were put under the supervision of a 'particular surveyor', and these men were included on the commissions as being best informed about local conditions. The brunt of the work seems to have fallen upon them too. It would be wrong to regard them as either servile or narrowminded officials more concerned to seize lands for the crown than to discover and preserve useful charities. They were gentlemen of local standing, often justices of the peace, who conscientiously applied themselves to sending accurate information to the crown, to which alone belonged the final decision about confiscation or preservation.[4]

The arrangements for the new survey were probably similar to those of 1546, involving the sending of questionnaires to each parish, whose representatives then brought their certificates before the commissioners at central points. In Devon, for example, the commissioners are mentioned at Exeter, Paignton and Tiverton. The information required was more extensive than two years before. The certificate of each parish began with

[1] *Journals of the House of Lords*, i, 306-13; *Journals of the House of Commons*, i, 2-4; *Acts of the Privy Council, 1547-1550*, pp. 193-5.
[2] *Visitation Articles and Injunctions*, ii, 116.
[3] For the commissions and their members see *CPR 1548-9*, pp. 135-7.
[4] On the particular surveyors see W. C. Richardson, *History of the Court of Augmentations* (1961), especially pp. 141-2.

an estimate of the number of communicants at church, in case the crown should feel disposed to appoint an extra priest to work in the parish. After the name of each chantry came details of the original founders and the date and purpose of the foundation. Then followed the incumbent's name, his age, stipend and any other benefices or pensions he held. Sometimes there were observations about his morals and learning. The revenues of the foundation were given and also the value of the goods and ornaments. Sometimes the parishioners added a memorandum, particularly recommending the usefulness of a chantry in keeping a grammar school or of a guild in maintaining public works. Sometimes they took the initiative in asking for a free school to be founded in their locality, evidently in view of the promise to convert chantry lands to 'good and godly uses'. But it was not left to the initiative of the local inhabitants to point out places where the government ought to consider establishing new charities. The commissioners had to do this, and they added to the certificates a suggested list of places in need of schools or of extra parish clergy. In Gloucestershire for example they named four places for schools, and in Staffordshire six. The parish certificates and the commissioners' observations were eventually enrolled, and they form the second or Edwardian series of chantry certificates, though as we shall see there was to be a further series before the whole process was finished.[1]

The chantry certificates have long been used as a source for the history of schools and charities, as well as of the chantries themselves, and rightly so. It is worth, however, pointing out their deficiencies in this respect. To begin with they were first compiled in the parishes, not by the commissioners, and the temptation to conceal information from the crown was very great. At Powick in Worcestershire, for example, the parishioners appear to have packed off the chantry priest, and they certainly failed to make a presentment about the chantry, which only came to light two years later.[2] At Wotton-under-Edge the oldest of all chantry grammar schools was deliberately misrepresented as being merely a grammar school, and as the commissioners never discovered the truth, it escaped the act.[3] In Staffordshire so many foundations were concealed that an entirely new commission had to be appointed in 1549 to make a

---

[1] The Edwardian chantry certificates are in PRO, Exch. Augm., E 301. Most of the educational entries are printed in *ESR*, part 2, but there were some omissions, e.g. Fotheringhay (*VCH Northants.*, ii, 223), and St Briavels, Gloucs. (Sir J. Maclean, 'Chantry certificates, Gloucestershire', *Transactions of the Bristol and Gloucs. Archaeological Society*, viii (1883-4), pp. 295-6).

[2] PRO, Exch. Augm., Proceedings, E 321/37/28.

[3] *ESR*, part 2, pp. 79-80.

fresh survey.[1] And for the next fifty years concealed chantry lands were a happy hunting ground for informers, who were given a share of the proceeds when the crown recovered the property. Even setting aside these frauds, the information returned was often vague and inaccurate. The figures for 'houselling people' or communicants are only given in round numbers, and in Oxfordshire in particular two sets of figures appear, often wildly incompatible. Parishes sometimes failed to give accurate information about the founders of chantries or returned them vaguely as 'diverse persons' although, as at Burford, the original deeds and muniments were quite accessible. Even incumbents are not always what they seem, for it was not unknown for the deputy of some absent cleric to represent himself as the true incumbent, and in Oxfordshire it has been noticed that their ages were given in round numbers. Still, the commissioners were not entirely the passive recipients of tall stories, and the particular surveyors and their deputies were especially active in verifying the certificates. In this way John Maynard, deputy surveyor of Oxfordshire, discovered the grammar school at Banbury which had not been presented, as well as two cases of deputies pretending to be incumbents.[2]

The task of the local commissioners was merely to survey the chantries; it was then up to the crown to carry out the promises it had made in the act. But even before the surveys had been completed, the pressing demands of government had made it unlikely that the crown would be as generous as it had first promised. War with Scotland had broken out in August 1547, French intervention was imminent and there was a threat of rebellion in Ireland. Money was desperately needed, and the chantry lands offered the most obvious source. On 17 April 1548 the privy council decided that chantry lands worth £5,000 a year should be sold, and it was agreed to appoint two officials to supervise the sales. The task was given to Sir Walter Mildmay, one of the general surveyors of the court of augmentations, and Robert Kellway, surveyor of liveries in the court of wards.[3] At the same time the government did not altogether forget its obligations to education and charity, nor to the chantry priests who would be deprived by the confiscations. On 20 June a second commission was issued to Mildmay and Kellway in which the young king specifically recalled his intention 'to erect diverse and sundry grammar schools in every county in England and Wales, for the education and bringing up of youth in virtue

[1] Ibid., pp. 203-4.
[2] *Chantry Certificates for Oxfordshire*, ed. Rose Graham (Alcuin Club, xxiii, 1920), especially pp. xii-xiv, 51, 54.
[3] *Acts of the Privy Council 1547-1550*, pp. 184-6, 206.

and learning and godliness, and also to make provision for the relief of the poor'. He went on however to disclaim the possibility of the crown being able to fulfil this promise at once. In the meantime Mildmay and Kellway were ordered to pension off all the incumbents of chantries who had been merely chantry priests. Those who had also been schoolmasters and preachers were to remain at their work and to receive stipends from the crown equal to those they had enjoyed before the Chantry Act, 'until such time as other order and direction should be taken therein'. The promised reforms and improvements of schools made in the act were thus put off.[1]

A third set of chantry certificates was now drawn up, abstracted from the fuller returns sent in by the commissioners, and against each chantry or guild and its incumbent a note was made either to award a pension or, in the case of grammar schools and preachers, the words 'continuatur quousque', meaning that the incumbents should continue in office at the same stipends that they had received before, until a final decision could be taken by the crown. Chantry lands then began to be sold off indiscriminately, whether or not they had supported schools. On 20 July 1548 Mildmay and Kellway signed a number of warrants authorizing the continuance of the grammar schools and other charities and ordering the receivers of the court of augmentations in each county to pay the schoolmasters their old stipends as from the previous 1 April. For the present therefore the crown took over the responsibility of maintaining the chantry schools.[2]

How many schools survived this crisis and secured a warrant for their continuance? The Chantry Act had proposed to save grammar schools maintained by chantries and guilds as part of the original foundation, and these were accordingly respited. The classic chantry grammar schools of the fifteenth century – Alnwick, Newland and Towcester – came into this class. But there were also the other chantries and guilds which while not having been founded to maintain schools, had since come to do so. Examples of these can be found at Bromsgrove, King's Norton and Stourbridge in Worcestershire, where priests employed by the parishioners to say additional masses and help with parish work had also become charged with keeping a grammar school.[3] Some of these arrangements do not seem to have been of long standing, and strictly speaking such

---

[1] *ESR*, part 2, pp. vii-1.
[2] For examples of the third set, or abstracts, of chantry certificates, see ibid., *passim*, and for a specimen of a continuance warrant, ibid., pp. 5-7.
[3] Ibid., pp. 268-71, 274-6.

THE DISSOLUTION OF THE CHANTRIES, 1547–1548
IN GLOUCESTERSHIRE, HEREFORDSHIRE & WORCESTERSHIRE

- ● Chantries with grammar schools in 1548
- ○ Chantries with elementary schools in 1548
  (Schools continued by the chantry commissioners are underlined)
- ■ Grammar schools not affected by the Chantry Act of 1547

Map labels:

Stourbridge
King's Norton
Bucknall
Rock
Bromsgrove
Richard's Castle
Kingsland
Leominster
Worcester
(King's Schl)
(Trinity Guild)
Pembridge
Bromyard
Kington
Dilwyn
Eardisley
Weobley
Evesham
Kinnersley
Much
Cowarne
Chipping Campden
Staunton-
on-Wye
Hereford
(Cath. Schl)
(St Owen's)
Bosbury
Ledbury
Winchcombe
Cheltenham
Gloucester
(King's Schl)
(Crypt)
Newland
St. Briavels
Cirencester
Wotton-under-Edge
Bristol
(Gr. Schl)
(Cath. Schl)

0 5 10 15 20 25 Miles

grammar schools did not qualify for continuance under the act, not being part of the original foundation. Nevertheless the commission to Mildmay and Kellway of 20 June empowered them to continue the stipends of any grammar masters, and in most cases they did so. Very few grammar schools, whatever their origin, seem to have been callously ignored; nearly all survived the dissolution of the chantries, at least to begin with. The odd exceptions include the grammar school of the Trinity guild at Worcester, which had only recently been revived after falling into desuetude, and the famous school at Banbury which had been concealed in the first instance from the commissioners. Even so, both schools were destined to be re-established within the next few years.[1]

The case of the chantries whose priests taught only reading or song was quite different. Elementary education was a far less precious commodity than grammar, and probably more easily available; the Chantry Act therefore made no provision for the continuance of such schools. Their masters were pensioned off like mere chantry priests. There is a good example of this at Rotherham, where Archbishop Rotherham's college founded in 1483 to give free instruction in grammar, song and writing was still in full working order in 1548. The chantry commissioners continued the grammar school, but the masters of writing and song got only pensions, thus greatly restricting the value of a school originally intended to benefit the community in the widest possible sense.[2] The cases of schoolmasters of an unspecified kind who were also pensioned off suggest that they too had taught only the elementary subjects, rather than being grammar masters whom the commissioners somehow overlooked.

But scrupulous as the commissioners might be in arranging for the continuance of the chantry grammar schools, the fact remained that the government had gone back on its promises. It had undertaken to provide more schools and to save the lands of those foundations already in existence. Yet in 1547 only two new schools were founded (Crediton and Norwich), both originating in the previous reign; in 1548 there was none and in 1549 only three. Meanwhile the lands of the chantry schools were fast being sold off, and the temporary arrangement of paying the masters out of the crown lands looked like becoming permanent. No wonder that there was disappointment at the outcome, and not a little indignation. In January 1549 an attempt was made to force the government's hand by introducing a bill in the House of Commons 'for making of schools and giving lands thereto'. It was read three times and approved, but was quietly shelved when it got to the Lords. A second attempt in December of the

[1] *ESR*, part 2, pp. 175-6, 273-4.   [2] Ibid., pp. 299-300, 305.

same year did not get beyond its first reading in the Commons.[1] In February 1550 Thomas Lever, one of the leading Protestant divines, introduced the subject into his Lenten sermon before the king. Lever was master of St John's College, Cambridge, which had the patronage of the chantry grammar school at Sedbergh in Yorkshire, and the college had made valiant but unsuccessful attempts to prevent the school lands from being seized and sold. He therefore took the opportunity to attack the way in which the Chantry Act had been carried out, and to hold up the case of Sedbergh as an example. Later on in the year he repeated his criticisms at the great public forum of Paul's Cross. It was all very well, he declared, for the Chantry Act to talk of erecting grammar schools, augmenting the universities, and making better provision for the poor. 'This shall ye find in the acts of parliament, in the king's statutes, but what shall be found in your practice and your deeds? Surely the pulling down of grammar schools, the devilish drowning of youth in ignorance, the utter decay of the universities, and most uncharitable spoil of provision that was made for the poor.'[2]

Whether or not the government was moved by its critics, the year 1550 did at last see the real beginning of the promised educational foundations, the 'free grammar schools of King Edward VI', as they were generally called. Some of the towns chosen for the endowment of new schools had been recommended in the chantry certificates of 1548, but in the end which places got new schools or their old ones refounded depended on vigorous petitioning or influential backing. Most of the letters patent founding the new schools explain at whose request the foundation has been made, and these tell us that Sir John Mason forwarded the case of Abingdon, while Chelmsford owed its choice to Sir William Petre and Sir Walter Mildmay, who both lived in the vicinity. The foundation at Bath seems to have been due to the exertions of the corporation there.[3]

The Edwardian schools fall into two classes, some being refoundations of chantry schools which had come under the act of 1547, and others being new endowments in places not affected by the act. There were about fifteen schools in the first group, and the extent of the crown's generosity varied from one to another. At Saffron Walden and Ludlow the crown did no more than return the original endowment of the earlier school.[4] But in most cases greater generosity was shown, and thirteen chantry

---

[1] *Journals of the House of Commons*, i, 6-7, 13; *Journals of the House of Lords*, i, 342.
[2] *EYS*, ii, 358-64.
[3] For these and other similar examples see *CPR 1547-53*, *passim*.
[4] *CPR 1548-9*, pp. 211-12 (Walden); *CPR 1550-3*, pp. 345-6 (Ludlow).

K*

schools whose endowments had produced £10 or less before 1548 were now re-established with incomes of around £20. In the case of Sedbergh, the fellows of St John's must have been pleased to see the old lands worth £11 replaced with new ones worth £20, and at Giggleswick nearby the endowment went up even more, from £6 to £23.[1]

The second group consisted of about nine schools which were either entirely new foundations or replaced earlier schools which had not come under the act. Here again the cases vary. There was Bruton where the school endowments had come into the hands of the crown in 1539 after the dissolution of the abbey, and Bury and Sherborne where schools may well have been disrupted at the same time. There were Guildford and Nuneaton, apparently secular schools endowed before the Reformation, now re-established and augmented. Lastly, endowments were given to places where no endowed schools appear to have existed before, such as Bath, Birmingham, Shrewsbury and Spilsby.[2] While these schools complete the list of the more obvious Edwardian foundations, there were other cases where, as at Maidstone and Marlborough, the crown sold chantry lands to the corporations for various projects which often included permission to erect and endow a grammar school. If, as sometimes appears likely, the sales were made on favourable terms, it may be that the Edwardian patronage of education can be slightly extended to these other places where the crown encouraged rather than initiated the foundation of new schools.

Private benefactors also stepped in before the tardy government to re-establish certain schools. At Stamford the chantry grammar school which fell to the crown in 1548 was re-established in the following year by means of a private act of parliament through the efforts of William Cecil, afterwards Lord Burghley. At Pocklington, where there had been a similar school of recent foundation, the founder's nephew Thomas Dowman secured its refoundation by another private act in 1552. And there were doubtless other instances where local men exerted themselves to strengthen schools whose future existence, after the confiscation, seemed doubtful. Thus at Towcester between 1550 and 1552 some of the parishioners actually bought back the chantry house which had been confiscated and

---

[1] *EYS*, ii, 248, 364-9. Existing schools refounded by Edward VI included Berkhamsted, Chelmsford, Giggleswick, Grantham, Louth, Ludlow, Macclesfield, Morpeth, Retford, Saffron Walden, Sedbergh, Stafford, Stourbridge, Stratford and perhaps Wisbech (*CPR 1547-53, passim*).

[2] Foundations not apparently connected with the dissolution of chantries and guilds included Bath, Birmingham, Bruton, Bury, Guildford, Nuneaton, Sherborne, Shrewsbury and Spilsby (*CPR 1547-53, passim*).

sold, and conveyed it to feoffees for the perpetual use of the school-master.[1]

At the death of Edward VI in 1553, when Catholicism was restored under Mary, the new foundations either private or royal still fell far short of the expectations of 1547. Most of the places noted by the chantry commissioners as suitable for endowed schools were still without them, and at least eighty of the old chantry schools, if not more, were still probably dependent on the temporary payments 'quousque' from the crown. One of the complaints of the convocation of Canterbury which met at the end of 1554 was that although the statute of 1547 provided for the foundation of schools, hospitals and other works of charity, this had not been performed according to the meaning of the statute, and the bishops were asked to petition the queen to amend the matter.[2] However, in this respect Mary's reign marked no improvement on that of her brother. Three chantry schools only seem to have been re-endowed by her, at Basingstoke, Boston and Bromsgrove, and three entirely new endowments were made, at Clitheroe, Leominster and Walsall.[3] At the same time the arrangements for paying the other schoolmasters were far less satisfactory than they had been under Edward. For reasons which are obscure, but which may have been simply due to shortage of money, the receivers of crown lands in some places stopped paying salaries to the ex-chantry schoolmasters during Mary's reign. Although in some counties such as Worcestershire the masters received their salaries each year under Mary, in others, of which Gloucestershire and Northamptonshire are examples, payments ceased in 1554 and were only resumed at the beginning of Elizabeth's reign after the masters had brought petitions into the court of the exchequer. In at least one case – the fifteenth-century grammar school at Newland – a school appears to have become permanently defunct during the Marian period, and later on a new private foundation had to be made there.[4]

But while Mary failed to settle the problem of the chantry schools, she and her government cannot be accused of neglecting the importance of education in general. As far as the schools were concerned, there was no Marian 'reaction', but on the contrary, increasing efforts to organize and supervise them along the lines laid down under Henry VIII and Edward VI.

[1] *VCH Lincs.*, ii, 474-5; *VCH Yorks.*, i, 464; *VCH Northants.*, ii, 228.
[2] *Concilia*, iv, 95-7.
[3] *CPR 1553-8, passim.*
[4] See the histories of schools during this period in *VCH Gloucs.*, ii, and *VCH Northants.*, ii.

It was as vital as ever to make the schools conform to the religious settlement in force, in this case the old religion, and to see that schoolmasters were efficient and orthodox missionaries of Catholicism to the next generations. Hence arose a new practice of licensing schoolmasters to teach, irrespective of their appointments to particular schools. In March 1554 Mary commanded the bishops to examine all schoolmasters and to replace those of suspect opinions by Catholic men. Soon afterwards Bishop Bonner, when carrying out his visitation of the diocese of London, ordered that no schoolmaster be admitted to teach until licensed by the ecclesiastical authority.[1] Licensing was made general throughout England in February 1556 by a decree of the English synod called by Cardinal Pole in the winter of that year. This forbade anyone to undertake the office of teaching until he had been examined and approved by the bishop, the penalty being excommunication and prohibition from teaching for three years.[2] That these measures achieved at least a partial success is apparent from what happened after Elizabeth's accession in 1558, when several schoolmasters preferred to lose their posts rather than conform to the new regime. They included both masters of Winchester College, and those of several other leading English schools: Durham, St Paul's and Salisbury among them.[3]

As well as licensing schoolmasters, the Marian authorities were concerned about the quality of their work. Bishop Bonner in his visitation of London in 1554 and 1555 required that schoolmasters be sober and discreet, of honest conversation and diligent in teaching. Scholars were to be made to fast and pray and to come often to mass. They were not to be taught heresy, nor instructed in the New Testament either in English or Latin, nor in any other books of scripture unsuitable for young children to meddle with. Instead they were to know how to help the priest at mass, to repeat the *paternoster*, the *ave Maria*, the Creed, the ten commandments and to say grace.[4] In 1554 an act of parliament empowered the queen to make new statutes for such grammar schools as had been established under Henry VIII and Edward VI,[5] and soon afterwards, under the influence of Cardinal Pole, plans began to be made to turn the cathedral schools into seminaries for the training of Catholic clergy. At the English synod of 1556 it was also provided that each cathedral church should maintain a

[1] *Visitation Articles and Injunctions*, ii, 328, 371-2.
[2] *Concilia*, iv, 125-6.
[3] A. C. F. Beales, 'A biographical catalogue of Catholic schoolmasters in England, 1558-1603', *Recusant History*, vii, no 6 (1964), pp. 268-89.
[4] *Visitation Articles and Injunctions*, ii, 355-6, 371-2.
[5] *Statutes of the Realm*, iv, part 1, 233-4.

certain number of boys, 'or rather a seminary', according to the wealth and size of the diocese. The boys chosen were to be aged eleven or more, able to read and write, and the children of poor rather than rich parents. They were to be given food and clothes, educated in grammar, and diligently instructed in ecclesiastical discipline. They were to be ordained first as acolytes and then, when they had reached the legitimate age, to take higher orders and be sent out to minister in a church under the bishop's supervision. The expenses of these schools were to be paid for by a tax of 6d. in the pound on the income of bishops and all who held benefices worth more than £20 a year.[1] This was to make more general the obligation to support scholars which Henry and Edward had already imposed on all benefices worth more than £100 a year. The orders of the synod were certainly carried out at Lincoln and York. At Lincoln Bishop White founded the 'College of Thirty Poor Clerks' in 1556, into which he gathered the secondaries and altarists who had always been maintained in the cathedral, and added to their number.[2] At York, St Mary's Hospital was taken over by the dean and chapter to house fifty boys learning grammar with a view to becoming priests.[3] What, if anything, was done elsewhere is not certain. In any case the brief re-establishment of Catholicism came to an end in November 1558 with the deaths of Mary and Pole.

The accession of Elizabeth saw the making of a new Protestant settlement of religion, but educational policies hardly changed at all. In the royal injunctions to the clergy of 1559 Henry VIII's grammar continued to be prescribed. Beneficed men with incomes of over £100 were again commanded to support scholars, and most important of all, the licensing of schoolmasters was continued under the new Protestant regime. 'No man', declared the injunctions, 'shall take upon him to teach but such as shall be allowed by the ordinary, and found meet as well for his learning and dexterity in teaching, as for sober and honest conversation, and also for right understanding of God's true religion.'[4] Licensing of schoolmasters by the diocesan bishops was to be almost universal until the eighteenth century, and did not finally disappear until 1869.

The new reign also saw the foundation of a considerable number of 'free grammar schools of Queen Elizabeth'. In most cases these schools were endowed by private benefactors and the queen's contribution was

---

[1] *Concilia*, iv, 125-6.
[2] *Chapter Acts of the Cathedral Church of Lincoln, 1547-1557*, ed. R. E. G. Cole (Lincoln Record Society, xv, 1920), *passim*.
[3] *EYS*, i, 42-65, especially p. 65.
[4] *Visitation Articles and Injunctions*, iii, 12-13, 21.

merely to grant the charter setting up a body of governors and the licence to acquire lands under the Statute of Mortmain. However, the crown did make a few additions to what Edward and Mary had done in re-endowing the old chantry schools. At Worcester in 1561 and at Penrith in 1564 two earlier schools were refounded, and annuities were given equal in value to the stipends which the incumbents had formerly enjoyed.[1] At Darlington in 1563 and at Middleton, Lancashire, in 1572 two chantry schools whose masters had been receiving their stipends out of the crown lands were refounded with endowments of land.[2] At Stafford in 1571 lands were given to the corporation who then took over from the crown the responsibility for paying the schoolmaster.[3] And there were other less obvious examples of royal patronage where, on the foundation of new schools or on the refoundation of old ones, buildings were made over and lands assigned, if not as a pure gift, at least on favourable terms.

What then is to be our final judgement about the effect of the dissolution of the chantries upon English education? Clearly no very great improvements resulted. The hopes and expectations that a large number of new schools would be endowed out of the chantry lands were not fulfilled, beyond the nine erected by Edward VI and those few more which his sisters added. On the other hand the ill effects of the Chantry Act seem to have been overestimated. The chantry grammar schools were only a part of the facilities for education then existing. Nearly all of them were kept in being after 1548 by the payment of salaries by the crown, but with the loss of their original endowments. Some were re-endowed in the following years by the crown, and others by private benefactors. Many however were never re-endowed, and these were the real casualties. Their fixed stipends in an age of inflation put them at a severe disadvantage beside schools with endowments, and at least under Mary it could prove difficult to get the crown's stipends paid by the local receivers. If these schools continued in being, it must have involved increasing reliance on fees, thus making them less useful to the poor than had been the case in the past. Yet though individual localities may well have suffered in this way, in general there was no recession of education. The endowment of schools by private hands did not stop in 1547; it continued throughout the sixteenth century, and the neglected chantry schools came to form a smaller and smaller proportion of the facilities for education in existence. For despite the increasing concern of the crown with education, most of

---

[1] *CPR 1560-3*, p. 215 (Worcester); ibid., *1563-6*, p. 71 (Penrith).
[2] Ibid., p. 509 (Darlington); Ibid. *1569-72*, pp. 334-5 (Middleton).
[3] Ibid., pp. 394-5.

the progress in this field was still due, as in the past, to the multitude of private benefactors.

We have now reached the threshold of the Elizabethan era and it is tempting to go on into the 1560s, the decade that saw the education of Hooker and Raleigh and the birth of Marlowe and Shakespeare. Much will be found in common between the aims and methods of education both before and after the Reformation, and not a few of the fifteenth-century schools continued in being in the new age. But what particularly characterized the medieval era in English education has now disappeared. The old grammarians and poets are no longer read in the classrooms. The schools of the cathedrals, colleges and chantries have all undergone reforms, while those of the religious orders have utterly ceased to exist. Education has become a matter of concern to the civil power, and the conditions under which the schoolmasters do their work are becoming very different. It is a suitable moment for the *medieval* historian to conclude his work.

A list of medieval English schools
1066-1530

A list of medieval English schools
1066-1530

There has hitherto been no handy list of the schools of medieval England such as Professor Knowles and Dr Hadcock have provided for the benefit of students of monasticism. That it is possible to attempt one at all is due in no small measure to the researches of Dr A. B. Emden, who generously made available a copious collection of references for the author to add to his own. This has enabled a preliminary list to be drawn up of all the secular schools, both public and private, including the schools of collegiate churches and private households, which are known to have existed or to have been projected between the Conquest and the beginning of the Reformation in 1530. Four items of information are here given about each school in so far as they are known: the range of studies (reading, song, grammar or higher), the foundation of an endowment to support a schoolmaster, the period of time during which the school can be traced and the appropriate references.

Two important groups of schools, however, whose inclusion might be thought desirable, will not be found in these pages. The schools which were kept by the religious orders for their novices, almonry boys and choristers have been reluctantly omitted, not out of disregard for their importance (which was considerable), but because of the time and difficulty involved in producing a full and accurate list. It may be possible to include them in a future edition; meanwhile a number of examples of such schools will be found above, in chapter 8. Others may regret the absence of many of the chantry schools which appear for the first time in the surveys of 1546 and 1548, but are there said to have been coeval with the chantries to which they were attached, or at least to have existed 'time out of mind'. Although some historians have been content to accept these claims to antiquity, many chantries probably came to include schools only a short time before 1546, and with this in mind, they have generally been required to furnish corroborative proof of their existence before 1530 in order to gain admission. Some of those excluded probably deserve to be brought in, but the author has tried throughout to err on the side of caution, so that those who come after may have the pleasure of adding to the list rather than the vexation of making subtractions.

The fugitive nature of most medieval schools and their intermittent appearances in record sources have prompted many doubts as to whether they enjoyed either stability or continuity. In the following pages, therefore, not only has the first known date of each school been given, but the subsequent ones which suggest its continuity. When these occur more frequently than once every twenty-five years or thirty years, continuity has been taken for granted, and the earliest and latest dates involved have been linked together. The author must be forgiven for having sometimes taken a subjective view of continuity, and not all who investigate the sources may wish to agree with him. It is also important to remember that the dates given are merely those when a school or master occurs in the records, and are not dates of foundation unless stated. Nor are these medieval schools necessarily the ancestors of those which claim descent from them today.

The incompleteness of the list makes it unwise to draw conclusions from the statistics collected so far, but it may be of interest to finish by setting down the approximate number of places which at the present moment are known to have possessed schools in medieval times:

1066-1149	19	32	1066-1200	
1150-99	22			
1200-49	32	67	1200-1299	
1250-99	48			
1300-49	62	105	1300-1399	Total: 253
1350-99	72			
1400-49	82	114	1400-1499	
1450-99	85			
1500-30	124			

Abbreviations

c.   circa

×   a single, unknown point of time between two dates, e.g. 1066 × 1087

-   the whole period of time between two dates, e.g. 1250-1350

→   the continuity of a school from a particular date until after the year 1530

ABINGDON, Berks.
School, 1388-1415 (*VCH Berks.*, ii, 261-2).

ACASTER SELBY, Yorks. W.R.
Endowed writing, song and grammar school, founded *c.* 1483; grammar school → (*EYS*, ii, 89-96).

ALDWINKLE, Northants.
Endowed reading school, founded 1489, ?-1546 (*ECD*, pp. 434-5; *VCH Northants.*, ii, 281-2).

ALFORD, Lincs.
School, 1511 (H. M. Colvin, *The White Canons in England* (1951), p. 319).

ALNWICK, Northumberland
Endowed grammar and perhaps song school, founded 1448 → (*CPR 1446-52*, p. 170; *ESR*, part 2, pp. 156-7).

APPLEBY, Westmorland
Grammar school, 1478, endowed by 1518 → (*SME*, pp. 268-9; J. Nicolson and R. Burn, *History and Antiquities of Westmorland and Cumberland* (1777), i, 329).

ARUNDEL, Sussex
School, 1269 (*VCH Sussex*, ii, 398).

AWRE, Gloucs.
School, *c.* 1287 (*Calendar of Inquisitions Post Mortem*, vol v (1908), p. 167).

AYLSHAM, Norfolk
Grammar school, 1460×1465; endowed grammar school founded 1530 → (PRO, C 1/27/343; W. K. Jordan, *The Charities of Rural England* (1961), p. 153).

BANBURY, Oxon.
Endowed grammar school, founded 1501 → (*VCH Oxon.*, i, 461-2).

BARNACK, Northants.
Reading, song and grammar school, 1359 (*VCH Northants.*, ii, 280).

BARNSLEY, Yorks. W.R.
School, 1370 (E. Hoyle, *History of Barnsley and the Surrounding District* (Barnsley, 1924), chapter 36, section 12).

BARTON-ON-HUMBER, Lincs.
Grammar school, 1329-34 (*ECD*, pp. 280-3; *VCH Lincs.*, ii, 449-50).

BATTLE, Sussex
School, 1251 (*VCH Sussex*, ii, 397).

BECCLES, Suffolk
School, *c.* 1235, 1396-1404; grammar school, 1432 (BM, MS Harl. 1005, fo 102v, dated by Dr Antonia Gransden; *VCH Suffolk*, ii, 337; S. B. Meech, 'John Drury and his English writings', *Speculum*, vol ix (1934), pp. 70-84).

BEDFORD

School, *c.* 1160 (*ECD*, pp. 116-17; *VCH Beds.*, ii, 152).

BERKHAMSTED, Herts.

School, early thirteenth century; endowed grammar school, founded *c.* 1523 → (charter in the possession of Dr Antonia Gransden, to whom I am indebted for the reference; *VCH Herts.*, ii, 72ff).

BEVERLEY, Yorks. E.R.

Song school, 1423-4; grammar school, *c.* 1100, *c.* 1150, 1276, 1304-66, 1436-56 (*EYS*, i, pp. xxxix-li, 80c-109).

BILBOROUGH, Notts.

Private tuition in the rectory, probably in grammar, 1505 (*VCH Notts.*, ii, 221-2).

BILLINGSHURST, Sussex

Endowed school, projected 1521 (*Transcripts of Sussex Wills*, ed. R. G. Rice, vol i (Sussex Record Society, xli, 1935), p. 145; *VCH Sussex*, ii, 398).

BLACKBURN, Lancs.

Endowed grammar school, founded 1514 → (G. A. Stocks, *The Records of Blackburn Grammar School* (Chetham Society, new series, lxvi, 1909), pp. 1-8; W. K. Jordan, *The Social Institutions of Lancashire* (ibid., 3rd series, xi, 1962), pp. 35-6; *VCH Lancs.*, ii, 590).

BLISWORTH, Northants.

Endowed grammar school, probably founded 1505 → (*CPR 1494-1509*, p. 461; *ESR*, part 2, pp. 147, 151-2; *VCH Northants.*, ii, 229-30).

BLOFIELD, Norfolk

Grammar school, 1350 (Norfolk and Norwich Record Office, Reg/2 Book 4, fo 118v).

BOLTON-LE-MOORS, Lancs.

Endowed grammar school, founded 1524 → (W. K. Jordan, *The Social Institutions of Lancashire* (1962), p. 65; *VCH Lancs.*, ii, 596).

BOSTON, Lincs.

Grammar school, 1329 →, endowed by 1514 (*ECD*, pp. 280-3; *VCH Lincs.*, ii, 450-3).

BOTESDALE, Suffolk

Grammar school, 1389 (Sylvia Thrupp, 'The problem of replacement rates in late medieval English population', *Economic History Review*, 2nd series, xviii (1965), p. 113).

BOUGHTON, Kent

School, 1301 (*Reg. Winchelsey, Canterbury*, ed. Rose Graham, vol ii (Canterbury & York Society, lii, 1956), p. 953).

BOURNE, Lincs.

Grammar school, 1330 (*SME*, p. 199; *VCH Lincs.*, ii, 450).

BRAUGHING, Herts.

Tuition in grammar by the parish chaplain, 1460s (P. Heath, *The English Parish Clergy on the Eve of the Reformation* (1969), p. 208).

BREDGAR, Kent

Grammar scholarships for two clerks, founded 1392, -*c.* 1542 (*Literae Cantuarienses*, ed. J. B. Sheppard, vol iii (Rolls Series, 1889), pp. 15-25; *VCH Kent*, ii, 230).

BRIDGNORTH, Salop

School, 1503 (*Historical MSS Commission, Tenth Report*, part 4, pp. 425-426).

BRIDGWATER, Somerset

School, 1298, 1379 (*Reg. Drokensford, Wells*, ed. E. Hobhouse (Somerset Record Society, i, 1887), pp. 208-9; PRO, E 179/4/4).

Tuition in reading and song in the vicarage, *c.* 1450 × 1474 (Bridgwater Corporation MSS, vol x no 1, document no 115).

BRIDPORT, Dorset

School, 1240; grammar school, fifteenth century (J. Hutchins, *History of Dorset*, 3rd ed. (1861-73), ii, 20; R. M. Woolley, *Catalogue of the MSS of Lincoln Cathedral* (1927), p. 49).

BRINGTON, Northants.

Endowed song school, founded 1522 (R. M. Serjeantson and H. I. Longden, 'The parish churches and religious houses of Northants.', *Archaeological Journal*, lxx (1913), p. 287).

BRISTOL, Gloucs.

Schools, probably more than one, 1243, 1379; grammar schools, 1426 → (F. B. Bickley, *A Calendar of Bristol Deeds* (1899), no 4; PRO, E 179/58/5; C. E. Boucher, 'The Lond or Loud brass', *Transactions of the Bristol and Gloucs. Archaeological Society*, xxx (1907), pp. 265-72).

ST NICHOLAS CHURCH. Song school, perhaps, 1481 (J. R. Bramble, 'Records of St Nicholas Church, Bristol', *Clifton Antiquarian Club Proceedings*, i (1884-8), p. 148).

HOUSE OF KALENDARS. Endowed theology lecture, founded 1464 (Worcs. Record Office, Reg. Carpenter, i, folios 197-8).

BROUGH-UNDER-STAINMORE, Westmorland

Endowed writing, song and grammar school, founded 1506 → (J. Nicolson and R. Burn, *Antiquities of Westmorland and Cumberland* (1777), i, 573-5; *Valor Ecclesiasticus*, vol v (1825), p. 297; *ESR*, part 2, pp. 251-252).

BROUGHTON [near Preston], Lancs.

Endowed grammar school, founded 1527 → (W. K. Jordan, *The Social Institutions of Lancashire* (1962), p. 39).

BRUTON, Somerset

Endowed grammar school, founded 1520 → (F. W. Weaver, 'Foundation deed of Bruton School', *Somerset and Dorset Notes and Queries*, iii (1892), pp. 241-8; *VCH Som.*, ii, 448ff).

BUCKINGHAM

School, 1423 (*VCH Bucks.*, ii, 145).

BURROUGH, Leics.

Private tuition, probably in grammar, in the rectory, 1508 (Oxford, Brasenose College, Principal Yate's Book (1668), pp. 97-8).

BURY ST EDMUNDS, Suffolk

Song school, 1268-1426; grammar school, late twelfth century → (*VCH Suffolk*, ii, 306-13).

BUSHMEAD, Beds.

Grammar school, projected 1332 (*VCH Beds.*, ii, 49-50).

CAERNARVON, Wales

Grammar school, mid-fifteenth century (Sir John Wynn, *The History of the Gwydir Family*, ed. J. Ballinger (1927), p. 50).

CAMBRIDGE

Grammar schools, 1276-1470 (*Vetus Liber Archidiaconi Eliensis*, ed. C. L. Feltoe and E. H. Minns (Cantab. Antiquarian Society Publications, xlviii, 1917), pp. 20-3; H. P. Stokes, *Medieval Hostels of the University of Cambridge* (ibid., xlix, 1924), pp. 43-57).

Higher Studies, 1209 → (Hastings Rashdall, *The Universities of Europe in the Middle Ages*, ed. F. M. Powicke and A. B. Emden (1936), iii, 274-324; *VCH Cambs.*, iii, 150-66).

GODSHOUSE. Endowed college for grammarians, founded 1439, refounded as Christ's College, 1505 (A. H. Lloyd, *The Early History of Christ's College, Cambridge* (1934); statutes in *The Early Statutes of Christ's College, Cambridge*, ed. H. Rackham (1927)).

JESUS COLLEGE. Endowed grammar school, founded 1496-1514/15 → (*The Earliest Statutes of Jesus College, Cambridge*, [ed. A. Gray] (1935), pp. 31-3, 61; A. Gray and F. Brittain, *A History of Jesus College, Cambridge* (1960), pp. 30-2).

CANTERBURY, Kent

Song school, 1077×1087; grammar school, 1077×1087, 1219, 1259 → (*Cartulary of the Priory of St Gregory, Canterbury*, ed. Audrey M. Woodcock (Camden third series, lxxxviii, 1956), pp. 1-2; C. E.

Woodruff and H. J. Cape, *Schola Regia Cantuariensis* (1908), pp. 16-44).

ST AUGUSTINE'S ABBEY. Grammar school, projected 1431 (*Calendar of Papal Letters*, viii, 348-9).

ST MARTIN'S. Reading, song and grammar school, 1321 (*ECD*, pp. 260-267).

CARLISLE, Cumberland

School, 1188, 1264-1371; grammar school by 1362, 1425 (Archdeacon Prescott, 'The grammar school of Carlisle', *Transactions of the Cumberland and Westmorland Antiquarian and Archaeological Society*, new series, xvi (1916), pp. 1-4; J. Wilson, 'Peculiar ordination of a Cumberland benefice', *Scottish Historical Review*, v (1907-8), pp. 297-303; *Reg. Langley, Durham*, ed. R. L. Storey, vol iii (Surtees Society, clxix, 1954), p. 42).

CASTLE DONINGTON, Leics.

Endowed grammar school, perhaps founded 1511 → (*LPFD*, i, no 784(3); *ESR*, part 2, pp. 126-7).

CHESTER

Grammar school, 1368 (*Reg. Stretton, Lichfield*, ed. R. A. Wilson (Wm. Salt Archaeological Society, new series, viii, 1905), p. 20).

CHESTERFIELD, Derbs.

School, thirteenth century, 1336-7 (*VCH Derbs.*, ii, 223).

CHICHESTER, Sussex

Grammar school, 1232-47, 1384-1479, endowed 1498 → (Statutes, etc., in *VCH Sussex*, ii, 399-406).

Higher Studies. Theological lectureship, founded 1224 × 1244, 1373 (Kathleen Edwards, *English Secular Cathedrals*, p. 197; *Calendar of Papal Letters 1362-1404*, pp. 189-90).

CHILDREY, Berks.

Endowed reading, song and grammar school, founded 1526 → (*VCH Berks.*, ii, 275-6).

CHIPPING CAMPDEN, Gloucs.

Endowed grammar school, founded *c.* 1441 → (the account in *VCH Gloucs.*, ii, 417-18, should not be followed. For the founder, John Ferriby, see *Reg. Chichele, Canterbury*, ed. E. F. Jacob, vol ii (1937), pp. 577-8, 652; *ESR*, part 2, pp. 78, 80-1).

CHIPPING NORTON, Oxon.

Endowed grammar school, founded 1450 → (*CPR 1446-52*, p. 402; *ESR*, part 2, pp. 173-4; *VCH Oxon.*, i, 467).

CHRISTCHURCH, Hants.

School, twelfth century (*ECD*, pp. 74-5).

CIRENCESTER, Gloucs.

School, 1242, 1340, 1432 (*Historia et Cartularium Monasterii Gloucestriae*, ed. W. K. Hart, vol i (Rolls Series, 1863), p. 281; *Calendar of Inquisitions Post Mortem*, xi, no 130; *Reg. Chichele, Canterbury*, ed. E. F. Jacob, vol ii (1937), p. 492).

Endowed grammar school, founded *c.* 1457 → (*CPR 1452-61*, p. 338; *VCH Gloucs.*, ii, 388-90).

CLARE, Suffolk

School, 1381 (E. Powell, *The Rising in East Anglia in 1381* (1896), p. 62).

CLITHEROE, Lancs.

School, *c.* 1283 (*Calendar of Inquisitions Post Mortem*, vol iv (1913), pp. 171-2).

COBHAM, Kent

Endowed song and grammar school, apparently for the clerks and choristers of the collegiate church, perhaps also public, perhaps founded 1362, 1383-8 (*SME*, p. 203; P. J. Tester, 'Notes on the medieval chantry college at Cobham', *Archaeologia Cantiana*, lxxix (1964), p. 119).

COCKERMOUTH, Cumberland

School, thirteenth century, second half (*Reg. of the Priory of St Bees*, ed. J. Wilson (Surtees Society, cxxvi, 1915), pp. 560-1).

COLCHESTER, Essex

School, twelfth century, 1206, 1353-7, 1464 (*Curia Regis Rolls, 1205-6*, (1929), pp. 74-5; *Court Rolls of the Borough of Colchester*, ed. I. H. Jeayes, vol ii (1938), pp. 9, 57; *VCH Essex*, ii, 502).

COVENTRY, War.

School, 1318, and also private tuition; grammar school, 1357, 1410 → (*The Liber Albus of Worcester Priory*, ed. J. M. Wilson (Worcs. Historical Society, xxxv, 1919), p. 65 no 801; *Reg. Norbury, Lichfield*, ed. E. Hobhouse (Wm. Salt Archaeological Society, i, 1880), p. 284; *VCH War*, ii, 318ff).

CREDITON, Devon

Grammar school, 1377 (*Reg. Brantyngham, Exeter*, ed. F. C. Hingeston-Randolph, vol i (1901), pp. 378-9).

CREWKERNE, Somerset

Endowed grammar school, founded 1499 → (R. Grosvenor Bartelot, *History of Crewkerne School* (1899); *VCH Som.*, ii, 453-4).

CROFTON, Yorks. W.R.

Grammar school, 1372 (*John of Gaunt's Register, 1371-1375*, ed. S. Armitage-Smith, vol i (Camden third series, xx, 1911), p. 111).

CROMER, Norfolk
Endowed grammar school, founded 1505 → (W. K. Jordan, *The Charities of Rural England* (1961), p. 152).

CROYDON, Surrey
Grammar school, 1393-5 (*VCH Surrey*, ii, 189; Lambeth Palace Library, Reg. Morton, ii, fo 182v; Edith Rickert, 'Extracts from a fourteenth-century account book', *Modern Philology*, xxiv (1926-7), pp. 251-2).

CROYLAND, Lincs.
School, perhaps public, 1526-35 (*A Subsidy Collected in the Diocese of Lincoln in 1526*, ed. H. E. Salter (Oxford Historical Society, lxiii, 1909), p. 92; *LPFD*, ix, no 1107).

CUCKFIELD, Sussex
Endowed grammar school, founded *c.* 1521 → (statutes, etc., in *VCH Sussex*, ii, 416-19).

DARLINGTON, Durham
School, 1417 (*Account Rolls of the Abbey of Durham*, ed. J. T. Fowler, vol i (Surtees Society, xcix, 1898), p. 226).

DARTMOUTH, Devon
School, 1489 (H. R. Watkin, *Dartmouth* (Devonshire Association, 1935), i, 310-11.

DERBY
School, 1154×1159, 1161×1182, 1406, fifteenth century; grammar school, 1481 (*The Cartulary of Darley Abbey*, ed. R. R. Darlington (1945), i, pp. xli-iii, 80-1; ii, 596, 599; PRO, C 1/16/336; *VCH Derbs.*, ii, 208-216).

DEVIZES, Wilts.
Grammar school, 1462 (Salisbury, Diocesan Record Office, Reg. Beauchamp, i, part 2, fo 153).

DONCASTER, Yorks, W.R.
Grammar school, 1351 (*EYS*, i, 22).

DOVER, Kent
School, 1284 (C. R. Haines, *Dover Priory* (1930), p. 350).

DROITWICH, Worcs.
School, fourteenth century, 1530 (*VCH Worcs.*, iii, 76; *The Letter Book of Robert Joseph*, ed. H. Aveling and W. A. Pantin (Oxford Historical Society, new series, xix, 1967), pp. 79-81, 286).

DUNHAM, Notts.
Grammar school, before 1351 (*VCH Notts.*, ii, 179).

DUNSTABLE, Beds.
School, 1097×1119, 1131×1133, 1183×1195, 1244-37 (*ECD*, pp. 78-81, 92-5, 132-5; *Regesta Regum Anglo-Normannorum*, ed. H. W. C. Davis

and others (1913-69), ii, no 1827; *VCH Beds.*, ii, 178-9; *Cartulary of Oseney Abbey*, ed. H. E. Salter, vol iv (Oxford Historical Society, xcvii, 1934), pp. 461-2).

DUNSTER, Somerset

School, 1355, 1410 (*CPR 1354-8*, p. 231; Sir H. C. Maxwell-Lyte, *History of Dunster* (1909) i, 303).

DUNWICH Suffolk

School, 1066 × 1087 (*ECD*, pp. 58-61; *VCH Suffolk*, ii, 303).

DURHAM

School, twelfth and early thirteenth centuries, *c.* 1260s; endowed song and grammar schools, founded 1414 → (*Historiae Dunelmensis Scriptores Tres*, ed. J. Raine (Surtees Society, ix, 1839), p. 74, appendix p. xiv; *Libellus de Vita et Miraculis S. Godrici*, ed. J. Stevenson (ibid., xx, 1847), pp. 59-60, 366-8; *ECD*, pp. 124-7; *VCH Durham*, i, 371-5).

EARL'S COLNE, Essex

Endowed grammar school, founded *c.* 1519 → (*VCH Essex*, ii, 526).

EAST RETFORD, Notts.

Grammar school, 1393 (*CCR 1392-6*, p. 135).

ELY, Cambs.

Grammar school, 1403-6 (Reg. Fordham, Ely, folios 149, 196; *Ely Diocesan Remembrancer* (1899-1900), pp. 158, 198).

ETON, Bucks.

Endowed grammar school, founded 1440 → (Sir H. C. Maxwell-Lyte, *History of Eton College*, 4th ed. (1911); *VCH Bucks.*, ii, 147ff).

EVESHAM, Worcs.

School, 1379; endowed grammar school, probably founded 1462 → (PRO, E 179/58/11; *VCH Worcs.*, iv, 497ff).

EWELME, Oxon.

Endowed reading and grammar school, founded 1437 → (*CPR 1436-41*, p. 80; statutes in *Historical MSS Commission, Ninth Report* (1883), pp. 216-22; *VCH Oxon.*, i, 470).

EXETER, Devon

Song school, 1276, 1337 (*Reg. Bronescombe, Exeter*, ed. F. C. Hingeston-Randolph (1889), pp. 77-8; *Ordinale Exon.*, ed. J. N. Dalton, vol i (Henry Bradshaw Society, xxxvii, 1909), p. 3).

Grammar school, twelfth century, 1283, 1329 → (Kathleen Edwards, *English Secular Cathedrals*, p. 185; Exeter, City Record Office, Mayor's Court Rolls, 16/17 Edward I m. 25d; H. L. Parry, *The Founding of Exeter School* (1913), pp. 7-9).

Higher Studies. Twelfth century; lectures in theology, *c.* 1230, in theology or canon law, 1337 (Kathleen Edwards, *English Secular Cathedrals*, pp. 186-7, 198-9; *Ordinale Exon.*, p. 4).

FAIRBURN, Yorks. W.R.

School, 1348 (*Select Cases from the Coroners' Rolls, 1265-1413*, ed. C. Gross (Selden Society, ix, 1896), p. 111).

FARINGDON, Berks.

Grammar school, 1343 (*Registrum Brevium*, 4th ed. (London, 1687), fo 35).

FARNWORTH, Lancs.

Endowed grammar school, founded 1507 → (W. K. Jordan, *The Social Institutions of Lancashire* (1962), pp. 33-4).

FARTHINGHOE, Northants.

Endowed elementary school, founded 1443 → (*ECD*, pp. 414-17; *ESR*, part 2, pp. 146-7; *VCH Northants.*, ii, 280-1).

FAVERSHAM, Kent

Reading and song school, 1506; grammar school, *c.* 1420, endowed 1526 → (F. F. Giraud, 'On the parish clerks and sextons of Faversham, 1506-1593', *Archaeologia Cantiana*, xx (1893), p. 205; PRO, E 36/196, p. 45; E. Hasted, *History of Kent*, vol ii (1782), p. 713).

FAWSLEY, Northants.

Endowed song school, founded 1528 (*VCH Northants.*, ii, 282).

FINCHAM, Norfolk

Grammar school, 1432 (Norfolk and Norwich Record Office, Reg/5 Book 9, fo 59).

FOTHERINGHAY, Northants.

Endowed song and grammar school for the clerks and choristers of the collegiate church, founded 1415 → (A. Hamilton Thompson, 'The statutes of Fotheringhay', *Archaeological Journal*, lxxv (1918), pp. 272-3). Endowed public grammar school, either the same or another foundation by 1548 (*VCH Northants.*, ii, 223-4).

GIGGLESWICK, Yorks. W.R.

Grammar school, 1507, endowed by 1548 (*EYS*, ii, 232-40).

GLOUCESTER

School, 1106 × 1135, 1199, 1286-9; grammar school, 1392-1535 (*CPR 1385-9*, p. 525; *ECD*, pp. 76-7, 94-7; *VCH Gloucs.*, ii, 314-20; *Reg. Romeyn, York*, ed. W. Brown, vol ii (Surtees Society, cxxviii, 1917), p. 64; PRO, C 115 (The Lanthony Cartulary), vols A 4, 6, 7, 13, *passim*).

ST MARY CRYPT. Endowed grammar school, founded 1528-40 → (R. Austin, *The Crypt School, Gloucester* (1939), *passim*).

ST NICHOLAS. Endowed grammar school, projected 1447 (*Calendar of*

Records of the Corporation of Gloucester, ed. W. H. Stevenson (1893), no 1134).

GRANTHAM, Lincs.

Grammar school, 1329-34, endowed *c.* 1478-94 → (*ECD*, pp. 280-3; *VCH Lincs.*, ii, 479).

GREAT TORRINGTON, Devon

School, 1524 (John Foxe, *Acts & Monuments*, ed. J. Pratt (1870), v, 18-26).

GRIMSBY, Lincs.

Grammar school, 1329-34, 1390 (*ECD*, pp. 280-3; *VCH Lincs.*, ii, 480).

GUILDFORD, Surrey

School, 1299; endowed grammar school, founded 1509-12 → (*Reg. J. de Pontissara, Winchester*, ed. C. Deedes, vol ii (Canterbury & York Society, xxx, 1924), p. 577; *VCH Surrey*, ii, 164-5).

GUISBOROUGH, Yorks. N.R.

School, 1266 × 1268, 1280 (C. R. Cheney, 'Letters of William Wickwane, chancellor of York', *English Historical Review*, xlvii (1932), p. 633; *Cartularium Prioratus de Gyseburne*, ed. W. Brown (Surtees Society, lxxxix, 1891), p. 360).

HADLEIGH, Suffolk

Grammar school, 1382 (*VCH Suffolk*, ii, 325).

HALIFAX, Yorks. W.R.

Endowed school, projected *c.* 1497; grammar school, 1516 × 17 (M. W. Garside, 'Halifax schools prior to 1700', *Halifax Antiquarian Society Papers* (1924), pp. 186-7).

HAREWOOD, Yorks. W.R.

School, *c.* 1505 (J. S. Purvis, *Select XVIth Century Causes in Tithe* (Yorks. Archaeological Society, Record Series, cxiv, 1947), p. 68).

HARLESTON, Norfolk

Grammar school, 1433-6 (Norfolk and Norwich Record Office, Reg/5 Book 9, fo 65; PRO, E 179/45/111).

HARNHILL, Kent

Reading and song school, 1386 (Edith Rickert, *Chaucer's World* (1948), p. 118).

HASTINGS, Sussex

Song and grammar schools, *c.* 1095 × 1140 (*ECD*, pp. 68-9; *VCH Sussex*, ii, 409-10).

HAVERFORDWEST, Wales

School, 1325; grammar school, 1488 (K. B. McFarlane, *The Nobility of Later Medieval England* (1973), p. 246; *Episcopal Registers of the Diocese of*

St David's, 1397-1518, ed. R. F. Isaacson, vol ii (Cymmrodorion Record Series, vi, 1917-20), pp. 524-5.

HEDON, Yorks. E.R.

Grammar school, 1271-1465 (N. Denholm-Young, 'The Yorkshire estates of Isabella de Fortibus', *Yorks. Archaeological Journal*, xxxi (1934), p. 392; J. R. Boyle, *The Early History of Hedon* (1895), pp. cxii, cxxiii-ix, clxxxv, cxii-iii, 162, 169-70; *Testamenta Eboracensia*, ed. J. Raine, vol ii (Surtees Society, xxx, 1855), p. 270).

HELMSLEY, Yorks. N.R.

School, thirteenth century (*Historical MSS Commission, MSS of the Duke of Rutland* vol iv (1905), p. 91).

HEMINGBROUGH, Yorks. E.R.

Grammar school, 1394 (*SME*, p. 211).

HENLEY-ON-THAMES, Oxon.

School, 1419-20 (*Henley Borough Records*, ed. P. M. Briers (Oxon. Record Society, xli, 1960), p. 28).

HEREFORD

Song school, 1240 × 1268 (*Statutes of Lincoln Cathedral*, ed. H. Bradshaw and C. Wordsworth (1892-7), ii, 76. For the date see A. T. Bannister, *The Cathedral Church of Hereford* (1924), p. 45).

Grammar school, 1240 × 1268, 1384, 1492 (*Statutes of Lincoln*, ii, 71; *Reg. Gilbert, Hereford*, ed. J. H. Parry (Canterbury & York Society, xviii, 1915), p. 48; *BRUO*, i, 307 sub Richard Burghill).

Higher Studies. Twelfth century; lectures in theology or canon law, 1356 (Kathleen Edwards, *The English Secular Cathedrals*, pp. 189-91, 197-8).

HEXHAM, Northumberland

Grammar school, 1294 (J. Raine, *The Priory of Hexham*, vol i (Surtees Society, xliv, 1863), p. lxxix).

HEYTESBURY, Wilts.

Grammar school by 1449, endowed 1472 → (R. C. Hoare, *History of Modern Wiltshire: Heytesbury Hundred* (1824), p. 102; *VCH Wilts.*, iii, 337-8; Canon Jackson, 'Ancient statutes of Heytesbury almshouse' *Wilts. Archaeological and Natural History Magazine*, xi (1869), pp. 289, 308).

HIGHAM FERRERS, Northants.

Grammar school, 1372-1400; endowed song and grammar school, founded 1422 → (*John of Gaunt's Register, 1371-1375*, ed. S. Armitage-Smith, vol i (Camden third series, xx, 1911), pp. 103-4; *CPR 1416-22*, p. 441; *VCH Northants.*, ii, 217-21).

HORNBY, Lancs.

Endowed grammar school, founded 1523 → (W. K. Jordan, *The Social Institutions of Lancashire* (1962), pp. 37-8).

HORNCASTLE, Lincs.

Grammar school, 1329-54 (*ECD*, pp. 280-3; *VCH Lincs.*, ii, 449-50, 482).

HOUGHTON REGIS, Beds.

Endowed grammar school, probably founded 1515 → (*VCH Beds.*, ii, 150-1; *ESR*, part 2, pp. 1-5).

HOVINGHAM, Yorks. N.R.

School, *c.* 1310 (*Calendar of Inquisitions Post Mortem*, vol v (1908), p. 192).

HOWDEN, Yorks. E.R.

Reading, song and grammar school, 1393-1456 (*EYS*, ii, 84-7).

HULL, Yorks. E.R.

School, perhaps by 1347, 1437; reading and grammar school by 1454; endowed song and grammar school, founded 1479 → (J. Lawson, *A Town Grammar School through Six Centuries* (1963), pp. 12-42; *VCH Yorks.* (*East Riding*), i, 348).

HUNTINGDON

Song school, *c.* 1109 or later; school, *c.* 1094×1123, *c.* 1130, 1255, 1392 (Mary Bateson, 'The Huntingdon song school', *English Historical Review*, xviii (1903), pp. 712-13; *Regesta Regum Anglo-Normannorum*, ed. H. W. C. Davis and others (1913-69), ii, 241; *Select Pleas of the Forest*, ed. G. J. Turner (Selden Society, xiii, 1901), p. 21; *VCH Hunts.*, ii, 107-8).

IPSWICH, Suffolk

Grammar school, 1412; reading, song and grammar school, 1477, endowed *c.* 1483 → (I. E. Gray and W. E. Potter, *Ipswich School* (1950), pp. 1-30; *VCH Suffolk*, ii, 325ff).

JERSEY, Channel Islands

Grammar school, projected 1496 (*CPR 1494-1509*, p. 83).

KELK, Yorks. E.R.

School, 1305 (*EYS*, i, 81).

KING'S LYNN, Norfolk

School, probably by 1383; endowed song and grammar school, founded *c.* 1510 → (Toulmin Smith, *English Guilds* (EETS, 1870), pp. 51-3; W. K. Jordan, *The Charities of Rural England* (1961), pp. 152-3).

KINGSTON-ON-THAMES, Surrey

Reading, song and elementary grammar school, 1377; school, probably of grammar, 1364; endowed school, projected 1528 (*VCH Surrey*, ii, 155-9).

KINOULTON, Notts.

School, 1289 (*Reg. Romeyn, York*, ed. W. Brown, vol i (Surtees Society, cxxiii, 1913), pp. 285-6).

KIRKOSWALD, Cumberland

Endowed school in the collegiate church, perhaps founded *c.* 1523, -1548 (*VCH Cumberland*, ii, 208-11; *ESR*, part 2, pp. 43-4).

LAMBOURN, Berks.

Endowed grammar school, probably founded 1501 → (*CPR 1494-1509*, p. 233; *ESR*, part 2, pp. 7-8, 13).

LANCASTER

School 1284; endowed grammar school, founded 1469-1500 → (*VCH Lancs.*, ii, 561-4, including statutes; W. K. Jordan, *The Social Institutions of Lancashire* (1962), pp. 30-1)

LAUNCESTON, Cornwall

Grammar school, 1342 (*Reg. Grandisson, Exeter*, ed. F. C. Hingeston-Randolph, vol ii (1897), p. 955).

LEEDS, Yorks. W.R.

School, 1341-1400 (J. Le Patourel, *Documents Relating to the Manor and Borough of Leeds, 1066-1400* (Thoresby Society, xlv, 1956), pp. 41, 44, 74).

LEICESTER

School, 1229, late thirteenth century, 1367; grammar school, 1440 (M. Claire Cross, *The Free Grammar School of Leicester* (Leicester University, Department of English Local History, Occasional Papers, iv (1953), p. 5).

LEIGHTON BUZZARD, Bucks.

Grammar school, probably in 1441 (*BRUO*, i, 29 sub Thomas Alwyn).

LEWES, Sussex

School, 1248, 1285; grammar school, 1313; school, 1405; endowed grammar school, founded 1512 → (*VCH Sussex*, ii, 411-13; R. W. Hunt, 'Oxford grammar masters in the middle ages', *Oxford Studies Presented to Daniel Callus* (Oxford Historical Society, new series, xvi, 1964), p. 175 note 3).

LEYLAND, Lancs.

Endowed grammar school, founded 1524 → (*VCH Lancs.*, ii, 600; W. K. Jordan, *The Social Institutions of Lancashire* (1962), p. 38).

LICHFIELD, Staffs.

Song school, *c.* 1190 (*Statutes of Lincoln Cathedral*, ed. H. Bradshaw and C. Wordsworth (1892-7), ii, 23).

Grammar school, *c.* 1190, 1272, endowed 1495 → (ibid.; *Magnum*

L

Registrum Album, ed. H. E. Savage (Wm. Salt Archaeological Society, xlviii, 1924), pp. 360-1; *VCH Staffs.*, iii, 280-2).

Choristers. Separate tuition in song by 1490 × 1520 (ibid., pp. 164-5).

LINCOLN

Song school, 1147 × 1148, 1236-1440 (*The Registrum Antiquissimum of Lincoln*, ed. C. W. Foster, vol i (Lincoln Record Society, xxvii, 1931), pp. 262-3; *VCH Lincs.*, ii, 422-4; *Statutes of Lincoln Cathedral*, ed. H. Bradshaw and C. Wordsworth (1892-7), ii, 157; iii, 299).

Grammar school, twelfth century, 1236 → (Kathleen Edwards, *English Secular Cathedrals*, p. 185; *VCH Lincs.*, ii, 421-40).

Choristers. Separate tuition in song and grammar, 1308, 1389-1407, 1524-6 (ibid., pp. 424-6; *Chapter Acts of Lincoln, 1520-1536*, ed. R. E. G. Cole (Lincoln Record Society, xii, 1915), pp. 52, 210).

Higher Studies. Twelfth century; lectures in theology, by 1200, 1209 × 1235, 1236, *c.* 1300, 1390, 1440 (Kathleen Edwards, *English Secular Cathedrals*, pp. 185-6; *Rotuli Hugonis de Welles*, ed. F. N. Davis, vol iii (Lincoln Record Society, xx, 1914), pp. 101-2; *Statutes of Lincoln*, i, 284; ii, 158; iii, 300-1; *VCH Lincs.*, ii, 424).

LIVERPOOL, Lancs.

Endowed grammar school, founded *c.* 1517 → (*VCH Lancs.*, ii, 593; W. K. Jordan, *The Social Institutions of Lancashire* (1962), p. 37).

LONDON, Middx.

AUTHORIZED SCHOOLS

ST ANTHONY'S. Endowed grammar school, founded 1441 → ; endowed song school, founded 1449 (London, Guildhall Library, MS 9531/6, fo 183; *CPR 1436-41*, p. 238; R. R. Sharpe, *Calendar of Wills Proved in the Court of Husting, London*, vol ii (1890), pp. 524-5).

ST DUNSTAN-IN-THE-EAST. Grammar school, 1446 (*ECD*, pp. 416-18; *CPR 1441-6*, p. 482).

ST MARTIN-LE-GRAND. Grammar school, 1134 × 1141-1446 (*Early Charters of St Paul's*, ed. Marion Gibbs (Camden third series, lviii, 1939), pp. 251-9; A. F. Leach, 'St Paul's school before Colet', *Archaeologia*, lxii, part 1 (1910), pp. 191-238; *ECD*, pp. 90-2, 416-18; *SME*, pp. 142-3).

ST MARY ARCHES. Grammar school, 1134 × 1141-1446 (references as for St Martin-le-Grand).

ST PAUL'S. Song school, 1296 × 1300, 1505 × 1519 (*Registrum Statutorum Sancti Pauli Londinensis*, ed. W. S. Simpson (1873), pp. 22, 49-50, 226).

Grammar school, *c.* 1102 → ; endowed 1508-1512 (J. Le Neve, *Fasti*

Ecclesiae Anglicanae, 1066-1300: St Paul's, London, ed. Diane E. Greenway (1968), p. 25; *Early Charters of St Paul's*, pp. 215-20; *Archaeologia*, lxii, part 1 (1910), pp. 191-238).

Higher Studies. Twelfth century; lectures in theology, 1281-1308, *c.* 1465, 1505×1522 (Kathleen Edwards, *English Secular Cathedrals*, pp. 188-9, 199-200; *Registrum Statutorum S. Pauli*, pp. 413-15).

ST THOMAS ACON. School perhaps, 1453; grammar school, 1535 (R. R. Sharpe, op. cit., p. 542; C. L. Kingsford, 'Two London chronicles', *Camden Miscellany XII* (Camden third series, xviii, 1910), p. 11).

OTHER SCHOOLS

Grammar school near Crutched Friars, 1392 (*Calendar of Plea and Memoranda Rolls of London, 1381-1412*, ed. A. H. Thomas (1932), p. 182); grammar school or schools in Cornhill, 1404-39×1441 (V. H. Galbraith, 'John Seward and his circle', *Medieval and Renaissance Studies*, vol i (1943), pp. 85-104; *ECD*, pp. 396-7; Sylvia Thrupp, *The Merchant Class of Medieval London* (1948), p. 156); grammar school at The Cardinal's Hat in Lombard Street, *c.* 1410 (V. H. Galbraith in *Medieval and Renaissance Studies*, pp. 89-91, 104); grammar and song school in St Bartholomew's Hospital, projected 1444, grammar school, 1476 (R. R. Sharpe, op. cit., p. 508; *CCR 1476-85*, p. 78); school near the Tower Royal, 1465 (*CPR 1452-61*, p. 285); endowed song school at St Mary Woolnoth, founded 1492 → (R. R. Sharpe, op. cit., pp. 600-1; *ESR*, part 2, p. 145); school at St Mary-at-Hill, 1523 → (H. Littlehales, *The Medieval Records of a London City Church* (EETS, cxxv, cxxviii, 1904-5), pp. xx, xxxiv, 321; *ESR*, part 2, p. 145).

PROJECTED SCHOOLS

Grammar schools in the parishes of All Hallows the Great, St Andrew Holborn, St Mary Colechurch and St Peter Cornhill, projected 1447 (*Rotuli Parliamentorum* (1767-77), v, 137; *ECD*, pp. 418-20); endowed writing, song and grammar school at Leadenhall, projected 1459 (John Stow, *Survey of London*, ed. C. L. Kingsford (1908), i, 74).

HIGHER STUDIES

GUILDHALL LIBRARY. Endowed for the study of theology, founded *c.* 1425, -*c.* 1549 (for references see above, p. 84 note 2).

LONG MELFORD, Suffolk

School, 1484 (*VCH Suffolk*, ii, 340).

LOUGHBOROUGH, Leics.

Endowed school, projected 1514, perhaps founded by 1548 (*Testamenta Vetusta*, ed. N. H. Nicolas (1826), p. 543; J. Nichols, *History and Antiquities of Leicestershire*, vol iii (1804), pp. 711, 891, 895).

LOUTH, Lincs.
School, 1276; grammar school, 1433, endowed 1533 → (*VCH Lincs.*, ii, 400-1).

LUDLOW, Salop
School, 1200 × 1207, 1349-50 (C. R. Cheney, *English Bishops' Chanceries, 1100-1250* (1950), pp. 157-8; *Reg. Trillek, Hereford*, ed. J. H. Parry (Canterbury & York Society, viii, 1912), pp. 500, 508, 519).

MACCLESFIELD, Cheshire
Endowed grammar school, founded 1503 → (D. Wilmot, *A Short History of the Grammar School, Macclesfield* (1910), pp. 10-11, appendix pp. xli-li).

MAIDSTONE, Kent
School, 1343; grammar school, 1393-1418 (F. R. H. Du Boulay, *The Lordship of Canterbury* (1966), p. 259; Lambeth Palace Library, Reg. Morton, ii, fo 182; T. F. Kirby, *Annals of Winchester College* (1892), p. 188).

MALDON, Essex
Grammar school, 1408-35 (*VCH Essex*, ii, 516).

MALLING, Kent
School, 1348 (*Reg. Hethe, Rochester*, ed. C. Johnson, vol ii (Canterbury & York Society, xlix, 1948), p. 985).

MALMESBURY, Wilts.
School, *c.* 1260s (*Registrum Malmesburiense*, ed. J. S. Brewer, vol i (Rolls Series, 1879), pp. 128, 132; Bodleian, MS Bodl. 191, fo 41).

MALPAS, Cheshire
Endowed reading and grammar school, founded 1528 → (statutes, etc., in 'Malpas Grammar School', *Transactions of Historic Society of Lancs. and Cheshire*, lxv (1913), pp. 194-211).

MALTON, Yorks. N.R.
School, 1245 (Bodleian, MS Laud misc. 642, folios 4v, 5-v, 6).

MANCHESTER, Lancs.
Endowed reading and grammar school, founded 1510-15 → (W. K. Jordan, *Social Institutions of Lancashire* (1962), pp. 34-5; *VCH Lancs.*, ii, 578-84).

MARLBOROUGH, Wilts.
School, 1232, 1301 (*ECD*, pp. 152-5; *Reg. de Gandavo, Sarum*, ed. C. T. Flower and M. C. B. Dawes, vol ii (Canterbury & York Society, xli, 1934), p. 849).

MELBOURNE, Derbs.
Endowed school, projected 1514 (*VCH Derbs.*, ii, 207; *Testamenta Vetusta*, ed. N. H. Nicolas (1826), p. 542).

MELLS, Somerset
Grammar school, 1524 (*Somerset Medieval Wills*, ed. F. W. Weaver, vol ii (Somerset Record Society, xix, 1903), p. 225; *VCH Som.*, ii, 455).

MELTON MOWBRAY, Leics.
School, 1347 (*CPR 1345-8*, p. 362).

MIDDLEHAM, Yorks. N.R.
Song school for the choristers of the collegiate church, projected 1478 (J. Raine, 'The statutes for the college of Middleham', *Archaeological Journal*, xiv (1857), p. 163).

MIDDLETON, Lancs.
Endowed grammar school, founded 1440 → (*CPR 1436-41*, p. 399; *VCH Lancs.*, ii, 574-5).

MILDENHALL, Suffolk
School, *c.* 1235 (BM, MS Harl. 1005, fo 102v, kindly dated by Dr Antonia Gransden).

MILTON ABBAS, Dorset
Endowed grammar school, founded 1521 → (J. Hutchins, *History of Dorset* 3rd ed. (1861-73), iv, 396).

NEWARK, Notts.
Grammar school, 1238, 1333-1499, endowed 1530 → (*VCH Notts.*, ii, 199-208).

NEWLAND, Gloucs.
Endowed reading, song and grammar school, founded 1445 → (*CPR 1441-6*, p. 388; statutes in *Reg. Spofford, Hereford*, ed. A. T. Bannister (Canterbury & York Society, xxiii, 1919), pp. 281ff).

NEWPORT PAGNELL, Bucks.
Grammar school, perhaps, 1421 (*BRUO*, i, 29 sub Thomas Alwyn).

NORHAM, Northumberland
School, twelfth century, 1302-48 (*Reginaldi Dunelmensis Libellus*, ed. J. Raine (Surtees Society, i, 1835), pp. 149-50; Durham, Dean and Chapter Muniments, Priory Reg. I, part 2, fo 8v; Reg. II, fo 75).

NORTHALLERTON, Yorks. N.R.
Reading, song and grammar school, 1322-1440 (*EYS*, ii, 60-74).

NORTHAMPTON
Schools, probably of grammar and, until the thirteenth century, of arts, 1176 → (H. G. Richardson, 'The schools of Northampton in the twelfth century', *English Historical Review*, lvi (1941), pp. 595-605; PRO, C 1/27/282; *Cambridge University Grace Book Γ*, ed. W. G. Searle (1908), pp. 176, 189; *A Subsidy Collected in the Diocese of Lincoln in 1526*, ed. H. E. Salter (Oxford Historical Society, lxiii, 1909), p. 158; *VCH Northants.*, ii, 234).

NORTHENDEN, Cheshire

School, *c.* 1514-18 (F. J. Furnivall, *Child Marriages, Divorces, and Ratifications in the Diocese of Chester* (EETS, 1897), p. 139).

NORTH WALSHAM, Norfolk

School, *c.* 1324 (*Calendar of Inquisitions Post Mortem*, vol viii (1913), p. 449).

NORWICH, Norfolk

Grammar school, 1156-1497 (H. W. Saunders, *A History of the Norwich Grammar School* (1932), pp. 85-102).

NOTTINGHAM

School, 1289; grammar school, 1382 →, endowed 1512 (*VCH Notts.*, ii, 216ff).

OSWESTRY, Salop

Endowed grammar school, founded *c.* 1423 → (Mrs Bulkeley-Owen, 'The founder and first trustees of Oswestry grammar school', *Transactions of the Salop Archaeological and Natural History Society*, 3rd series, iv (1904), pp. 194-5; R. R. Oakley, *A History of Oswestry School* (1964), pp. 13-48).

OTTERY ST MARY, Devon

Endowed song school for the choristers of the collegiate church, and grammar school, 1338 → (J. N. Dalton, *The Collegiate Church of Ottery St Mary* (1917), pp. 93, 98, 100, 300-1).

OXFORD

Grammar schools by the late twelfth century, -*c.* 1492 (A. B. Emden, *An Oxford Hall in Medieval Times* (1927), pp. 84-6; *VCH Oxon.*, iii, 40-3; R. W. Hunt, 'Oxford grammar masters of the middle ages', *Oxford Studies Presented to Daniel Callus* (Oxford Historical Society, new series, xvi, 1964), pp. 163-93; statutes, etc., in *Statuta Antiqua Universitatis Oxon.*, ed. S. Gibson (1931), pp. 20-3, 169-74).

Study and teaching of dictamen and business studies, 1215-1432 (H. G. Richardson, 'Letters of the Oxford *Dictatores*', in *Formularies which Bear on the History of Oxford*, ed. H. E. Salter and others, vol ii (Oxford Historical Society, new series, v, 1942), pp. 329-450).

Higher Studies, 1096 × 1102 → (*BRUO*, iii, 1754 sub Theobaldus Stampensis; Hastings Rashdall, *The Universities of Europe in the Middle Ages*, ed. F. M. Powicke and A. B. Emden (1936), iii, 1-273; *VCH Oxon.*, iii, 1-19).

MAGDALEN COLLEGE SCHOOL. Endowed song and grammar school, founded *c.* 1479 → (R. S. Stanier, *A History of Magdalen College School, Oxford*, 2nd ed. (1958), *passim*; *VCH Oxon.*, i, 472-3).

MERTON COLLEGE. Endowed grammar school for the boys of the college, projected 1270, 1490-1 (*The Early Rolls of Merton College*, ed. J. R. L. Highfield (Oxford Historical Society, new series, xviii, 1964), pp. 69-73, 382; *Registrum Annalium Collegii Mertonensis*, ed. H. E. Salter (ibid., lxxvi, 1921), p. 142).

THE QUEEN'S COLLEGE. Endowed song and grammar school for the boys of the college, projected 1341 (J. R. Magrath, *The Queen's College, Oxford* (1921), i, 45-9, 141-2).

PARTNEY, Lincs.

Grammar school, 1329-34 (*ECD*, pp. 280-3; *VCH Lincs.*, ii, 449-50).

PENRITH, Cumberland

Grammar school, 1340; song and grammar school, 1361 (J. Nicolson and R. Burn, *History and Antiquities of Westmorland and Cumberland* (1777), ii, 410-11).

PETERBOROUGH, Northants., now Hunts.

School, 1402, *c.* 1512-26 (*Peterborough Local Administration*, ed. W. T. Mellors (Northants. Record Society, ix, 1939), p. 223; *VCH Northants.*, ii, 202-3; *A Subsidy Collected in the Diocese of Lincoln in 1526*, ed. H. E. Salter (Oxford Historical Society, lxiii, 1909), p. 136).

PLESHEY, Essex

Endowed school, perhaps founded 1498 → (*CPR 1494-1509*, p. 173; *VCH Essex*, ii, 516).

PLYMPTON, Devon

School, 1263 (*Calendar of Inquisitions Post Mortem*, vol i (1904), p. 174).

POCKLINGTON, Yorks. E.R.

Endowed grammar school, founded 1514 → (*LPFD*, i, part 2, no 2964(70); *VCH Yorks.*, i, 463-4).

PONTEFRACT, Yorks. W.R.

School, *c.* 1139×1140, 1267, 1437-64 (*EYS*, ii, pp. vii-xiii, 1-15).

PRESTON, Lancs.

School, 1358; grammar school, 1400-74 (*VCH Lancs.*, ii, 570; A. Hamilton Thompson, 'The registers of the archdeaconry of Richmond, 1361-1442', *Yorks. Archaeological Journal*, xxv (1919), p. 200).

READING, Berks.

School, 1102×1139, 1189×1193, 1216×1234, 1246; grammar school, *c.* 1502-3, probably endowed by 1524 → (*VCH Berks.*, ii, 245-51; J. C. Russell, *Dictionary of Writers of Thirteenth-Century England* (London, Bulletin of Institute of Historical Research, Supplement, 1936), p. 67; *Close Rolls, 1242-1247*, p. 402).

RICHMOND, Yorks. N.R.

Grammar school, 1393-7, 1486 × 1487 (A. Hamilton Thompson, 'The registers of the archdeaconry of Richmond, 1361-1442', *Yorks. Archaeological Journal*, xxv (1919), pp. 129-268; L. P. Wenham, 'Two notes on the history of Richmond school', ibid., xxxvii (1951), pp. 369-72).

RIPON, Yorks. W.R.

Song school, 1503 → ; grammar school, 1348 → (*EYS*, i, pp. lvi-lxiii, 141-56, 236-7).

ROCK, Worcs.

Endowed grammar school, founded 1513 → (*LPFD*, i, part 2, no 2055(53); *VCH Worcs.*, iv, 473-4).

ROLLESTON, Staffs.

Endowed reading, accounting and grammar school, founded 1524 → (statutes, etc., in Chichester Diocesan Record Office, Cap I/14/5, folios 25-29v).

ROTHERHAM, Yorks. W.R.

Grammar school, *c.* 1430; endowed writing, song and grammar school, founded 1483 → (statutes, etc., in *EYS*, ii, 104-31).

ROYSTON, Yorks. W.R.

Endowed grammar school, founded 1503 → (*The Certificates of the Chantries in the County of York*, ed. W. Page, vol i (Surtees Society, xci, 1894), p. 62; J. Hunter, *South Yorkshire*, vol ii (1831), p. 381).

RUDHAM, Norfolk

School, 1240 (H. W. Saunders, 'A history of Coxford Priory', *Norfolk Archaeology*, xvii (1910), p. 343).

RUSHWORTH, Norfolk

Grammar school for thirteen children in the collegiate church, founded 1485 → (E. K. Bennet, 'The college of Rushworth', *Norfolk Archaeology*, x (1888), pp. 367-73, 375).

SAFFRON WALDEN, Essex

School, 1317-45, 1401-40, grammar school by 1423, 1511; endowed grammar school, projected 1517, founded 1525 → (A. F. Leach, 'Some results of research in the history of education in England', *Proceedings of the British Academy*, vi (1913-14), pp. 475-6; *VCH Essex*, ii, 518-21; statutes in T. Wright, 'Rules for the free school at Saffron Walden', *Archaeologia*, xxxiv (1852), pp. 37-41).

ST ALBANS, Herts.

School, 1097 × 1119, 1183 × 1195; grammar school by *c.* 1286 → (*VCH Herts.*, ii, 47-56; statutes in *ECD*, pp. 240-53, and *Reg. John Whethamstede*, ed. H. T. Riley, vol ii (Rolls Series, 1873), pp. 305-15).

ST DAVIDS, Wales

Endowed song school for the choristers of the cathedral, founded 1363 (W. B. Jones and E. A. Freeman, *The History and Antiquities of St Davids* (1856), pp. 303, 326).

ST MICHAEL-ON-WYRE, Lancs.

Endowed grammar school, founded 1528 → (*VCH Lancs.*, ii, 603; W. K. Jordan, *The Social Institutions of Lancashire* (1962), pp. 39-40).

SALISBURY, Wilts.

Song school, *c.* 1200 (*The Use of Sarum*, ed. W. H. Frere (1898), i, 8). Grammar school, 1078 × 1099-1474 (*Statutes and Customs of Salisbury*, ed. C. Wordsworth and D. Macleane (1915), pp. 30-3, etc.; Dora H. Robertson, 'Notes on some buildings in the city and close of Salisbury', *Wilts. Archaeological and Natural History Magazine*, xlviii (1939), pp. 11-18; Kathleen Edwards, *English Secular Cathedrals*, pp. 195-6).

Choristers. Separate tuition in song and grammar, 1314 → (Dora H. Robertson, *Sarum Close*, 2nd ed. (1969), pp. 39ff).

Higher Studies. Lectures in theology, 1240, 1300, 1349-58, 1454 (Kathleen Edwards, *English Secular Cathedrals*, pp. 201-2).

DE VAUX COLLEGE. Endowed college for the study of arts and theology, founded 1262 → (*VCH Wilts.*, iii, 369-85).

ST EDMUND COLLEGE. Endowed college for the study of theology, founded 1269 → (ibid., pp. 385-8).

SCARBOROUGH, Yorks. N.R.

Grammar school, 1444 (J. Lawson, *A Town Grammar School through Six Centuries* (1963), p. 16).

SEAFORD, Sussex

School, 1320 (*VCH Sussex*, ii, 398).

SEDBERGH, Yorks. W.R.

Endowed grammar school, founded *c.* 1525-8 → (statutes, etc., in *EYS*, ii, pp. xli ff, 287-332).

SEVENOAKS, Kent

Endowed grammar school, founded 1432 → (*ECD*, pp. 398-403; W. K. Jordan, 'Social institutions in Kent, 1480-1660', *Archaeologia Cantiana*, lxxv (1961), pp. 68-9).

SHAFTESBURY, Dorset

School, 1234 (BM, MS Cotton Vespasian xxv, fo 114v).

SHERBORNE, Dorset

School, 1437 × 8; grammar school, 1535 (A. F. Leach, 'Sherborne school before, under and after Edward VI', *Archaeological Journal*, 2nd series, v (1898), pp. 1-83).

L*

SHERBURN, Yorks. W.R.

School, before 1321 (W. Wheater, *The History of the Parishes of Sherburn and Cawood*, 2nd ed. (1882), p. 34).

SHIPDEN, Norfolk

Grammar school, 1455 (Norfolk and Norwich Record Office, Reg/6 Book 11, fo 84).

SHOREHAM, Sussex

School, 1302 (*VCH Sussex*, ii, 398).

SHOULDHAM, Norfolk

Grammar school, 1462 (Norfolk and Norwich Record Office, Reg/6 Book 11, fo 131v).

SHREWSBURY, Salop

School, 1232 (*CPR 1225-32*, p. 506).

SIBTHORPE, Notts.

Endowed reading school, founded 1335-43 (A. Hamilton Thompson, *The English Clergy and their Organization in the Later Middle Ages* (1947), pp. 256, 267).

SOUTH DALTON, Yorks. E.R.

School, 1304 (*EYS*, i, 80m-81, 92).

SOUTHWARK, Surrey

Reading and song school, 1365 (*Select Cases in the Court of King's Bench under Edward III*, ed. G. O. Sayles, vol vi (Selden Society, lxxii, 1965), pp. 141-3).

SOUTHWELL, Notts.

Grammar school, 1313, 1413, 1475 → (*Reg. Greenfield, York*, ed. W. Brown and A. Hamilton Thompson, vol iv (Surtees Society, clii, 1938), p. 137; *VCH Notts.*, ii, 183-9).

SPARHAM, Norfolk

Grammar school, 1408 (Norfolk and Norwich Record Office, Reg/4 Book 7, fo 102).

SPRATTON, Northants.

School, 1520 (H. I. Longden, *Northamptonshire and Rutland Clergy from 1500* (1940), vi, 189-91).

STAFFORD

Probable school, 1380 (G. Wrottesley, 'Extracts from the *Coram Rege* Rolls', *Wm. Salt Archaeological Society*, xiv (1893), pp. 150, 155).

STAMFORD, Lincs.

School, 1298-1389 (*Select Cases in the Court of King's Bench under Edward I*, ed. G. O. Sayles, vol iii (Selden Society, lviii, 1939), p. cix; *VCH Lincs.*, ii, 474).

Higher Studies. Secession of scholars from Oxford, 1334-5 (ibid., pp. 468-74).

STEVENAGE, Herts.

School, 1312 (*VCH Herts.*, ii, 69).

STOCKPORT, Cheshire

Endowed grammar school, founded 1488 → (B. Varley, *The History of Stockport Grammar School*, 2nd ed. (1957), pp. 1-54).

STOKE BY CLARE, Suffolk

Endowed reading and song school for the choristers of the collegiate church, founded 1422 → ; endowed grammar school by 1548 (Dugdale, *Monasticon*, vol vi, part 3 (1830), p. 1419; *VCH Suffolk*, ii, 339; *ESR*, part 2, p. 220).

STOKE BY NAYLAND, Suffolk

School, 1465, possibly in the household of Sir John Howard but apparently open to others (*Manners and Household Expenses of England*, ed. T. H. Turner (Roxburghe Club, lvii, 1841), pp. 179, 269).

STRATFORD-ON-AVON, War.

School, 1295, 1402-73; grammar school, 1478, endowed grammar school founded 1482 → (*VCH War.*, ii, 329ff).

STRUBBY, Lincs.

Grammar school, 1309-34 (*VCH Lincs.*, ii, 449).

SUDBURY, Suffolk

Endowed grammar school, founded 1491 → (*VCH Suffolk*, ii, 341).

SUTTON COLDFIELD, War.

School, 1521-3 (*Historical MSS Commission, Report on the MSS of Lord Middleton* (1911), pp. 335-59).

TATTERSHALL, Lincs.

Endowed song and grammar school, founded *c.* 1460 → (*Historical MSS Commission, Report on the MSS of Lord De L'Isle and Dudley*, vol i (1925), p. 182).

TAUNTON, Somerset

School, 1286, 1523 (*Catalogue of Ancient Deeds*, vol i (1890), p. 232; *ESR*, part 2, p. 190; *VCH Som.*, ii, 444-5).

TAVERHAM, Norfolk

School, 1288 (H. W. Saunders, *An Introduction to the Obedientiary and Manor Rolls of Norwich Cathedral Priory* (Norwich, 1930), p. 112).

TEMPSFORD, Beds.

Endowed grammar school, projected 1517 (Oxford, Magdalen College, Deeds, Tempsford 96).

TENTERDEN, Kent

School, projected 1525; endowed grammar school by 1548 (A. H. Taylor, 'The grammar free school at Tenterden', *Archaeologia Cantiana*, xliv (1932), pp. 129-31).

THETFORD, Norfolk

School, 1090 × 1119; grammar school, 1328-1496 (*VCH Suffolk*, ii, 303-4).

THORNAGE, Norfolk

Grammar school, 1474 (Norfolk and Norwich Record Office, Reg/7 Book 12, fo 40).

THORNHILL, Yorks. W.R.

School, *c.* 1361 (*Calendar of Inquisitions Post Mortem*, vol xiv (1952), p. 182).

TICEHURST, Sussex

School, projected 1489 (*Transcripts of Sussex Wills*, ed. R. G. Rice, vol iv (Sussex Record Society, xlv, 1940-1), p. 244).

TONBRIDGE, Kent

School, 1323; endowed grammar school, projected 1525 (*Reg. Hethe*, *Rochester*, ed. C. Johnson, vol i (Canterbury & York Society, xlviii, 1948), pp. 190-1; *LPFD*, iv, part 1, nos 1459, 1470-1).

TONG, Salop

Endowed reading, song and grammar school, founded 1411 (Dugdale, *Monasticon*, vol vi, part 3 (1830), p. 1407).

TOPCLIFFE, Yorks. N.R.

School, *c.* 1513 × 1517-19 (*LPFD*, xiii, part 1, no 403(2); *VCH Yorks.*, i, 415).

TOWCESTER, Northants.

Endowed grammar school founded, probably for this purpose, 1448 → (*CPR 1446-52*, p. 204; *ECD*, part 2, pp. 146, 151; *VCH Northants.*, ii, 225-8).

WAINFLEET, Lincs.

Endowed grammar school, founded *c.* 1484 → (R. Chandler, *Life of William Waynflete* (1811), pp. 367-70; *VCH Lincs.*, ii, 483-4).

WAKEFIELD, Yorks. W.R.

School by 1275, 1296-1317, 1335-8 (J. W. Walker, *Wakefield, its History and People*, 2nd ed. (1939), ii, 363-4).

WALSALL, Staffs.

School, *c.* 1503 (*Historical MSS Commission, MSS of the Duke of Rutland*, vol i (1911), p. 17).

WALTHAM HOLY CROSS, Essex

School, 1423 (*CPR 1422-9*, pp. 216-17).

WALTHAMSTOW, Essex

Endowed grammar school, founded *c.* 1527 → (*VCH Essex*, ii, 527-8).

WARRINGTON, Lancs.

Endowed grammar school, founded 1520-6 → (W. K. Jordan, *Social Institutions of Lancashire* (1962), pp. 38-9; *VCH Lancs.*, ii, 601-2, including statutes).

WARWICK

School, 1113 × 1123, 1119 × 1153, 1155; song school, *c.* 1315; grammar school, *c.* 1315, 1464 × 5, endowed by 1501 → (A. F. Leach, *History of Warwick School* (1906); *ECD*, pp. 58-9, 86-91, 272-7; *VCH War*, ii, 299ff; *CPR 1494-1509*, p. 264).

WEEK ST MARY, Cornwall

Endowed grammar school, founded 1508 → (*CPR 1494-1509*, p. 604; *ESR*, part 2, pp. 25-6, 33-4, 40).

WELLINGTON, Somerset

Grammar school, 1371 (J. Coleman, 'Four Wells wills of the fourteenth century', *Somerset and Dorset Notes and Queries*, viii (1903), pp. 151-3).

WELLS, Somerset

Song school, *c.* 1140 (H. E. Reynolds, *Wells Cathedral* (1881), pp. 45, 55). Grammar school, *c.* 1140, *c.* 1185 → (ibid.; *Historical MSS Commission, MSS of the Dean and Chapter of Wells* (1907), i, 492; ii, *passim*; *VCH Som.*, ii, 435-8).

Choristers. Separate tuition in reading and song, 1460 → (statutes in *Dean Cosyn and Wells Cathedral Miscellany*, ed. A. Watkin (Somerset Record Society, lvi, 1941), pp. 98-109; *MSS of Dean and Chapter*, ii, 104, 205, 208, 231, 236, 248; *VCH Som.*, ii, 440-2).

Higher Studies. Lectures in theology or canon law, 1335-48, early fifteenth century (*MSS of Dean and Chapter*, i, 239-40, 545; *Calendar of Papal Letters*, iii, 284; *BRUO*, iii, 1406, sub John Orum).

WESTBURY-ON-TRYM, Gloucs.

Endowed grammar school, founded 1463, -1544 (Worcs. Record Office, Reg. Carpenter, i, fo 183v).

WESTMINSTER, Middx.

School, *c.* 1443 × 1460; school, probably of song, 1451, in the chapel of St Mary de Pew (PRO, C 1/17/262; C. L. Kingsford, *English Historical Literature in the Fifteenth Century* (1913), p. 372).

WHITCHURCH, Salop

Grammar school, 1328 (*Reg. Norbury, Lichfield*, ed. E. Hobhouse (Wm. Salt Archaeological Society, i, 1880), p. 254, where incorrectly stated to be at Oswestry).

WHITKIRK, Yorks. W.R.

Endowed grammar school, founded 1521 (G. E. Kirk, *A History of the Parish Church of Whitkirk* (1935), pp. 244-7).

WIMBORNE, Dorset

Endowed grammar school, founded 1511 → (J. Hutchins, *History of Dorset*, 3rd ed. (1861-73), iii, 270-3).

WINCHCOMBE, Gloucs.

Endowed grammar school, founded 1521 → (PRO, LR 6/29/2; *VCH Gloucs.*, ii, 420-1).

WINCHESTER, Hants.

School, *c.* 1154×1159, 1205, 1366; grammar school, 1373-1488, ?1530-1535 (*The Letters of John of Salisbury*, ed. W. J. Millor and H. E. Butler, vol i (1955), pp. 95-6; *VCH Hants.*, ii, 253-7).

ST MARY alias WINCHESTER COLLEGE. Endowed grammar school, founded 1373-82 → (A. F. Leach, *A History of Winchester College* (1899), *passim*; *VCH Hants.*, ii, 261ff).

WISBECH, Cambs.

Grammar school, 1407, 1446, endowed by 1506 → (*Ely Diocesan Remembrancer*, no 191 (1901), p. 75; *VCH Cambs.*, ii, 327).

WITNEY, Oxon.

School, before 1373 (*Calendar of Inquisitions Post Mortem*, vol xiii (1954), p. 265).

WOLLATON, Notts.

Grammar school, 1473; school, 1524 (*VCH Notts.*, ii, 217; *Historical MSS Commission, Report on the MSS of Lord Middleton* (1911), p. 369).

WOLVERHAMPTON, Staffs.

Endowed grammar school, founded 1512 → (*LPFD*, i, part 1, 1415(19), 1804(25); G. P. Mander, *The History of Wolverhampton Grammar School* (1913), pp. 347-50).

WOOLAVINGTON, Somerset

Perhaps a school, *c.* 1380s (H. C. Maxwell-Lyte, 'The Hody Family', *Somerset and Dorset Notes and Queries*, xviii (1925), pp. 127-9).

WORCESTER

School, 1266-91; grammar school, 1312 →, probably endowed by *c.* 1510 (A. F. Leach, *Documents Illustrating Early Education in Worcester* (Worcs. Historical Society, 1913), *passim*; *VCH Worcs.*, iv, 475-80).

Higher Studies. Theology lectures, 1301×1317; endowed theology lectures in the Carnary Library, founded 1458-64, -1539 (A. F. Leach, *Early Education in Worcester*, pp. 29-33; *VCH Worcs*, iv, 411-12; Worcs.

Record Office, Reg. Carpenter, i, fo 175; Reg. Silvestro de Gigli, folios 132v-133v; PRO, E 315/101, fo 147).

WOTTON-UNDER-EDGE, Gloucs.

School, 1291 × 2; endowed grammar school, projected 1349, founded 1384 → (E. S. Lindley, *Wotton under Edge* (1962), p. 224; *CPR 1348-50*, p. 268; statutes in *ECD*, pp. 330-41; *VCH Gloucs.*, ii, 396-403).

WYE, Kent

Endowed reading, song and grammar school, founded 1448 → (Wye College, statutes, folios 10v-11v; E. Hasted, *History of Kent*, vol iii (1790), pp. 172-5; W. K. Jordan, 'Social institutions in Kent', *Archaeologia Cantiana*, lxxv (1961), p. 70; *VCH Kent*, ii, 235-6).

YARM, Yorks. N.R.

Reading school, 1133 × 1140 (*Reginaldi Dunelmensis Libellus*, ed. J. Raine (Surtees Society, i, 1835), p. 34).

YORK

Song school, 1307, 1367 (*EYS*, i, 12, 22).

Grammar school, 1070 × 1100-1486 (ibid., pp. 10-29).

Higher Studies. Twelfth century; lectures in theology, 1293, 1332, 1355, 1369, 1410 × 1429 (ibid., pp. 17, 18, 24, 26; A. G. Little, *The Grey Friars in Oxford* (Oxford Historical Society, xx, 1892), p. 242).

HOUSEHOLD SCHOOLS

(This list is arranged under the titles of the magnates concerned, since it is not always certain where the schools were based. Private tutors retained for one or two children only have in general been omitted.)

ROYAL HOUSEHOLD

Children of the chapel, instruction in song and grammar, 1401, *c.* 1449, 1467 × 1477.

Henchmen, instruction in grammar, 1467 × 1477, *c.* 1521 → (A. Cobban, *The King's Hall, Cambridge* (1969), pp. 60-3; J. H. Wylie, *History of England under Henry IV*, vol ii (1894), p. 487; iv (1898), p. 208; *Liber Regis Capelle*, ed. W. Ullmann (Henry Bradshaw Society, xcii, 1961), p. 57; A. R. Myers, *The Household of Edward IV* (1959), pp. 126-7, 136-8; and see also above, pp. 218-19).

BUCKINGHAM, Edward Stafford, duke of

Schoolmaster of his wards and henchmen, 1521 (*LPFD*, iii, part 1, 500).

CANTERBURY, John Morton, archbishop of

Grammar master for the boys of his household at Lambeth Palace, *c.* 1496 (John Holt, *Lac Puerorum* (*c.* 1496), sig. A.i.5; *BRUO*, ii, 953-4 sub John Holt).

ELY, Thomas Arundel, bishop of
Song schoolmaster of the choristers in his chapel, 1381-4 (Margaret Aston, *Thomas Arundel* (1967), pp. 247, 411).

LUTTRELL, Sir Hugh
A 'John Scolemaystre' in his household at Dunster, Somerset, 1424 (H. C. Maxwell-Lyte, *History of Dunster* (1909), i, 101).

NORTHUMBERLAND, Henry Percy, earl of
Grammar master in his household, 1511 (*Regulations and Establishment of the Household of Henry Algernon Percy*, ed. T. Percy (1770), p. 44).

RICHMOND AND SOMERSET, Henry Fitzroy, duke of
Grammar master for himself and the other youths in his household, 1525-7 (*LPFD*, iv, part 1, pp. 678-9, nos 1947-8; part 2, nos 3135, 3520; *Dictionary of National Biography*, sub Richard Croke).

ROS, William, lord
A grammar master to be hired to teach his children, 1413 (*Reg. Chichele, Canterbury*, ed. E. F. Jacob, vol ii (1937), p. 22).

ST JOHN, Prior of the Knights of
Tuition in his household at Clerkenwell, London, 1519-21 (*LPFD*, iii, part 1, 499-504).

WALSH, Sir John
Of Old Sodbury, Gloucs. Employed William Tyndale as tutor to his children, *c.* 1522-3 (*Dictionary of National Biography*, sub William Tyndale).

WINCHESTER, Thomas Langton, bishop of
Schoolmaster in his household, 1493 × 1501 (Richard Pace, *De Fructu* (Basel, 1517), p. 28).

YORK, Thomas Wolsey, archbishop of
Master of the children of his chapel; instructor of his wards, before 1529 (George Cavendish, *The Life and Death of Cardinal Wolsey*, ed. R. S. Sylvester (EETS, 1959), pp. 18-21).

LIST OF MEDIEVAL SCHOOLS ARRANGED BY COUNTIES

BEDFORD
Bedford, Bushmead, Dunstable, Houghton Regis, Tempsford

BERKSHIRE
Abingdon, Childrey, Faringdon, Lambourn, Reading

BUCKINGHAM
Buckingham, Eton, Leighton Buzzard, Newport Pagnell

CAMBRIDGE
Cambridge, Ely, Wisbech

CHESHIRE
Chester, Macclesfield, Malpas, Northenden, Stockport

CORNWALL
Launceston, Week St Mary

CUMBERLAND
Carlisle, Cockermouth, Kirkoswald, Penrith

DERBY
Chesterfield, Derby, Melbourne

DEVON
Crediton, Dartmouth, Exeter, Great Torrington, Ottery St Mary, Plympton

DORSET
Bridport, Milton Abbas, Shaftesbury, Sherborne, Wimborne

DURHAM
Darlington, Durham

ESSEX
Colchester, Earl's Colne, Maldon, Pleshey, Saffron Walden, Waltham Holy Cross, Walthamstow

GLOUCESTER
Awre, Bristol, Chipping Campden, Cirencester, Gloucester, Newland, Westbury-on-Trym, Winchcombe, Wotton-under-Edge

HAMPSHIRE
Christchurch, Winchester

HEREFORD
Hereford

HERTFORD
Berkhamsted, Braughing, St Albans, Stevenage

HUNTINGDON
Huntingdon

KENT
Boughton, Bredgar, Canterbury, Cobham, Dover, Faversham, Harnhill, Maidstone, Malling, Sevenoaks, Tenterden, Tonbridge, Wye

LANCASHIRE
Blackburn, Bolton-le-Moors, Broughton, Clitheroe, Farnworth, Hornby, Lancaster, Leyland, Liverpool, Manchester, Middleton, Preston, St Michael-on-Wyre, Warrington

LEICESTER
Burrough, Castle Donington, Leicester, Loughborough, Melton Mowbray

LINCOLN
Alford, Barton-on-Humber, Boston, Bourne, Croyland, Grantham, Grimsby, Horncastle, Lincoln, Louth, Partney, Stamford, Strubby, Tattershall, Wainfleet

MIDDLESEX
London, Westminster

NORFOLK
Aylsham, Blofield, Cromer, Fincham, Harleston, King's Lynn, North Walsham, Norwich, Rudham, Rushworth, Shipden, Shouldham, Sparham, Taverham, Thetford, Thornage

NORTHAMPTON
Aldwinkle, Barnack, Blisworth, Brington, Farthinghoe, Fawsley, Fotheringhay, Higham Ferrers, Northampton, Peterborough, Spratton, Towcester

NORTHUMBERLAND
Alnwick, Hexham, Norham

NOTTINGHAM
Bilborough, Dunham, East Retford, Kinoulton, Newark, Nottingham, Sibthorpe, Southwell, Wollaton

OXFORD
Banbury, Chipping Norton, Ewelme, Henley-on-Thames, Oxford, Witney

SHROPSHIRE
Bridgnorth, Ludlow, Oswestry, Shrewsbury, Tong, Whitchurch

SOMERSET
Bridgwater, Bruton, Crewkerne, Dunster, Mells, Taunton, Wellington, Wells, Woolavington

STAFFORD
Lichfield, Rolleston, Stafford, Walsall, Wolverhampton

SUFFOLK
Beccles, Botesdale, Bury St Edmunds, Clare, Dunwich, Hadleigh, Ipswich, Long Melford, Mildenhall, Stoke by Clare, Stoke by Nayland, Sudbury

SURREY
Croydon, Guildford, Kingston-on-Thames, Southwark

SUSSEX
Arundel, Battle, Billingshurst, Chichester, Cuckfield, Hastings, Lewes, Seaford, Shoreham, Ticehurst

WARWICK
Coventry, Stratford-on-Avon, Sutton Coldfield, Warwick

WESTMORLAND
Appleby, Brough-under-Stainmore

WILTSHIRE
Devizes, Heytesbury, Malmesbury, Marlborough, Salisbury

WORCESTER
Droitwich, Evesham, Rock, Worcester

YORKSHIRE
York
EAST RIDING. Beverley, Hedon, Hemingbrough, Howden, Hull, Kelk, Pocklington, South Dalton
NORTH RIDING. Guisborough, Helmsley, Hovingham, Malton, Middleham, Northallerton, Richmond, Scarborough, Topcliffe, Yarm
WEST RIDING. Acaster Selby, Barnsley, Crofton, Doncaster, Fairburn, Giggleswick, Halifax, Harewood, Leeds, Pontefract, Ripon, Rotherham, Royston, Sedbergh, Sherburn, Thornhill, Wakefield, Whitkirk

WALES
Caernarvon, Haverfordwest, St Davids

CHANNEL ISLANDS
Jersey

Contents of bibliography

The arrangement of the bibliography is as follows: *page*

LIST OF UNPRINTED SOURCES CITED

MSS   328

Theses   330

SELECT BIBLIOGRAPHY OF PRINTED SOURCES

Section I: Works mainly concerned with the history of literacy and education

1 Bibliographies   331

2 Historiography   331

3 The school curriculum   331
  (a) MSS and early printed books   331
  (b) Modern editions of original texts   332
    (i) *The theory of education*   332
    (ii) *Grammars and dictionaries*   332
    (iii) *Reading texts*   333
  (c) Modern critical works   334
  (d) Business studies and the French language   335

4 The history and organization of education   335
  (a) General works   335
  (b) The universities   337
  (c) Schools in particular regions   338
  (d) Particular schools   340
  (e) Education in the religious orders   341

**Section II: Works incidentally concerned with the history of
literacy and education**

1 Records of the central government   342

2 Political, administrative and legal history   343

3 Biographies   344

4 Ecclesiastical history   345
   (a) General records   345
   (b) Diocesan records   346
   (c) Records of secular cathedrals   347
   (d) Records of the religious orders   348
   (e) Modern works   348

5 Literary and social history   349
   (a) Texts and documents   349
   (b) Modern general works   351
   (c) Libraries and book collections   352

6 Local history   353

Bibliography

LIST OF UNPRINTED SOURCES CITED

MSS

Aberystwyth, National Library of Wales
  MS Peniarth 356
Bridgwater, Town Hall
  Corporation MSS, vol x, no 1
Bristol, Archives Office
  Great Orphan Book of Wills
Chichester, Diocesan Record Office
  Statutes of Rolleston school, Cap 1/14/5
Durham, The Prior's Kitchen
  Durham Priory registers, I and II
Edinburgh, National Library of Scotland
  MS Advocates 18.7.21
Exeter, Cathedral Library
  Dean and Chapter MSS, no 2228
Exeter, City Record Office
  DD 22783
  Mayor's court rolls, 16/17 Edward I
Glasgow, Hunterian Museum Library
  MS 472
Lichfield, Joint Record Office
  The register of William Smith
London, British Museum
  MS Arundel 249

MS Cotton Vespasian xxv
MS Harley 1005
MS Harley 1587
MS Harley 3954
MS Royal 2 B xx
London, Guildhall Library
   MS 9531/6, the register of Robert Gilbert
London, Lambeth Palace Library
  The register of John Stafford
  The register of John Morton
London, Public Record Office
  Chancery
  C 1   Early chancery proceedings
  C 47 Chancery miscellanea
  C 115 Chancery masters' exhibits
  Exchequer, K.R.
  E 134 Depositions
  E 154 Inventories of goods and chattels
  E 179 Subsidy rolls
  Exchequer, Augmentation Office
  E 301 Chantry certificates
  E 315 Miscellaneous books
  E 321 Proceedings
  Exchequer, Land Revenue
  LR 1 Receiver's accounts, Series I
  Exchequer, T.R.
  E 36 Books
  Prerogative Court of Canterbury
  Prob 11 Registered copy wills
  Special Collections
  SC 1 Ancient correspondence
  SC 2 Court rolls
  SC 6 Ministers' accounts
  State Paper Office
  SP 1 State papers
Norwich, Norfolk and Norwich Record Office
  Reg/2, Institution Book 4
  Reg/4, Institution Book 7
  Reg/5, Institution Book 9
  Reg/6, Institution Book 11

Reg/7, Institution Book 12
Nottingham, University Library
  Middleton MS, Mi L M 2
Oxford, Balliol College
  MS 354
Oxford, Bodleian Library
  MS Bodley 191
  MS Bodley 581
  MS Lat. th. e 25
  MS Laud misc. 642
  MS Rawlinson C 209
  MS Top. Glouc. c. 4-5
  MS Wood D 11
  University archives: Registers G, H
                        Hyp. B 2
  All Souls College: MS DD All Souls
Oxford, Brasenose College
  Principal Yate's Book
Oxford, Lincoln College
  MS lat. 129
Oxford, Magdalen College
  Deeds, Tempsford 96
Salisbury, Diocesan Record Office
  Chartularium Redingense
  The register of Richard Beauchamp
Worcester, Worcestershire Record Office
  The register of John Carpenter, 2 vols
  The register of Jeronimo Ghinucci
  The register of Silvestro de Gigli
  The register of Henry Wakefield
Wye College, Kent
  Statutes

Theses

MINER, J. N. T. (Br. Bonaventure). 'The teaching of grammar in England in the later middle ages', London, PhD, 1959.
ORME, N. I. 'Schools and education in Gloucestershire and the neighbouring counties from 1280 to the Reformation', Oxford, DPhil, 1969.

SELECT BIBLIOGRAPHY OF PRINTED SOURCES

Section I: Works mainly concerned with the history of literacy and education

1 Bibliographies

The Cambridge Bibliography of English Literature, ed. Bateson, F. W., vol i, Cambridge, 1940, pp. 124-7, 364-80.

The Cambridge Medieval History, vol v, ed. Tanner, J. R., Cambridge, 1926, pp. 934-6.

The Cambridge Medieval History, vol viii, ed. Previté-Orton, C. W., and Brooke, Z. N., Cambridge, 1936, pp. 982-7.

GROSS, CHARLES. *The Sources and Literature of English History to 1485*, 2nd ed. London, 1915, pp. 678-82.

LEACH, A. F. *The Schools of Medieval England*, 2nd ed. London, 1916, pp. vii-ix. (A bibliography of the author's works on medieval schools.)

READ, CONYERS. *Bibliography of British History : Tudor Period, 1485-1603*, 2nd ed. Oxford, 1959, pp. 320-3.

SIMON, JOAN. *Education and Society in Tudor England*, Cambridge, 1966, pp. 404-36.

WALLIS, P. J. *Histories of Old Schools: a revised list for England and Wales*, Department of Education, University of Newcastle upon Tyne, 1966.

2 Historiography

CHAPLIN, W. N. A. F. Leach: a reappraisal, *British Journal of Educational Studies*, xi (1962-3), pp. 99-124.

CHAPLIN, W. N. A. F. Leach: agreement and difference, ibid., xi (1962-3), pp. 173-83.

LITTLE, A. G. Review of Leach, A. F., *The Schools of Medieval England*, *English Historical Review*, xxx (1915), pp. 525-9.

SIMON, JOAN. A. F. Leach on the Reformation, *British Journal of Educational Studies*, iii (1954-5), pp. 128-43; iv (1955-6), pp. 32-48.

SIMON, JOAN. A. F. Leach: a reply, ibid., xii (1963-4), pp. 41-50.

WALLIS, P. J. Leach – past, present, and future, ibid., xii (1963-4), pp. 184-194.

WALLIS, P. J. The Wase school collection: a neglected source in educational history, *Bodleian Library Record*, iv (1952), pp. 78-104.

3 The school curriculum

(a) MSS and early printed books

These will be found listed in the following handbooks:

BENNETT, H. S. A check-list of Robert Whittinton's grammars, *The Library*, 5th series, vii (1952), pp. 1-14.

COPINGER, W. A. *Supplement to Hain's Repertorium Bibliographicum*, 2 vols in 3, London, 1895-1902, reprinted Milan, 1950.

DUFF, E. GORDON. *Fifteenth-Century English Books*, London, Bibliographical Society Monographs, xviii, 1917.

Gesamtkatalog der Wiegendrucke, A – Eigenschaften (all completed), 7 vols, Leipzig, 1925-38.

HAIN, L. *Repertorium Bibliographicum . . . usque ad annum MD.* 2 vols, Stuttgart and Paris, 1826-31.

MARIGO, A. *I Codici Manoscritti delle 'Derivationes' di Uguccione Pisano*, Rome, 1936.

PAFORT, EDITH. A group of early Tudor school books, *The Library*, 4th series, xxvi, no 4 (1946), pp. 227-61.

Patrologia Cursus Completus, sive Universalis, ed. Migne, J. P. Series (Latina) prima, 106 vols, Paris, 1844-64. Series (Latina) secunda, 111 vols, Paris, 1855-64. Indices, 4 vols, Paris, 1862-5.

POLLARD, A. W., AND REDGRAVE, G. R. *A Short Title Catalogue of Books Printed in England, Scotland, and Ireland, 1475-1640*, London, Bibliographical Society, 1926.

WALTHER, H. *Carmina Medii Aevi Posterioris Latina*: vol i, Initia Carminum ac Versuum, Göttingen, 1969.

(b) Modern editions of original texts

   (i) *The theory of education*

ASCHAM, ROGER. *The Whole Works*, ed. Giles, J. A., 3 vols, London, 1864-1865.

ELYOT, SIR THOMAS. *The Boke Named the Gouernour*, ed. Croft, H. H. S., 2 vols, London, 1883.

ERASMUS, DESIDERIUS. *The Education of a Christian Prince*, ed. and trans. Born, L. K., Records of Civilization, xxvii, New York, 1936.

HOCCLEVE, THOMAS. The regement of princes, in *Works*, ed. Furnivall, F. J., vol iii, EETS, extra series, lxxii, 1897, pp. 1-197.

SALTER, F. M. Skelton's *Speculum Principis*, *Speculum*, ix (1934), pp. 25-37.

VIVES, J. L. *Vives on Education*, trans. Watson, Foster, Cambridge, 1913.

   (ii) *Grammars and dictionaries*

ALEXANDER DE VILLA DEI. *Das Doctrinale des Alexander de Villa Dei*, ed. Reichling, D., Berlin, 1893.

Catholicon Anglicum, ed. Herrtage, S. J. EETS, original series, lxxv, 1881.

DONATUS, AELIUS. *Ars Minor*, in *Grammatici Latini*, ed. Keil, H., vol iv, Leipzig, 1864, pp. 355-66.

ÉVRARD OF BÉTHUNE. *Eberhardi Bethuniensis Graecismus*, ed. Wrobel, J., Breslau, 1887.

A Fifteenth-Century School Book, ed. Nelson, W., Oxford, 1956.

Grammatici Latini, ed. Keil, H., 7 vols, Leipzig, 1855-80.

HORMAN, WILLIAM. *Vulgaria*, ed. James, M. R., Oxford, for Roxburghe Club, clxix, 1926.

ISIDORE OF SEVILLE. *Isidori Hispalensis Episcopi Etymologiarum sive Originum*, ed. Lindsay, W. M., 2 vols, Oxford, 1911.

MEECH, S. B. John Drury and his English writings, *Speculum*, ix (1934), pp. 70-83.

MEECH, S. B. Early application of Latin grammar to English, *PMLA*, 1 (1935), pp. 1012-32.

MEECH, S. B. An early treatise in English concerning Latin grammar, *University of Michigan Publications, Language and Literature*, xiii (Ann Arbor, 1935), pp. 81-125.

PRISCIAN. *Ars Grammatica*, in *Grammatici Latini*, ed. Keil, H., vols ii-iii, Leipzig, 1855-8.

Promptorium Parvulorum sive Clericorum Lexicon Anglo-Latinum, c. 1440, ed. Way, A. 3 vols, Camden Society, xxv, liv, lxxxix, 1843-65.

A Shorte Introduction of Grammar, ed. Flynn, V. J., New York, 1945.

Synonyma (attributed to John of Garland), in *Patrologia Latina*, ed. Migne, J. P., vol cl, Paris, 1854, cols 1577-90.

A Volume of Vocabularies . . . from the Tenth Century to the Fifteenth, ed. Wright, Thomas, privately printed, 1857.

The Vulgaria of John Stanbridge and Robert Whittinton, ed. White, Beatrice, EETS, original series, clxxxvii, 1932.

(iii) *Reading texts*

ALAIN DE LILLE. *Textes inédits*, ed. d'Alverny, Marie-Thérèse, Études de Philosophie mediévale, lii, Paris, 1965.

Cartula, in *Patrologia Latina*, ed. Migne, J. P., vol clxxxiv, Paris, 1859, cols 1307-14.

CATO, DIONYSIUS. *Disticha Catonis*, ed. Boas, M., and Botschuyer, H. J., Amsterdam, 1952.

CATO, DIONYSIUS. *The Distichs of Cato*, trans. Chase, W. J., Madison, University of Wisconsin Studies in the Social Sciences and Literature, vii, 1922.

Parabolarum, Liber, in *Patrologia Latina*, ed. Migne, J. P., vol ccx, Paris, 1855, cols 581-94.

Penitencialis, Liber, in ibid., vol ccvii, Paris, 1855, cols 1153-6.

Stans Puer ad Mensam, in *Manners and Meals in Olden Time*, ed. Furnivall, F. J., EETS, original series, xxxii, part 2, 1868, pp. 30-2.

SULPIZIO, G. *Doctrina Mensae, table manners for boys*, ed. Thomas, H., Oxford, 1949.

Theoduli Eclogam, ed. Osternacher, J., Linz, 1902.

(c) Modern critical works

ALLEN, C. G. The sources of 'Lily's Latin Grammar', a review of the facts and some further suggestions, *The Library*, 5th series, ix (1954), pp. 85-100.

BOAS, M. De librorum Catonianorum historia atque compositione, *Mnemosyne*, new series, xlii (1914), pp. 17-46.

BONAVENTURE, BR. [also MINER, J. N. T.]. The teaching of Latin in later medieval England, *Medieval Studies*, xxiii (1961), pp. 1-20.

BORN, L. K. The perfect prince: a study in thirteenth- and fourteenth century ideals, *Speculum*, iii (1928), pp. 470-504.

DALY, LL. W. AND B. A. Some techniques in medieval Latin lexicography, ibid., xxxix (1964), pp. 229-39.

FLYNN, V. J. The grammatical writings of William Lily, ?1468-?1523, *Papers of the Bibliographical Society of America*, xxxvii (1943), pp. 85-113.

GALBRAITH, V. H. John Seward and his circle, *Medieval and Renaissance Studies*, i (1941-3), pp. 85-104.

HAMILTON, G. L. Theodulus: a medieval textbook, *Modern Philology*, vii, no 2 (1909), pp. 1-17.

HAURÉAU, B. Additions et corrections [on Guillaume Brito], *Histoire littéraire de la France*, xxix, Paris, 1885, pp. 583-602.

HAURÉAU, B. Notice sur les œuvres authentiques ou supposées de Jean de Garlande, *Notices et extraits des mss de la Bibliothèque nationale*, xxvii, part 2 (Paris, 1879), pp. 1-86.

HUNT, R. W. Hugutio and Peter Helias, *Medieval and Renaissance Studies*, ii (1950), pp. 174-8.

HUNT, R. W. The 'lost' preface to the *Liber Derivationum* of Osbern of Gloucester, ibid., iv (1958), pp. 267-82.

HUNT, R. W. Oxford grammar masters in the middle ages, *Oxford Studies Presented to Daniel Callus*, Oxford Historical Society, new series, xvi, 1964, pp. 163-93.

HUNT, R. W. Studies on Priscian in the eleventh and twelfth centuries, *Medieval and Renaissance Studies*, i (1941-3), pp. 194-231.

HUNT, R. W. Studies on Priscian in the twelfth century: II: the school of Ralph of Beauvais, ibid., ii (1950), pp. 1-56.

MACKINNON, H. William de Montibus: a medieval teacher, *Essays in Medieval History Presented to Bertie Wilkinson*, ed. Sandquist, T. A., and Powicke, M. R., Toronto, 1969, pp. 32-45.

PAETOW, L. J. *Morale Scolarium* of John of Garland, Berkeley, Memoirs of the University of California, iv, part 2 (1927), pp. 65-273.

STEVENSON, W. H. The introduction of English as the vehicle of instruction in English schools, *An English Miscellany Presented to F. J. Furnivall*, Oxford, 1901, pp. 421-9.

THUROT, CHARLES. Notices et extraits de divers manuscrits latins pour servir à l'histoire des doctrines grammaticales au moyen âge, *Notices et extraits des manuscrits de la Bibliothèque impériale*, xxii, part 2 (Paris, 1868), pp. 1-592.

WOODWARD, W. H. *Erasmus concerning the Aim and Method of Education*, Cambridge, 1904.

(d) Business studies and the French language

Formularies which bear on the History of Oxford, c. 1204-1420, ed. Salter, H. E., Pantin, W. A., and Richardson, H. G., 2 vols, Oxford Historical Society, new series, iv-v, 1942.

LAMBLEY, KATHLEEN. *The Teaching and Cultivation of the French Language in England during Tudor and Stuart Times*, London and Manchester, 1920.

MEYER, P. Les manuscrits français de Cambridge, *Romania*, xxxii (1903), pp. 47-58.

RICHARDSON, H. G. Business training in medieval Oxford, *American Historical Review*, xlvi (1941), pp. 259-80.

RICHARDSON, H. G. *An Oxford Teacher of the Fifteenth Century*, 1939, reprinted with corrections from *Bulletin of John Rylands Library*, xxiii (1939), pp. 436-57.

SUGGETT, HELEN. The use of French in the later middle ages, *Transactions of the Royal Historical Society*, 4th series, xxviii (1946), pp. 61-83.

4 The history and organization of education

(a) General works

BEALES, A. C. F. A biographical catalogue of Catholic schoolmasters in England, 1558-1603, *Recusant History*, vii, no 6 (1966), pp. 268-89.

CARLISLE, N. *A Concise Description of the Endowed Grammar Schools in England and Wales*, 2 vols, London, 1818.

DEANESLY, MARGARET. Medieval schools to *c.* 1300, *The Cambridge Medieval History*, vol v, ed. Tanner, J. R., Cambridge, 1926, pp. 765-79.

GALBRAITH, V. H. The literacy of the medieval English kings, *Proceedings of the British Academy*, xxi (1935), pp. 201-38.

GARDINER, DOROTHY. *English Girlhood at School*, London, 1929.

HEXTER, J. H. The education of the aristocracy in the Renaissance, *Reappraisals in History*, London, 1961, pp. 45-70.

JORDAN, W. K. *Philanthropy in England, 1480-1660*, London, 1959.

LEACH, A. F. *Educational Charters and Documents, 598-1909*, Cambridge, 1911.

LEACH, A. F. *English Schools at the Reformation, 1546-8*, Westminster, 1896.

LEACH, A. F. *The Schools of Medieval England*, 2nd ed. London, 1916.

LEACH, A. F. Some results of research in the history of education in England; with suggestions for its continuance and extension, *Proceedings of the British Academy*, vi (1913-14), pp. 433-80.

LITTLE, A. G. Theological schools in medieval England, *English Historical Review*, lv (1940), pp. 624-30.

MINER, J. N. T. [also BONAVENTURE, BR.] Schools and literacy in late medieval England, *British Journal of Educational Studies*, xi (1962-3), pp. 16-27.

POTTER, G. R. Education in the fourteenth and fifteenth centuries, *The Cambridge Medieval History*, vol viii, ed. Previté-Orton, C. W., and Brooke, Z. N., Cambridge, 1936, pp. 688-717.

RIMBAULT, E. F. Two sermons preached by the Boy Bishop, *Camden Miscellany*, Camden Society, new series, xiv, 1875.

SEABORNE, M. V. J. *The English School, its architecture and organization, 1370-1970*, London, 1971.

SIMON, JOAN. *Education and Society in Tudor England*, Cambridge, 1966.

SIMON, JOAN. The Reformation and English education, *Past and Present*, xi (1957), pp. 48-65.

THOMPSON, A. HAMILTON. *Song Schools in the Middle Ages*, Church Music Society Occasional Papers, xiv, 1942.

THOMPSON, J. W. *The Literacy of the Laity in the Middle Ages*, Berkeley, University of California Publications in Education, ix, 1939.

WASE, CHRISTOPHER. *Considerations concerning Free Schools as Settled in England*, Oxford, 1678.

WATSON, FOSTER. *The English Grammar Schools to 1660: their curriculum and practice*, Cambridge, 1908.

WOOD, N. *The Reformation and English Education*, London, 1931.

(b) The universities [*this section contains only works relevant to the present study*]

BALL, W. W. ROUSE. *Cambridge Notes, chiefly concerning Trinity College and the University*, Cambridge, 1921.

BLAKISTON, H. E. D. Some Durham college rolls, *Collectanea III*, ed. Burrows, M., Oxford Historical Society, xxxii, 1896, pp. 1-76.

BLOXAM, J. R. *A Register of the Presidents, Fellows, Demies . . . and other members of St Mary Magdalen College in the University of Oxford*, 8 vols, Oxford, 1853-85.

COBBAN, A. B. *The King's Hall within the University of Cambridge in the Later Middle Ages*, Cambridge, Studies in Medieval Life and Thought, 3rd series, i, 1969.

COOPER, C. H. *Annals of Cambridge*, 5 vols, Cambridge, 1842-53.

Documents relating to the University and Colleges of Cambridge, 3 vols, London, 1852.

The Earliest Statutes of Jesus College, Cambridge, issued by James Stanley, bishop of Ely, 1514-1515, [ed. Gray, A.], Cambridge, 1935.

The Early Rolls of Merton College, Oxford, ed. Highfield, J. R. L., Oxford Historical Society, xviii, 1964.

The Early Statutes of Christ's College, Cambridge, with the statutes of the prior foundation of God's House, ed. Rackham, Harris, Cambridge, 1927.

EMDEN, A. B. *A Biographical Register of the University of Cambridge to 1500*, Cambridge, 1963.

EMDEN, A. B. *A Biographical Register of the University of Oxford to 1500*, 3 vols, Oxford, 1957-9.

EMDEN, A. B. *An Oxford Hall in Medieval Times, being the early history of St Edmund Hall*, Oxford, 1927.

EVANS, EVANGELINE. St Mary's College in Oxford for Austin canons, *Oxford Archaeological Society Report*, no lxxvi (1931), pp. 367-91.

GALBRAITH, V. H. Some new documents about Gloucester College, *Snappe's Formulary and other Records*, ed. Salter, H. E., Oxford Historical Society, lxxx, 1924, pp. 337-86.

Grace Book A, containing the Proctors' Accounts and other Records of the University of Cambridge, 1454-1488, ed. Leathes, S. M., Cambridge, Luard Memorial Series, i, 1897.

Grace Book B . . . 1488-1511, ed. Bateson, Mary, 2 vols, Cambridge, Luard Memorial Series, ii, 1903-5.

Grace Book Γ, containing the Records of the University of Cambridge 1501-1542, ed. Searle, W. G., Cambridge, 1908.

Grace Book Δ, containing the Records of the University of Cambridge 1542-1589, ed. Venn, J., Cambridge, 1910.

GRAY, A., AND BRITTAIN, F. *A History of Jesus College, Cambridge*, London, 1960.

HACKETT, M. B. *The Original Statutes of Cambridge University*, Cambridge, 1970.

LITTLE, A. G. *The Grey Friars in Oxford*, Oxford Historical Society, xx, 1892.

LLOYD, A. H. *The Early History of Christ's College, Cambridge*, Cambridge, 1934.

MAGRATH, J. R. *The Queen's College, Oxford*, 2 vols, Oxford, 1921.

MOORMAN, J. R. H. *The Grey Friars in Cambridge, 1225-1538*, Cambridge, 1952.

PEACOCK, G. *Observations on the Statutes of the University of Cambridge*, London, 1841.

RASHDALL, HASTINGS. *The Universities of Europe in the Middle Ages*, ed. Powicke, F. M., and Emden, A. B., 3 vols, Oxford, 1936.

Register of the University of Oxford, ed. Boase, C. W., vol i: 1449-63, 1505-71, Oxford Historical Society, i, 1885.

Registrum Cancellarii Oxoniensis, 1434-1469, ed. Salter, H. E., 2 vols, Oxford Historical Society, xciii-iv, 1932.

Statuta Antiqua Universitatis Oxoniensis, ed. Gibson, Strickland, Oxford, 1931.

Statutes of the Colleges of Oxford, 3 vols, London and Oxford, 1853.

STEVENSON, W. H., AND SALTER, H. E. *The Early History of St John's College, Oxford*, Oxford Historical Society, new series, i, 1939.

STOKES, H. P. *The Medieval Hostels of the University of Cambridge*, Cambridge Antiquarian Society Publications, xlix, 1924.

THOMPSON, H. L. *Christ Church*, London, University of Oxford College Histories, 1900.

Vetus Liber Archidiaconi Eliensis, ed. Feltoe, C. L., and Minns, E. H., Cambridge Antiquarian Society Publications, xlviii, 1917.

WOOD, ANTHONY. *Survey of the Antiquities of the City of Oxford*, ed. Clark, A., 3 vols, Oxford Historical Society, xv, xvii, xxxvii, 1889-99.

(c) Schools in particular regions

JORDAN, W. K. Charitable institutions of the west of England, *Transactions of the American Philosophical Society*, new series, l, part 8 (1960).

JORDAN, W. K. *The Charities of London, 1480-1660*, London, 1960.

JORDAN, W. K. *The Charities of Rural England, 1480-1660*, London, 1961.

JORDAN, W. K. Social institutions in Kent, 1480-1660, *Archaeologia Cantiana*, lxxv (1961).

JORDAN, W. K. *The Social Institutions of Lancashire, 1480-1660*, Chetham Society, 3rd series, xi, 1962.

LEACH, A. F. *Early Yorkshire Schools*, 2 vols, Yorks. Archaeological Society, xxvii, xxxiii, 1899-1903.

TATE, W. E. *A. F. Leach as a Historian of Yorkshire Education: with an index of the Yorkshire schools, c. 730 to c. 1770, referred to in his works*, York, St Anthony's Hall Publications, xxiii, 1963.

Victoria History of the Counties of England: articles on medieval schools:

Bedfordshire, vol ii (1908), pp. 149-86, by Leach, A. F.

Berkshire, vol ii (1907), pp. 245-84, by Leach, A. F.

Buckinghamshire, vol ii (1908), pp. 145-222, by Leach, A. F.

Cambridgeshire, vol ii (1948), pp. 319-56, by Hampson, E. M.

Derbyshire, vol ii (1907), pp. 207-82, by Leach, A. F.

Durham, vol i (1905), pp. 365-413, by Leach, A. F.

Essex, vol ii (1907), pp. 501-64, by Smith, C. Fell-, edited by Leach, A. F.

Gloucestershire, vol ii (1907), pp. 313-448, by Leach, A. F.

Hampshire, vol ii (1903), pp. 250-408, by Leach, A. F.

Hertfordshire, vol ii (1908), pp. 47-102, by Leach, A. F.

Huntingdonshire, vol ii (1932), pp. 107-19, by Parsloe, C. G.

Lancashire, vol ii (1908), pp. 561-624, by Chaytor, H. J., and Leach, A. F.

Lincolnshire, vol ii (1906), pp. 421-92, by Leach, A. F.

Northamptonshire, vol ii (1906), pp. 201-88, by Leach, A. F.

Nottinghamshire, vol ii (1910), pp. 179-264, by Leach, A. F., and Fletcher, F.

Oxfordshire, vol i (1939), pp. 457-90, vol iii (1954), pp. 40-3, by Lobel, M. D., and Midgley, M.

Rutland, vol i (1908), pp. 259-300, by Fletcher, F.

Somerset, vol ii (1911), pp. 435-66, by Holmes, T. S., and Leach, A. F.

Suffolk, vol ii (1907), pp. 301-55, by Leach, A. F., and Hutton, E. P. Steele-.

Surrey, vol ii (1905), pp. 155-242, by Leach, A. F.

Sussex, vol ii (1907), pp. 397-440, by Leach, A. F.

Warwickshire, vol ii (1908), pp. 297-373, by Leach, A. F.

Wiltshire, vol v (1957), pp. 348-68, by Butcher, E. E.

Worcestershire, vol iv (1914-24), pp. 473-540, by Leach, A. F.

Yorkshire, vol i (1907), pp. 415-500, by Leach, A. F.

M

WALLIS, P. J., AND TATE, W. E. A register of old Yorkshire grammar schools, *Leeds University Institute of Education, Researches and Studies*, xiii (1956), pp. 64-104, and reprinted.

(d) Particular schools [*the following are only a selection, chiefly bearing on the medieval period. For a complete list see Wallis, P. J.*, Histories of Old Schools, *in subsection 1 above*].

The Ancient Laws . . . for King's College Cambridge and . . . Eton College, ed. Heywood, J., and Wright, Thomas, London, 1850.

AUSTIN, ROLAND. *The Crypt School, Gloucester, 1539-1939*, Gloucester, 1939.

BARTELOT, R. GROSVENOR. *History of Crewkerne School, 1499-1899*, Crewkerne, 1899.

BATESON, MARY. The Huntingdon song school and the school of St Gregory's, Canterbury, *English Historical Review*, xviii (1903), pp. 712-713.

CROSS, M. CLAIRE. *The Free Grammar School of Leicester* (Leicester University Department of English Local History, Occasional Papers, iv, 1953).

FAIRBROTHER, E. H. The foundation of Bruton school, Somerset, *Somerset and Dorset Notes and Queries*, xii (1911), pp. 49-52.

GRAY, I. E., AND POTTER, W. E. *Ipswich School, 1450-1950*, Ipswich, 1950.

KIRBY, T. F. *Annals of Winchester College, from its foundation in the year 1382*, London, 1892.

KIRBY, T. F. *Winchester Scholars. A list of the wardens, fellows, and scholars*, London, 1888.

LAWSON, J. *A Town Grammar School through Six Centuries. A History of Hull Grammar School*, London, 1963.

LEACH, A. F. *Documents Illustrating Early Education in Worcester, 685-1700*, Worcs. Historical Society, xxxi, 1913.

LEACH, A. F. *History of Warwick School*, London, 1906.

LEACH, A. F. *A History of Winchester College*, London, 1899.

LEACH, A. F. St Paul's school before Colet, *Archaeologia*, lxii, part 1 (1910), pp. 191-238.

LEACH, A. F. Sherborne school before, under, and after Edward VI, *Archaeological Journal*, lv (2nd series v) (1898), pp. 1-83.

LYTE, SIR H. C. MAXWELL-. *History of Eton College, 1440-1910*, 4th ed. London, 1911.

MCDONNELL, SIR, M. F. J. *The Annals of St Paul's School*, London, 1959.

MCDONNELL, M. F. J. *A History of St Paul's School*, London, 1909.

Malpas Grammar School, *Transactions of Historic Society of Lancs. and Cheshire*, lxv (new series, xxix) (1914), pp. 194-211.

MANDER, G. P. *The History of Wolverhampton Grammar School*, Wolverhampton, 1913.

OAKLEY, R. R. *A History of Oswestry School*, London, 1964.

OWEN, MRS BULKELEY-. The founder and first trustees of Oswestry grammar school, *Transactions of the Salop Archaeological and Natural History Society*, 3rd series, iv (1904), pp. 185-216.

PARRY, H. L. *The Founding of Exeter School*, London, 1913.

PRESCOTT, ARCHDEACON. The grammar school of Carlisle, *Transactions of the Cumberland and Westmorland Antiquarian and Archaeological Society*, new series, xvi (1916), pp. 1-28.

RICHARDSON, H. G. The schools of Northampton in the twelfth century, *English Historical Review*, lvi (1941), pp. 595-605.

RICKERT, EDITH. Chaucer at school, *Modern Philology*, xxix (1931-2), pp. 258-74.

SAUNDERS, H. W. *A History of the Norwich Grammar School*, Norwich, 1932.

STANIER, R. S. *A History of Magdalen College School, Oxford*, 2nd ed., Oxford, 1958.

STERRY, SIR WASEY. *The Eton College Register*, 1441-1698, Eton, 1943.

STOCKS, G. A. *The Records of Blackburn Grammar School*, 3 vols, Chetham Society, new series lxvi-viii, 1909.

TAYLOR, A. H. The grammar free school at Tenterden, *Archaeologia Cantiana*, xliv (1932), pp. 129-46.

VARLEY, B. *History of Stockport Grammar School*, 2nd ed. Manchester, 1957.

WATNEY, J. Mercers' school, *London and Middx. Archaeological Transactions*, new series, i (1905), pp. 115-50.

WEAVER, F. W. Foundation deed of Bruton school, *Somerset and Dorset Notes and Queries*, iii (1892-3), pp. 241-8.

WENHAM, L. P. Two notes on the history of Richmond school, Yorkshire, *Yorks. Archaeological Journal*, xxxvii (1951), pp. 369-73.

WILMOT, D. *A Short History of the Grammar School of Macclesfield, 1503-1910*, Macclesfield, 1910.

WOODRUFF, C. E., AND CAPE, H. J. *Schola Regia Cantuariensis: a History of Canterbury School*, London, 1908.

WRIGHT, THOMAS. Rules of the free school at Saffron Walden in Essex in the reign of Henry VIII, *Archaeologia*, xxxiv (1852), pp. 37-41.

(e) Education in the religious orders [*see also section* (*b*)]

EVANS, S. J. A. Ely almonry boys and choristers in the later middle ages, *Studies Presented to Sir Hilary Jenkinson*, ed. Davies, J. Conway, London, 1957, pp. 155-63.

LITTLE, A. G. Educational organisation of the mendicant friars in England (Dominicans and Franciscans), *Transactions of the Royal Historical Society*, new series, viii (1894), pp. 49-70.

PANTIN, W. A. Abbot Kidderminster and monastic studies, *Downside Review*, xlvii (1929), pp. 199-211.

Section II: Works incidentally concerned with the history of literacy and education

1 Records of the central government

Acts of the Privy Council, new series, 1542-, ed. Dasent, J. R., and others, London, 1890-, in progress.

Calendar of Close Rolls, 1272-1509, 47 vols, London, 1892-1963.

Calendar of Inquisitions Post Mortem, 1216-1384, 15 vols, London, 1904-70.

Calendar of Letters and Papers, Foreign and Domestic, Henry VIII, ed. Brewer, S. J., Gairdner, J., and Brodie, R. H., 21 vols, London, 1864-1920.

Calendar of Miscellaneous Inquisitions, 7 vols, London, 1916-69.

Calendar of Patent Rolls, 1216-1509, 1547-72, 68 vols, London, 1891-1966.

Catalogue of Ancient Deeds, 6 vols, London, 1890-1915.

Chantry Certificates:

    MACLEAN, SIR J. Chantry certificates, Gloucestershire, *Transactions of the Bristol and Gloucs. Archaeological Society*, viii (1883-4), pp. 229-308.

    The Chantry Certificates for Oxfordshire, ed. Graham, Rose, Alcuin Club, xxiii, 1920; Oxfordshire Record Society, i, 1919.

    The Survey and Rental of the Chantries, etc., in Somerset in 1548 ed. Green, E., Somerset Record Society, ii, 1888.

    The Certificates of the Commissioners appointed to Survey the Chantries, etc., in the County of York, ed. Page, W., 2 vols, Surtees Society, xci-ii, 1894-5.

CHAPLAIS, P. T. V. M. *English Royal Documents, King John-Henry VI, 1199-1461*, Oxford, 1971.

Close Rolls, 1227-1272, 14 vols, London, 1902-38.

COLE, HENRY. *King Henry VIII's Scheme of Bishopricks*, London, 1838.

A Collection of Ordinances and Regulations . . . of the Royal Household, London, Society of Antiquaries, 1790.

DEVON, F. *Issues of the Exchequer*, London, 1837.

Journals of the House of Lords, vol i: 1509-1577, no place or date.

Journals of the House of Commons, vol i: 1547-1628, London, 1803.

Letters Relating to the Suppression of Monasteries, ed. Wright, T., Camden Society, xxvi, 1843.

Liber Reges Capelle, ed. Ullman, W., Cambridge, Henry Bradshaw Society, xcii, 1961.

Memorials of King Henry VII, ed. Gairdner, J., London, Rolls Series, 1858.

MYERS, A. R. *The Household of Edward IV*, Manchester, 1959.

Proceedings and Ordinances of the Privy Council of England, ed. Nicolas, N. H., 7 vols, London, 1834-7.

Regesta Regum Anglo-Normannorum, 1066-1154, ed. Davis, H. W. C., and others, 4 vols, Oxford, 1913-69.

Rotuli Parliamentorum, ed. Strachey, J., 6 vols, London, 1767-77. *Index to the Rolls of Parliament*, ed. Strachey, J., and others, London, 1832.

Select Cases in the Court of King's Bench, ed. Sayles, G. O., 7 vols, Selden Society, lv, lvii-viii, lxxiv, lxxvi, lxxxii, lxxxviii, 1936-71.

The Statutes of the Realm, from Magna Carta to the end of the reign of Queen Anne, 10 vols, London, Record Commission, 1810-24.

A Subsidy Collected in the Diocese of Lincoln in 1526, ed. Salter, H. E., Oxford Historical Society, lxiii, 1909.

Valor Ecclesiasticus tempore Henrici VIII auctoritate regis institutus, ed. Caley, J., 6 vols, London, Record Commission, 1810-24.

2 Political, administrative and legal history

ARMSTRONG, C. A. J. *The Usurpation of Richard III*, 2nd ed. Oxford, 1969.

BROWN, A. L. The privy seal clerks in the early fifteenth century, *The Study of Medieval Records: Essays in Honour of Kathleen Major*, ed. Bullough, D. A., and Storey, R. L., Oxford, 1971, pp. 260-81.

FORTESCUE, SIR JOHN. *De Laudibus Legum Anglie*, ed. and trans. Chrimes, S. B., Cambridge, Studies in English Legal History, 1942.

HASTINGS, MARGARET. *The Court of Common Pleas in Fifteenth-Century England*, Ithaca and New York, 1947.

HOLDSWORTH, W. S. *A History of English Law*, 16 vols, London, 1922-66.

HOLMES, G. A. *The Estates of the Higher Nobility in Fourteenth-Century England*, Cambridge, 1957.

IVES, E. W. The common lawyers in pre-Reformation England, *Transactions of the Royal Historical Society*, 5th series, xviii (1968), pp. 145-73.

John of Gaunt's Register, 1371-5, ed. Smith, S. Armitage-, 2 vols, Royal Historical Society, Camden third series, xx-xxi, 1911.

MCFARLANE, K. B. *Lancastrian Kings and Lollard Knights*, Oxford, 1972.

MADOX, T. *The History and Antiquities of the Exchequer of the Kings of England*, 2 parts, London, 1711.

MATHEW, G. *The Court of Richard II*, London, 1968.

MYERS, A. R. The household of Queen Elizabeth Woodville, 1466-7, *Bulletin of the John Rylands Library*, l (1967-8), pp. 207-35, 433-81.

POLLOCK, SIR F., AND MAITLAND, F. W. *The History of English Law before Edward I*, 2 vols, 2nd ed. Cambridge, 1898.

The Regulations and Establishment of the Household of Henry Algernon Percy, Fifth Earl of Northumberland, ed. Percy, T., London, 1770, reprinted 1905.

RICHARDSON, H. G., AND SAYLES, G. O. *The Governance of Medieval England, from the Conquest to Magna Carta*, Edinburgh, 1963.

RICHARDSON, W. C. *History of the Court of Augmentations, 1536-1554*, Baton Rouge, 1961.

RUTHVEN, A. JOCELYN OTWAY-. *The King's Secretary and the Signet Office in the Fifteenth Century*, Cambridge, 1939.

SHARP, MARGARET. The central administrative system of Edward the Black Prince, in Tout, T. F., *Chapters in the Administrative History of Medieval England*, vol v, Manchester, 1930, pp. 289-400.

SOMERVILLE, R. *History of the Duchy of Lancaster*, vol i, London, 1953.

TOUT, T. F. *Chapters in the Administrative History of Medieval England*, 6 vols, Manchester and London, 1920-33.

TOUT, T. F. The household of the chancery and its disintegration, *Essays in History Presented to R. L. Poole*, ed. Davis, H. W. C., Oxford, 1927, pp. 46-85.

WILLARD, J. F., MORRIS, W. A., and others. *The English Government at Work, 1327-1336*, 3 vols, Cambridge, Mass., 1940-50.

WOLFFE, B. P. *The Royal Demesne in English History*, London, 1971.

WYLIE, J. H. *History of England under Henry IV*, 4 vols, London, 1884-98.

3 Biographies

BREWER, THOMAS. *Memoir of the Life and Times of John Carpenter, Town Clerk of London*, 2nd ed. London, 1856.

CAVENDISH, GEORGE. *The Life and Death of Cardinal Wolsey*, ed. Sylvester, R. S., EETS, ccxliii, 1959 for 1957.

CHURTON, R. *The Lives of William Smyth, Bishop of Lincoln, and Sir Richard Sutton, Knight, Founders of Brasen Nose College*, Oxford, 1800.

COCKAYNE, G. E. *The Complete Peerage*, ed. Doubleday, H. A. and Gibbs, V., 14 vols in 15, London, 1910-59.

DAVID, C. W. The claim of King Henry I to be called learned, *Anniversary Essays in Medieval History by Students of C. H. Haskins*, Boston and New York, 1929, pp. 45-56.

Dictionary of National Biography, ed. Stephen, L., and Lee, S., 63 vols, London, 1885-1900.

ERASMUS, DESIDERIUS. *The Lives of Jehan Vitrier . . . and John Colet*, trans. Lupton, J. H., London, 1883.

JAMES, M. R. *Henry VI: a Reprint of John Blacman's Memoir*, Cambridge, 1919.

KINGSFORD, C. L. *Henry V*, new ed., London, 1923.

KIRBY, J. L. *Henry IV of England*, London, 1970.

KITTREDGE, G. L. Chaucer and some of his friends, *Modern Philology*, i (1903-4), pp. 1-18.

LUPTON, J. H. *A Life of John Colet*, London, 1887.

MCFARLANE, K. B. William Worcester: a preliminary survey, *Studies Presented to Sir Hilary Jenkinson*, ed. Davies, J. Conway, London, 1957, pp. 196-221.

MOBERLY, G. H. *Life of William of Wykeham*, 2nd ed. Winchester, 1893.

NELSON, W. *John Skelton, Laureate*, New York, 1939.

RICKERT, EDITH. Thou Vache, *Modern Philology*, xi (1913-14), pp. 209-25.

SMITH, S. ARMITAGE-. *John of Gaunt*, Westminster, 1904.

VICKERS, K. H. *Humphrey, Duke of Gloucester: a Biography*, London, 1907.

WILLIAMS, ETHEL CARLETON. *My Lord of Bedford, 1389-1435, a life of John of Lancaster, first duke of Bedford*, London, 1963.

4 Ecclesiastical history

(a) General records

Archiv für Litteratur- und Kirchengeschichte des Mittelalters, ed. Denifle, P. H., and Ehrle, F., 7 vols, Berlin and Freiburg im Breisgau, 1885-1900.

Bullarum Privilegiorum ac Diplomatum Romanorum Pontificum Amplissima Collectio, ed. Cocquelines, C., 14 vols, Rome, 1739-44.

Calendar of Papal Letters, 1198-1492, 14 vols in 15, London, 1894-1951.

Concilia Magnae Britanniae et Hiberniae, 446-1717, ed. Wilkins, D., 4 vols, London, 1737.

Corpus Juris Canonici, ed. Friedberg, E., 2 vols, Leipzig, 1879-81.

Councils and Synods, with other documents relating to the English Church, Part 2: 1205-1313, ed. Powicke, F. M., and Cheney, C. R., 2 vols, Oxford, 1964

DUGDALE, SIR WILLIAM. *Monasticon Anglicanum, enriched with a large accession of materials*, ed. Caley, J., Ellis, H., and Bandinel, B., 6 vols in 8, London, 1817-30.

LE NEVE, J. *Fasti Ecclesiae Anglicanae, 1066-1300*, ed. Greenway, Diane E., London, 1968-, in progress.

LE NEVE, J. *Fasti Ecclesiae Anglicanae, 1300-1541*, ed. Horn, Joyce M., Jones, B., and King, H. P. F., 12 vols, London, 1962-7.

MANSI, J. D. *Sacrorum Conciliorum Nova et Amplissima Collectio*, 31 vols, Florence and Venice, 1759-98.

(b) Diocesan records

OLIVER, G. *Monasticon Dioecesis Exoniensis*, Exeter and London, 1846.

Registers of English bishops:

BATH AND WELLS

Calendar of the Register of John Drokensford, Bishop of Bath and Wells, 1309-1329, ed. Hobhouse, E., Somerset Record Society, i, 1887.

The Register of Ralph of Shrewsbury, Bishop of Bath and Wells, 1329-1363, ed. Holmes, T. Scott., 2 vols, ibid., ix-x, 1896.

The Register of Thomas Bekynton, Bishop of Bath and Wells, 1443-1465, ed. Lyte, H. C. Maxwell- and Dawes, M. C. B., 2 vols, ibid., xlix-l, 1934-5.

CANTERBURY

The Register of Henry Chichele, Archbishop of Canterbury, 1414-1443, ed. Jacob, E. F. and Johnson, H. C., 4 vols, Canterbury & York Society, xlii, xlv-vii, 1937-47.

ELY

[*Calendar of the Registers of the Bishops of Ely*, ed. Crosby, J. H.], *Ely Diocesan Remembrancer*, nos 1-355, Cambridge, 1885-1914.

EXETER

The Register of Walter de Stapeldon, Bishop of Exeter, 1307-1326, ed. Randolph, F. C. Hingeston-, 3 vols, Exeter and London, 1892.

The Register of John Grandisson, Bishop of Exeter, 1327-1369, ed. Randolph, F. C. Hingeston-, 3 vols, Exeter and London, 1894-9.

The Register of Thomas de Brantyngham, Bishop of Exeter, 1370-1394, ed. Randolph, F. C. Hingeston-, 2 vols, Exeter and London, 1901-6.

HEREFORD

Registrum Thome Spofford, episcopi Herefordensis, 1422-1448, ed. Bannister, A. T., Canterbury & York Society, xxiii, 1919.

LINCOLN

Rotuli Hugonis de Welles, episcopi Lincolniensis, 1209-1235, ed. Phillimore, W. P. W. and Davis, F. N., 3 vols, Canterbury & York Society, i, iii, iv, 1907-9; Lincoln Record Society, iii, vi, ix, 1912-14.

Rotuli Roberti Grosseteste, episcopi Lincolniensis, 1235-1253, ed. Davis, F. N., Canterbury & York Society, x, 1913; Lincoln Record Society, xi, 1894.

SALISBURY

The Registers of Roger Martival, bishop of Salisbury, 1315-1330, ed. Edwards, Kathleen, Elrington, C. R., and Reynolds, Susan, 3 vols, Canterbury & York Society, lv, lvii, lix, 1959-63.

WINCHESTER

Wykeham's Register, ed. Kirby, T. F., 2 vols, Hants. Record Society, xi, 1896-9.

WORCESTER

The Register of Walter Reynolds, Bishop of Worcester, 1308-1313, ed. Wilson, R. A., Worcs. Historical Society, xxxix, 1927; Dugdale Society, ix, 1928.

A Calendar of the Register of Wolstan de Bransford, Bishop of Worcester, 1339-1349, ed. Haines, R. M., Worcs. Historical Society, new series iv, 1966; Historical MSS Commission, Joint Publications Series, ix, 1966.

THOMPSON, A. HAMILTON. The registers of the archdeaconry of Richmond, 1361-1442, *Yorks. Archaeological Journal*, xxv (1919), pp. 129-268.

Visitation Articles and Injunctions of the Period of the Reformation, 1536-1575, ed. Frere, W. H., and Kennedy, W. M., 3 vols, Alcuin Club Collections, xiv-xvi, 1910.

Visitations in the Diocese of Lincoln, 1517-1531, ed. Thompson, A. Hamilton, 3 vols, Lincoln Record Society, xxxiii, xxxv, xxxvii, 1940-7.

Visitations of Religious Houses in the Diocese of Lincoln, 1420-1449, ed. Thompson, A. Hamilton, 3 vols, Canterbury & York Society, xvii, xxiv, xxxiii, 1915-27; Lincoln Record Society, vii, xiv, xxi, 1914-29.

(c) Records of secular cathedrals

Calendar of the MSS of the Dean and Chapter of Wells, 2 vols, London, Historical MSS Commission, 1907-14.

Chapter Acts of the Cathedral Church of Lincoln, 1520-1559, ed. Cole, R. E. G., 3 vols, Lincoln Record Society, xii, xiii, xv, 1915-20.

Dean Cosyn and Wells Cathedral Miscellanea, ed. Watkin, A., Somerset Record Society, lvi, 1941.

Early Charters of the Cathedral Church of St Paul, London, ed. Gibbs, Marion, Royal Historical Society, Camden third series, lviii, 1939.

The Register of St Osmund, ed. Jones, W. H. R., 2 vols, London, Rolls Series, 1883-4.

Registrum Statutorum et Consuetudinum Ecclesiae Cathedralis Sancti Pauli Londiniensis, ed. Simpson, W. S., London, 1873.

The Statutes of the Cathedral Church of Durham, ed. Thompson, A. Hamilton, Surtees Society, cxliii, 1929.

M*

Statutes of Lincoln Cathedral, ed. Bradshaw, H., and Wordsworth, C., 3 vols, Cambridge, 1892-7.

(d) Records of the religious orders

BIHL, P. M. Statuta generalia ordinis edita, *Archivum Franciscanum Historicum*, xxxiv (1941), pp. 13-94, 284-358.

CARLINI, A. Constitutiones generales ordinis fratrum minorum anno 1316 Assisii conditae, ibid., iv (1911), pp. 269-302, 508-36.

Chapters of the English Augustinian Canons, ed Salter, H. E., Oxford Historical Society, lxxiv, 1922.

Chapters of the English Black Monks, 1215-1540, ed. Pantin, W. A., 3 vols, Royal Historical Society, Camden third series, xlv, xlvii, liv, 1931-7.

Collectanea Anglo-Premonstratensia, ed. Gasquet, F. A., 3 vols, ibid., vi, x, xii, 1904-6.

EVANS, S. J. A. Ely chapter ordinances and visitation records, 1241-1515, *Camden Miscellany XVII*, ibid., lxiv, 1940.

Extracts from the Account Rolls of the Abbey of Durham, ed. Fowler, J. T., 2 vols, Surtees Society, xcix-c, 1898-9.

Gesta Abbatum Monasterii Sancti Albani, ed. Riley, H. T., 3 vols, London, Rolls Series, 1867-9.

Literae Cantuarienses, the letter books of the monastery of Christ Church, Canterbury, ed. Sheppard, J. Brigstocke, 3 vols, London, Rolls Series, 1887-9.

The Monastic Constitutions of Lanfranc, ed. Knowles, M. C., London, 1951.

Monumenta Historica Carmelitana, ed. Zimmerman, B., Lingen, 1905-7.

Monumenta Ordinis Fratrum Praedicatorum Historica, ed. Reichert, B. M., 14 vols, Rome and Stuttgart, 1897-1904.

Registrum Johannis Whethamstede, ed. Riley, H. T., 2 vols, London, Rolls Series, 1872-3.

The Rites of Durham, ed. Fowler, J. T., Surtees Society, cvii, 1903.

ROTH, F. *Sources for a History of the English Austin Friars*, reprinted from *Augustiniana*, Louvain, 1958-61.

SEARLE, W. G. *Christ Church, Canterbury*, Cambridge Antiquarian Society Publications, xxxiv, 1902.

Statuta Capitulorum Generalium Ordinis Cisterciensis, 1116-1786, ed. Canivez, J. M., 8 vols, Louvain, 1933-41.

(e) Modern works [*see also below, subsection 6*]

ASTON, Margaret E. *Thomas Arundel: a study of church life in the reign of Richard II*, Oxford, 1967.

BENNETT, H. S. Medieval ordination lists in the English episcopal registers, *Studies Presented to Sir Hilary Jenkinson*, ed. Davies, J. Conway, London, 1957, pp. 20-34.

BOWKER, MARGARET. *The Secular Clergy in the Diocese of Lincoln, 1495-1520* Cambridge, Studies in Medieval Life and Thought, new series, xiii, 1968.

COLVIN, H. M. *The White Canons in England*, Oxford, 1951.

DICKENS, A. G. *The English Reformation*, London, 1965.

EDWARDS, KATHLEEN. *The English Secular Cathedrals in the Middle Ages*, 2nd ed. Manchester, 1967.

EMDEN, A. B. *A Survey of Dominicans in England, 1268-1538*, Institutum Historicum FF Praedicatorum Romae ad S. Sabinae, Dissertationes Historicae, fasc. xviii. Rome, Istituto Storico Domenicano, Santa Sabina, 1967.

GABEL, LEONA C. *Benefit of Clergy in England in the Later Middle Ages*, Smith College Studies in History, xiv, Northampton, Mass., 1929.

HAINES, R. M. Aspects of the episcopate of John Carpenter, *Journal of Ecclesiastical History*, xix (1968), pp. 11-40.

HEATH, PETER. *The English Parish Clergy on the Eve of the Reformation*, London, 1969.

HUGHES, PHILIP. *The Reformation in England*, 3 vols, London, 1950-4.

KNOWLES, M. C. *The Monastic Order in England, 940-1216*, 2nd ed. Cambridge, 1963.

KNOWLES, M. C. *The Religious Orders in England*, 3 vols, Cambridge, 1948-1959.

KNOWLES, M. C., AND HADCOCK, R. N. *Medieval Religious Houses, England and Wales*, 2nd ed. London, 1971.

LITTLE, A. G. *Studies in English Franciscan History*, Manchester, 1917.

MOORMAN, J. R. H. *Church Life in England in the Thirteenth Century*, Cambridge, 1945.

POWER, EILEEN. *Medieval English Nunneries, c. 1275 to 1535*, Cambridge, 1922.

ROTH, F. *The English Austin Friars*, 1249-1538, New York, 1966.

THOMPSON, A. HAMILTON. *The English Clergy and their Organization in the Later Middle Ages*, Oxford, 1947.

5 Literary and social history

(a) Texts and documents

BENTLEY, SAMUEL. *Excerpta Historica, or, Illustrations of English History*, London, 1831.

CHAUCER, GEOFFREY. *The Works of Geoffrey Chaucer*, ed. Robinson, F. N., 2nd ed. London, 1957.

DUDLEY, EDMUND. *The Tree of the Commonwealth*, ed. Brodie, D. M., Cambridge, 1948.

England in the Reign of King Henry VIII: Part I, Starkey's Life and Letters, ed. Herrtage, S. J., London, EETS, extra series, xxxii, 1878.

The English Works of Wycliffe hitherto Unprinted, ed. Matthew, F. D., ibid., original series, lxxiv, 1880.

ERASMUS, DESIDERIUS. *Opus Epistolarum*, ed. Allen, P. S., 12 vols, Oxford, 1906-58.

FROISSART, JEAN. *Œuvres*, ed. Lettenhove, Kervyn de, 25 vols, Brussels, 1867-77.

GERALD OF WALES. *Giraldi Cambrensis Opera*, ed. Brewer, J. S., Dimock, J. F., and Warner, G. F., 8 vols, London, Rolls Series, 1861-91.

GREENE, R. L. *A Selection of English Carols*, Oxford, 1962.

GROSSETESTE, ROBERT. *Roberti Grosseteste, episcopi quondam Lincolniensis epistolae*, ed. Luard, H. R., London, Rolls Series, 1861.

HALL, EDWARD. *Chronicle Containing the History of England [from] Henry IV to Henry VIII*, London, 1809.

HIGDEN, RANULF. *Polychronicon Ranulphi Higden monachi Cestrensis; together with the English translations*, ed. Babington, C. and Lumby, J. R., 9 vols, London, Rolls Series, 1865-6.

Italian Relation of England, ed. Sneyd, Charlotte A., Camden Society, xxxvii, 1847.

Itineraria Simonis Simeonis et Willelmi de Worcestre, ed. Nasmith, J., Cambridge, 1778.

JOCELIN OF BRAKELOND. *The Chronicle of Jocelin of Brakelond*, ed. Butler, H. E., London, 1949.

LANGLAND, WILLIAM. *Piers the Plowman*, ed. Skeat, W. W., 2 vols, Oxford, 1886, reissued 1924.

The Letter Book of Robert Joseph, monk-scholar of Evesham and Gloucester College, Oxford, 1530-33, ed. Aveling, H., and Pantin, W. A., Oxford Historical Society, new series, xix, 1967 for 1964.

Le Livre de Seyntz Medicines, ed. Arnould, E. J., Anglo-Norman Text Society, ii, 1940.

Manners and Meals in Olden Time, ed. Furnivall, F. J., London, EETS, original series, xxxii, 1868.

PACE, RICHARD. *De Fructu*, Basel, 1517.

The Paston Letters, 1422-1509, ed. Gairdner, J., 3 vols, London, 1872-5 and reprinted; 6 vols, London, 1904.

Paston Letters and Papers of the Fifteenth Century, ed. Davis, Norman, vol i Oxford, 1971.

REGINALD OF DURHAM. *Reginaldi monachi Dunelmensis libellus*, ed. Raine, J., Surtees Society, i, 1835.

RICKERT, EDITH. *Chaucer's World*, London, 1948.

RICKERT, EDITH. Extracts from a fourteenth-century account book, *Modern Philology*, xxiv (1926-7), pp. 111-19, 249-56.

ROBBINS, R. H. *Secular Lyrics of the Fourteenth and Fifteenth Centuries*, 2nd ed., Oxford, 1955.

SCATTERGOOD, V. J. *The Two Ways*: an unpublished religious treatise by Sir John Clanvowe, *English Philological Studies*, x (1967), pp. 33-56.

SCATTERGOOD, V. J. 'The Boke of Cupide' – an edition, ibid., ix (1965), pp. 47-83.

SCATTERGOOD, V. J. The authorship of 'The Boke of Cupide', *Anglia*, lxxxii (1964), pp. 137-49.

Songs, Carols and other Miscellaneous Pieces from the Balliol MS 354, Richard Hill's Commonplace-Book, ed. Dyboski, R., London, EETS, extra series, ci, 1908.

STARKEY, THOMAS. *A Dialogue between Reginald Pole and Thomas Lupset*, ed. Burton, Kathleen M., London, 1948.

The Stonor Letters and Papers, 1290-1483, ed. Kingsford, C. L., 2 vols, Royal Historical Society, Camden third series, xxix-xxx, 1919.

Wills:

    Calendar of Wills Proved and Enrolled in the Court of Husting, London, 1258-1688, ed. Sharpe, R. R., 2 vols, London, 1889.

    Notes or Abstracts of the Wills in the Great Orphan Book and Book of Wills, Bristol, ed. Wadley, T. P., Bristol, Bristol and Gloucs. Archaeological Society, 1886.

    Testamenta Eboracensia, ed. Raine, J., 6 vols, Surtees Society, iv, xxx, xlv, liii, lxxix, cvi, 1836-1902.

    Testamenta Vetusta, being illustrations from wills of manners, customs, etc., ed. Nicolas, N. H., 2 vols, London, 1826.

(b) Modern general works

The Cambridge History of English Literature, ed. Ward, A. W. and Waller, A. R., 15 vols, Cambridge, 1907-27.

DEANESLY, MARGARET. *The Lollard Bible*, Cambridge, 1920.

GREEN, ALICE STOPFORD. *Town Life in the Fifteenth Century*, 2 vols, London, 1894.

HARRISON, F. LL. *Music in Medieval Britain*, 2nd ed. London, 1963.

HUNT, R. W. English learning in the late twelfth century, *Transactions of the Royal Historical Society*, 4th series, xix (1936), pp. 19-42.

KINGSFORD, C. L. *English Historical Literature in the Fifteenth Century*, Oxford, 1913.

KINGSFORD, C. L. *Prejudice and Promise in Fifteenth-Century England*, Oxford, 1925.

MCFARLANE, K. B. *The Nobility of Later Medieval England*, Oxford, 1973.

WARTON, THOMAS. *History of English Poetry from the Twelfth to the Close of the Sixteenth Century*, ed. Hazlitt, W. Carew, 4 vols, London, 1871.

WEISS, ROBERTO. *Humanism in England during the Fifteenth Century*, 3rd ed. Oxford, Medium Aevum Monographs, iv, 1967.

(c) Libraries and book collections

ATKINSON, R. L. A French Bible in England about the year 1322, *English Historical Review*, xxxviii (1923), pp. 248-9.

BATESON, MARY. *Catalogue of the Library of Syon Monastery, Isleworth*, Cambridge, 1898.

BIRLEY, R. The history of Eton College library, *The Library*, 5th series, xi (1956), pp. 231-61.

BORRAJO, E. M. The Guildhall library, *Library Association Record*, x (1908), pp. 380-4.

DILLON, VISCOUNT, AND HOPE, W. H. ST J. Inventory of the goods of Thomas, duke of Gloucester, *Archaeological Journal*, liv (1897), pp. 275-308.

GUNNER, W. H. Catalogue of books belonging to the college of St Mary, Winchester, in the reign of Henry VI, ibid., xv (1858), pp. 59-74.

HODNETT, E. *English Woodcuts, 1480-1535*, London, Bibliographical Society Monographs, xxii, 1935.

JAMES, M. R. *The Ancient Libraries of Canterbury and Dover*, Cambridge, 1903.

JAMES, M. R. Catalogue of the library of Leicester Abbey, *Transactions of Leics. Archaeological Society*, xix (1936-7), pp. 111-61, 377-435; xxi (1940-1941), pp. 1-88.

JAMES, M. R. [Eton] chapel inventories, *Etoniana*, xxv-xxxii (1920-3), especially xxviii (1921), pp. 442-4.

MADAN, F. The daily ledger of John Dorne, *Collectanea I*, ed. Fletcher, C. R. L., Oxford Historical Society, v, 1885, pp. 71-177.

SMITH, R. The library at Guildhall in the fifteenth and sixteenth centuries, *Guildhall Miscellany*, i (1952), pp. 3-9; vi (1956), pp. 2-6.

WEISS, ROBERTO. The earliest catalogues of the library of Lincoln College, *Bodleian Library Quarterly Record*, viii, no 94 (1937), pp. 343-59.

WILLIAMS, T. W. Gloucestershire medieval libraries, *Transactions of the Bristol and Gloucs. Archaeological Society*, xxxi (1908), pp. 78-189.

6 Local history

BENNET, E. K. Notes on the original statutes of the college . . . of Rushworth, Norfolk, *Norfolk Archaeology*, x (1888), pp. 50-64.

BLOMEFIELD, F. *An Essay Towards a Topographical History of the County of Norfolk* [continued by Parkin, C.], 11 vols, London, 1805-10.

BOUCHER, C. E. The Lond or Loud Brass in St Peter's Church, Bristol, *Transactions of the Bristol and Gloucs. Archaeological Society*, xxx (1907), pp. 265-72.

BOYLE, J. R. *The Early History of the Town and Port of Hedon*, Hull and York, 1895.

DALTON, J. N. *The Collegiate Church of Ottery St Mary*, Cambridge, 1917.

HASTED, E. *The History and Topographical Survey of the County of Kent*, 4 vols, Canterbury, 1778-99.

HOARE, R. C. *The History of Modern Wiltshire*, 14 parts, London, 1822-44.

HUTCHINS, J. *The History and Antiquities of the County of Dorset*, ed. Shipp, W., and Hodson, J. W., 4 vols, Westminster, 1861-73.

LEVETT, A. ELIZABETH. *Studies in Manorial History*, ed. Cam, Helen M., and others, Oxford, 1938.

LINDLEY, E. S. *Wotton under Edge, men and affairs of a Cotswold wool town*, London, 1962.

LYTE, SIR H. C. MAXWELL-. *A History of Dunster and of the Families of Mohun and Luttrell*, 2 vols, London, 1909.

NICOLSON, J., AND BURN, R. *The History and Antiquities of Westmorland and Cumberland*, 2 vols, London, 1777.

ROBERTSON, DORA H. Notes on some buildings in the city and close of Salisbury, *Wilts. Archaeological and Natural History Magazine*, xlviii (1937-9), pp. 1-30.

ROBERTSON, DORA H. *Sarum Close: a picture of domestic life . . . and the history of the choristers*, 2nd ed. Bath, 1970.

SAUNDERS, H. W. A history of Coxford Priory, *Norfolk Archaeology*, xvii (1908-10), pp. 284-370.

STENTON, F. M. *Norman London*, with a translation of William FitzStephen's *Description* by Butler, H. E., London, Historical Association Leaflets, xciii-iv, 1934.

STOW, JOHN. *A Survey of London*, ed. Kingsford, C. L., 2 vols, Oxford, 1908.

TESTER, P. J. Notes on the medieval chantry college at Cobham, *Archaeologia Cantiana*, lxxix (1964), pp. 109-20.

THOMPSON, A. HAMILTON. The statutes of the college of St Mary and All Saints, Fotheringhay, *Archaeological Journal*, lxxv (2nd series, xxv) (1918), pp. 241-309.

THRUPP, SYLVIA L. *The Merchant Class of Medieval London*, Chicago, 1948.

WEST, THOMAS. *The Antiquities of Furness*, 3rd ed. Ulverston, 1822.

WILLIAMS, G. A. *Medieval London: from Commune to Capital*, London, University of London Historical Studies, xi, 1963.

WILSON, J. Peculiar ordination of a Cumberland benefice, *Scottish Historical Review*, v (1907-8), pp. 297-303.

Index

NOTE – The schools listed in the index are those which occur in the main body of the text. The alphabetical list of schools, pp. 295-321, has not been indexed.

Abbot, John, mercer, 66, 203
Abergwili, Carms., college at, 267
Abingdon, Berks., abbey of, 226
    school at, 283
Acaster Selby, Yorks. W. R., school at, 78, 121, 268
Adam of Stratton, usurer, 51
Ælfric of Eynsham, scholar, 99
Aesop, *Fables* of, 104 n 1, 114
Alain de Lille, French poet, 104
    Liber Parabolarum of, 104-5, 113
Albinus, bishop of Ferns, 20
Alcock, John, bishop of Rochester, Worcester and Ely, 26-7, 62, 210
Aldwinkle, Northants., school at, 66, 274
Alexander III, Pope, 144
Alexander, prior of Canons Ashby, 172-3
Alexander de Villa Dei, grammarian, 89
    Doctrinale of, 89-90, 98, 103, 107, 112, 125, 126, 127
Alkborough, Richard, schoolmaster, 220
Alnwick, Northumberland, priory of, 241
    school at, 200
Alnwick, William, bishop of Lincoln, 67, 200, 241, 280
alphabet, study of, 60-2
Alwyn, Thomas, schoolmaster, 161
André, Bernard, humanist, 28
Anwykyll, John, schoolmaster, 107, 127, 156, 208
Appleby, Westmorland, corporation and school at, 204
apprentices, education of, 48
    Statute of (1406), 52

Aquinas, Thomas, theologian, 22-3
archdeacons, educational interests of, 146
Aristotle, philosopher, 22
Arnold, Richard, haberdasher, 47
Arthur, prince of Wales, 28, 111
Arundel, Thomas, bishop of Ely, archbishop of Canterbury, 25, 39, 143, 253-4, 322
Ascham, Roger, schoolmaster, 159
Ashby family, 220
Aubrey, John, antiquarian, 2 n 2
'Auctores Octo', 103-4, 126
augmentations, court of, 259-60, 277
Augustinian canons and education, 64-5, 136, 148, 149, 206, 236-9, 241-8, 250
Augustinian friars and education, 227-8, 231-2, 233
Austin, John, chaplain, 66
Avianus, Latin author, 102-3
Awre, Gloucs., school at, 170
Aylsham, Norfolk, school at, 136

Bacon, Roger, friar, 13, 87, 228
Bagby, John, schoolmaster, 218
Bakewell, Derbs., church of, 180
Banbury, Oxon., hospital and school at, 108, 121, 154-5, 279, 282
Barbour, Robert, schoolboy, 136
Barbour, William, schoolmaster, 54
Bardney, Lincs., abbey at, 25
Barkby, John, schoolmaster, 212
Barlow, William, bishop of St Davids, 267
Barton, Beds., manor of, 52
Barton-on-Humber, Lincs., vicar of, 82
Barton, John, French scholar, 74

355

Basing, Edmund, clerk, 234
Basingstoke, Hants., school at, 285
Bath, Som., cathedral priory at, 241, 259
    school at, 283, 284
Baynham family, 206
Beauchamp, Guy, earl of Warwick, 31
Beauchamp, Richard, earl of Warwick, 25-6,
    128-9
Beaufort, Henry, cardinal-bishop of Win-
    chester, 35, 122
Beaufort, Lady Margaret, 202, 222
Beaulieu, Hants., abbey of, 148
Beccles, Suffolk, school at, 95, 104, 118 n 3,
    119 n 2, 134, 148
Beckingham, Richard, canon lawyer, 121
Beckington, Thomas, bishop of Bath and
    Wells, 16, 19, 129, 188 n 1, 200
Bedford, school at, 170
Benedict XII, Pope, 238
Benedictines and education, 148, 156, 160,
    177-8, 179-80, 206, 224-6, 233-6, 237-51
Berkeley family, 150, 188-9, 206, plate 14
Berkhamsted, Herts., school at, 284 n 1
Beverley, Yorks. E.R., school at, 6, 101-2,
    119 n 2, 148, 170, 176, 192
Bibbesworth, Walter of, author, 32, 72
Bibles, 24, 31, 32, 46, 94
Bilborough, Notts., rector and school at, 220
Billingshurst, Sussex, guild and school at,
    205
Bingham, William, cleric, 153, 221-2
biography, medieval interest in, 134-9
Birchwood, Thomas, schoolboy, 136
Birmingham, War., school at, 284
bishops and education, 12, 15-20, 142-6, 148,
    169, 200-1, 240, 241, 242, 256, 263-4
bishops, registers of, 15-19
Blaby, John, landowner, 248
Blackburn, Lancs., school at, 202
Blackman, John, royal chaplain, 26
Blisworth, Northants., school at, 154 n 1
Blofield, Norfolk, school at, 144 n 5
Bocking, John, schoolmaster, 156
Bodyn, Thomas, apprentice, 48
Boniface IX, Pope, 232
Bonner, Edmund, bishop of London, 256,
    286
books: Bibles, *see* Bibles
    chronicles and histories, 25, 32, 47
    devotional and liturgical, 23, 25, 31-2, 46,
        62-3
    grammars, *see* grammar books
    hunting, 25
    miscellanies, 47
    romances, 23-4, 25, 31, 32
    schoolbooks, *see* schools, books used in
    theological, 25, 46, 84
Bordesley, Worcs., abbey of, 31

Boston, Lincs., guild and schools at, 54-5, 126,
    205, 215, 285
Boteler, Sir Thomas, of Bewsey, 203
Botesdale, Suffolk, school at, 148
boy-bishops, 131-2
Boys, William, abbot of Evesham, 249
Bracebridge, John, schoolmaster, 126
Brackendale, Nicholas of, grammarian, 96
Bradwell, Bucks., priory of, 245
Bransford, Wulstan, bishop of Worcester, 16
Brantingham, Thomas, bishop of Exeter, 16
Braughing, Herts., school at, 220
breakfast in bed, 138-9
Brecon, Christ's College, 267
Bredgar, Kent, college at, 100, 183-4
Bredgar, Robert, cleric, 183
Bridgnorth, Salop, corporation and school at,
    204
Bridgwater, Som., schools at, 66-7, 170, 179,
    261
Bridport, Dorset, school at, 95, 170
Bristol, Gloucs., Augustinian convent at, 231
    cathedral, 264-5
    civic administration, 45
    Franciscan convent at, 230
    House of Kalendars and library at, 84-5
    schools at, 120, 170, 215, 217, plate 9
        cathedral, 265, 269
        elementary, 68
        grammar book used in, 77, 95, 96, plate 3
        schoolmasters of, 22, 128, 130, plate 14
Brito, William, grammarian, 94
    dictionary of, 94, 97
Broc, William, monk, 236
Broke, John, of Braughing, 220
Bromsgrove, Worcs., school at, 280, 285
Bromwich, Richard, monk, 236
Brooke, Henry, schoolmaster, 219
Brougham, Lord, politician, 3
Bruton, Som., abbey of, 206
    school at, 69, 116 n 1, 133, 201, 206, 259-60,
        270, 284
Buckfast, Oxford student, 136
Buckingham, John, bishop of Lincoln, 183
Buckler, Walter, queen's secretary, 269
Bulkeley, Charles, gentleman, 136-7
Burghersh, Sir Bartholomew, knight, 183
Burley, Sir Simon, royal tutor, 23, 32
Burrough, Leics., rector and school at, 220
Burton-on-Trent, Staffs., abbey and school at,
    249 n 5
    college and school at, 195, 267, 269
Bury St Edmunds, Suffolk, abbey of, 67, 148
    abbots of, 135, 178, 184
    schools at, 65, 67, 119, 148, 170, 178, 184,
        248, 259-60, 270 n 5, 284
Bury, William, mercer, 83
Byland, Oxford student, 136

Caesar, classical author, 28, 114

Calthorpe, Ranulf, monk, 236

Cambridge, colleges and religious houses
  Augustinian convent, 232
  Buckingham College, 239
  Carmelite convent, 232
  Christ's College, 222
  Clare College, 185
  Dominican convent, 230
  Ely Hostel, 236
  Godshouse, 153, 221-2
  Jesus College, 210
  King's College, 198-200
  King's Hall, 217-18, 267
  Peterhouse, 185
  St Edmund's priory, 237
  St John's College, 207, 283
  Trinity College, 267
  glomery, master of, 146, 210
  grammar, study of, 96, 107, 152-3, 210
  schools at, 146, 170, 177, 208-10
    Jesus College school, 210
    Trinity College School, 267
  university of, 79, 146, 192
    degrees at, 127-8, 152-3

canon law, educational provisions of, 67, 142-4, 225, 237-9
  study of, 79-82, 234, 238, 242

Canons Ashby, Northants., priory of, 242-3

Canonsleigh, Devon, priory of, 53

canons regular, *see* Augustinians, Gilbertines, Premonstratensians

Canterbury, cathedral (new foundation), 263-5
  Christ Church cathedral priory, 100, 225, 234, 235, 236, 242, 243, 245, 250
  Franciscan convent, 230
  King's School, 263-4, 265, 266
  medieval schools at
    patrons of, 64, 145 n 1, 168-9
    St Martin's, 69
    scholars of, 120, 136
    schoolmasters of, 120, 121, 136, 154, 266
  St Augustine's abbey, 225, 236
  St Gregory's priory, 64, 168-9

Carlisle, Cumberland, cathedral at, 264-5
  schools at, 145 n 1, 181, 265

Carlisle, Nicholas, historian, 2-3

Carlton Husthwaite, Yorks. N.R., 136

Carmelite friars and education, 113, 227, 228 n 5, 232

Carpenter, John, bishop of Worcester, 84-5, 200, 212

Carpenter, John, common clerk of London, 44, 46, 83-4

Cartula, Latin poem, 104 n 1, 105

cathedrals monastic, schools of, 157, 168-9, 175, 214-15

secular, chancellors of, 79-86, 145, 173-4, 264
  choristers of, 175-6
  Henrician foundations, 262-6
  precentors of, 64
  schools of, 64, 79-86, 151, 153, 155, 157, 168, 173-6, 214-15, 262-6, 275, 286-7
  succentors of, 64

Catholicon, *see* John of Genoa

Catholicon Anglicum, dictionary, 97-8

Cato, Dionysius, pseudonymous writer, 102
  Distichs of Cato, 100, 102-4, 114, 127

Caxton, William, printer, 75, 106-7

Cayso, William, schoolboy, 127

Cecil, William, Lord Burghley, 84, 284

Chamber, William, of Northants., 66

chancery, royal, 37, 39-40, 41, 42

chantries and chantry priests, 160, 195-7, 207, 276-80
  certificates of (1546-8), 122, 162, 197, 204-5, 274, 277-9, 280
  commissioners to survey, 274, 276, 277
  dissolution of, 84, 85, 150, 268, 276-89
  schools of 6-7, 66, 68, 156, 256, 276-89
  history of, 195-7, 276-89
  origins of, 189-90, 294-5

chapel royal, education in, 217-19

Chaucer, Geoffrey, poet, 25, 33, 34, 60, 63, 117, 135

Chedworth, John, bishop of Lincoln, 200

Chedzoy, Som., church of, 180

Chelmsford, Essex, school at, 283, 284 n 1

Chertsey, John, schoolmaster, 96

Chester cathedral, 264

Chicheley, Henry, archbishop of Canterbury, 65, 188

Chichester, Sussex, schools at, 3, 29, 81, 116 n 1, 124, 160, 161, 174 n 1, 215

Childermas, festival, 131-2

childhood, medieval interest in, 135

Childrey, Berks., school at, 62, 207

Chipping Campden, Gloucs., school at, 122, 203, 206, 217

Chipping Norton, Oxon., guild and school at, 205

choristers, education of, 65-7, 129, 175-6, 177, 186, 194, 200, 245-7, 263, 270

Christchurch, Hants., priory and school at, 249 n 5

Church, and schools, 142-6, 174, 206-7, 225, 237-9, 252-6

Church, Richard, schoolmaster, 154

Cicero, Latin author, 28, 107, 108, 109, 111, 112, 114, 152

Cirencester, Gloucs., abbey of, 246-7
  school at, 170, 200, 206, 217, 259-60, 270 n 4

Cistercians and education, 148, 225, 233-5, 237-8, 244, 245

Clanvowe, Sir John, knight, 33
Clare, Suffolk, school at, 161
Claudian, Latin author, 102-3
Clement V, Pope, 237, 254
clergy, administrative work by, 40-1
  benefit of, 48-9
  education of, 12-21, 134, 160, 184, 220, 256-7
  interest in education by, 200-1, 213, 256-7, 275, 287
  minor orders of, 14, 120-1
  ordination of, 14-16
  teaching by, 66-7, 69, 220-1, 254, 256
  visitations of, 20, 256, 275, 286
  see also religious orders
Clerk, John, schoolmaster, 136
clerks, administrative, 36-41
  parish and holy-water, 65, 180-1
Clifford, Sir Lewis, knight, 33
Clitheroe, Lancs., school at, 285
Cobham, Kent, college and school at, 186-7
Cobham, John, Lord (d. 1408), 186
cock-fighting, 132, 137
Colchester, Essex, school at, 170
Coldwell, Robert, schoolmaster, 160
Cole, John, cleric, 241
Cole, John, of Wodyl, 127
Colet, John, dean of St Paul's
  Aeditio of, 111-13, 255
  educational views of, 69, 111, 113, 120, 122, 124, 130, 131, 132, 139, 156, 157
  New Learning and, 111-14
  portrait, plate 13
  refounds St Paul's school, 213-14
colleges and collegiate churches, 65-6, 184-5, 262-3, 268-70
  education in, 6, 65-6, 176-7, 184-90, 194-5, 267, 268-70
Coln Rogers, Gloucs., manor of, 51
Columbers family, 182
Combe, John, cleric, 201
Common Pleas, court of, 37-8
Coningsby, Humphrey, lawyer, 203
convocation of province of Canterbury (1529-30), 12, 221, 243, 254-6
  (1554), 285
Cook, John and Joan, of Gloucester, 206, 268, plate 15
Coote, John, London rector, 213, 221
Coppledyke, John, gentleman, 233
Cornwall, John, schoolmaster, 95, 155, 190
  Speculum Grammaticale of 95-6, 99
councils and synods, ecclesiastical
  Lateran III (1179), 80, 144, 174
  Lateran IV (1215), 80, 174
  London (1200), 144
  London (1237), 15
  Mâcon (581), 67

Oxford (1408), 143, 253-4
Vienne (1311), 237
Westminster (1138), 144
Westminster (1555-6), 286
see also convocation
Coventry, Carmelite convent at, 232
  cathedral priory at, 156-7
  corporation of, 204, 276
  Franciscan convent at, 231
  schools at, 156-7, 204, 215, 219, 268
Cox, Leonard, schoolmaster, 249, 260
Cox, Richard, archdeacon of Ely, 264
Coxford, Norfolk, priory of, 149
Coyfurelly, T., French canon, 72
crab apples, used as missiles, 139
Cranmer, Thomas, archbishop of Canterbury, 263-4, 276
Crediton, Devon, college and school at, 145, 270, 282
Crewkerne, Som., school at, 122, 201
Cromer, Norfolk, school at, 154 n 1
Cromwell, Thomas, royal servant, 262-4
Crosse, John, cleric, 196
Crowden, John, prior of Ely, 236
crown, English, and education, 148, 181, 197, 213, 228, 252-89
Croyden, Surrey, school at, 118 n 3, 119 n 2
Cuckfield, Sussex, school at, 124

Dacres, Robert, royal servant, 269
Dalston, Cumberland, rectory of, 181
Darcy, Richard, schoolmaster, 126, 161
Darcy, Thomas, Lord, 202-3
Darlington, Durham, school at, 288
Davy, Richard, schoolmaster, 161
Day, George, bishop of Hereford, 264
de la Pole, William, duke of Suffolk, 202
Denny, Anthony, royal servant, 214
Depeden, Sir John, knight, 48
Derby, school at, 170, 178
Deschamps, Eustace, poet, 33
Despauterius, Johannes, grammarian, 112-13
D'Ewes, Giles, schoolmaster, 28
dictamen, study of, 70, 76-7, 100, 101
dictionaries, Latin, 13, 92-4
  Latin and English, 97-8
Dingley family, 54
dissolution of the monasteries, and education, 258-62
Distichs of Cato, see Cato
Doctrinale, see Alexander de Villa Dei
Dominican friars and education, 32, 83, 97, 226-30, 233
Donatus, Aelius, grammarian, 88
  Ars Minor of, 88-9; mentioned, 69, 74, 96-7, 98, 106-7, 108, 112, 127, 183, 187, 228
Doncaster, Yorks. W.R., school at, 145
Donne, Lady Joan, plate 1

Dorne, John, bookseller, 112, 127
Dove, R., author, 74
Dover, Kent, priory of, 250
    school at, 170
Dowman, Thomas, benefactor, 284
Droxford, John, bishop of Bath and Wells, 19, 180
Druett, Peter, schoolmaster, 240
Drury, John, schoolmaster, 104
Dudley, Edmund, royal servant, 85-6, 207, 222-3
Dunfermline, Scotland, school at, 163
Dunstable, Beds., school at, 135, 170
Dunwich, Suffolk, school at, 148, 170
Durham, cathedral priory, 65, 161, 236, 246
    almonry school, 181, 244-5
    cloister school, 239-40, 242, 243
    song school, 246-7
    cathedral (new foundation), 263-5
    schools at, 66, 145 n 1, 181, 214, 246, 265, 266, 286
Dyer, John, schoolmaster, 246
Dymock, Roger, theologian, 24

Eccleston, Thomas of, friar, 230
Eclogue of Theodulus, poem, 102-4, 113
Edmund of Abingdon, Saint, archbishop of Canterbury, 129
Edmund, earl of Cornwall, 235
Edmunds, Henry, schoolmaster, 247
Edmunds, John, cleric, 201
education, aspects of in medieval times, 1
    hostility to, 192-3
    religious, 62, 104-5, 114, 121, 130, 254, 258, 286
    social, 105-6, 114, 127-9
Edward I, King, 22 n 5, 181
Edward II, King, 22 n 5, 23, 198, 218
Edward III, King, 23, 24, 74
Edward IV, King, 26, 158, 199
Edward V, King, 22 n 5, 26-7, plate 2
Edward VI, educational and religious policies of the reign of, 157, 158, 159, 196, 210, 260, 266, 267, 276-85
Edward the Black Prince, 22 n 5, 24, 38
Edward, prince of Wales, son of Henry VI, 22 n 5, 26
Edward, duke of York (d. 1415), 194
Eglesfield, Robert of, chaplain, 185
Eleanor of Aquitaine, Queen, 226
Elizabeth I, educational and religious policies of, 158, 287-9
Eltham, Kent, palace at, 25
Elwyn, John, chaplain, 125
Ely, Cambs., archdeacon of, 146
    cathedral priory, 236, 241, 243, 244, 245
    cathedral (new foundation), 264
    school at, 145

Elyot, Sir Thomas, author, 34, 159, 162
Emden, A.B., historian, xiii, 7, 293
English language, use of, 42-3, 45-8, 96-8, 101
Equivoca, see Synonyma
Erasmus, Desiderius, scholar, 111, 112, 113, 114, 123, 129
Eton, Bucks., college and school at, 116 n 1, 129, 188, 202, 276
    curriculum, 69, 98, 100-1, 109, 111, 112, 114, 117, 124, 132, 133-4
    foundation and history, 197, 198-200
    library, 125
    scholars, 100-1, 120, 121, 122, 133-4
    schoolmasters, 121, 129, 153-4, 156, 157, 161
Everal, William, friar, 235
Evesham, Worcs., abbey of, 160, 240, 248-9, 250-1, 262
    school at, 160, 248-9, 259-60, 270 n 3
Évrard of Béthune, grammarian, 90
    Grecismus of, 90, 107, 125, 126, 127, 250
Ewelme, Oxon., school at, 70, 120, 202, plate 6
exchequer, royal, 37, 42
    court of, 285
Exeter, Devon, Franciscan convent, 231
    St John's hospital, 182-3, 261
    schools at, 64, 120, 135, 146, 156-7, 172, 182-3, 261
Exton, Richard, schoolmaster, 190 n 2
Eye, Suffolk, priory of, 148
Eyford, Gloucs., church of, 249
Eyre, Simon, draper, 78, 213

Fabyan, Robert, chronicler, 47
Facetus, Latin poems entitled, 105
Fairchild, John, administrator, 79
Farceux, Robert, schoolmaster, 248
Faringdon, Berks., school at, 148
Faringdon, Hugh, abbot of Reading, 249
Farlington, Simon of, archdeacon of Durham, 181
Farnworth, Lancs., school at, 154 n 1, 259, 261, 270 n 3
Farthinghoe, Northants., school at, 66, 203, 206
Fastolf, Sir John, knight, 41, 50
Faversham, Kent, abbey of, 206, 241, 260
    schools at, 68, 206, 241, 259-60, 270 n 4
Fayred, Robert, schoolboy, 136
Felaw, Richard, merchant, 196, 203
Ferrers, Thomas, son of the earl of Derby, 18
Ferriby, John, royal servant, 203
Fettiplace, William, gentleman, 62
Fincham, Norfolk, school at, 144 n 5
FitzJames, Richard, bishop of London, 69, 81-2, plate 12

FitzNeal, Richard, bishop of London, 173
FitzRalph, Richard, archbishop of Armagh, 228
FitzRichard, John, schoolboy, 48
FitzRoy, Henry, duke of Richmond and Somerset, 322
FitzStephen, William, biographer, 130-2, 169
Fladbury, Worcs., rector of, 21
Fleming, Robert, humanist, 106
Floretus, Latin poem, 104 n 1
Foderley, Thomas, schoolmaster, 247
football, 132
Forde, Dorset, abbey of, 244, 259
Fortescue, Sir John, chief justice, 26
Fosse, Thomas, schoolmaster, 128
Fotheringhay, Northants., college and school at, 194, 268
Francis, protégé of the duke of Buckingham, 137
Franciscan friars and education, 83, 227, 228, 230-1, 233
French language, decline of, in England, 73-4
  grammars of, 71-5
  study and use of, in England, 23-5, 28, 32, 41-3, 45-8, 53, 71-7, 264
friars and education, 5-6, 83, 226-33
friars, *see* Augustinians, Carmelites, Dominicans, Franciscans
Froissart, Jean, chronicler, 23-4, 74
Furness, Lancs., abbey of, 244, 245
Furnivall, F. J., historian, 3-4

Garrard, Elizabeth, schoolgirl, 54
Gascoigne, Thomas, theologian, 256
Gateshead, Durham, hospital of, 181
Gaunte, John, schoolboy, 232
Gaywood, John, merchant, 130
gentry, education of, *see* nobility and gentry
'Geoffrey the Englishman', 91
Geoffrey, friar of King's Lynn, 97, 250
  Promptorium Parvulorum of, 97, 250
Geoffrey of Maine, schoolmaster, 178
Gerald of Wales, scholar, 135, 226
Giffard, Sir John, of Brimpsfield, 235
Giggleswick, Yorks. W.R., school at, 284
Gilbert, Robert, bishop of London, 212
Gilbertine canons and education, 237
Giles of Rome, author, 23
Giles, John, schoolmaster, 27
Gillingham, William, monk, 242
Glasgow, Dominican convent at, 230
Glastonbury, Somerset, abbey and schools at, 121, 241, 244
glomery, master of, *see* Cambridge
Gloucester, cathedral, 264
  Franciscan convent, 231
  Lanthony priory near, 148-9, 154, 246, 250, 268

St Oswald's priory, 148-9, 245
St Peter's abbey, 51, 226, 234, 247
schools at, 170, 215, 217, 245
  Crypt, 206, 268
  fees, 118 n 3
  King's, 265
  patronage of, 148-9, 154
  St Nicholas, 203
  schoolhouse, 120, 156-7
  schoolmasters, 121, 135, 154, 161, 226
Gloucester, Thomas, royal servant, 203
Gloucestershire, schools in, 4, 217, 278, 285
Godmersham, Richard, monk, 242
Gower, John, poet, 47
grammar, French, *see* French language
grammar, Latin, decline of alleged in later middle ages, 95-6, 151-3, 208, 221-3
  degrees in, 101, 127-8, 151-3
  grammars and dictionaries, 77, 97, 100, 124-7
  importance of in medieval times, 87-8
  knowledge of by clergy, 12-21, 224-43
  knowledge of by laymen, 22-9, 32, 34-5, 41-3, 45-8
  knowledge of by women, 53
  literature read in schools, 102-14
  study of, 88-115, 249-51
  speaking of, 101
grammar schools, *see* schools, grammar
Grandisson, John, bishop of Exeter, 62, 98, 143, 180, 182, 186
Grantham, Lincs., school at, 284 n 1
Gray of Heton, Sir Thomas, chronicler, 32
Gray, William, bishop of Lincoln, 242
Great Malvern, Worcs., priory of, 262
Great Shelford, Cambs., church of, 210
Grecismus, *see* Évrard of Béthune
Greek, study of, 263, 265
Green, Alice Stopford, historian, 4
Gregory, William, skinner, 47
Gregory IX, Pope, 67, 144
Grey, Henry, duke of Suffolk, 219
Grey, Thomas, 2nd marquess of Dorset, 35-6, 219-20
Grey, Thomas, priest, 136
Greyndour family, 196, 203, 206
Grosseteste, Robert, bishop of Lincoln, 12, 17-18, 87
  Stans puer ad mensam attributed to, 106, 114
Guadel, Clement, friar, 228
Guarino of Verona, humanist, 28
Guildford, Surrey, Dominican convent at, 230
  school at, 170, 215, 284
guilds, religious, and education, 204-5
Guisborough, Yorks. N.R., priory and school at, 145, 170, 243, 248
Guyldesburgh, Thomas, schoolmaster, 160

Hadleigh, Suffolk, school at, 145
Hales, John, of Coventry, 267
Hall, John, of Lewes, 205
Hambury, Richard of, schoolmaster, 95
Hamelyn, John, schoolmaster, 154
Hamo of Gloucester, schoolmaster, 135, 226
Hamundson, John, schoolmaster, 126
Hanley, John, benefactor, 125
Hanney, Thomas, grammarian, 96
  Memoriale Juniorum of, 96
Harleston, Norfolk, school at, 144 n 5
Harset, Robert, clothmaker, 207
Hastings, Sussex, college and school at, 6, 176
Haverfordwest, Pembs., school at, 144
Hazleshaw, Walter, bishop of Bath and Wells, 180
Heath, Nicholas, bishop of Worcester, 264
Hebrew, study of, 263
Hedon, Yorks. E.R., school at, 125, 170, 192
Helmsley, Yorks. N.R., school at, 170
Henley, Walter of, author, 32
Henna, Jewess of Exeter, 135-6
Henry I, King, 22
Henry II, King, 22
Henry III, King, 119
Henry IV, King, 25, 146
Henry V, King, 23, 25, 35, 117, 198
Henry VI, King, 128-9, 157
  education of, 22 n 5, 25-6
  educational interests of, 197, 198-9, 221
Henry VII, King, 27-8, 199
Henry VIII, King, education of, 23, 28-9
  educational and religious policies of, 86, 157, 158, 186, 195, 201, 242, 256-74
Henry of Blois, bishop of Winchester, 169
Henry of Grosmont, duke of Lancaster, 32
Henry of Huntingdon, chronicler, 64-5
Henryson, Robert, schoolmaster and poet, 163
Hereford, Franciscan convent at, 230
  schools at, 64, 81, 151, 172
Hexton, Herts., manor of, 51
Heytesbury, Wilts., school at, 202
Higden, Ranulf, chronicler, 73
Higham Ferrers, Northants., college and school at, 65, 146-8, 220 n 7, 268-9, 270 n 3
Hill, Richard, grocer, 47, 140
Hitchin, Herts., Carmelite convent at, 232
Hoccleve, Thomas, poet, 23, 41
Hody family, 193
Holbach, David, lawyer, 203
Holcot, Robert, friar, 61
Holt, John, schoolmaster, 28-9, 110, 219, plate 5
Homer, classical author, 28
Hone, William, schoolmaster, 29
Horace, Latin author, 107, 112, 114, 127

Horman, William, schoolmaster, 63, 111, 133
hornbooks, 61-2
Hornby, Lancs., school at, 202
hospitals and education, 179, 182, 261-2
House, Walter, king's ward, 35
households, administration of, 36-41, 76-7, 79
households, lay, 36, 38-41
  education in, 158-9, 219-20, 222, 321-2
household, royal, 35, 36-7, 42, 321
  education in, 158, 217-19
Howden, Yorks., school at, 65
Hugutio of Pisa, grammarian, 93
  Derivationes of, 93, 97, 125
Hull, Yorks. E.R., school at, 215
Humbert of Romans, friar, 226
Humphrey, duke of Gloucester, 25
Hungerford, Robert, Lord Hungerford and Moleyns, 35
Hungerford, Walter, Lord, treasurer, 202
Hunt, R. W., historian, xiii, 7, 95 n 1, 151
Huntingdon, priory of, 64-5, 148
  schools at, 64-5, 148, 161, 170
Hurst, Berks., chaplain of, 20
Hyet, Isabel, benefactress, 207

Ing, Hugh, archbishop of Dublin, 188
institutions to benefices, 16-19
Ipswich, Suffolk, college and school at, 112, 114, 118 n 3, 121, 143, 188, 196, 201-2, 204, 215, 255
  corporation of, 204
  Dominican convent at, 230
Ireton, Ralph, bishop of Carlisle, 181
Isabel, duchess of York (d. 1393), 33
Isidore of Seville, scholar, 92
  Liber Etymologiarum of, 92, 125, 126
Islip, Simon, archbishop of Canterbury, 236
Italy, Renaissance in, 106-7
Ive, William, cleric, 83

Jane, Thomas, bishop of Norwich, 188 n 1
Januensis, see John of Genoa
Jersey, Channel Is., schools in, 203
Jocelin of Brakelond, chronicler, 135
John XXII, Pope, 24
John, duke of Bedford, 25
John of Garland, grammarian, 90-1, 139
  Synonyma ascribed to, *see Synonyma*, plate 4
John of Gaunt, duke of Lancaster, 25, 38, 146
John of Genoa, grammarian, 92
  Catholicon of, 92-3, 97, 125, 126
Joliffe, Thomas, priest, 205
Jordan, W. K., historian, 7
Joseph, Robert, monk of Evesham, 21, 240, 250-1
Juvencus, Latin author, 113

Kelk, Yorks. E.R., school at, 148
Kellway, Robert, royal servant, 279-80
Kemp, John, archbishop of Canterbury, 269
Keston, Roger, schoolmaster, 210
Kidderminster, Richard, abbot of Winchcombe, 242
Kilwardby, Robert, archbishop of Canterbury, 87
kings of England, education and literacy of, 21-9
King's Bench, court of, 37
Kingsbury Episcopi, Som., church of, 180
Kingscote, John, bishop of Carlisle, 188 n 1
King's Lynn, Norfolk, Augustinian convent at, 231
    burgesses of, 276
    Dominican convent at, 97, 230
Kingsmill, William, scrivener, 75, 77
King's Norton, Worcs., school at, 122, 280
Kingston-on-Thames, Surrey, school at, 69
Kinoulton, Notts., school at, 170
Knight, William, bishop of Bath and Wells, 188 n 1
Knighton, Henry, chronicler of Leicester, 13
Kyme, Lincs., priory of, 241
Kyo, Durham, manor of, 181

Lactantius, Latin author, 113
laity and education, 146-8, 149-50, 158-9, 178, 198, 202-6, 219-20, 241, 248
Lancaster, school at, 116 n 1, 124, 170, 215
Lanfranc, archbishop of Canterbury, 64, 168-9, 225
Langham, Simon, bishop of Ely, 82
Langland, William, author
    Piers Plowman of, 13, 40, 128, 193, 207
Langley, Thomas, bishop of Durham, 66, 214, 246
Langton, Thomas, bishop of Winchester, 219, 322
Lanthony, Gloucs., priory of, *see* Gloucester
Latimer, Hugh, bishop of Worcester, 159, 256, 262, 268
Latin, *see* grammar
'latins', 98-9
Launceston, Cornwall, priory and school at, 180
Launde, Leics., priory of, 261
lawyers, common, interest in education of, 203
    literacy of, 42-3
Leach, A. F., historian, 3-7, 52 n 1
Ledbury, Herefs., school at, 118
Leicester, abbey of, 249 n 5, 250
    Augustinian convent at, 231
    Franciscan convent at, 230
    school at, 170, 249 n 5
Leighton Buzzard, Bucks., school at, 161

Leland, John, schoolmaster, 95-6, 151, 155, 186, 190, 208
Leominster, Herefs., school at, 285
Lestrange family, 220
Lever, Thomas, divine, 283
Lewes, Sussex, school at, 96, 215, 259, 261, 270 n 3
libraries, of laity, 24-5, 31-2
    public, 83-5
    of religious houses, 25, 124, 250
    of schools, *see* schools, libraries of
licences to teach, 144-8, 152, 286-7
Lichfield, Staffs., schools at, 64, 214-15
Lichfield, William, cleric, 213
Lily, William, schoolmaster, 111-12, 114, 214, 255, 257
'Lily's Latin grammar', 112-13, 257-8
Linacre, Thomas, humanist, 111, 112, 113
Lincoln, Augustinian convent at, 231-2
    cathedral choristers of, 175-6
    corporation of, 204
    Dominican convent at, 230
    schools at, 64, 66, 79, 81, 82, 104, 126, 151, 172, 174 n 1, 175-6, 179, 183, 287
Lincolnshire, schools in, 145, 190-1
literacy, of administrators and lawyers, 36-43, clergy, 12-21
    kings and princes, 21-9
    merchants, craftsmen, artisans, 43-50
    nobility and gentry, 29-36
    villeins, 50-2
    women, 52-5
literature, reading of, in schools, 102-14
Liverpool, Lancs., school at, 196
Livy, Latin author, 28
Lollards and Lollardy, 13, 24, 33, 41, 85, 143, 253-4
Londe, Robert, schoolmaster, plates 3, 9, 10
London, churches and religious houses
    All Hallows the Great, 213
    Augustinian convent, 231
    Carmelite convent, 232
    Dominican convent, 228-9, 230
    Franciscan convent, 230-1
    St Andrew, Holborn, 213
    St Bartholomew, priory of, 131, 212
    St Benedict Fink, 212
    St Gregory, 64
    St Mary Colechurch, 213
    St Paul's cathedral, 124-5
    St Peter, Cornhill, 213
    St Thomas of Acon, 213
    civic administration of, 44-5
    Guildhall Library, 83-4
    guilds and companies, 48, 206, 213, 229, 262
    inns of court, 8, 36, 43, 77, 79, 134
    schools of, in general, 130-2, 149, 169, 190, 210-14

London, schools of—*continued*
  Christ's Hospital, 214
  Cornhill, 210
  Leadenhall, 213
  Merchant Taylors', 214
  St Anthony's, 131, 200, 212
  St Dunstan in the East, 212
  St Martin-le-Grand, 129-30, 169, 210, 212, 214
  St Mary Arches, 169, 210, 212, 214
  St Paul's
    almonry school, 124-5
    grammar school before Colet, 151, 155, 168, 173, 210, 212
    grammar school of Colet
      curriculum of, 63, 69, 109, 111, 113-14, 255
      foundation of, 213-14
      organization of, 120, 122, 123, 124, 130, 132, 133
      schoolmasters of, 121, 154, 155, 157-8, 286
      statutes of, 63, 69, 116 n 1, 120, 124, 130, 131, 132, 133, 157-8
    song school, 64
    theology school, 81-3
  St Thomas of Acon, 131, 213, 214, 261-2, 270 n 3
  other schools in, 54-5, 78, 190 n 2, 212
Long Melford, Suffolk, school at, 207
Louth, Lincs., school at, 284 n 1
Lucan, classical author, 28
Lucian, classical author, 114
Ludlow, Salop, school at, 283, 284 n 1
Luttrell family, 219, 322
Luttrell, Robert, cleric, 237
Lyndwood, William, canonist, 254
Lynn, William, bishop of Chichester, 81
Lyster, Robert, schoolmaster, 160

Macclesfield, Cheshire, school at, 154, 284 n 1
Maghfield, Gilbert, merchant, 45-6
Maidstone, Kent, school at, 284
Maitland, F. W., historian, 5
Maldon, Essex, Carmelite convent at, 232
  school at, 118 n 3
Malmesbury, Wilts., school at, 170
Malpas, Cheshire, school at, 116 n 1, 154 n 1
Malton, Yorks. N.R., school at, 170
Manchester, Lancs., school at, 70, 116 n 1, 124, 132, 133, 156, 255
Mancinelli of Velletri, Antonio, grammarian 106-7
Mancini, Dominic, humanist, 27
Manorbier, Pembs., castle at, 135
Mantuanus, Baptista, poet, 113, 114, 251
Map, Walter, satirist, 22
Maresflete, Matilda, schoolmistress, 55

Markenfield, Ninian, 36
Markenfield, Sir Thomas, 36
Marlborough, Wilts., school at, 284
Martival, Roger, bishop of Salisbury, 19
Martyn, John, schoolmaster, 161-2
Mary I, Queen, educational and religious policies of, 285-7
Mary, daughter of Henry VII, 29
Mason, Sir John, royal servant, 283
Matthew of Vendôme, poet, 104 n 1
Maximian, Latin author, 102-3
Mayhew, Richard, bishop of Hereford, 188 n 1
Maynard, John, surveyor, 279
Medulla Grammatice, dictionary, 97
Melanchthon, Philip, scholar, 113
Mellers, Agnes, foundress, 206
Melton, John, clerk, 134
Melton, William, chancellor of York, 13
merchants, educational interests of, 203
  literacy and education of, 43, 74-5
Merton, Walter of, chancellor, 185
Methley, Yorks. W.R., manor of, 52
Mettingham, Suffolk, college of, 134
Middleton, Lancs., school at, 288
Mildenhall, Suffolk, school at, 148
Mildmay, Sir Walter, royal servant, 279-80
monks and education, 5-6, 158, 206, 224-6, 233-51, 258
  see also Benedictines, Cistercians, and religious orders
Montague, John, earl of Salisbury, 33
More, Sir Thomas, statesman, 29, 162
Morpeth, Northumberland, school at, 284
Mortimer, Edmund, earl of March, 65
mortmain, licences for, 197, 288
Morton, schoolmaster of London, 210
Morton, John, archbishop of Canterbury, 110, 219, 321
Mosellanus, Peter, grammarian, 112
Mounchensy, Denise de, noblewoman, 72
Muscham, John, schoolmaster, 151

Naundes, Richard of, cleric, 179
Neckham, Alexander, scholar, 94 n 2, 135, 178
Neel, John, cleric, 213
Nevill, Ralph, bishop of Chichester, 81, 179
Neville, Joan, countess of Westmorland, 25
Newark, Notts., school at, 116 n 1, 124, 133, 145, 192
Newburgh, Yorks. N.R., priory of, 136
Newcastle-on-Tyne, Dominican convent at, 230
Newland, Gloucs., school at, 116 n 1, 120, 280
  foundation of, 197, 203
  organization of, 70, 118 n 3, 124, 133, 196
  patrons of, 203, 206
  Reformation and, 285
  scholars of, 158, 207

New Learning in England, 25, 28, 106-15, 158-9, 162, 250-1, 253
Newnham, Beds., priory of, 241
Newport Pagnell, Bucks., school at, 161
Newsham, John, schoolmaster, 128
Nicholas, Saint, as patron of scholars, 101, 131
nobility and gentry, education and literacy of, 29-36, 117, 218-20, 248
  interest in education of, 202-3
Norfolk, schools in, 7 n 2, 144, 149, 217
Norham, Northumberland, schools at, 161, 170
North, Edward, royal servant, 214
Northallerton, Yorks. N.R., schools at, 65
Northampton, Franciscan convent at, 231
  schools at, 79, 170, 172-3, 177
North Cadbury, Som., church of, 61
North Elmham, Norfolk, possible school at, 220
Norton near Baldock, Herts., manor of, 51
Norwich, Augustinian convent at, 231
  bishops of, and education, 143, 144
  cathedral priory of, 246
  cathedral (new foundation), 266
  Dominican convent at, 230
  Franciscan convent at, 231
  schools at, 144, 145, 149, 179, 266, 282
Nottingham, schools at, 78, 118 n 3, 123, 145, 156, 170, 192, 206, 215, 220
  university, Middleton MSS at, 127
Nottingham, William of, friar, 230
Nottinghamshire, schools in, 145, 190-2
Nugge, Henry, schoolmaster, 150
Nuneaton, War., school at, 284
nuns and nunneries, education of and in, 52-4
Nyweton, clerk of Exeter, 135-6

O., Simon, Oxford master, 77
oblates, monastic, 224-5
'Octo Auctores', *see* 'Auctores Octo'
Ombersley, Worcs., vicar of, 21
Ortus Vocabulorum, dictionary, 97
Orum, John, cleric, 83
Osbern of Gloucester, grammarian, 94 n 2
Osgoodby, Henry, schoolmaster, 136
Osmund, bishop of Salisbury, 168
Osney, Berks., cathedral at, *see* Oxford cathedral
Oswestry, Salop, school at, 203, 206
Ottery St Mary, Devon, college and school at, 186, 268-70, 270 n 3
Otto, Cardinal, 18
Ovid, Latin author, 18, 28, 108, 111, 112, 114
Oxford, cathedral at (Osney), 264-5
  schools at (medieval), 116 n 1, 170, 190, 207-8
    curricula of, 73-4, 95-6, 98, 126-7

fees of, 118
matriculation at, 120
patrons of, 146
scholars of, 126-7, 129, 161-2
schoolmasters of, 95-6, 128, 146, 151, 155, 161-2, 185, 208
Magdalen College school, 101, 107-11, 119, 129, 138, 154, 156, 200, 201, 207, 208, 276
  Vulgaria of, 101, 110-11, 117, 119, 129, 133, 138-9, 163
Osney cathedral school, 265
study of grammar at, 95-6
university of, 73, 77, 79, 146, 172-3, 177, 190, 228
colleges and halls of
  Augustinian convent, 232
  Canterbury College, 236
  Carmelite convent, 232
  Christ Church, 265-6
  Dominican convent, 230, 233
  Durham College, 236, 242
  Exeter College, 73, 182
  Franciscan convent, 230, 231
  Gloucester College, 235-6
  Ing Hall, 208
  Lincoln College, 106
  Lyon Hall, 208
  Magdalen College, 107, 207
  Merton College, 118, 119, 127, 185
  New College, 28, 107, 187
  Oriel College, 73
  Peckwater Inn, 208
  Queen's College, 35, 73, 102 n 1, 185-6, 207
  Rewley Abbey, 235
  St Bernard's College, 136, 239
  St Cuthbert's Hall, 208
  St Hugh's Hall, 208
  St Mary College, 239
  Tackley Inn, 208
  University College, 35
  White Hall, 208
  degrees in, 151-5, 185
  nobility and gentry at, 35-6
Oxford, John of, author, 76
Oxford, John, schoolmaster, 161
Oxfordshire, chantries and schools in, 279

Pace, Richard, humanist, 34, 219
Paget, William, royal servant, 214
papacy and education, 142, 225, 232, 237-8
Papias, grammarian, 92-3
  Elementarium of, 92-3, 126
Parabolarum, Liber, see Alain de Lille
Paradise, John, schoolmaster, 160
Paris, France, study and teaching at, 55, 91, 104, 135, 186, 230, 231, 238-9

Parkhouse, William, schoolmaster, 240
parliament, and education and religion, 40, 42, 73, 213, 228, 273-4, 275-7, 282-3, 286
parsing, 98
Parvula, grammatical work, 48, 108-9
Paston family of Norfolk, 41, 43, 55, 100-1, 193
Pavy, Hugh, bishop of St Davids, 144, 188 n 1
Paynel, John, royal tutor, 23
Peasants' Revolt (1381), 161, 192
Pecham, John, archbishop of Canterbury, 180
peculium, monastic, 241
Pembridge, Isabel, of Salop, 195
Penitencialis, Liber, see William de Montibus
Penkridge, Richard, schoolmaster, 95
Penrith, Cumberland, school at, 288
Percival, Thomasine, benefactress, 118
Percy, Henry Algernon, earl of Northumberland, 38, 39, 136, 158, 219, 241, 322
Perotto, Niccolo, grammarian, 28, 106-7, 111, 112, 250
Peter of Blois, cleric, 22
Peter Helias, grammarian, 92, 125
Peter Lombard, master of the *Sentences*, 229-32, 242
Peterborough, Northants., abbey of, 243
cathedral at, 264
Petre, Sir William, royal servant, 283
Philip, Francis, schoolmaster, 218
Picot, Nicholas, alderman, 100
Pierce the Ploughmans Crede, poem, 193
Piers Plowman, see Langland, William
'Pinnock', *see* Osbern of Gloucester
Pitt, John, monk, 241, 259
plainsong, study of, 63
Plank, Maurice, schoolmaster, 154
Plantagenet, Lady Bridget, 54
Pliny, Latin author, 28, 108
Plutarch, classical author, 109
Plympton, Devon, school at, 146, 170
Pocklington, Yorks. E.R., school at, 284
poetry, English medieval, 139-41
Latin medieval, 102-6
Pole, Reginald, cardinal-archbishop of Canterbury, 13-14, 159, 286
Polesworth, War., abbey of, 54
Polsloe, Devon, priory of, 53
Pontefract, Yorks. W.R., school at, 170, 179
Pontesbury, Nicholas, subdean of Wells, 125
Poore, Richard, bishop of Durham, 181
Portsmouth, Raulin, son of Master Stephen of, 119
Pottinger, John, schoolmaster, 240, 247
Powick, Worcs., chantry at, 278
Premonstratensian canons and education, 237, 240
Preston, Lancs., school at, 146

primers, 23, 62, 258
printing and printed books, 75, 106-13, 123, 127, 255
Priscian, grammarian, 91
grammar of, 91-2, 125, 126, 153, 221-2
privy seal office, 37, 40
Proba, Latin authoress, 113
Promptorium Parvulorum, see Geoffrey, friar of King's Lynn
Prudentius, Latin author, 113
Pyne, John, priest, 121
Pynson, Richard, printer, 75

Quarrington, Geoffrey of, 226
Quinel, Peter, bishop of Exeter, 180
Quintilian, Latin author, 107, 116-17

Ramsey, Hunts., abbey of, 226, 236
Rand, Lincs., church of, 18
Ravenstone, William, almoner of St Pauls', 125
Reading, Berks., abbey of, 243, 249
school at, 170, 177, 249, 259-60, 270 n 3
recorder, office of, 44-5
Rede, John, schoolmaster, 28
Redman, Richard, bishop of Ely, 240
Ree, John, schoolmaster, 160
Reformation and education, 253-89
Reginald of Durham, author, 170
religious education, *see* education, religious
religious orders and education, 224-51, 254, 258
almonry schools of, 243-5
cloister schools of, 233-43
public schools of, 233, 248-9, 259
song schools of, 245-7
see also canons regular, friars, and monks
Relyk, William, schoolmaster, 212
'remedies', 133
Retford, Notts., school at, 284 n 1
Reviers, Baldwin de, earl of Devon (d. 1262), 146
Reynolds, Walter, bishop of Worcester, 16
Ricart, Robert, common clerk, 44
Richard II, King, 22 n 5, 23-4
Richard III, King, 27, plate 2
Richard, abbot of St Albans, 177-8
Richard, duke of York, son of Edward IV, 27
Richard, king of the Romans, 22 n 5, 185
Richard de Belmeis I, bishop of London, 173
Richmond, Yorks. N.R., archdeacon of, 146
school at, 146
Ripon, Yorks. W.R., college and school at, 176
Rivers, Oxford student, 136
Robert Curthose, duke of Normandy, 22
Rochester, Kent, cathedral priory of, 243
cathedral (new foundation), 264-5
Rock, Worcs., school at, 160, 203

Rocliffe, Margaret, schoolgirl, 55
Roger, archbishop of York, 173
Roger of Chewton, cleric, 179
Rolleston, Staffs., school at, 70, 78, 116 n 1, 124 n 1
Romeyn, John, archbishop of York, 82
Romsey, Thomas, schoolmaster, 126, 161
Ros, William de, Lord Ros, 35, 219, 322
Rotherham, Yorks. W.R., college and school at, 78, 116 n 1, 121, 125-6, 134, 137, 156, 268, 282
Rotherham, Thomas, archbishop of York, 78, 121, 125-6, 137, 156
Rous, John, chronicler, 85, 208
Rudham, Norfolk, school at, 149, 170
Rushworth, Norfolk, college and school at, 268
Russell, John, bishop of Lincoln, 188 n 1

Saffron Walden, Essex, school at, 114 n 1, 283, 284 n 1
St Albans, Herts., abbey of, 51, 137, 146, 177-8, 179-80
    almonry school at, 120-1, 133, 243, 245
    public school at, 101-2, 116 n 1, 120, 125, 135, 146, 163, 170, 177-8, 179-80, 184, 245, 259-60, 270 n 5
St Germans, Cornwall, priory of, 51
St Germans, John of, monk, 236
St John of Jerusalem, prior of, 137, 322
St Paul's School, London, *see* London, schools, St Paul's
Salisbury, Wilts., schools at, 64, 79, 81-2, 120, 150, 157, 168, 173, 177, 286
Sallust, Latin author, 28, 108, 114, 152
Sampson, Thomas, schoolmaster, 76-7
Samson, abbot of Bury, 135, 178, 184, 248
sanitation, *see* school lavatories
Savage, Ralph, schoolboy, 127
schoolboys
    age of, 100, 116-17, 183, 225, 227-8
    biographies of, 136-7
    board and lodging of, 118-19, 156, 179-80, 181-4
    books belonging to, 126-7
    cheek of, 140-1
    clerical status of, 120-1
    clothes of, 119
    exhibitions for, 180-4, 207, 256-7
    food of, 179-80, 182
    married, 134
    violence of, 135-6, 139, 161
schoolgirls, 54-5
schoolmasters, 150-63, plates 10-11
    appointment of, 143-50
    books belonging to, 126, 141
    clerical, 155-6, 160, 195-6
    graduate, 151-5

grammatical works by, 94-113, 210-12
    lay, 155-6
    length of service of, 160-1
    numbers of in schools, 121
    salaries and wages of, 78, 80, 121, 156-60, 214, 238, 240-1, 247, 249, 259, 262, 263, 265, 275
    taxation of, 158
    villainous and incompetent, 150, 161-2
schoolmistresses, 54-5
schools, almonry, 243-5
    books used in, 119, 124-7, 239-40
    buildings, 156-7, 178-9, 197, 207, plates 6, 7, 9
    business, 60, 70-9
    classrooms, 70, 82, 122, 123, plate 8
    cloister, 224-43
    cost of founding, 197-8
    curricula, 102, 114, 201
    definitions of the word, 59-60, 167, 172
    discipline in, 127-9, 139-41
    disputations in, 98, 131
    distribution of, 168-72, 190-2, 207-17, 294
    endowment of, 150, 153-4, 157-8, 173-217
    fees and expenses at, 77, 117-20, 184, 196
    festivals and holidays, 131-3
    free, 59, 118, 157, 175, 184-217, 249, 266, 275
    grammar, 60, 68-71, 87 *et passim*
    higher studies, 79-86, 172-3
    historians of, 2-8
    hours of teaching, 123-4, 140
    lavatories, 129-30
    length of time spent at, 133-4, 183, 245
    libraries of, 124-6
    matriculation at, 120
    monopolies by, 122, 123, 148-9, 198, 212-13
    patrons of, 64-5, 143-50, 177-8, 205-7
    plague in, 255
    prayers in, 62, 130
    size of, 121-3, 240, 244, 246
    song, 60-8, 245-7, 282
    sports and games of, 132, 137
    statutes of, 116, 124
    teaching methods used in, 98-111, 124-33
    terms and vacations of, 82, 132-3
    violence in, 136
Schorn, John, shrine of, 137
Scogan, Edward IV's jester, 100
Scolemaystre, John, 219
Scollowe, William, schoolmaster, 160, 249
Scotland, Estates of, 117
scriveners and scrivening, 48, 75, 78
Sedbergh, Yorks. W.R., school at, 207, 283, 284
Sedulius, Latin author, 113
Sempringham, Lincs., priory of, 237
Sevenhampton, Wilts., manor of, 51

Sevenoaks, Kent, school at, 154 n 1, 155, 276

Sevenoaks, William, grocer, 155, 203

Seward, John, schoolmaster, 210

'Sex Auctores', 102-3, 126

Seymour, Edward, duke of Somerset, 84, 275

Shaftesbury, Dorset, school at, 170

Shaxton, Nicholas, bishop of Salisbury, 256

Shaw, Edmund, goldsmith, 203

Sherborne, Dorset, school at, 284

Sherborne, Robert, bishop of Chichester, 70, 78, 188 n 1

sheriffs' clerks, 38

Sherrington, Bucks., Robert, clerk of, 135

Shipden, Norfolk, school at, 144

Shipton, William, schoolmaster, 212

Shouldham, Norfolk, school at, 144

Shrewsbury, Salop, school at, 170, 284

Shrewsbury, Ralph, bishop of Bath and Wells, 81

Shrove Tuesday, 132

Sibthorpe, Notts., college and school at, 65

signet office, 36-7

Simon, Joan, historian, 7

Skeffington family, 220

Skelton, John, poet, 23, 28

Smith, William, bishop of Lincoln, 108, 214-15

Sonning, Berks., church of, 20-1

South Dalton, Yorks. E.R., school at, 148

Southwell, Notts., college and school at, 3, 101, 145, 176, 192, 268

Sparham, Norfolk, school at, 144

Spilsby, Lincs., school at, 284

Sponne, William, archdeacon of Norfolk, 201

Stafford, school at, 284 n 1, 288

Stafford, Edward, duke of Buckingham, 137, 219, 321

Stafford, Henry, duke of Buckingham, 35, plate 2

Stafford, Humphrey, brother of Henry, 35

Stafford, John, archbishop of Canterbury, 212

Stafford, John, London cleric, 212

Staffordshire, schools in, 278

Stamford, Augustinian convent at, 231
Carmelite convent at, 232
Franciscan convent at, 231
Gilbertine priory at, 237
higher studies at, 173, 177
school at, 170, 284

Stanbridge, John, schoolmaster, 107-8, 110, 111, 208
grammatical writings of, 97, 107-9, 111, 127, 255, 257

Stanbridge, Thomas, schoolmaster, 154-5

Stanley family, earls of Derby, 202

Stanley, James, bishop of Ely, 210

Stannowe, Ralph, schoolmaster, 219

Stapledon, Walter, bishop of Exeter, 16, 18-19, 53, 182

Starkey, Thomas, author, 13-14, 159, 262

Starre, Margery, old woman, 192

Statius, Latin author, 102-3

Stavensby, Alexander, bishop of Coventry and Lichfield, 143

Stephen, King, 173

Stevenage, Herts., school at, 119 n 2

Stillington, Robert, bishop of Bath and Wells, 78, 121

Stixwould, Lincs., priory of, 54

Stockport, Cheshire, school at, 203, 206

Stoke by Clare, Suffolk, college and school at, 65

Stonor, Edmund, schoolboy, 118, 126-7

Story, Edward, bishop of Chichester, 215

Stourbridge, Worcs., school at, 280, 284 n 1

Stow, John, historian, 131

Stow-on-the-Wold, Gloucs., rector of, 21

Stratford-on-Avon, War., guild and school at, 123 n 5, 205, 284 n 1

Stury, Sir Richard, knight, 33

Suffield, Walter, bishop of Norwich, 179

Sulpizio, Giovanni, grammarian, 28, 107, 111, 112, 114, 250

Sutton Coldfield, War., school at, 134, 220

Synonyma and *Equivoca*, grammatical poems, 48, 90-1, 112, 127, plate 4

Syon, Middx., abbey of, 126, 250

Tattershall, Lincs., college and school at, 65, 268-9, 270 n 3

Taunton, Som., school at, 122, 170

Tehy, Vincent, merchant, 203

Terence, Latin author, 107, 108, 111, 112, 114, 251

Tewkesbury, Gloucs., abbey of, 243

Theodulus, Latin author, *see Eclogue of Theodulus*

theology, study of, 79-86, 172-3, 174, 229-32, 234-9, 242

Thetford, Augustinian convent at, 231
Dominican convent at, 230
school at, 144

Thomas, earl of Lancaster (d. 1322), 31

Thomas of Bayeux, archbishop of York, 168

Thomas of Holland, scholar, 179

Thomas of Woodstock, duke of Gloucester, 32, 33, 35

Thoresby, John, archbishop of York, 66

Thornage, Norfolk, school at, 144

Thornton, Lincs., abbey of, 242
college and school at, 195, 267

Thucydides, classical author, 28

Ticehurst, Sussex, school at, 67

Tichborne family, 54

Tickhill, Yorks. W.R., Augustinian convent at, 232-3
Tiptoft, John, earl of Worcester, 35
Toddington, Gloucs., vicar of, 21
Tolleshunt, William, almoner of St Paul's, 125
Tong, Salop, college and school at, 195, 268-9, 270 n 5, 275 n 1
Topcliffe, Yorks. N.R., school at, 136
Torksey, Lincs., church of, 180
Toulouse, France, study of grammar at, 91, 96
Towcester, Northants., school at, 201, 280, 284-5
town clerk, office of, 44-5
towns, administration of, 43-5
  education and, 204
Treveris, Peter, printer, 255
Trevisa, John, translator, 73-4, 95, 189
Triplett, Henry, schoolboy, 233
Tucke, John, schoolmaster, 247
Turvill family, 51
Tyler, William, schoolmaster, 259

uniformity in education and religion, 112-13, 253-8
Urban V, Pope, 81
urine, uses of, 130
ushers, school, 121, 122, 136, 139, 154, 157, 159, 161, 263

Vache, Sir Philip la, knight, 33
Valla, Lorenzo, grammarian, 28, 106-7, 108, 111, 112, 250
venison, penchant of scholars for, 161, 179
verse, study of in schools, 100-1
Victoria County Histories, 4-5
villeins, education of, 50, 117, 192-3
Villiers family, 220
Virgil, Latin author, 28, 108, 111, 112, 114, 153, 221-2
Vives, Juan Luiz, educationalist, 129
vocabularies, French, 72
  Latin, 109
vulgaria or vulgars, 98-100, 107, 109, 110, 250

Wainfleet, Lincs., school at, 123 n 5, 200, 207, plate 7
Wainfleet, William, bishop of Winchester, 162, 200, plates 7, 16
Wakefield, Yorks. W.R., school at, 170
Walkelin of Derby, 178
Walpole, Ralph, bishop of Ely, 234
Walsall, Staffs., school at, 285
Walsh, Sir John, knight, 322
Walsingham, Thomas, chronicler, 192
Walton, Robert, Premonstratensian, 240
Walworth, Sir William, lord mayor, 46
Wanda, William de, dean of Salisbury, 20-1
Wapplode, John, 127

wardrobe, king's great, 37
wards, royal, education, of, 35, 217-19
Warham, William, archbishop of Canterbury, 188
Warren, abbot of St Albans, 178
Warrington, Lancs., school at, 116 n 1, 124 n 1, 203
Warwick, college and schools at, 65, 69, 120, 170, 176, 268-9, 270 n 3
Wase, Christopher, historian, 2
Week St Mary, Cornwall, school at, 118
Wellington, Som., school at, 125
Wells, Som., cathedral choristers of, 129, 200
  schools at, 64, 82, 83, 101, 121, 122, 129, 157, 174 n 1, 179
Wells, Hugh of, bishop of Lincoln, 17-18, 20, 82
Westbury-on-Trym, Gloucs., college and school at, 176, 200, 217, 268-9, 270 n 4
West Dereham, Norfolk, abbey of, 240
Westminster, Middx., abbey of, 83, 244
  cathedral and college at, 263
  schools at, 67-8, 131, 214, 265
Wetherden, Suffolk, church of, 184, 248
White, John, bishop of Lincoln, 287
Whitkirk, Yorks. W.R., school at, 202-3
Whittington, Sir Richard, lord mayor, 83
Whittinton, Robert, schoolmaster, 111-12, 127, 208, 218-19, 255, 257
Willarsey, Gloucs., rector of, 21, 160
William I, King, 21-2
William of Diss, schoolmaster, 135
William de Montibus, chancellor of Lincoln, 104
  Liber Penitencialis ascribed to, 104, 113
Willoughby, Sir Henry, of Middleton, 207, 220
Willoughby, Sir Hugh, explorer, 120, 134, 220
wills as sources for history of education, 207
Wimborne, Dorset, college and school at, 176, 202
Winchcombe, Gloucs., abbey of, 206, 242
  school at, 156, 206, 217, 259, 261, 270 n 3
Winchelsey, Robert, archbishop of Canterbury, 82-3, 234, 243
Winchester, Hants., Carmelite convent at, 232
  cathedral priory at, 240, 243, 247
  cathedral (new foundation), 264-6
  city school at, 145, 179
  college of St Mary and school at
    commoners of, 119, 187-8, 266
    curriculum of, 60, 69, 109, 112, 114, 117
    foundation and history of, 88, 187-8, 266, 276, 286
    library, 97 n 1, 125, 126
    organization, 122, 124 n 1, 132, 133-4, 187-8

scholars, 60, 69, 107, 117, 120, 133-4, 187-8

schoolmasters, 28, 111, 121, 126, 129, 153-4, 156, 157, 161, 187-8, 199, 240, 286

statutes, 60, 69, 107, 117, 120, 133-4, 187-8

St Cross, hospital of, 49

St Mary, abbey of, 54

Windsor, Berks., castle and college of St George at, 125, 198-9, 276

Wingfield, Lady Anne, 268

Wisbech, Cambs., guild and school at, 154, 205, 284 n 1

Woburn, Beds., abbey of, 248

Wollaton, Notts., school at, 123

Wolsey, Thomas, cardinal-archbishop of York, 36, 38, 39, 79, 121, 163, 201-2, 208, 255, 322, plate 11

Wolston, Wars., manor of, 51

women, education of, 52-5

Wood, Anthony, historian, 2

Woodville, Anthony, Lord Rivers, 26

Worcester, carnary library at, 84-5

cathedral priory of, 83, 84-5, 179, 236, 243, 245, 246

cathedral (new foundation), 264

schools at, 83, 84-5, 122, 131, 146, 150, 179, 215, 243, 282, 288

Trinity guild at, 215, 282

Worcester, William, topographer, 41

Worcestershire, schools in, 4

Worde, Wynkyn de, printer, 75

Worksop, Notts., priory of, 95

Worthington, Gilbert, London rector, 213, 221

Wotton-under-Edge, Gloucs., school at, 116 n 1, 170, 217, 278

foundation of, 188-90, 197

holidays at, 133

patrons of, 150, 188-9, 206

scholars of, 123, 134, 188-9

schoolmasters of, 158, 160, 188-9

writing, study of, 63, 100, 119-20, 282

Wye, Kent, college and school at, 154 n 1, 268-9, 270 n 3

Wykeham, William, bishop of Winchester, 24, 50, 60, 88, 125, 129, 153, 157, 180, 187

Wylie, J. H., historian, 4

Yarm, Yorks. N.R., Dominican convent at, 228

schools at, 170, 228

Yarnscombe, Devon, church of, 182

Yate, Walter son of Henry atte, 51

York, Augustinian convent at, 231-2

Franciscan convent at, 231

St Leonard's hospital at, 82, 261

St Mary's hospital at, 287

schools at, 121, 157, 168, 170, 173

higher studies at, 79, 81, 82, 83

Reformation and, 287

schoolmasters of, 126, 151, 155

song schools, 64, 66

York, John of, schoolmaster, 151

Yorkshire, schools in, 7 n 2, 190-2